Enterprise and American Law, 1836–1937

Enterprise and American Law
1836–1937

Herbert Hovenkamp

Harvard University Press
Cambridge, Massachusetts
London, England
1991

Library of Congress Cataloging-in-Publication Data

Hovenkamp, Herbert, 1948–
Enterprise and American law, 1836–1937 / Herbert Hovenkamp.
p. cm.
Includes bibliographical references and index.
ISBN 0–674–25748–0
1. Corporation law—United States—History. 2. Trade regulation—
United States—History. 3. Antitrust law—United States—History.
4. Industry and state—United States—History. I. Title.
KF1414.H68 1991
343.73'08'09—dc20
[347.303809]   90–48564
CIP

To my wife, Beverly,
and my children, Arie and Erik

Contents

Preface

This is principally a book about legal ideas rather than legal institutions. It should be read as intellectual history and not as political, social, or economic history, although I have attempted to integrate historians' work in all these disciplines.

The dates in the title, 1836 and 1937, are symbolic and somewhat arbitrary. In 1836 Roger Brooke Taney was appointed Chief Justice of the United States Supreme Court. The rise of classicism as America's dominant constitutional philosophy can be said to begin with him. The year 1937 saw the great court-packing crisis of the Franklin D. Roosevelt administration—an event that, though not treated here, symbolizes the death of constitutional classicism.

For financial support and released time I am indebted to the Nellie Ball Trust, the University of Iowa Faculty Scholars Program, and particularly my Dean, N. William Hines. I also thank the editors of the following law reviews for permission to reprint portions of these previously published articles: "Labor Conspiracies in American Law, 1880–1930," 66 *Texas Law Review* 919–965 (1988), and "The Antitrust Movement and the Rise of Industrial Organization," 68 *Texas Law Review* 105–168 (1989), Copyright 1988, 1989 by the Texas Law Review Association; "Regulatory Conflict in the Gilded Age: Federalism and the Railroad Problem," 97 *Yale Law Journal* 1017–1072 (1988), by permission of The Yale Law Journal Company and Fred B. Rothman & Company; "The Classical Corporation in American Legal Thought," 76 *Georgetown Law*

Journal 1593–1689 (1988); and "The Sherman Act and the Classical Theory of Competition," 74 *Iowa Law Review* 1019–1065 (1989). I am grateful to numerous earlier readers, but have profited in particular from comments by Ian Ayres, Frank H. Easterbrook, Lawrence M. Friedman, Robert W. Gordon, Lino A. Graglia, J. R. T. Hughes, Kenneth Kress, Thomas K. McCraw, Louis B. Schwartz, and Lester Telser.

Enterprise and American Law, 1836–1937

Introduction: Classicism, Democracy, and the Rule of Law

The Classical Tradition in American Politics

"Classicism" refers to a way of thinking about policy problems that dominated American law and economics during the first two-thirds of the nineteenth century. A unified theory of political economy, classicism had broad implications for both public and private law. Because they were classicists, nineteenth-century American jurisprudents could honestly believe that the law and all of the state's economic policy formed a single, seamless web.

American classicists adopted most of their economic and legal ideas from the British. Following Adam Smith, the principal English classical economists were Thomas R. Malthus, David Ricardo, James Mill, and his son John Stuart Mill. Classicism in the United States began later than in England and lasted longer, until Progressivism discovered British welfare economics and reformulated American legislative policy to match.

Historians sometimes equate classical political economy with the thought of Adam Smith, and his name is most widely associated with classicism. But in several ways Smith was not typical of the classical tradition. His basic impulses were more agrarian and less industrial than those of his followers. And mixed into *The Wealth of Nations* was an explicitly Protestant moral content that was suppressed in later English classicism. One might wish to divide the great classical political economists into a "natural law" group and a "utilitarian" group. Adam Smith and perhaps Malthus clearly belong in the former, and John Stuart Mill clearly in the latter. The others are transitional figures. For reasons elaborated in Chapter 7, most American classicists clung to Adam Smith's moralism and rejected most forms of utilitarianism.

Classical political economy in the United States is a Jacksonian phenomenon. Although one can speak of classical political economy during the Jeffersonian era, there are two good reasons for attributing classicism to the Age of Jackson rather than to that of Jefferson. First, classical political economy was struggling to take hold in Jefferson's day, and was still a controversial economic doctrine in the United States. Second, the Jeffersonian impulse, like Adam Smith's, was far more agrarian than industrial. In fact Jefferson was quite hostile toward industrial development and would have preferred a nation of farmers with only a minimum of indigenous industry to support them.

Andrew Jackson was an entrepreneurial president. His terms of office—or, in political economic terms, his regime—stood for economic growth, unobstructed by "artificial" constraints. The two greatest classical *legal* institutions in the United States—the modern business corporation and the constitutional doctrine of substantive due process—are both distinctively Jacksonian products. The modern business corporation had its origin in the general corporation acts, one of the most important legal accomplishments of a regime bent on democratizing and deregulating American business. The founders of substantive due process—Thomas Cooley, Christopher Tiedeman, and John Dillon—were Jacksonian to the core.

Beginning with the Jackson era, the work of the classical political economists became one of the most salable products in the American market for economic and political ideas. Classicism offered a complete view of human nature, an ethical defense of self-interest, a theory of political economy that seemed to work—and all of this in a package that complemented American moral and religious beliefs about independence and individual freedom. Lawyers and judges were inevitably among this market's most enthusiastic traders. As a result, classicism as economic doctrine gradually merged into classicism as legal and constitutional philosophy.

Classicism and the Rule of Law

Classicism was not merely an economic philosophy. It was also a model for statecraft, and for private as well as public law. We seldom appreciate how closely early American jurists tied their law to economic principles. For example, one of America's first constitutional law treatises, Daniel Raymond's *Elements of Constitutional Law and of Political Economy*,[1] was also a treatise on economics. Many Jeffersonian and early Jacksonian legal scholars, such as Raymond, John Taylor, Alexander Hamilton, George Tucker, Theodore Sedgwick, and Thomas Cooper, were also political economists.[2]

Classical political economy purported to develop rules for evaluating a legal regime's justness or fairness without regard to how its wealth happened to be distributed. As a political and legal doctrine, classicism identified the best regime as the one that maximized total wealth. Distribution had secondary importance or no importance at all. But classicism did contain a theory of justice. Classicists were convinced that for too long the federal government and the states had been playing political favorites. The body politic as a whole was weaker when the state favored one politically powerful group at the expense of others—perhaps by giving it a special corporate charter with monopoly privileges or relief from taxation. The duty of the state was to enlarge the wealth of all its constituents, not merely of some. This duty was inherent in the notion of *political*, as opposed to private, economy.

Theodore Sedgwick, one of America's greatest antebellum legal scholars, expressed this view as well as any elite lawyer could. In the 1830's Sedgwick observed that the content of political economy and of law were precisely the same, except that the first was normative while the second was positive:

> What then is the difference between good laws and good public economy?—None—because all good laws tend to the production and just distribution of wealth; all good laws are good economy. But there is a difference between the science of law, and the science of public economy. The former teaches what the law is, which is the business of the lawyer to learn; the latter teaches what law should be, which is the business of the public economist, or legislator to learn. . . . The public economy of a country is clearly indicated by its laws; if the laws are good, the public economy is likely to be. . . .[3]

Above all, Sedgwick argued, political economy dealt with the welfare of the "public"—not with that of particular individual members. Only by maximizing the wealth of the group as a whole could the wealth of individual members be maximized. Political economy, he continued, teaches that all the wealth of a nation, public and private, may be supposed to be gathered into one great store-house, which is divided into public and private apartments; that the common stock is stored in the public rooms; that every industrious man has a private apartment, under the same roof, which is under his own lock and key. That as the public apartments are filled from the private, the better supplied the latter, the richer will be the stores of the nation. That if a man set fire to, or in any way destroy those parts of this building, where the public property is stored, he is a loser of course, because he is a partner in it, though the flames do not reach his own apartment; and if, through heedlessness, spite, or malice, he kindles a blaze in one of the private apartments, he then destroys one of those heaps, out of which the great public store-house is furnished.

For the elite nineteenth-century American lawyer, classical political economy was the best possible determinant of the rule of law. The best legal rule enlarged total social wealth, and the science of political economy provided the necessary instructions for making society wealthier. Explicit state involvement in the transfer of wealth was inherently suspect—because it made one person or interest group richer only by making another poorer.

Liberal critics today are inclined to view the classicists through the lens created by the Progressives and the policy makers of the New Deal. The classicists were bad, or at least deficient in theory, because they objected to state intervention in the market on behalf of the disadvantaged. As a naked proposition this is certainly true. But the political argument that turned Americans to the classicists was much different. To be a classicist was to be opposed to state intervention on behalf of the rich and the politically powerful. Classicism achieved its popularity in the United States in a political movement, Jacksonianism, that was heavily supported by society's disfavored classes. The issues were not welfare and subsidized education. Rather, they were special corporate charters or licenses that gave unique privileges to engage in business to certain favored people, while denying access to others. When Federalists intervened in the market, the immediate beneficiaries were generally people of property. In such a regime, arguments for a noninterventionist state leaned to the left, not to the right. To be a classicist in the 1830's was to be a liberal.

Classicism was a system for policy making dedicated to the principles that (1) the market, left to itself, works pretty well; and (2) the state should not play favorites. If classicism is to be faulted, it is not for preferring the interests of the wealthy or even of the entrepreneurial class over those of the poor. It is to be faulted for the naiveté of its faith in the market, or for its belief that the quality of a society can somehow be measured without regard to the way its wealth is distributed. But even here, classicism erected a monument that is difficult to tear down. The fundamental premise of classicism—that the government should not play favorites—is a lesson seldom learned by any alternative regime, whether fascist or Marxist, socialist or libertarian. Classicism at its best never came close to creating such a regime, but it probably did as well as any alternative.

This book explores the relationship between classical political economy and American law in six broadly defined areas relating to business enterprise in the nineteenth and early twentieth centuries. Part I examines the development of the classical concept of the American business corporation—a concept designed simultaneously to make the business corporation an efficient engine of economic development and to free the corporate form of business firm structure from its preclassical attachment to interest group politics. Part II considers how classical political economy provided the intellectual background for constitutional theory and helped define the limits of state and federal jurisdiction to regulate business behavior. Part III looks at one set of classicism's failures—the markets in which competition seemed not to work—and relates the development of "regulated industry," or separate branches of economics and law designed to ensure that even these markets would function in the "public" interest rather than for the benefit of special interest groups. Part IV argues that the Gilded Age and Progressive Era constitutional doctrine of substantive due process was driven by classical political economy, and that it became obsolete and an object of ridicule as classicism gave way to more modern, more interventionist neoclassicism. Part V describes one of the most embarrassing political failures of classical economics: its notion that combinations of capital and combinations of labor should be treated in exactly the same way. State policy should not prefer one to the other, because business combinations and labor unions organized for exactly the same reasons. Finally, Part VI reexamines the antitrust movement, the most explicit intersection of law and economics before the New Deal, and argues that we have greatly underestimated the role of economics in the common law of trade restraints.

The Importance of Theory in Legal History

Writing about the history of American economic law has been dominated by a mode of analysis that makes every issue into a political conflict. Marxists, conservatives, and even many liberals appear to believe that every economic question the law addresses is ultimately answered by a process of interest group politics—with each interest group dedicated to enriching its own members, whatever the consequences for society as a whole.

The propositions that people organize into interest groups, that interest groups place the welfare of their own members above the welfare of society, and that throughout history interest groups have spoken up enthusiastically on most of the major economic issues that legal policy makers have addressed are indisputable. But to look exclusively at political concerns in economic policy making results in a misleading and limited perspective on American legal development.

Theory has always been an essential part of state policy. Although theory is sometimes a thin disguise for politics, it can be much more. To take a simple example, special interest politics alone does not explain why toll bridges and gaslight utilities in the nineteenth century succeeded so often in acquiring legal monopoly status, while ordinary manufacturers and retailers did not. It was not merely that the bridge owners wielded enormous political power or had unusual control over the governmental process. All the political dispute and rhetoric was dwarfed by a simple consideration of accepted theory. Within the classical and neoclassical economic models toll bridges and gaslight utilities were natural monopolies, while manufacturers and retailers were competitively structured.

In such cases theory was the dog and politics but the tail. Every important political dispute of the nineteenth century—whether the railroads should be government owned or price-regulated private enterprise, whether utilities should have express monopoly rights, whether antimonopoly provisions in state constitutions should apply to utilities—rested firmly on premises from theoretical economics. Anyone who studies the great monopoly cases in American constitutional history and ignores the role of economic theory is seeing only a small and faded part of a magnificent picture. The *Charles River Bridge* case (1837) may have been a political dispute about entitlements to a lucrative market; but it was more fundamentally a dispute about state policy toward natural monopoly in an era when classical natural monopoly theory was in its infancy. The *Slaughter-House Cases* (1873) may tell a tale of legislative corruption; but, even if there is such a story to tell, its importance is dwarfed by the great public health problems that confronted New Orleans. One should more appropriately compare the slaughter-house monopoly with the Pure Food and Drug Act than with the Yazoo County land fraud.

To be sure, economic theory can never relieve the state of the burden of politics. There is no dichotomy between science and politics. On the contrary, science is a form of politics. One purpose of scientific model building is to explain observed phenomena and make predictions. But an equally important purpose is to produce consensus. A scientific model becomes successful when it convinces those who practice a particular discipline, and it may convince by a variety of mechanisms, including many that are political or even rhetorical.[4] The science of political economy in nineteenth-century England and America was no exception, and neither was the law.

PART I

THE CLASSICAL CORPORATION
AND STATE POLICY

CHAPTER 1

Classical Political Economy
and the Business Corporation

Classical political economy was dedicated to the principle that the state could encourage economic development best by leaving entrepreneurs alone, free of both regulation and subsidy. Capital would flow naturally toward investments that promised to be profitable, provided that the channels were clear. In the words of Chief Justice John Appleton of the Maine Supreme Court, condemning legislative grants of money to private corporations, "Capital naturally gravitates to the best investment. If a particular place or a special kind of manufacture promises large returns, the capitalist will be little likely to hesitate in selecting the place and in determining upon the manufacture."[1] Investments that did not promise to be profitable were not worth undertaking, and a public subsidy would not make them so. From the 1830's until the end of the century state economic policy was predominantly classical, although neither legislators nor judges followed the classical model with perfect consistency. For example, many states as well as the federal government encouraged railroad development with subsidies in the form of land grants or cash. Courts most generally approved.[2]

Adam Smith derisively called the economic ideology that he rejected "mercantilism," and the name stuck. Mercantilism was not so much a coherent economic ideology as it was a hodge-podge of ideas about how to stimulate economic growth.[3] Mercantilism had little faith in the market itself to deliver optimal growth. The state must regulate. In particular, it must encourage domestic production by controlling imports and subsidizing lagging industries. Business entrepreneurs became the principal beneficiaries of state largess.

Within the mercantilist model the private business corporation was a unique entity created by the state for a special purpose.[4] State involvement was presumed from the very act of incorporation. Both state subsidy and public obligation by the incorporators were natural corollaries. Business firms that relied on the market alone to determine their prospects were simply not incorporated. During the preclassical period states such as Massachusetts, Connecticut, and New York relied heavily on corporate charters to encourage specific kinds of economic development, including turnpikes, bridges, and banks.

The development of classical economic policy in the United States effected a dramatic change in the concept of the business corporation. Under classicism the corporation became nothing more than a device for assembling large amounts of capital so it could be controlled efficiently by a few active managers. Other mechanisms might have served the same purpose. One of these was the limited partnership, a form of business organization containing an "active" partner and several "silent" partners. The silent partners did not participate in the business, and their liability was limited to their actual investment. The purpose of the limited partnership was to encourage the investor who did not wish to manage and who wanted to limit his risk.

But in the 1830's and 1840's limited partnerships were found only in Louisiana and New York, while corporations were everywhere. In 1832 Joseph Angell and Samuel Ames, the authors of the first American treatise on business corporations, suggested some reasons for limited partnerships' unpopularity, and others can be surmised. One disadvantage lay in the fact that while the limited partners had limited liability, the active partners did not.[5] Further, unless reduced liability for limited partners was authorized by statute, states continued to apply the common law rule that all partners were personally liable for partnership debts. The limited partnership was unknown to the common law; therefore limited liability would not be presumed.[6] Yet another disadvantage was that limited partnerships did not receive federal protection under the Constitution's contract clause, from subsequent regulation of their activities.

But Angell and Ames also suggested one strong advantage of the limited partnership that would encourage firms to use it: those seeking to raise capital in this way did not need to obtain an act of special incorporation from the state legislature. Under the New York statute they needed only to register with the county clerk.[7] These early limited partnership statutes were thus an ancestor of the general corporation laws of mid-century. They were a first step in the formation of the classical corporation: a mechanism for achieving lower-risk investment by silent investors for an ordinary business enterprise that could anticipate no special treatment from the state other than limited liability itself.

The classical theory of the business corporation began to emerge early in the post-Federalist Supreme Court. It appears in Chief Justice Roger Brooke Taney's holding in the *Charles River Bridge* case (1837),[8] a year after President Jackson appointed him, that a monopoly privilege would not be implied in a bridge corporation's charter, for "in grants by the public, nothing passes by implication."

The classical model did not emerge mature in a single decision. It evolved gradually in the nineteenth century, reaching its apogee in the 1880's and 1890's. Then it began to fall apart, a victim of its own success. The developing model of the classical corporation included two fundamental premises: (1) the corporate form is not a special privilege from the state but merely one of many ways of organizing a business firm; (2) in a market economy, the peculiar advantage of the corporation is its ability to raise and direct capital more efficiently than other forms of business organization.

These important developments, which are taken up in subsequent chapters, formed the core of the classical corporate model: the attack on the Marshall era contract clause; the demise of the charter theory of business regulation; the rise of the general corporation act and decline of the special subsidy; the application of the fourteenth amendment to corporations; the expansion of limited shareholder liability; the narrowing scope of quo warranto and ultra vires; the facilitation of multistate corporate business activities; and separation of ownership and control. All of these were natural consequences of classical corporate theory. But inevitably some, particularly the rise of multistate business and the separation of ownership and control, undermined the classical theory and inaugurated a post-classical, more regulatory view of the relationship between the state and the corporation.

The Classical Corporate Personality

Under mercantilism the unique thing about the corporation was not its structure or its ability to assemble capital. Rather, the mercantile corporation was the result of a special contract (charter) with the state, permitting the incorporators to do something that no one else could do. Within the classical model, however, the business corporation became a "firm"—an equal participant in the markets for capital, labor, and a variety of products and services. The law of business corporations encouraged competition by giving the corporation the same status as other forms of business enterprise, while giving management any advantages perceived to be inherent in the corporate structure. The development of classical corporate law necessitated a radical change in the basic idea of the corporation itself, and sparked a century-long debate about the legal nature of the corporation.

To collapse a very long history, the jurisprudential concept of the corporation passed through three broad categories: an "associational" view, which dominated the thinking of the Marshall Court, a "fictional" view that ascended during the Taney period and dominated most of the century, and a "personal" or "entity" view that became important near the end of the century, when the classical theory of corporation began to collapse.[9]

The associational view is clear in Chief Justice John Marshall's holding in *Bank of the United States v. Deveaux* (1809)[10] that a corporation itself is "certainly not a citizen" under the Constitution. As a result, "diversity of citizenship," necessary before the federal courts have jurisdiction, must be determined by looking at the citizenship of the shareholders rather than at the state of incorporation or the principal place of business. This view tended to close the federal courts to claims by or against corporations. Since shareholders might be from more than one state, it reduced the number of situations in which complete diversity between all plaintiffs and all defendants would be found.

The associational view of corporate citizenship dominated until *Deveaux* was overruled by the Taney Court in *Louisville, Cincinnati & Charleston Railroad Co. v. Letson* (1844),[11] which held that shareholders' citizenship notwithstanding, a corporation should be "deemed . . . a person, although an artificial person," and "an inhabitant of the same State, for the purposes of its incorporation, capable of being treated as a citizen of that State, as much as a natural person." The Court conceded that "in some particulars it differs from a natural person," but in "the manner in which it can sue and be sued, it is substantially, within the meaning of the law, a citizen of the State which created it . . . ."

A decade later the Taney Court retained this position but changed the rationale, admitting that a corporation was not literally a "citizen," but creating a conclusive presumption that all shareholders were citizens of the state of incorporation. This proposition was widely known as the purest legal fiction. Nevertheless, it has remained good law ever since, even though its logic was substantially undermined by *Dodge v. Woolsey* (1855), two years later, which entertained a diversity action between a shareholder and a corporation. The emerging notion that a corporation was both a "person" and a "citizen" of the chartering state would infect all classical jurisprudence.[12]

The preclassical, associational view also appeared in the question of entitlement to sue for injuries to the corporation or to collect its debts. The associational view suggested that injuries to the corporation were injuries to its shareholders, and that they should have the cause of action. In fact, Angell and Ames's 1832 treatise recognized an issue in whether the corporation was *permitted* to be a party in many legal proceedings. They cited the traditional English rule that the corporation itself could not be sued for its torts, but such an "action must be brought against each person who committed the tort by name . . . ."[13] Only in 1812 did an English court sustain an action in trover, or to recover wrongfully held property, against a corporation.[14] In 1811 American courts began permitting tort and other actions by and against the corporation itself, under agency principles.[15]

As late as 1827 the issue was controversial, and occasioned a lengthy debate between Justice Joseph Story and Chief Justice Marshall in *Bank of the United States v. Dandridge*.[16] The Court, speaking through Justice Story, permitted an action by the bank on a performance bond on one of its cashiers. The bond had been approved by the directors individually, but had never been accepted by the corporation and placed under its seal. In a long dissent, Chief Justice Marshall complained that the corporation could act only within the scope of its charter; any inconsistent action was that of its individual directors, not of the corporation itself. As a result, the bank was not entitled to sue on the bond. "The voice which utters" in the name of the corporation "must be the aggregate voice . . . . The words they utter are the words of individuals. These individuals must speak collectively to speak corporately, and must use a collective voice." Implicit in Marshall's reasoning was that the individual actors of the corporation, rather than the corporation itself, were responsible for acts not strictly authorized by or in conformity with the corporate charter. Carried to its conclusion, a corporation's agents, not the corporation itself, were answerable for wrongdoing, for wrongdoing was never authorized by the charter.

When Angell and Ames wrote, Marshall's view was already widely rejected.[17] In fact, the ancient doctrine was being turned upside down.

Courts began holding that shareholders ordinarily lacked standing to sue for injuries to the corporation, and that suits by outsiders for injury by the corporation must be brought against the corporation itself. At the same time, the expansion of limited shareholders' liability effectively insulated shareholders from most tort and contract claims against the corporation. Within a generation the rule that a shareholder was not the proper party to corporate litigation was relatively absolute.[18]

Separation of Ownership and Control

The shareholder's disqualification from direct participation in the classical corporation's legal affairs began the gradual separation of corporate ownership from corporate control, a process whose importance was not generally recognized until the second and third decades of the twentieth century. As the Supreme Judicial Court of Massachusetts had already explained in 1847, in denying a shareholder's suit for injuries suffered by a bank, corporate shares represent

> a limited and qualified right which the stockholder has to participate, in a certain proportion, in the benefits of a common fund . . . . To the extent of [any] separate and peculiar interest, a stockholder, no doubt, might maintain his separate and special action . . . ; as trover or trespass, for the conversion or tortious taking of his certificate . . . . But an injury done to the stock and capital, by negligence or misfeasance, is not an injury to such separate interest, but to the whole body of stockholders in common.[19]

The shareholders' derivative suit for the directors' neglect to bring or defend claims in violation of their legal duty came to prominence in mid-century as the shareholders' only interest in the corporation's legal affairs. This effectively segregated the legal claims of the corporation from those of its shareholders. In 1891 the corporate law scholar William W. Cook lamented "the separation of the stockholders from the corporate agents, of the investor from the investment, of the principal from the agent, with the expectation on the part of the investor, the principal, the stockholder, that profits will be made, honestly if possible, but that profits will be made."[20] The American business corporation had become a person but had lost its soul.

CHAPTER 2

Vested Corporate Rights

The Attack on the Marshall Era Contract Clause

With the ratification of the Fourteenth Amendment in 1868, the due process clause became the primary source of constitutional protection of individual liberties against state and local government. The greatest contribution of classical political economy to constitutional jurisprudence was the fourteenth amendment doctrine of substantive due process, which effectively constitutionalized classicism's abhorrence of state interference in the market. At the same time the contract clause, the principal source of protection in the antebellum period, became gradually less important until by century's end it was only a withered skeleton of its Marshall era frame. It has become a commonplace that the great contract clause decisions of the Marshall era were all but overruled.[1]

Both the contract clause and the due process clause were used by the federal courts to secure economic liberties. The thrust of contract clause jurisprudence was that once a right had become "vested" by either private bargaining or an arrangement with the state, the state could not take the right away or alter its fundamental character. It might alter the remedy, provided that the change did not undermine the opportunity to enforce the right.[2] For example, although the sovereign could not give debtors broad relief from debts incurred before the legislation was passed, it could deny creditors the right to have debtors sent to debtors' prison, and it could pass statutes of limitation on the right of recovery.[3] In contract clause jurisprudence, the United States Constitution did not define the substantive content of contractual rights; they were determined by a freely negotiated agreement. But once committed to contract, or "vested," such rights could not be substantially undermined by the state.

Under the doctrine of substantive due process, which followed more than a half century later, the Constitution itself created rights against the sovereign, such as the right to engage in a lawful occupation or to bargain freely for the terms of one's employment. Although these rights were characterized as a "liberty of contract,"[4] they were fundamentally different from the rights secured by the contract clause. They involved the liberty *to* contract—that is, to enter into prospective agreements— rather than the sanctity of contracts already in existence. The substantive content of such rights was defined in the first instance by the courts and protected whether or not the rights had been made the subject of an earlier private bargain.

The contract clause and substantive due process protected different interests. Both doctrines limited state power to control business corporations, but they were developed within antagonistic economic models and often yielded irreconcilable results. The most notable opposing pair of Supreme Court decisions is the *Charles River Bridge* case of 1837 and the *Slaughter-House Cases* of 1873.[5] In *Charles River Bridge* a divided Supreme Court rejected the argument that the contract clause forced implication of a monopoly privilege in a corporate charter that conferred no explicit monopoly right. In the *Slaughter-House Cases* a divided Supreme Court rejected the argument that the fourteenth amendment's due process clause forbade a state from placing a monopoly privilege in a corporate charter. Under the strong view of the contract clause developed during the Marshall era, monopoly rights were considered essential to economic development, and many prominent lawyers, including Joseph Story and Alexander Hamilton, believed they should be implied in charters for works of public improvements such as bridges.[6] But under the strong view of substantive due process emerging in the 1870's, monopoly was an abomination, and was not justified merely because it was expressly authorized in a state charter. In less than forty years a change in prevailing economic model had stood the Constitution on its head.

This change in constitutional doctrine followed after several interrelated developments in economic and legal theory. First was the change from a mercantilist economic model, in which state grants of vested rights were considered essential to economic development, to a classical regime, in which the state granted little or nothing, but protected the rights to bargain and engage freely in lawful enterprise. Second was the rise of the modern business corporation itself and the collapse of several legal doctrines that had distinguished the corporation from other forms of business organization. Third, was the broader movement by American legal writers and courts to conceptualize the corporation as a "person," just like any natural person engaging in business. This view originated in Chief Justice Taney's diversity jurisdiction decisions and became fully developed after the Court's holding that a corporation is a person for purposes of the fourteenth amendment.

Two Branches of Contract Clause Jurisprudence

The legislative history of the contract clause is scant and ambiguous. The framers of the Constitution were concerned principally with popular state attempts to relieve debtors from their creditors. They also expressed concern with *ex post facto* legislation, and both the contract clause and the *ex post facto* clause were frequently discussed together.[7] Nowhere appears even a hint that the contract clause referred to a land grant or a corporate charter from the state. Indeed, the framers were concerned almost exclusively with *private* contracts—those between two individuals, such as a debtor and a creditor—and not with states' reneging on past grants.

Nevertheless, Benjamin Wright observed in 1938 that "[m]uch the largest and most important group of cases under the contract clause is that having to do with the regulation of corporate enterprise."[8] By the Taney period a century earlier, the contract clause had already become the principal federal limitation on a state's power over its corporations. Distinct "private" and "public" branches of contract clause jurisprudence had emerged. The private branch governed state impairment of previously negotiated contracts between individuals. The public branch governed legislative impairment of state corporate grants and, to a lesser extent, public land grants, where the state was a party to the bargain for which protection was sought.

Although scholars have widely noted that the Taney Court and its successors "emasculated" the Marshall Court's contract clause doctrine, they have not observed that this occurred almost exclusively within the "public" branch of contract clause jurisprudence. Beginning with *Charles River Bridge* (1837), Chief Justice Taney began tugging at the foundation of the Marshall era contract clause by reducing federal supervision of state corporate regulation. However, the same Taney Court continued vigorous, even broadened protection to creditors victimized by states' debtor relief. The supposed transformation from vested to substantive rights against the state was nothing other than a change in the way the federal courts limited state power over business corporations.

The Political Economy of Marshall Court Contract Clause Jurisprudence

The most important Marshall era contract clause decisions are *Fletcher v. Peck* (1810), *Dartmouth College v. Woodward* (1819), *Sturges v. Crowinshield* (1819), and *Ogden v. Saunders* (1827).[9] In *Fletcher* the Court held that the contract clause forbade a state from rescinding a prior land grant, because the earlier grant was a contract with the grantees that the rescinding act presumed to impair. *Dartmouth College* held that a state could not unilaterally amend a corporate charter that it had previously granted, because the charter constituted a contract and could not be changed without the grantees' consent unless the charter itself permitted such modification. Although Dartmouth College was a charitable corporation, the decision clearly applied to business corporations as well, as the Supreme Court held in *Providence Bank v. Billings* (1830).[10] In *Sturges* the Court held that a state could not pass legislation discharging the preexisting debt of one who put up all his property for payment, when the amount of the debt exceeded the value of the property. When a debtor and creditor enter into a contract they ordinarily contemplate that payment will be taken not merely from the property that the debtor may own at a given time, but from any property he may acquire in the future. "Future acquisitions are, therefore, liable for contracts; and to release them from this liability impairs their obligation." In *Ogden v. Saunders* the Court held over Chief Justice Marshall's dissent that a state bankruptcy law could be applied *prospectively* to debts incurred after that statute took effect, although it could not impair the obligation of private contracts that had been executed previously.

Most Marshall era contract clause decisions were not concerned explicitly with state policy toward economic growth—other than to assert that states that honored debtor-creditor arrangements and stood behind their land grants encouraged progress. But Federalists who came into political power after the American Revolution were greatly concerned with growth. The question was how growth could be achieved. The scant history of the contract clause suggests that its framers did have a particular danger to economic growth in mind: the threat to American creditworthiness that might result from debtor relief legislation passed by the states during the 1780's recession. Such a concern was equally consistent with the mercantilist political economy of the day and the classicism that was to follow.[11]

Federalist and classical interpretations of the contract clause were in close agreement on the issue of sanctity of private contract, but they were poles apart on the question of state subsidy. Within both economic models enforcement of private contracts was critical as a general rule, although the mercantile theory may have been more willing than the classical to upset a contract when it perceived substantive unfairness.[12] In his *First Report on the Public Credit* (1790),[13] Alexander Hamilton urged that American economic development required good internal as well as external credit, which could be facilitated only if all debts were paid in full. But Hamilton then proposed an array of taxes and duties in order to help fund that debt.

Federalist and classical policy diverged sharply on questions about the relationship between the state and economic development, and thus on the state's relationship with the developing business corporation.[14] Within the preclassical view the state was an active participant in economic development. In his 1791 *Report on Manufactures*[15] Hamilton argued that although growth in manufacturing would come as American reliance on agriculture drove its economy to a subsistence level, it would come much more quickly and at lower cost if encouraged by the government. He recommended that the government fund investments in new plant and equipment, with debt that would eventually be paid off by the investors themselves. But Hamilton also encouraged widespread use of bounties on local manufactured goods, to be funded by duties on imports—a suggestion that would have been anathema to most classicists a half century later. For Hamilton bounties were "indispensable to the introduction of a new branch" of manufacturing not yet present in the United States, although they might not be as important for industries that were well established.

America's first comprehensive treatise on political economy was written by Daniel Raymond in 1820 and enlarged in 1823 as *The Elements of Political Economy*.[16] Raymond's two-volume work is the only significant book on political economy written by a nineteenth-century American who clearly preceded the classical tradition. Raymond himself was a lawyer from Massachusetts who studied at the staunchly Federalist Litchfield Law School in the 1810's. His work was admired by John Jay, John Adams, and John Marshall.

Like Hamilton, Raymond believed that high tariffs and government intervention were necessary to ensure economic growth. By the time Raymond wrote, the classical revolution in political economy was already well under way in England. Much of Raymond's *Elements* was an attack on the laissez-faire attitude expressed in Adam Smith's *Wealth of Nations*. For example, Raymond noted that Smith's work had made "monopoly" almost a forbidden word in the political economist's lexicon. But many great works of government were monopolies. Although many monopolies held by private entrepreneurs were bad, Raymond conceded, "[t]here are numerous instances in which, for the purpose of accomplishing some specific object, or for the attainment of some national benefit, it may be expedient and useful to grant a private monopoly for a certain period":

> A nation may be desirous of establishing some useful manufactory, or to open some new source of trade, which is expected to be useful and important to the nation, at some future period; and for the attainment of these objects, it may be expedient to create a private monopoly for a limited period. This monopoly may be granted to a single individual, to a company, to a corporation, or to some particular town; and although the rest of the nation may be excluded from the benefit of it, still as the object is to promote national interests, and as it is the duty of every citizen to forego his own private advantage for the public good, no one will have a right to complain.

From the outset American states and local governments used a wide array of public and private inducements to encourage economic development. These included government construction of public works, taxation plus subsidies, and numerous grants of monopoly rights to turnpike corporations, bridge corporations, and later to some railroad corporations.[17] Although classicism, with its laissez-faire attitude toward economic development, may have come to dominate American political economy and even the American judiciary, it was never as successful in controlling executive or legislative policy making at the state and local level. Interventionist theories had attractions for the politician that laissez-faire classicism could not match.

The constitutional law writer who best expressed the preclassical theory of the corporation was Justice Story. The second edition of his *Commentaries on the Constitution*[18] was published in 1851, after he had had some time to reflect on the major corporation decision of the Taney Court, *Charles River Bridge,* from which he had dissented. The holding that a monopoly provision was not implied in a corporate charter enraged Story because it undermined the state's obligation to bargain in good faith. Such good faith could be protected only if charters were construed liberally in favor of the incorporators "so far as to secure them in the enjoyment of what is actually granted," at least when the function of the corporation confers a valuable benefit on the public. The good faith consideration for the grant of corporate privileges "was not merely the granting of a right to build a bridge, but an implied contract, to restrict themselves from interfering to impair or destroy the value of that grant." Had the legislature originally included a proviso that if the bridge were successful the state would be free to charter a second bridge, "the inadequacy and insecurity of the consideration would have prevented any prudent man from accepting the charter." A policy of strict construction would make future investors more reluctant, for they could find their investment undermined by an unanticipated state usurpation of their assumed rights.

Classicism and the Obligation of Contract

Even the Federalist period saw substantial dissent from the Hamiltonian approach to state encouragement of economic growth. Jeffersonians, particularly James Madison, objected that Hamilton's plan of subsidies and bounties would encourage only those "artificial" types of manufacturing that needed subsidies in order to survive. The state should encourage whatever manufacturing developed naturally.[19] Madison conceded that the resulting manufactures might be less sophisticated or refined, at least in the early stages, but they would be good precisely because they were self-supporting.

Jeffersonian thought drew heavily upon the writing of Adam Smith. But Jefferson was guided by an ideology fundamentally agrarian rather than industrial. He envisioned the United States as a nation of farmers— "those who labour in the earth." Jeffersonians feared that subsidies and bounties for manufacturing would drain the farming economy and encourage the development of a privileged class of the kind that accounted for so many of England's problems.[20] Aggressive, pro-industrial classical political economy did not emerge until the early 1820's, with the rise of the Jacksonian movement.

One would hardly think that classical political economy would weaken the role of contract in society. Classicism represented the "triumph" of contract in a variety of senses. Under the classical theory the contract was the preeminent expression of the individual will, and its sanctity was protected rigorously by courts from perceived legislative interference.[21] The fundamental premise of the "invisible hand" was that private bargaining would yield the optimal distribution of goods and services.

But the classical revolution could take place only if given a fair chance. The state had to extricate itself as much as possible from preclassical entanglements. The entanglements were manifold, but in general they were state and municipal subsidies designed to attract new business. These subsidies included outright grants of money, tax exemptions, grants of the right to injure the property of others, and grants of monopoly rights.

The differing preclassical and classical theories of economic growth were at least casually empirical. Federalist political economy developed at a time when capital was relatively hard to come by and economic growth was perceived as quite slow. As a result, the federalist tended to view new investments as entailing a high degree of risk. High initial cost was certain, but future income depended on the development of uncertain demand.

But the American classicist faced a much different world. Although capital was still hard to find, economic growth was not. Even more important was classicism's theory of competition and politics. In a properly functioning market those businesses would enter and survive which produced goods and services that people wanted and at a price they were willing to pay. Businesses that did this best would grow and enter new markets, while others would not. Monopoly grants, tax exemptions, direct subsidies, or other special privileges were bad, for they permitted special interest politics rather than entrepreneurial skill to determine who and what kinds of businesses would enter. By definition, the business that deserved to survive within the classical scheme was the one that did not need a subsidy.

The Classical Contract Clause during the Taney Era

Debtor-creditor regulation. The classical contract clause as developed by the Taney Court implied a high regard for the sanctity of private contracts, but the narrowest possible interpretation of earlier grants of developmental privileges from the state. As noted above, any suggestion that the Taney Court undermined Marshall era contract clause jurisprudence must distinguish between "private" and "public" contract clause opinions. In the realm of private contract the Taney Court did not retreat one whit from the strong Marshall position. In *Bronson v.*

Kinzie (1843) Chief Justice Taney wrote the opinion holding that a statutory right of redemption on a foreclosed mortgage was unconstitutional when applied to a mortgage executed before the statute was passed. Likewise, in *Gantley's Lessee v. Ewing* (1845) the Court unanimously struck down an Indiana statute forbidding foreclosed property to be sold for less than half its appraised value, when applied to a foreclosure decree that antedated the statute.[22]

In the controversial decision in *Gelpcke v. City of Dubuque* (1864),[23] decided at the end of Chief Justice Taney's tenure, the Supreme Court held that a state's invalidation of its own municipality's bonds impaired the obligation of a contract between the municipality and the bond holders. The municipal bond cases pitted the two classical principles of respect for contract and laissez-faire developmental policy against each other. The bonds had been issued in order to subsidize railroad construction. An earlier Iowa Supreme Court holding declaring the bonds invalid struck down the subsidy, but in the process upset the debtor-creditor relationship. In overruling the Iowa court the Taney Court effectively held that although state subsidization is bad, disrespect for contract is even worse.

During the balance of the classical period the Supreme Court did not retreat from the strong Taney Court position on private contracts. For example, in *Gunn v. Barry* (1873) and *Edwards v. Kearzy* (1878) it struck down retroactive application of state homestead exemptions from private debts. In every case in which substantial modification of a debtor-creditor relationship to the creditor's detriment was made retroactive, the Court struck it down. The Court did not alter this position until the *Blaisdell* case in 1934, when constitutional classicism was in its death throes. The Taney Court's contract clause decisions as well as those that followed were absolutely consistent with classicism's desire to protect the sanctity of private bargains.[24]

The classical contract clause and the corporation. The Taney Court's decisions in the public branch of contract clause jurisprudence are quite a different matter. The first great classicist Supreme Court corporations decision was the *Charles River Bridge* case of 1837,[25] in which Taney held that corporate charters must be strictly construed. The Court expanded this position at every opportunity. *West River Bridge Co. v. Dix* (1848)[26] held that a charter that gave the corporation a one-hundred-year privilege to operate a bridge could be taken under the state's eminent domain power. A state could thus buy itself out of a previous entanglement. Since the fifth amendment was not incorporated against the states for another half century,[27] this effectively gave the states a great deal of power to take back ill-advised charters without substantial concern about the federal courts. For example, in *Boston & Lowell Railroad* (1854)[28] the plaintiff's charter provided that "No other railroad than the one hereby granted shall, within thirty years from the passage of this act, be authorized to be made leading from Boston to Lowell." The defendant's competing railroad was chartered within the thirty-year limit. The Supreme Judicial Court of Massachusetts held that such a grant without compensation to the plaintiff impaired its charter, but that the problem could be cured if the defendant compensated the plaintiff for loss of the monopoly right.

In *Fanning v. Gregoire* (1853) the Taney Court went a step further, holding that a state charter granting the corporation the right to operate a ferry and guaranteeing that no county court could authorize the establishment of a competitor did not prevent the state legislature itself from authorizing a second, competing line. Similarly, in the *Richmond Railroad* case (1851) it held that a grant explicitly giving a railroad the exclusive right to carry passengers between Richmond and Fredericksburg did not prevent a competing line from being authorized to carry freight, nor a parallel line from operating part of the distance between those two points. And in *Hoboken* (1864) it held that a charter expressly giving a toll road company the exclusive right to operate a bridge did not prevent the legislature from chartering a railroad to build a parallel bridge. The Court reasoned that since the plaintiffs' plank bridge could not carry rail traffic, and the offending bridge carried only rail traffic, the two bridges did not compete and the proprietors' rights were not impaired. Of course, this ignored the fact that absent the railroad bridge *all* freight, whatever its overland mode of transport, had to pass over the river by either bridge or boat. Clearly the two bridges did compete, and the construction of the rail bridge certainly damaged the value of the plaintiffs' franchise.[29]

Taney applied every available argument to permit states to withdraw from previous entanglements with private corporations. When he was Attorney General to President Jackson he wrote a legal opinion stating that states did not have the power to grant monopoly rights—implying that corporations did not have such rights even if they were explicit in their grants.[30] Twenty years later Chief Justice Taney, writing for the Supreme Court, suggested that many if not most corporate charters were politically ill-advised. Taney took judicial notice of the fact that almost every bill of incorporation "is drawn originally by the parties who are personally interested in obtaining the charter; and that they are often passed by the legislature in the last days of its session, when, from the nature of our political institutions, the business is unavoidably transacted in a hurried manner, and it is impossible that every member can deliberately examine every provision in every bill upon which he is called on to act." However, "those who accept the charter have abundant time to examine and consider its provisions, before they invest their money."[31]

State reservations. Statutory reservation clauses began to appear at the beginning of the nineteenth century. An 1809 Massachusetts statute provided that the legislature could "from time to time" repeal or amend any corporate charter simply by giving notice to the corporation. A Virginia statute of 1805 contained a similar provision. Justice Story appeared to approve such reservations in his *Dartmouth College* opinion, when he suggested that a state could repeal or change a charter if it had reserved the power to do so in advance. It was unclear at the time whether the reservation had to appear in the charter of each corporation, or if the state could pass a general statute applying to all future corporations. Supreme Court decisions in the 1870's and 1880's found both to be acceptable, provided that they applied only to corporations chartered after the reservation statute was passed. The general reservation became the principal mechanism by which the states hedged on earlier commitments to business corporations.[32]

During the Jackson era state hostility toward private monopoly was the most obvious manifestation of the new classicism in political economy. In addition to placing antimonopoly provisions in their constitutions, many states also inserted reservation clauses. Delaware led the way in 1831, and by the Civil War fourteen states had adopted similar clauses, some even purporting to give state legislatures the power to revoke the charters of existing corporations.[33] For many states the problem of state commitments to specially chartered corporations became a nonissue, at least if the corporation was chartered after the reservation act was passed. The effect was that the remaining burden of state-created monopoly was far heavier on the original colonies and eastern states, which had issued many charters during colonial and Federalist times, than in the western and Mississippi Valley states, which had issued relatively few. This problem of monopoly belonged mostly to New England, New York, and Pennsylvania.

The Classical Contract Clause after the Civil War

The treatise tradition. Classicism became the dominant judicial theory during the last half of the nineteenth century. By that time state and local governments had entangled themselves in economic development in a way that was absolutely inconsistent with classicism's theory of economic growth. Literally thousands of business subsidies had been granted, and as many charters had been created, giving their recipients tax exemptions, monopoly rights, or other special privileges that undermined the classical theory of efficient business development.

The classical judiciary responded by developing a set of doctrines designed to limit state power to subsidize new business. The public purpose doctrine, to be discussed in Chapter 3, was the most important of these, although eminent domain doctrine and substantive due process later did the same thing. These doctrines were designed to force governments to place new and prospective businesses on an equal footing, so that the best would rise to the top.

But an equally serious problem was damage already done. Once a business had received a tax break, a special right to injure the property of others, or a monopoly privilege, competitive incentives in that market were forever destroyed. No one could compete on equal terms with those having such artificial advantages. Classicism's principle of economic development could be made to work properly only if, liberty of contract notwithstanding, the sovereign was permitted to extricate itself from unfortunate commitments made in the past. The principal role of classical contract clause jurisprudence was to facilitate this disentanglement, consistent with classicism's own especially high regard for the sanctity of contract. We have already seen how the Taney Court began this task. It was to be completed by that Court's successors.

The great treatise writers in the Jacksonian tradition often spoke explicitly about economic policy. For example, Thomas M. Cooley, author of *Constitutional Limitations*, believed that the task of undoing the damage caused by the *Dartmouth College* decision was every bit as important as the protection of substantive property rights against the state. Although much has been written about Cooley's considerable influence on the police power and substantive due process, relatively little attention has been paid to his position on the contract clause. He attacked the Marshall era contract clause at every opportunity. In *East Saginaw Manufacturing Co. v. City of East Saginaw* (1869),[34] his most important contract clause opinion as chief justice of the Michigan Supreme Court, Cooley adopted essentially the position developed by Taney in the *Charles River Bridge* case, but Cooley's dicta had much broader implications for future Supreme Court decisions.

In 1859 Michigan had passed a statute designed to encourage the manufacturing of salt by offering a ten-cent bounty on each bushel produced and exempting salt-producing land from property taxes. In 1861 the statute was amended to limit the amount of the bounty and reduce the property tax exemption to a maximum period of five years. When the plaintiffs' tax exemption expired and the city of East Saginaw attempted to collect property taxes, the plaintiff sued to enjoin enforcement, claiming that the amendments impaired a contractual obligation created in the original 1859 statute.

Cooley held that the 1859 statute was neither a contract nor a tax exemption, but rather a mere promise not to tax. The taxing power was one of the "essential powers of sovereignty, which the State must exercise again and again, as its needs or its interests may require. . . ." As a result, it cannot be "crippled or abridged" by a mere promise. Cooley found that it was "so often and so earnestly denied by learned and able jurists" that "any legislative body, chosen as representatives of the people" could "enter into any contract by which they bargain away any portion of the power to levy taxes . . . ." Most radically, Cooley observed that every statute implies a right of repeal, and a promise not to tax should be treated no differently. "The absence of any express reservation of the right to repeal, or of any limitation in time, is not therefore a fact of any significance . . . ."

Cooley's academic writing on the contract clause was even more to the point. He appended this footnote to the discussion of the *Dartmouth College* case in the 1871 revision of his treatise on *Constitutional Limitations:*

[U]nder the protection of the decision in the Dartmouth College Case the most enormous and threatening powers in our country have been created; some of the great and wealthy corporations actually having greater influence in the country and upon the legislation of the country than the states to which they owed their corporate existence. Every privilege granted or right conferred—no matter by what means or on what pretence—being made inviolable by the Constitution, the government is frequently found stripped of its authority in very important particulars, by unwise, careless or corrupt legislation. . . . [35]

The result, Cooley concluded, was that "a clause of the federal Constitution, whose purpose was to preclude the repudiation of debts" instead perpetuated the evil of entrenched corporate power.

Cooley urged broad interpretation of the view that a state could not contract away its police power, and that attempts to do so in charters to private corporations were void.[36] He suggested, for example, that a state could not exempt a corporation from the state's eminent domain power. If it expressly promised in a charter that the power would never be exercised, the promise "must be considered as only a valuable portion of the privilege secured by the grant, and as such liable to be appropriated under the power of eminent domain." The manifest illogic of concluding that a right to be free from eminent domain is nothing more than a property interest for which compensation must be paid when eminent domain is exercised did not appear to trouble him. Isaac Redfield, a prominent railroad law scholar and chief justice of the Vermont Supreme Court, took the same position, noting that the "law-making power of all free states" is something that resides "perpetually and inalienably in the legislature," and cannot be granted away.[37]

But what of the state's power to create monopolies? Some Jacksonians, such as Taney and the dissenters in the *Slaughter-House Cases* (1873),[38] denied that the state had the "police power" to create monopolies at all. But the *Slaughter-House Cases* majority was clearly of the opposite opinion; so Cooley was forced to regard the issue as settled in the third and subsequent editions of *Constitutional Limitations*. Nevertheless, he gave the *Slaughter-House* decision an extraordinarily narrow reading on the police power issue. He distinguished corporate charters involving franchises from those that involved general occupations. The state clearly had the power to create monopoly rights in bridges or ferries, Cooley concluded, because only the state had the power to confer the right to build and operate such facilities in the first place. However, ever since 1602 it had been established that the sovereign lacked the constitutional power to create private monopolies for common callings, such as the activity of being a butcher: "the grant of a monopoly in one of the ordinary and necessary occupations of life must be as clearly illegal in this country as in England . . . ."[39]

The charter upheld in the *Slaughter-House Cases* created a butchers' monopoly, which the state lacked the power to create under Cooley's reasoning. Cooley was not one to say that a recent Supreme Court case was wrongly decided. Rather, the true import of the *Slaughter-House Cases* was that, although a group of competitors of the incorporated firm could not impeach the monopoly grant as beyond the state's power, the state itself was not bound by the grant: "the legislature could not by a grant of this kind make an irrepealable contract." [40]As a result, the state was quite justified in later repealing the monopoly provision even though the contract clause forbade it from repealing a monopoly grant to a properly defined franchise, such as a gas light company. The Supreme Court accepted both of these positions.[41] This distinction between the durability of monopolies given to ordinary business and those given to "franchises" signaled the emergence of a distinct group of "public utility" corporations, which were to be treated differently from ordinary manufacturers. By the turn of the century they were governed by an entirely distinct body of law.

Just as the Taney Court did, Cooley experienced a tension between his respect for freedom of contract and his hatred of monopoly and special privilege. His ambivalence is reflected in two essays he wrote in 1878 and 1883[42] on the general subject of business regulation. Cooley was adamantly opposed to rate regulation in all but a few industries, but he made clear that his opposition was not based on any implied rights granted in corporate charters. Rather it was founded on the general limitations imposed by the fourteenth amendment on the state's regulatory power. In other words, the constraints operated on all firms alike, whether incorporated or not.

The common law required certain firms such as common carriers to charge only reasonable rates, Cooley conceded. However, reasonable rates are generally those set by competition, not by a court or legislature. Only when a company receives special privileges from the state—such as the power of eminent domain or a monopoly franchise freeing it from competition—does the state acquire the power to determine which rates are reasonable, because the special privileges free the firm from competition. The power to regulate then comes from the privileged monopoly status, not by virtue of the corporate charter.

But some charters gave corporations freedom from regulation as well as monopoly status. Legislatures were subject to corruption, and often gave special privileges where no public interest required them. In such cases "the State must abide by the grant, and if it was improvident, must suffer the consequences." But such charters are always to be strictly construed. Cooley suggested that even if a charter gave a railroad the power to set its own rates, the rates must be subject to the state's higher power to determine if the rates are reasonable. The Supreme Court eventually adopted this position in the *Railroad Commission Cases,* which are discussed below. The result was the substantial weakening of the contract clause as a limitation on state corporate control.

Francis Wharton, a clergyman who turned to the law and became one of the nineteenth century's most prolific treatise writers, was nothing if not orthodox. His writing is important not for its creativity, of which it generally showed little, but rather because it reflected the consensus position so well. If Cooley provided the creative impulse for substantive due process, Wharton furnished its orthodox restatement.

In the case of the contract clause, however, Wharton saw more clearly than Cooley the relationship between the classical corporation and American economic growth. While Cooley was concerned with equal access to business and abolition of special privilege, Wharton was concerned about making way for new technology. Permanent grants of monopoly or special privilege undermined both. In his 1884 *Commentaries*[43] Wharton suggested that the *Dartmouth College* decision should no longer be regarded as controlling, because it came out of an era when economic growth was much slower:

> The policy of irrevocably granting away public franchises, and fixing social rights in a constant perpetual mold, has become far more questionable with the lapse of years than it was at the time the business of the country was only slowly recovering from the paralysis produced by the war of 1812; when, in fact, as to machinery or facilities of transportation, there had been no material change since the constitution had been adopted. In those days, therefore, when an apparently permanent type had been assumed by society, there was nothing startling in the position that an adjustment of social rights made by any particular legislature should bind forever. Now, however, we have been taught by the great inventions of steam and of the telegraph, by the marvelous improvements of machinery by which industries of all kinds have been remodelled, and by the introduction of new staples displacing old, that the stationary and apparently immutable condition of society during the first quarter of the present century was exceptional, and that the normal type of social life, as of all other kinds of life, is mutability tending to development.

The *Dartmouth College* rule may be harmless when applied to charitable institutions, Wharton acknowledged, but it had no application to the charters of business corporations. Wharton preferred the English rule "that business franchises granted by the legislature can, in all cases, be recalled and modified when the public interests require, provided that in this way private property is not taken without adequate compensation."

In 1890 Christopher Tiedeman, another father of substantive due process, published *The Unwritten Constitution of the United States*. The title reveals the considerable extent to which the advocates of classicism were willing to carry constitutional noninterpretivism in order to support their economic views. Among the "unwritten" rights Tiedeman found implicit in the Constitution was the right to pursue a lawful occupation. The system of monopoly grants and special tax privileges fostered by the *Dartmouth College* decision effectively undermined this right by removing many areas of enterprise from full and free competition.[44]

Tiedeman elaborated in his important 1900 treatise on the police power.[45] For him, classical corporate theory justified both the narrowing of the contract clause and the expansion of substantive due process rights. Although Tiedeman generally maintained an extremely limited view of the state's authority to regulate, he nevertheless regarded any doctrine that a corporate charter created an exemption from future exercises of the police power as an affront:

> . . . the intention of a legislature to place a private corporation beyond the reach of the police power of the State—to grant to a corporation the right to do what it pleases in the exercise of its corporate powers, it matters not how much injury is inflicted upon the public, and yet be subject to no control or restraint, which is not provided by the laws in force when the charter was granted—is so manifestly unreasonable, that we cannot suppose that the legislature so intended, unless this extraordinary privilege is expressly granted.

Private business corporations were not unique creatures deserving special protection. Rather, "an act of incorporation simply guarantees to the incorporators the right to act and do business as a corporate body, subject, of course, to the laws of the land, and the legitimate control of government." As a result "the legal *status* of the corporation, as an artificial person, does not differ from the natural person, except so far as the charter may reserve or grant special privileges or impose peculiar burdens."

Chase, Waite, and Fuller. From the Civil War until the end of the century the Supreme Court never veered from the course that Taney had set. Although it continued to apply the contract clause to enforce private debtor-creditor agreements, the notion that a corporate charter was a contract according vested privileges to the corporation substantially fell apart. Business corporations lost contract clause arguments in the great majority of cases, usually on rationales that were flatly inconsistent with Marshall era interpretations. In *Fertilizing Co. v. Hyde Park*

(1878) the Supreme Court held that a charter granting a corporation the right to produce chemicals for fifty years at a designated site did not stop the incorporating state from shutting the plant down as a public nuisance to houses that had been built after the plant was incorporated. In *Ruggles v. Illinois* (1883) the plaintiff railroad corporation had a charter giving it authority to set its own rates in its by-laws and to make its own by-laws, provided that these did not conflict with state law. The Court held that the road must nevertheless be subject to the rates set by the state legislature after the railroad was chartered, because otherwise its by-laws would conflict with state law—specifically, the law setting the charges.[46] The *Railroad Commission Cases*[47] of 1886 made a final travesty of *Dartmouth College*. The plaintiff railroads had charters that expressly authorized them to fix their rates. To their claim that state commissions could not now be created to prescribe rates, the Court responded that the charters implicitly required the rates to be reasonable and said nothing about who should determine reasonableness. As a result, the railroads had only the power to "fix" the rate that the commissions established. However, the charters had not given the railroads in question the power to fix "reasonable" rates at all. For example, the charter in *Farmers' Trust* had empowered the company "to fix, regulate and receive the toll and charges by them to be received," and the one in *Illinois Central* had provided that the corporation's officers could "adopt and establish such a tariff . . . as they may think proper, and the same to alter and change at pleasure." The Court reasoned that charters implicitly incorporated the common law, and that the common law, not the express language of the charter, required that a common carrier's rates be reasonable. "The right to fix reasonable charges has been granted, but the power of declaring what shall be deemed reasonable has not been surrendered."

As Justice Stephen J. Field noted in dissent, the common law required rates to be sufficient to provide the company a fair return on the current market value of its assets. In this case, however, "improvements in machinery" and "decline in the cost of materials" had reduced the cost of railroad construction by one third. The result was that the railroads in question, which had been constructed when costs were much higher, would not receive an adequate return on their historical investment if the commissions adopted the common law rule. "Does anybody believe," Field asked rhetorically, that the railroads "would have undertaken the work . . . had they been informed that, notwithstanding their vast outlays, they should only be allowed . . . to receive a fair return upon its value, however much less than cost that might be?" Nevertheless, as the *Railroad Commission Cases* made clear, the mercantile theory that the charter was a contract with the state according unique privileges to the incorporated firm was dead.

CHAPTER 3

Politics and Public Goods

Writing around 1825, Thomas Cooper, the most Jeffersonian of America's political economists, minced no words about the American business corporation:

> [T]hese institutions are founded on the right claimed by government, to confer privileges and immunities on one class of citizens, not only not enjoyed by the rest, but at the expense of the rest. This is always done on the pretence of promoting the GENERAL WELFARE; a pretence of unlimited operation, and undefinable extent; and which has already rendered the constitution of the United States, a dead letter.
>
> Generally in this country, it has glutted itself by incorporating banking companies, insurance companies, canal companies, and manufacturing companies of various descriptions. All these are increasing daily, the list of public nuisances.[1]

Characteristically, the Jeffersonian Cooper responded to the Federalist corporation problem by attacking corporations on principle. Jacksonians, who were more entrepreneurial, chose rather to preserve the corporation but to democratize it to suit their purposes. General business incorporation acts, which permitted firms to incorporate without seeking a special charter from the legislature, first became popular during the Jacksonian period. Not long after followed a broad-based attack on legislative or municipal subsidies as devices for encouraging economic development. The subsidies consisted of municipal stock subscriptions or outright grants of cash, often supported by the issuance of municipal bonds. Beginning in the Taney period the Supreme Court decided some three hundred cases challenging the validity of these bonds under a variety of theories.[2]

As J. Willard Hurst has noted, there is no evidence that Jacksonians were opposed to incorporation on principle. Rather, they were concerned about equal access. They believed that the special charter system favored wealthy, well-established entrepreneurs at the expense of the newcomer.[3] Even Jackson's outspoken opposition to reincorporation of the Second National Bank was based on his hatred of hard money and the National Bank's dominance over state banks, not on any general hostility toward the corporation as a method of doing business. Indeed, one consequence of the general incorporation statute was a great increase in the number of business corporations. During the Jackson era the corporation became a democratic institution, consistent with the classical model of the business firm. Acquiring corporate status became easier than entering into business itself.

The close relationship between the rise of the general incorporation act and the subsequent judicial revolt against the special subsidy is striking. Both developments flowed naturally from the classical theory of the corporation. Within the mercantilist model the corporate structure was designed to give state protection to enterprises regarded as potentially unprofitable without it. Special franchise privileges, freedom from competition, and direct subsidy were merely alternative ways of achieving the same thing. For example, when the Federalist-controlled New York legislature began a comprehensive program of encouraging industrial development at the beginning of the nineteenth century, it simultaneously used subsidies and special incorporation as incentives. Two decades later, when the dominant Jeffersonian Republicans believed that the policy of encouraging growth "artificially" had become too politicized, they wrote into the 1821 New York Constitution a clause requiring a two-thirds vote of both houses of the legislature in order to appropriate "public moneys or property for local or private purposes" or to create or renew any corporate charter. This Jeffersonian and later Jacksonian opposition to business subsidy was certainly ideological, but it may also have been practical: an extraordinarily high number of public subsidies went to failed enterprises, such as canals, turnpikes, and later railroads, and the default rate on publicly financed loans was high. The failures peaked during the 1837–1843 panic, and inspired a great Jacksonian outcry against corporate subsidies.[4]

For the Jacksonian Democrats, support of general incorporation acts and opposition to subsidy were the two edges of a single sword. The

1846 New York Constitution, a Jacksonian document, replaced the two-thirds vote requirement with a prohibition against "the credit of the state" being "given or loaned to, or in aid of any individual, association, or corporation."[5] But it replaced the two-thirds vote requirement for creating corporations—a relic of Jeffersonian hostility to business corporations in general—with a provision mandating general incorporation except where "the objects of the corporation cannot be attained under general laws." Acting under this constitution the New York legislature passed a series of general incorporation acts—one for roads and turnpikes, another for manufactures, another for railroads, and so on.[6]

The rise of general acts of incorporation in the 1840's and 1850's rested on the premise that the corporation was no longer a "prerogative of the crown," requiring special permission and dedication to a public use. A corollary was that public subsidies for such corporations were no longer necessarily dedicated to a public use either. This set the stage for a general challenge to public subsidies on the theory that they were politically motivated grants to favored, established entrepreneurs at the expense of others—in the words of the Maine Supreme Court, "to load the tables of the few with bounty that the many may partake of the crumbs that fall therefrom."[7]

The judge-made weapon for this assault was an unwritten constitutional requirement that taxation could be only for a "public use." First state courts, and later the lower federal courts and the Supreme Court, held in a series of decisions that corporate status was not the determining factor whether an enterprise was engaged in a "public use." Rather, public use should be determined by looking at the firm's business activities. Under this rule subsidies for railroads were generally upheld, and those for ordinary manufacturing were commonly struck down. The principal Supreme Court decision is *Loan Association v. Topeka* (1875), where the Court condemned a statute authorizing a municipality to provide bonds to an incorporated bridge works. The bonds were not a loan but rather an outright cash grant to the bridge company. The Supreme Court held that a municipality might lawfully make such a subsidy if it had property of its own for financing it. But since the subsidy monies had to come out of taxes, they required the municipality to tax for a "private" rather than public purpose, which the United States Constitution forbade.[8]

The principal architects of the public purpose doctrine were two pioneers who had migrated to the Midwest during the Jackson era, Chief Justice Thomas M. Cooley of the Michigan Supreme Court and

Judge John F. Dillon, first of the Iowa Supreme Court, later of the federal circuit court. Cooley, citing no authority, had concluded in his *Constitutional Limitations* that "certain elements are essential in all taxation."⁹ If one of these elements is absent the citizens themselves could challenge a tax on constitutional grounds "notwithstanding there be no conflict with constitutional provisions." One of these "essential elements" of taxation, argued Cooley, is that taxes may not be raised except for a "public purpose." The "exaction of moneys from the citizens for other purposes is not a proper exercise of this power, and must therefore be unauthorized." This extraordinary piece of mid-nineteenth-century noninterpretivism was proposed in such an understated way that it even slipped by the Supreme Court. Justice Samuel F. Miller adopted Cooley's proposal in the *Topeka* case, citing Cooley, John Dillon on *Municipal Corporations*, and one state case as his only authority.

John Dillon, whose work probably contributed more than anyone's except Cooley's to the constraints late nineteenth-century courts placed on state regulatory power, was more explicit than Cooley about the relationship between general incorporation and the public purpose doctrine. General incorporation acts, he argued, removed the corporation as such from the realm of public purpose. Public purpose must be determined from the nature of the activity rather than the corporate status of the persons engaged in it.¹⁰

In 1873 Judge Dillon wrote a circuit court opinion later affirmed by the Supreme Court in one of the companion cases to *Topeka*.¹¹ Dillon's decision struck down the same Kansas statute, applied in this case to a municipal subsidy to a foundry and machine shop. Dillon located the limitation on the municipality's power to tax for the benefit of a private corporation in the general incorporation acts themselves. General corporation laws were "intended to correct an existing evil, and to inaugurate the policy of placing all corporations of the same kind upon a perfect equality as to all future grants of power" and "of making all judicial construction of their powers, or the restrictions imposed upon them, equally applicable to all corporations of the same class." One of the objects of general corporation acts "was to cut up by the roots the mischief of special legislation, particularly in respect to corporations, both public and private."

But special subsidies by their nature selected one or a small number among these equals for special treatment, with no consideration to be given in return. The proprietors of a general manufacturing corporation, unlike the shareholders in a franchise or public service company, "are under no obligations, by reason of the aid extended and the burden of taxation thereby imposed upon the municipality, to render it or the state any duty or service whatever—not even to repay the loan, or to maintain for any specified time the contemplated manufacturing enterprise." As the New York Court of Appeals observed three years later when it struck down a municipal subsidy to a lumber mill,[12] the corporation had been created under a general incorporation law. As a result, there was no presumption that its activities were for a public purpose. "[N]othing in the fact of this body being a corporation" was relevant. "Any individual, or partnership of individuals, with the requisite capital, could do all that this corporation proposed to do . . . ."

Dillon's argument that the general manufacturing company provided no "consideration" for its subsidy was important. It explained why subsidies to the railroads were routinely upheld. Municipalities were forced to compete with one another for railroad depots, and the subsidies given to railroads were generally conditioned on the railroad's building its terminal or laying its tracks through or within a specified distance from the municipality. The railroad was performing a "public" service, an act that brought it within the municipal taxing power.[13]

Courts had a difficult time distinguishing private from public purposes. The emerging consensus was that "public purpose" in taxation law meant about the same thing as "public purpose" in eminent domain law, since both involved a forced transfer of property from one person to another. This solution ultimately begged the question, for the power of eminent domain was also justified only if it were for a "public purpose." Nevertheless, several courts held that government subsidies were generally permissible for corporations that had the power of eminent domain, but not for others. Since the power of eminent domain was a prerogative of the crown, only corporations could exercise it, and only if their charters so provided. The effect was that corporate status was a necessary, but not a sufficient, condition for direct government subsidization.[14]

The public purpose distinction further widened the developing gap between utilities, or public service corporations, and general corporations. In his 1909 treatise on franchises Joseph Joyce found great ambiguity in the use of the term "franchise," and devoted two chapters to its definition.[15] While all corporations technically received a "franchise" from the state, the "franchise" accorded a public service corporation was different. Joyce concluded that although the corporate charter itself was a franchise from the state, a particular charter might also contain other franchises that distinguished it from general corporations. These additional, "special" franchises distinguished the public utility and justified more intensive state regulation than would be appropriate for the ordinary manufacturing firm. The "public purpose" debate thus led to the formulation of a narrower "public service" concept that applied largely to utilities—a special subclass of corporations that were indeed formed for a public purpose. This development paved the way for the emergence of a distinct class of regulated industries.

CHAPTER 4

The Corporate Personality

The legal doctrine that a corporation is a "person" for most legal purposes, including those of the fourteenth amendment, is one of the most misunderstood in American legal history. By the end of the nineteenth century the doctrine had given the corporation an almost metaphysical quality—it was an intangible creation of the law, yet so much a "person" that it even had constitutional rights.

The doctrine of constitutional corporate personhood was the solution courts chose for two quite different problems. The first was how to treat the incorporated business firm just like any other form of enterprise—to guarantee that the owners of property held in the name of a corporation would receive the same constitutional protections as the owners of property held in their own name. The second problem, which lies below the surface, was how to assign the power to assert constitutional rights in corporately held property. The doctrine that a corporation is a constitutional person meant that the corporation's directors or managers had the power to assert the corporation's constitutional claims. The far less cited corollary was that the shareholders *lacked* standing to assert these rights. Indeed, had the doctrine of corporate constitutional personhood not been developed, the result certainly would not have been that corporate property was unprotected by the fourteenth amendment. Rather, it would have been that an unconstitutional injury to corporate property is an injury to the constitutional rights of shareholders. Thus an important effect of the *Santa Clara* decision (1886), which declared the corporation a constitutional person, was to enlarge the gap between ownership and control that characterized the development of the classical corporation. Managers, not shareholders, should have a generally exclusive power to assert the corporation's constitutional rights.

Domestic Corporations

The classical business corporation became a device for managing capital and investment, not a special privilege from the state. But this did not mean that the corporation lost most of its state protection. On the contrary, it became entitled to the same set of protections that belonged to any person wishing to do business. A key doctrine in this development was that the corporation was a "person" entitled to many of the protections that the fourteenth amendment accorded natural persons, including liberty of contract, equal protection, and eventually the incorporation of the just compensation clause. The decline of contract clause jurisprudence and its gradual replacement by substantive due process was simply the Supreme Court's rejection of a set of protections that were unique to corporations as a class in favor of protections that were given to all forms of business organization alike. As Justice Field noted in his concurring opinion in *Santa Clara*,[1] "nearly all great enterprises are conducted by corporations." It was therefore essential for the Court to determine "whether [corporate] property is subject to the same rules of assessment and taxation as like property of natural persons."

In *Santa Clara* the Supreme Court first suggested that a corporation is a "person" within the meaning of the fourteenth amendment, noting only that it found the issue too plain for argument. The Court noted two years later in *Pembina*[2] that "corporations are merely associations of individuals united for a special purpose, and permitted to do business under a particular name, and have a succession of members without dissolution." As a result, the "equal protection of the laws which these bodies may claim is only such as is accorded to similar associations within the jurisdiction of the State."

As Morton J. Horwitz has observed,[3] *Santa Clara* in no way represents the Supreme Court's rejection of older "associational" or "fictional" theories of the corporation in favor of an "entity" theory that imputed personhood to the corporation itself. On the contrary, the Court relied explicitly on the notion that a corporation is nothing more than an association of individuals. Its interests are the same as those of its shareholders.

The best explanation of *Santa Clara* is that by 1886 it was well established that the corporation, rather than its shareholders, must generally be the named party to the corporation's litigation.[4] In fact, the shareholders themselves generally lacked standing to redress the grievances of the corporation in court. The corporation owned real property in its own name, transacted business in its own name, and dealt with the government in its own name. Even though the purpose of *Santa Clara* was to protect the federal constitutional rights of a corporation's shareholders, the most consistent and practical vehicle for achieving this within the existing legal framework was to declare the corporation itself a constitutional "person." There was also the precedent of many cases involving corporate "citizenship" for diversity purposes. The move from declaring corporations to be constitutional "citizens" to finding them "persons" was not large, particularly in an era when the fourteenth amendment's coverage was relatively insubstantial. The Court had refused to apply due process analysis in cases involving corporate regulation.[5] In 1886, the same year as *Santa Clara*, the Supreme Court first struck down a statute under the equal protection clause, but two years later made clear that the standard was not high. Selective incorporation of the Bill of Rights would not begin for another decade. Only thirty or forty years of hindsight can attach great consequences to the substantive protections produced by the *Santa Clara* decision.[6]

The Court might have selected some other route to giving what little fourteenth amendment protection there was to private property owned by corporations. For example, it might have said that the corporation represents the constitutional property rights of its shareholders. But then it would have involved itself in a quagmire of problems concerning one person's right to assert the constitutional claims of another. Worst of all, it might have invited the shareholders themselves to participate in constitutional litigation, given that their constitutional rights were at stake. The thought that each individual shareholder might challenge a rate regulation as confiscatory would make any federal judge shudder. One consequence of the *Santa Clara* decision was that since the corporation was a "person" entitled to assert constitutional rights respecting its property, the shareholders themselves *lacked* standing to assert the same rights.

The Supreme Court found shareholder standing in cases asserting the constitutional rights of the corporation if the suit were properly maintained as a shareholders' derivative action—a lawsuit filed by shareholders against the corporation in order to force its directors to perform a legal duty. *Dodge v. Woolsey* (1856), in which the Supreme Court first approved such suits, was a shareholders' challenge to the directors' payment of an allegedly unconstitutional tax. In *Pollock v. Farmers' Loan & Trust Co.* (1895) the plaintiff stockholders sued their corporation to enjoin it from paying the federal income tax, successfully alleged to be unconstitutional. The Court held that the shareholders had standing to sue their own corporation in equity "to prevent any threatened breach of trust in the misapplication or diversion of the funds of a corporation by illegal payments out of its capital . . . ." And in *Smyth v. Ames* (1898), the Court permitted stockholders to maintain class-action suits against their companies to establish that a state rate statute was unconstitutional, and to enjoin the corporations from charging the illegal rates. The Court noted that multiple stockholders' suits would not arise, because the decree would bind all the stockholders as well as the corporation in which they held shares.[7]

The implications of *Santa Clara* for shareholders' constitutional suits became clear in 1903, in *Corbus v. Alaska Treadwell Gold Mining Co.* The plaintiff shareholder sued his corporation to restrain it from paying a state license tax alleged to be unconstitutional. The Supreme Court held that only the corporation could bring suit. "The directors represent all the stockholders and are presumed to act honestly and according to their best judgment for the interests of all," noted the Court. This presumption could be defeated in a shareholders' derivative action, but in this case the plaintiff had not even alleged that he had made a demand on the directors "to protect the corporation against this alleged illegal tax." The same year the Supreme Court required that shareholders' suits asserting the constitutional claims of the corporation must meet the requirements of derivative actions, including "an allegation that the directors of a corporation have refused to institute the proceedings themselves in the name of such corporation . . . ." After that the Supreme Court routinely entertained shareholder suits challenging unconstitutional legislation, provided that the suits were cast as derivative actions and the corporation itself was named as a defendant. In the first instance, however, the obligation to assert the corporation's constitutional rights lay with the directors.[8]

In retrospect, it seems that the Court selected the shortest and most practical route to its end—constitutional protection of the property rights of shareholders equivalent to that given unincorporated firms or persons. Nevertheless, the Progressive critique of Gilded Age corporate law was inclined to describe *Santa Clara* and its progeny as "big business" decisions by a reactionary Supreme Court. John R. Commons's *Legal Foundations of Capitalism* (1924) blamed the Supreme Court's hostility toward labor unions on the decision that a corporation is a legal "person."[9] As a result, Commons complained, a group of laborers acting together in an unincorporated labor union constitute a "conspiracy," which the law abhors, while a union of capitalists that combines into a business corporation is a single entity incapable of conspiring. Clearly, however, neither *Santa Clara* nor *Pembina* expressed any Supreme Court bias in favor of big business at the time they were decided. On the contrary, they were the natural outgrowth of a Jacksonian ideology whose goal was the constitutional merger of the business corporation into ordinary enterprise. The eventual effect was that corporations received the same freedom from state regulation that liberty of contract and substantive due process accorded unincorporated businesses.

But there is one important difference between the natural person's right to contract and the right of the corporation: the corporation has only those powers granted it by the sovereign. Already in 1880 a Maryland court had held that although a state legislature might not forbid natural persons from paying wages by something other than money, it had that power over corporate employers, at least where the state had retained the power to amend the corporate charter. The difference was that "a corporation has no inherent or natural rights like a citizen." In the wake of *Santa Clara* and *Pembina* several state courts concluded that, general applicability of the fourteenth amendment notwithstanding, *liberty of contract* was a special liberty unique to people. "Natural persons do not derive the right to contract from the legislature. Corporations do," the Arkansas Supreme Court concluded in 1894. As a result, although the legislature lacked the power to control how wages were paid by natural persons to their employees, they could control the wage payment practices of corporate employers. In 1892 a Rhode Island court upheld a statute requiring corporate employers to pay employees weekly, noting that the statute would be unconstitutional when applied to natural persons. However, corporations had no inherent right to contract, and "we see no reason why the legislature, under its reserved power to amend charters, cannot limit the power to contract in the future just as they might have fixed it in the original charter."[10]

This view had Supreme Court precedent. In *Bank of Augusta v. Earle* (1839),[11] the Court, speaking through Chief Justice Taney, had held that corporations of one state could do business in another state, but only subject to that state's permission and regulation. In reaching that result Taney explicitly rejected the notion that a corporation had the same power to contract that its stockholders had. The issue was the privileges and immunities clause, not the fourteenth amendment, but the conclusions were clearly broad enough to apply to both. Taney concluded that the "only rights" a corporation could claim were those "given to it in [the] charter, and not the rights which belong to its members as citizens of a State . . . ."

But the Supreme Court applied liberty of contract in favor of a corporation in *Allgeyer v. Louisiana* (1897), its very first substantive due process decision, with no mention of any difference between natural persons and corporations. Likewise, in *Coppage v. Kansas* (1915), which struck down a labor statute applied against a domestic corporation on liberty of contract grounds, the Court again failed to consider whether a corporation might have a smaller liberty of contract than a natural person. In *Chicago, Burlington & Quincy Railroad Co. v. McGuire* (1911) the Court upheld a regulatory statute applied to a corporation and challenged on liberty of contract grounds. The Court listed several reasons why the statute was within the state's police power and therefore did not interfere with the plaintiff's freedom of contract, but the plaintiff's corporate status was not among them.[12]

In these fourteenth amendment cases the Supreme Court was protecting the constitutional rights of shareholders, to whom liberty of contract clearly applied. *Bank of Augusta* offered no precedent limiting their rights. Nevertheless, the Supreme Court's failure in the due process cases to consider state power over corporate charters is troublesome, and seems quite inconsistent with its contract clause jurisprudence of the same era, where it interpreted state reservations expansively.

But this triumph of the corporation's liberty of contract was important constitutional recognition of the classical corporation—all the more important because the arguments against the doctrine were persuasive, well established in state decisions, and so thoroughly ignored by the Supreme Court. For the Court to hold otherwise would have been to create a regime in which the state could freely regulate wages, hours, and working conditions of corporate employers but not of unincorporated ones. Such a distinction would have undermined the classical view of the general business corporation as nothing more than an efficient device for raising capital and doing business.

Foreign Corporations

Section 1 of the fourteenth amendment uses the word "person" three times. The first use defines citizens of the United States as "persons born or naturalized in the United States." The second provides that a state may not deprive a person of life, liberty, or property without due process of law. The third provides that it may not deny the equal protection of laws to any "person within its jurisdiction." Eventually the Supreme Court came to hold that a firm incorporated in one state but doing business in a different state is a "person within the jurisdiction" of the second state.

In *Bank of Augusta v. Earle* (1839) the Supreme Court had held that a state could more or less arbitrarily exclude foreign corporations from doing business within their territory. Under that rule the Supreme Court upheld discriminatory taxes against foreign corporations as late as the 1870's and 1880's.[13] The same cases established that a corporation is not a "citizen" for purposes of the privileges and immunities clause, which controlled discrimination by one state against citizens from another state. This view was reiterated in *Pembina Mining Co. v. Pennsylvania* (1888),[14] which held both that a corporation was a "person" under the fourteenth amendment but not a "citizen" under the privileges and immunities clause. Although a state could not unreasonably discriminate on the basis of corporate status, the prohibition against discrimination on the basis of state citizenship did not apply to corporations.

Even though the *Earle* doctrine was reiterated in *Pembina,* it had already began to unravel in a series of "unconstitutional conditions" cases. In 1874 Justice Bradley wrote that although a state might have the power "of prohibiting all foreign corporations from transacting business within its jurisdiction, it has no power to impose unconstitutional conditions upon their doing so." The unconstitutional conditions cases, the liberty of contract cases, and a series of cases striking down discriminatory taxes under the commerce clause gradually permitted American corporations to work in multistate markets. This development culminated in a series of decisions in the first two decades of the twentieth century holding that a foreign corporation is a "person within the jurisdiction" of a state in which it is doing business, and entitled not to be expelled arbitrarily.[15] These cases, which carried the "personhood" of the corporation much further than early Jacksonians such as Taney had been willing to do, deliberately put the corporation doing interstate business on the same constitutional footing as the natural person.

But the multistate corporation proved to be a powerful and unruly mount, often beyond any state's ability to control. The corporation's expanded rights to engage in multistate business contributed to the rise of the "trust" problem and the perceived growth of business concentration that eventually would signal the demise of the classical corporation.

CHAPTER 5

Limited Liability

Modern limited liability entails that shareholders are generally not accountable for debts or other claims against the corporation except to the extent of their investment in shares. English common law recognized limited liability, and this rule was effectively enacted in an 1825 statute. Limited liability was known in the United States from the eighteenth century. Joseph Davis notes that at least one manufacturing firm received a specific grant of limited liability in its charter in 1786. In 1832 Angell and Ames concluded that "[n]o rule of law . . . is better settled, than that, in general, the individual members of a private corporate body are not liable for the debts, either in their persons or in their property, beyond the amount of property which they have in the stock." They later noted that some states had passed statutes increasing shareholder liability beyond the common law rule.[1]

Voluminous writings on the history of American corporate law have not adequately explained either the evolution of limited liability in the nineteenth century or its meaning. Morton J. Horwitz regards the modern concept of relatively strict limited liability as a late nineteenth-century phenomenon.[2] But ample evidence suggests that it grew up during the Jackson era and was part of the classical theory of the corporation. Connecticut, New Hampshire, Maine, Vermont, Rhode Island, New Jersey, and Pennsylvania all made limited liability the general rule by statute during the second and third decades of the nineteenth century.[3]

Early in the nineteenth century American states experienced a general legislative and judicial reaction against limited liability. Jeffersonians, who were not favorably inclined toward business corporations in general, appear to have regarded it as simply another of the political favors granted to wealthy entrepreneurs. Thomas Cooper railed at limited liability, which he characterized as a "mode of swindling, quite common and honourable in these United States" and "a fraud on the honest and confiding part of the public."[4] But even the Federalists had a much narrower concept of limited liability than did the Jacksonians, as can be seen in the Massachusetts experience.

Massachusetts for a time even provided for *un*limited liability of shareholders. Much has been written about the Massachusetts experience with shareholder liability. But the Commonwealth was atypical, reflecting the relative weakness of the Jackson movement there.[5] Some Massachusetts charters provided for unlimited liability, and an 1809 Massachusetts statute applying to all manufacturing corporations made shareholders directly answerable to the corporation's creditors fourteen days after it was determined that the corporation's assets were insufficient to pay its debts. In 1822 this statute was amended to create unlimited liability for those who had been shareholders at the time the debt was incurred but who were no longer shareholders. However, in areas where this statute did not apply, such as corporations for turnpikes and banks, courts continued to apply the common law rule of limited liability. In his 1879 treatise on shareholders' liability Seymour Thompson noted that Massachusetts courts had held that the statutes expanding shareholders' liability must be strictly construed as statutes in derogation of the common law.[6]

During the 1820's a great public debate over the Massachusetts policy respecting shareholder liability ensued, Jacksonian liberals generally arguing that unlimited liability was driving capital from the state and into nearby Maine and New Hampshire, where limited liability prevailed.[7] An anonymous writer in the 1829 *American Jurist* concluded that unlimited liability in Massachusetts had "driven thousands of her sons to other quarters of the country."[8] Furthermore, the effect of the Massachusetts policy was to give corporations with wealthy shareholders an "extensive credit," while those whose shareholders were less wealthy had to search for financing. The relatively impecunious entrepreneurs who paid their entire fortunes into their incorporated enterprise were forever at a disadvantage to the rich investor who had a great deal left over. But limited liability gave the corporation held by small shareholders the same status as the one held by the wealthy, provided that the corporations themselves were equally creditworthy. That argument almost certainly gives away its author as a Jacksonian.

The author recognized that creditors had a right to their security; but they would not be injured if they were entitled to "know the fund to which they trust" when they made the loan. Just as a potential creditor checks into the assets of a natural person before lending money, so too he should inquire into the corporation's assets and liabilities. The real problem for creditors was not limited liability but misstated capitalization. In many cases, the author noted, "but a small part of [the corporation's stated capital] is paid in." Clearly, "institutions carried on in this manner must be much more liable to failure than if the whole capital was paid in, as a much smaller loss would overwhelm them." He then proposed a statute "requiring a certain part of the capital to be paid before the corporation commences operation, and the whole to be paid in before a certain date, and leaving corporators liable as partners, in case of a neglect to comply . . . ."

In 1830 Massachusetts provided for full limited liability once the whole amount of capital had been paid in. The state's first general incorporation act, passed in 1851, contained a similar provision. In general, a strong case can be made for the traditional view expressed by the Oscar and Mary Handlin that limited liability was well established even in conservative Massachusetts by the end of the Jackson era.[9]

New York, probably the state with the greatest influence on antebellum American corporate law, accepted limited liability less reluctantly. Like Massachusetts, New York went through a period in which the common law rule of limited liability was narrowed, and a subsequent Jacksonian period in which it was substantially restored with a distinctively classical architecture. An 1826 New York decision that a statute authorizing manufacturing corporations required "double liability" of shareholders set off a Jacksonian revolt. The result was a general statute in 1828 providing for limited liability to all shareholders whose shares were fully paid in. Likewise, New York's general incorporation acts of the 1840's and 1850's provided for limited liability with respect to fully paid shares, but double liability before shares were fully paid in.[10]

New York's 1848 general incorporation statute applying to manufacturers needs some discussion for two reasons. First, it was highly influential and created a model for general incorporation acts in many states; second, it has been described as imposing a general requirement of "double liability" on shareholders.[11] The statute rested on a distinctly classical view of the capital market and of the role of the corporation in facilitating economic development. Section 6 authorized the incorporators to "call in and demand" the stockholders' unpaid subscriptions—the money that the stockholders had promised to pay in, and upon which the announced capitalization of the company was based. If a shareholder did not pay on demand, he forfeited all shares both paid in and subscribed.

Section 10 of the statute, which contained the "double liability" clause, provided that all stockholders would be individually liable "to an amount equal to the amount of stock held by them respectively for all debts and contracts made by such company, until the whole amount of capital stock fixed and limited by such company shall have been paid in." Section 12 required the trustees to make annual reports showing both the capital paid in and the existing debts of the corporation. If they failed to do this or misrepresented debts and paid-in capital, they were jointly and severally liable for the corporation's debts that might exceed its paid in capital. Section 18 of the statute additionally provided for joint and several liability of the stockholders for payment of the wages of corporation employees. This clause, very common in nineteenth-century general incorporation acts, distinguished wages from other debts by providing for expanded shareholder liability. The New York courts construed the clause narrowly.[12] Finally, section 25 of the statute required the trustees to keep a book, listing the stockholders' names alphabetically with their addresses, their subscriptions, and the amount of money they had actually paid in. This book had to be available during all usual business hours, "every day except Sunday and the fourth day of July," and must be open for inspection to creditors. The book was "presumptive evidence of the facts stated therein, in favor of the plaintiff, in any suit or proceeding against such company, or against any one or more stockholders." Heavy fines were then imposed on officers or agents who failed to keep these records or falsified them. The statute nowhere provided for general shareholder liability after the shareholder's subscription was fully paid. Under the virtually unanimous rule, the absence of any provision meant absolutely limited liability.[13]

This New York statute and others modeled after it[14] rested on the premise that the paid-in capital of the corporation was a "fund" upon whose existence creditors were entitled to rely. Increased shareholder liability would result if the fund proved to be smaller than the par value multiplied by the number of outstanding shares indicated. The rule, which came to be called the "trust-fund" doctrine, had been developed judicially in Justice Story's opinion in *Wood v. Dummer* (1824), and was eventually adopted by the Supreme Court.[15] The trust-fund doctrine held that if the stated value of the shares exceeded the amount of capital actually paid in—that is, if the stock was "watered"—then the creditors could turn to the shareholders for satisfaction of the corporation's debts.

At first glance one would not think of limited shareholder liability as a characteristic of the classical corporation, for it smacks too much of a "subsidy"—reduced legal liabilities to those willing to invest in corporate enterprises. Under classicism, it would seem, each person may enjoy the full benefits but also must pay the full costs of his economic decisions. Why was strengthened limited liability so important to the classical business corporation? In this case, classical corporation theory perceived a "market failure" in the capital market. By their nature, new enterprises of the kind for which corporate charters were sought carried the risk of uncertain future liability that could be much greater than the paid-in capital. They trespassed on or flooded the lands of others, caused personal injuries, particularly after the rise of the railroad, or—most significant of all—failed and left behind lines of creditors. Limited liability greatly facilitated the flow of capital into new investments by telling the early nineteenth-century entrepreneur with $50,000 in reachable assets that he could invest $1,000 in a new incorporated enterprise without risk of losing the other $49,000 as well, should something go wrong.

The classical, limited liability corporation was the preeminent nineteenth-century risk-sharing device. It broadened the risk of failure to include the corporation's creditors as well as its investors. In the process limited liability encouraged the "silent" investor—the person who had some money to put at risk, but who did not wish to be concerned with the corporation's daily affairs. Significantly, it also blurred the distinction between the firm's owners and its creditors. Stockholders and bondholders became merely different classes of "investors" in the same business. Different consequences attached to the two kinds of instruments, to be sure, but nothing resembling the traditional debtor-creditor relationship existed as between their holders.

Creditors have always accepted part of the risk of failure of the new enterprise. Even the factor extending a crop loan to a farmer would suffer if the farmer were to go bankrupt.[16] Limited liability changed the stakes of the game by limiting the size of the pool from which creditors could collect to the assets of the defaulting corporation itself. This made it incumbent on creditors to learn something about the specific enterprise in which they were investing rather than merely the wealth of shareholders. It also required the trustees to determine accurately the financial condition of the company, particularly the amount of capital paid in, and make this information available to creditors or potential creditors. Creditors were entitled to rely on public information concerning the value of the corporation's assets against its outstanding debts. If this information was accurate and the corporation nevertheless failed, then the creditors had to be satisfied out of the corporate assets alone and the stockholders had no further liability. This policy was driven by the legal view that a corporation is a "person." A prudent lender would inquire into a natural person's financial position before loaning his money. So too would he inquire into the assets and liabilities of the corporation.

Significantly, when reliance was not an issue stockholders were generally held to have no liability whether or not their shares were fully paid in. Courts held almost without exception that statutory shareholders' liability in derogation of the common law applied only to contract debts, not to tort judgment creditors. In *Heacock & Lockwood v. Sherman* (1835),[17] for example, the New York Court of Appeals found that the shareholders were not answerable when a horse fell through a corporately owned bridge that was out of repair, even though the charter appeared to create unlimited shareholder liability. The provision applied only to contract actions, the court concluded, and not to torts.

Limited liability clearly encouraged the flow of capital into new enterprise. But it was not a "subsidy," which classicism loathed, unless it effectively transferred wealth from one class of people to another—for example, as cash subsidies transferred wealth from tax payers to recipient businesses. It is hard to make such a showing about limited liability. First, under the general corporation acts corporate status and thus limited liability were available to practically every entrepreneur who wanted it. If limited liability were truly a subsidy people with money to invest would have become shareholders rather than creditors.

Second, if limited liability were a subsidy, it would not be difficult to identify the subsidizing class. But it is. The wealth transfer, if there was one, certainly did not come from the corporation's consumers, for limited liability reduced the corporation's costs. The most obvious wealth transfer that comes to mind is from the corporation's contract creditors to its shareholders. But every competent creditor knew about limited liability and built it into his calculations about whether to loan, how much, and on what terms. Furthermore, if limited liability was as effective as one might think in encouraging new investment, then it greatly increased the demand for new loans. There is as much reason for thinking that limited liability on the whole made corporate creditors better off than worse off.

Inevitably, however, limited shareholder liability encouraged limited shareholder involvement—shareholders could be less concerned about the corporation's affairs. Limited liability was yet another of many doctrines inherent in the classical theory of the corporation that gradually made management rather than owners responsible for the corporation's affairs. The demise of the trust-fund doctrine late in the nineteenth century[18] was a natural consequence of the separation of ownership and control that attended the great success of the classical corporation. By 1900 much of the governance of the large corporation had been given over to professional management. The shareholders in such corporations were little more than investors, and any substantial possibility of liability would have undermined the attractiveness of corporate stocks as investment devices, particularly on the secondary market, where purchasers did not have insider information about the corporation's management, liabilities, or prospects for success. In the second edition of *Thompson on Corporations* Joseph Thompson indulged in a relentless attack on the trust-fund doctrine, finding it to be "at war with every principle of law and of sound reason."[19] If the doctrine had any proper meaning at all, Thompson concluded, it governed disposition of a corporation's assets upon dissolution. As long as a corporation is solvent it is a distinct entity which "holds its property as any individual holds his." On becoming insolvent, however, its distinct corporate identity disappears and its remaining property is placed "in the condition of trust, first for the creditors, and then for the stockholders." This rule was only a skeleton of the doctrine developed by Justice Story and the early classicists.

CHAPTER 6

Corporate Power and Its Abuse

The development of classical corporate theory sparked a change in the state's attitude toward corporate misbehavior. When the corporation held a special franchise, and was seen as authorized to do things that only the state itself could do, strict supervision of corporate activities seemed appropriate. But when the corporation became just another kind of private business organization, such supervision was no longer in order. Two phenomena characterize this development. First, responsibility for disciplining managers for behavior that was generally legal but unauthorized by the charter or imprudent within the firm was transferred from the state to the shareholders. Second, the standard of manager behavior was gradually lowered until by 1890 those in control of the corporation were legally answerable for virtually nothing but illegality, clearly ultra vires acts (that is, acts not authorized by the corporate charter), or gross negligence.

Classicism and Quo Warranto for Nonuser

As noted in Chapter 2, within the preclassical model the corporation had a special contractual relationship with the incorporating state and was entitled to substantial protections for its "vested" rights. But a contract is a two-way arrangement, and implies special obligations for the incorporators as well. Corporations were not generally chartered unless the legislature was interested in obtaining some particular work of public improvement. Many eighteenth-century charters contained "self-destruction" clauses, providing that the corporate charter would be forfeited if the contemplated project were not completed within a specified number of years. Whether or not the charter explicitly contained such language, it was implied in every charter by the common law, as Justice Story noted in 1815: "A *private* corporation created by the legislature may lose its franchises by a *misuser* or a *non-user* of them; and they may be resumed by the government under a judicial judgment upon a quo warranto to ascertain and enforce the forfeiture.—This is the common law of the land, and is a tacit condition annexed to the creation of every such corporation."[1]

Joseph Angell and Samuel Ames also noted that incorporation created a twofold obligation—first, by the incorporating state to guarantee the rights and privileges promised in the charter; but second, by the incorporators to fund and build the work of public improvement that the charter contemplated. "[I]t is now well settled, that it is a tacit condition of a grant of incorporation that the grantees shall act up to the end or design for which they were incorporated," they wrote, "and hence through neglect or abuse of its franchises a corporation may forfeit its charter, as for condition broken, or a breach of trust."[2]

This notion of corporate obligation rested on the premise that the proprietors had been given a right to do something that one could not do without the state's permission. Performance was the incorporators' consideration for these rights. Sometimes even corporations in compliance with their charters could not collect fees for activities that could have been performed without the corporation's help. In 1804 the Richmond James River Company was incorporated to widen and deepen a short section of the James River. The charter authorized it then to collect tolls from all boats with a draft of five feet or more. After the charter issued someone established that even the unimproved river had been deep enough to accommodate boats with seven-foot drafts. As a result, the legislature concluded, it would be unfair to permit the corporation to charge tolls for boats with drafts between five and seven feet, because the corporation was performing no additional service to such boats and thus offering no "consideration" for the public. Over the strenuous objections of the incorporators, the legislature amended the charter to exempt from toll any boat with a draft of less than seven feet.[3]

Quo warranto procedures were legal actions against the corporation by the incorporating state for abuse of its franchise or other illegal acts. The ordinary remedy was dissolution. Quo warranto actions for nonuser were common in the first half of the nineteenth century. Only the government could bring such a proceeding, Angell and Ames noted, because only it was a party to the "compact" made with the incorporators.[4] But the classical manufacturing corporation was just an ordinary business firm, and the state had no appreciable interest in whether it really undertook what its charter authorized. This was doubly true after the rise of general incorporation acts, which effectively removed the award of charters for ordinary corporations from state discretion. To be sure, one had to distinguish between public service corporations, or utilities, and general manufacturing corporations. Angell and Ames noted that American courts had rejected the English rule that quo warranto would not lie "where the franchise in no ways concerns the public." Under that rule the information in quo warranto would be refused if it was determined that a corporation had been created for purely private purposes. Gradually, however, American courts came to hold that quo warranto for *non*feasance was a more appropriate remedy for public utility corporations, which were created because the state had an interest in having a particular service delivered, than for general manufacturing firms, where the state was more or less indifferent toward whether the incorporated firm actually went into business.

Even after the Civil War American courts held consistently that a turnpike company, railroad company, bank, gas light company, water company, or similar utility that failed to build or operate the project contemplated in the charter could be dissolved in a quo warranto proceeding.[5] However, some courts began to hold that a mere manufacturing corporation was not answerable in a quo warranto simply because it failed to do business. "Purely business and manufacturing corporations formed under general statutes, and which are a species of business partnerships, are deemed dissolved when they cease to do business," conceded one Missouri court.[6] But this decision is made "in reference to the rights of creditors," and not because of any breach of the corporation's charter with the state. As long as the corporation had the requisite six members and no creditors' rights were being disturbed, dissolution could not be compelled. Likewise courts routinely began to hold that charter and statutory provisions demanding forfeiture of corporations that did not go into business within a specified number of years were not self-executing, but required a quo warranto action by the state.[7] Since only the state could bring a quo warranto, this meant that the existence of such corporations could not be challenged by private parties. In the second edition of his extraordinary treatise on injunctions, Thomas Carl Spelling generalized that "a much stronger case" for quo warranto against a company for nonuser of its franchise "must be shown where the franchise is of a private nature than where the public are interested in having them kept in constant use."[8] Once again, this development widened the gap between general corporations and "franchises," or public utilities, where a much higher degree of state participation was perceived as appropriate.

Classicism and Ultra Vires

Closely related to the quo warranto was the substantive doctrine of ultra vires, which forbade the corporation or its officers from performing acts outside the corporation's authority. Violation of a general law was ultra vires, but so were acts that were that were legal under the general law but contrary to the corporation's charter.[9] Although quo warranto actions could be brought only by the sovereign, ultra vires acts could be challenged by shareholders or others.[10]

Under preclassical theory the corporate charter was a grant from the crown of permission to do something that, absent the charter, would be illegal. The other side of the coin was that the corporation, because of its privileged status, could do *only* those things that it was authorized to do. When Angell and Ames wrote their treatise in 1832 they organized the powers of a corporation by reference to those things that a corporation was entitled to do without explicit authorization in its charter— own real property, make contracts, appoint its agents and supervise their activities, make its own by-laws, and sue in court. To do anything else was illegal unless expressly authorized by the charter. For a corporation "to assume a power which cannot be exercised, without a grant from the sovereign authority, or to intrude into the office of a private corporation contrary to the provisions of the statute which creates it, is, in a large sense, to invade the sovereign prerogative."[11]

Classical corporate theory both narrowed and privatized the law of ultra vires. When one thinks of the corporation as a special entity composed of private persons but created by the state for a public purpose, strict scrutiny of corporate powers and activities seems appropriate. But when the corporation is simply an alternative form of business organization, then it should presumptively be able to do what any business firm can lawfully do. By the 1880's and 1890's courts had become much more willing to imply powers from other explicit powers. As Victor Morawetz noted in his influential treatise on corporation law, the developing "collateral transactions" rule gave corporations broad power to engage in business not authorized in their charters if they could show that the new business enabled them to carry on authorized business more effectively. Even the Supreme Court, which generally construed corporate powers narrowly, held in 1896 that the express power granted to a corporation to run a railroad implied the power to operate a hotel, at least if the hotel was for the convenience of railroad passengers and employees.[12]

In 1894 the prominent corporations scholar William W. Cook noticed that the doctrine of ultra vires was rapidly disappearing, and by 1898 he was willing to proclaim it a dead letter, at least in the state courts.[13] Fundamental to this development was the prevailing use of general incorporation acts rather than special charters. Many state courts held that the powers of a corporation formed under a general statute should be construed more broadly than those of a corporation created by special charter, for the former was more like an ordinary person engaged in business.[14] Once again, however, a distinction had to be made between franchise, or public service, corporations and corporations engaged in general manufacturing. Cook noted that railroads were an exception to this trend, and if anything the courts were "more strict" about finding their acts ultra vires. The new "regulated industries" treatises of the early twentieth century showed the courts' continuing heavy concern with ultra vires acts by public service corporations, particularly their vertical integration into unregulated markets.[15]

Even more significant was the change in the nature of challenges to ultra vires acts. State challenges gradually diminished as private shareholder standing to challenge was expanded. At the time Angell and Ames wrote, ultra vires proceedings by private parties were generally disallowed, subject to a few exceptions.[16] Courts first began approving shareholder challenges to ultra vires actions in the 1830's and 1840's, in cases holding that the charter was a contract between the corporation and its stockholders as well as between the corporation and the state. The earlier cases arose, not when a shareholder challenged the activity, but when the corporation tried to recover from a stockholder who refused to pay his subscription. The corporation could not compel payment if it was engaged in activity unauthorized by the original contractual arrangement.[17]

In the 1850's the stockholders' derivative suit began to emerge, a development that had several implications for shareholder suits challenging activities as ultra vires. First, it justified shareholder challenges in principle. Second, it created a judicial procedure that effectively bound all shareholders, and thus foreclosed the possibility of multiple challenges with inconsistent outcomes. Third, it required shareholders to establish that the directors had violated a legal duty. If the activity was within the directors' discretion, the shareholders' lawsuit would not be sustained.

By the 1880's the stockholders' derivative suit had essentially privatized the law of the corporation's ultra vires but otherwise legal acts. In the process the state had virtually ceased to be concerned. Early in the nineteenth century it was clear that a quo warranto could be used against corporations that engaged in activities not expressly authorized by the charter. By 1900, however, the remedy, if any, lay principally with the stockholders. In 1901 Thomas Spelling concluded:

> There is a nice distinction necessary to be kept in view between corporate powers and corporate franchises. The occasional and temporary abuse of the former is a matter of complaint for the shareholders and creditors; but the state can object only when such abuse has been continued to the extent of involving and injuring public interests. The assumption of a mere power, such as any individual may assume, for instance the right to manufacture an article or to deal in evidences of indebtedness when not authorized by the charter, constitutes a ground of complaint by those privately interested only, unless long continued, in which case the state may proceed by quo warranto.[18]

The cases Spelling cited held that quo warranto is not an appropriate remedy for resolving purely private disputes between corporations and others over property ownership; that a corporation's illegal efforts to dodge its creditors were not actionable by the state in quo warranto if the creditors themselves had available legal remedies; that a corporation's wrongful entry onto private lands did not justify a quo warranto if the injured property owner was capable of redressing his grievance himself; and that a bank that loaned out more money than its charter authorized was not answerable in quo warranto unless the state could additionally show a resulting danger to the community. The remedy must otherwise lie with the stockholders, injured creditors, or the victims of tortious conduct.[19]

Whether the corporation engaged in activities outside its charter was a matter of internal firm management, but not of concern to the state unless the firm was a public utility, or unless the abuse was so substantial that it could be independently shown to injure the public interest. This privatization of the law of ultra vires effectively put the general manufacturing corporation on the same footing as any unincorporated firm: internal mismanagement or bad decisions in marketing or production were problems that belonged to the firm's owners, customers, or creditors, but not to the state, unless some independent body of law was broken. "It is not sufficient for [the state] to show that wrong has been done to some one; the wrong must appear to be done to the public in order to support an action by the people for redress." Later cases held that even illegal acts did not justify quo warranto if they created purely private wrongs—that is, wrongs that the victims could redress themselves in a civil suit.[20]

The Business Judgment Rule

The business judgment rule sets a standard for the liability of corporate directors to the stockholders for corporate mismanagement. The rule originally made directors responsible for negligent acts.[21] During the second half of the century a deep division emerged in state courts over the appropriate standard for directors' exercise of their business judgment. Victor Morawetz argued that corporate directors should not be held liable so long as they "act honestly within the powers conferred upon them by the charter," and thus suggested that the rule exempted everything but subjective bad faith. Many courts took that position. For example, in *Spering's Appeal* (1872) the Pennsylvania Supreme Court held that "while directors are personally responsible to the stockholders for any losses resulting from fraud, embezzlement or willful misconduct or breach of trust for their own benefit," they were not liable for "mistakes of judgment, even though they may be so gross as to appear to us absurd and ridiculous, provided they are honest and . . . within the scope of the powers and discretion confided to the managing body." The New York Court of Appeals squarely disagreed, concluding that the standard was the "ordinary skill and judgment" of a reasonable person—that is, that the directors were liable even for ordinary negligence. Until 1891 the United States Supreme Court waffled on the issue, holding that the standard should vary from ordinary negligence to gross negligence depending on the situation.[22]

But the Pennsylvania court's approach was clearly the dominant one. It eventually emerged triumphant and was adopted by the United States Supreme Court in *Briggs v. Spaulding* (1891). In his 1895 treatise Seymour Thompson concluded that for "mere errors of judgment by the officers of a private corporation, by which damage has been done to a member of a corporation, an action at law does not lie." To recognize an action would "destroy the discretion vested" in the directors by making it constantly subject to court review. Rather, "it must appear that the act complained of was *willful* and *malicious,* and done for the purpose of injuring the plaintiff."[23]

The liberalization of the business judgment rule gave relatively more discretion to corporate managers and relatively less control to shareholders. The irony of decreased director liability, C. Brewster Rhoads lamented in 1916, was that those states that had required a showing of willful dishonesty or gross negligence had begun with a premise perhaps valid in the early part of the century that directors were "'gratuitous mandatories,' serving without compensation."[24] However, the "latter part of the nineteenth century . . . witnessed a change in the status of directors." Directorships were now coveted professional positions, often offering high monetary rewards. The director, rather than the owner, was the real person in power, and he was clearly in a position to control the corporation to his advantage. The development of the business judgment rule separated even further the ownership of the American business corporation from its control.

The Monopoly Problem and the Changing Nature of Quo Warranto

Late in the nineteenth century the principal rationale for quo warranto actions changed. The concern expressed in earlier decisions was that the corporation would claim unauthorized privileges or would fail to perform activities to which it had contractually obligated itself. But after the Civil War quo warranto actions were often brought to challenge perceived anticompetitive activities, first vertical integration and later horizontal combination of various kinds.

Corporate charters initially appeared to contain powerful weapons for state trustbusters. The weapons were the remaining vestiges of the preclassical theory of corporation: statutes and charter provisions prohibiting the corporation from doing business outside the incorporating state, prohibiting activities outside the scope of the charter, and prohibiting one corporation from owning the shares of another. Coupled to these was the doctrine permitting states to exclude corporations chartered in other states from doing business within their borders.

For the giant business firms beginning to organize in the 1870's and 1880's, these restrictions were an albatross, and they sought every means to avoid them. In fact, the words "trust" and "antitrust" derive from the fact that late nineteenth-century monopolists used the common law trust arrangement in an attempt to evade these charter-imposed limitations. The common law trust proved to be inadequate, for reasons explored in Chapter 20. The great combinations then petitioned and obtained from states like New Jersey new incorporation acts that permitted multistate business, incorporation for any lawful purpose, and one corporation's ownership of another corporation's shares. These new statutes eradicated most of the remaining vestiges of the pre-classical corporation. Under them the business corporation could do almost everything that the unincorporated firm could.

As discussed above, by the late nineteenth century courts generally held that states could not use quo warranto merely to challenge the ordinary business corporation's violation of its charter. The state had to show injury to the public interest. When the unauthorized activities tended to create a monopoly, however, the rule was quite different. "[I]n a proceeding against a corporation by quo warranto for having formed with others a monopoly in the shape of a 'trust,'" Thomas Spelling concluded, "no actual public injury need be proven, but it will be presumed when an agreement is shown which, if carried out, will obviously result to the public detriment."[25] The state's concern with ultra vires activities reappeared when the activities undermined the competitive market system.

The revitalization of quo warranto in the state trust cases was the first great crisis faced by the classical theory of the business corporation in the age of giant enterprise, and the theory did not fare well. Principally, it revealed that the corporation had escaped the bonds of state control. For example, Standard Oil Company of Ohio complied with the Ohio Supreme Court's divestiture decree by setting up a new corporation under the liberalized corporation laws of New Jersey.

The classical corporation was about to become a victim of its own success. Its problem was not that it was bad at doing the job conceived for it—assembling and directing business capital efficiently. On the contrary, it did its job so well that by the end of the century it threatened to undermine the very competitive market structures for which it had been created.

PART II

THE ECONOMIC CONSTITUTION

CHAPTER 7

A Moral Theory of
Political Economy

American Economic Science and the British Classical Tradition

Rightly or wrongly, Adam Smith has been given most of the credit for
inventing classical political economy in the 1770's. Before political
economy would turn into modern economics, however, it would
undergo a utilitarian revolution in the late eighteenth and early nineteenth centuries and a marginalist revolution in the 1870's and 1880's.
Both revolutions substantially undermined support for the laissez-faire
theory that dominated Adam Smith's thinking. Political economy in both
Britain and the United States experienced the revolutions, but they
occurred later in the United States and took a different ideological turn.

Classical political economy considerably influenced British legislation
in the first half of the nineteenth century.[1] But in the second half of
the century consensus among political economists fell apart, and their
authority diminished. The influence of nineteenth-century American
political economy on American legislation is less documented than the
British experience.[2] One thing seems clear, however. Just as the revolutions in theory occurred much earlier in Britain than in America, so
too did the legislative response. Parliament passed the English Factory
Acts, which regulated hours of labor for adults and children, in 1833,
1844, and 1847.[3] Widespread legislative regulation of wages and
working conditions did not develop in the United States until the 1880's
and after. Britain faced a restive labor force beginning in the 1830's;
American capitalists faced the same threat beginning in the 1870's and

1880's. Most significant was that Britain reached the limits of its agricultural productivity and faced the prospect of imports early in the nineteenth century; America contained a great abundance of tillable land throughout the nineteenth century.

Clearly the distinction between classical political economy in Britain and in America was not merely that the Americans lagged behind in theory. But neither do differences in physical environment, labor supply, and rates of industrialization fully explain the divergence. Throughout the nineteenth century, American political economy was dominated by a moral, or normative, content that was much less visible in British political economy after 1800. American political economists, much more than the British, clung to the moral ideas of the Scottish "Common Sense" Realists.[4] Utilitarianism, which subordinated moral arguments based on natural law to a pragmatic concept of the good of the many, had far less influence on nineteenth-century American political economy than it did on the British.

Adam Smith himself was an orthodox Scottish Realist Protestant whose theory of "welfare" was derived as much from morals as from economics.[5] Smith intertwined the concepts of scarcity, desire, supply, demand, and value into a remarkably sophisticated economic as well as moral theory that included: (1) a Lockean view that each person has a natural right to his own labor; and (2) an essentially Lockean notion that value is a function of the labor put into something rather than the demand for it or the utility that it produces. Because each person has a natural right to his own labor, he also has a natural right to his own property.

Smith's theory of economic man was thoroughly intertwined with his theory of moral man. For example, Smith believed that liberty of contract was as much an ethical doctrine as an economic one. He adhered to a theory of natural price, rejecting the Hobbesian view that a price is "just" merely because it is the product of a voluntary bargain. But Smith also believed that the unrestricted market almost always yielded the natural price. As a result, individual determination of price was an inherent right of property ownership, on both economic and moral grounds.[6]

Smith's moral position on economic relations was to have a profound effect on the American judiciary's evaluation of statutory price controls and minimum wage laws during the era of substantive due process. Thomas M. Cooley adopted it in 1878: "[T]he capability of property, by means of the labor or expense or both bestowed upon it, to be made available in producing profits, is a potential quality in property, and as sacredly protected by the constitution as the thing itself in which the quality inheres."[7] The Supreme Court was almost as explicit, when it concluded that "the right of the owner to fix a price at which his property shall be sold or used is an inherent attribute of the property itself," and that there is a "moral requirement" of "just equivalence" between the price to be charged for labor and the value the employer places upon it.[8] One could not show liberty of contract to be a bad thing merely by proving it inefficient, for the doctrine was simultaneously grounded in moral and economic values. Smith's moral man worked for his wages, and in Smith's moral universe the wages set by the market were almost always normatively correct.[9]

Secularization in British Economics

As Smith's followers deviated from his thought, the economic argument for strict laissez-faire began to deteriorate. At the same time, the intellectual center of political economy in Britain moved away from orthodox, Presbyterian Scotland, where Smith did his work, toward more liberal, Anglican Oxford and Cambridge. By mid-century the moral content of Smith's position had been undermined in English political economy, particularly by utilitarianism. Not so in America, where Scottish Realism remained the ruling philosophy until after the Civil War.[10] American constitutional law came to be built on the political economy of an unreconstructed Adam Smith.

Two subsequent developments in British political economy undermined Smith's optimistic theory that "the invisible hand" would provide the best society. These developments, the population theory and the doctrine of rents, fueled the revolt against laissez-faire in British political thought.

The Population Theory

The first development was the population theory of Thomas Robert Malthus, who became England's first professor of political economy in 1806 at East India College. His 1798 *Essay on the Principle of Population* drew two conclusions rather ambiguously characterized as empirical:[11] (1) population, when left unchecked, will grow geometrically; and (2) once all good land has been put into production, the food supply can grow, at best, arithmetically. Malthus's observations had profound implications for Britain, which was heavily developed at the time of his writing.

Strictly applied, Malthus's "iron law" of population did not undermine Smith's laissez-faire theory. On the contrary, many later writers, particularly in the United States, believed it strengthened the case for non-intervention.[12] Any interference by the state on behalf of the masses would only increase their numbers in proportion to the supply of food and productive capital. Malthus sometimes personally proclaimed such a severe version of his theory. However, he was strongly influenced by Bentham's utilitarianism and was quite willing to manipulate Lockean property rights in order to improve the welfare of the poor, provided the price was not too high. Essentially Malthusian arguments carried the Poor Law Reform Bill of 1834, which centralized the distribution of poor relief.[13]

Later English political economists quickly softened the severest implications of Malthus's iron law, as did Malthus himself in a later edition of his famous essay.[14] For example, John Stuart Mill thought a moderate amount of poor relief would not unduly increase the population, and would greatly relieve suffering. Other classical economists such as Nassau Senior gave lip service to Malthus's work, but suggested that new technology and improvements in the efficiency of exchange would tend to offset the productivity problem; as a result, moderate governmental aid to the poor would not cause starvation.[15] The strong version of Malthus's iron law appeared prominently in the late nineteenth century in two places: the writings of Herbert Spencer, who was much more popular in America than in Britain, and the work of American Social Darwinists such as William Graham Sumner.[16]

The Doctrine of Rents

The political economy of David Ricardo, who wrote early in the nineteenth century, shows few remains of Scottish Realist orthodoxy. Ricardo's principal contribution to economic theory was the doctrine of land rents, which played a large role in the mid-century British revolt against laissez-faire ideology.

We are indebted to Ricardo for establishing that not only monopolists earn monopoly profits. Any time a production input is in short supply the price of the final product will rise to monopoly levels, whether the final product is sold by one vendor or thousands. For Ricardo, the relevant input was agricultural land. He argued that the first land to be placed into production in any market will also be the most fertile, for which production costs are the lowest. As demand increases, more marginal land must be used, and average production costs will rise. To sustain production off the marginal land, the market price of agricultural products must rise sufficiently to make the less fertile land profitable. As a result, the product of the most profitable land can be sold at monopoly profits, even though its owners constitute only a tiny fraction of all landowners. "It is then only because land is of different qualities with respect to its productive powers, and because in the progress of population, land of an inferior quality, or less advantageously situated, is called into cultivation, that rent is ever paid for the use of it."[17]

From his observations about agricultural land, Ricardo derived a theory of wages that further undermined Adam Smith's optimism that the invisible hand would yield ample provision for every industrious person. As increasingly marginal land was placed into production, Ricardo argued, prices would rise and demand would fall, landlords would earn monopoly returns, and the capitalist entrepreneur would be squeezed between high rental rates and reduced output. Falling demand and rising costs would drive wages to subsistence levels. An important corollary of Ricardo's doctrine of rents was that wages would decline as a percentage of total productivity, thus tending to support Malthus's claim that wages would always be driven to the subsistence level. Ricardo did not personally regard this fact, depressing as it might be, as sufficient to justify substantial state regulation of markets or wages. Later British political economists showed no such reluctance, however, and the doctrine of rents became an important element in the undermining of laissez-faire ideology. For example, John Stuart Mill preceded the American Henry George in advocating a tax on landlords to capture their "unearned income" from land rents. Mill was instrumental in founding the Land Tenure Reform Association, whose principal goal was the redistribution of land rents.[18]

Utilitarianism and Marginalism

Adam Smith believed that an individual's property in his own labor was the sacred, inviolate foundation of all property. He was opposed on moral as well as economic grounds to most legislation that interfered with an individual's power to bargain freely. The importance of Smith's moral commitment cannot be underestimated: even if someone proved laissez-faire wrong on purely economic grounds, the moral arguments would remain.

The development of British utilitarianism under Jeremy Bentham, John Stuart Mill, and their followers undermined this fundamental premise of Smith's political economy. Carried to its logical conclusion, utilitarianism excised natural law from political economy. For example, Smith believed that every commodity had both a "natural price" and a "market price," and that over the long run the latter would approximate the former. Later economists, starting with John Stuart Mill, separated the positive and normative elements of economic theory and assigned the behavior of the market exclusively to the former. At that point the "natural" price disappeared from economic dialogue. Likewise, Smith devised a labor theory of value, drawn from the premise that every person has a right to the product of his own labor. But Smith's theory of value gave way in the 1870's to the marginal utility theory of value, which assessed not the amount of labor that went into a thing, but rather the amount of incremental satisfaction that it produced.[19]

But the most important effect of utilitarianism was on political economists' perceptions of their discipline. The utilitarian revolution changed laissez-faire theory into an empirical or contingent truth, rather than a moral or necessary one. Once utilitarianism became the accepted predicate for welfare economics, the moral obstacle to state intervention disappeared.[20] Utilitarianism also changed political economy by incorporating distributive concerns into economic science. Adam Smith was concerned almost exclusively with maximizing the net social product, regardless of distribution. However, the utilitarians faced the possibility that different distributions of wealth could produce different amounts of total utility. Distribution became an inseparable part of economic science, at least for a time. John Stuart Mill, writing around 1830, defined political economy to include distributional as well as allocative concerns.[21] He understood utility to mean the aggregate utility of society as a whole, rather than of each individual considered separately. Since a poor person might obtain more utility from an additional dollar than would a rich person, the state could increase total utility by forcing wealth transfers from the rich to the poor. In fact, total utility would be maximized when every person had exactly the same amount of wealth, since total utility was maximized when marginal utilities from one person to the next were the same. William Jevons, Philip Wicksteed, and Alfred Marshall—the great revisionists of classical political economy—all dealt with the implications of this proposition.

These ideas about redistribution entered the mainstream of British economic thought, where they remained until economists began arguing in the 1930's that interpersonal comparisons of utility are impossible.[22] The same ideas entered the mainstream of British *political* thought, and never left. When the theory of marginal utility was developed in the 1860's and 1870's, principally under Jevons, who merged utilitarian ethics and welfare economics, British economists began to propose fairly elaborate schemes to use the state to redistribute wealth in order to enlarge total utility.[23] This development occurred in England at least a quarter century before it reached America.

Assumptions, Method, and Public Policy in Classical Economics

A traditional view of the political economy of Adam Smith is that his conclusions were either deductive, or based on observations so robust and uncontroversial, such as the inverse relation between supply and demand, that in the nineteenth century they were regarded as universal truths. This view is sometimes assigned to the entire classical tradition in political economy.[24] But the great classical economists were also policy makers who carried political agendas drawn from the economic disputes of their day. Their self-professed "general" solutions to economic problems were in fact pointed at specific issues, such as the wisdom of the Poor Laws or the Corn Laws.[25] For example, Ricardo's doctrine of rents was motivated largely by his opposition to the Corn Laws, part of the mercantilist policy of encouraging grain production by placing tariffs on imports and bounties on exports. His arguments were supported largely by casual empirical observations made in a relatively static industrial economy that appeared to have reached the limit of its agricultural productivity. The same thing can be said of Malthus's "iron law" of population or James Mill's defense of England's declining position as an exporter of agricultural goods.[26]

British political economists were also troubled by class unrest and the growing power of the labor movement. The theory of Marx and Engels about the crisis of labor and the need for revolution was drawn from their observations of British poverty during the first half of the nineteenth century.[27] But until late in the century American political economists did not bother to include the risk of substantial labor unrest as part of the social cost of a laissez-faire labor policy. In a rapidly expanding economy where wages were seen as rising and jobs as plentiful, revolution seemed unlikely.

American political economy differed from British political economy not because of fundamental disagreements over basic principles but rather because Americans collected their data in a different laboratory. Our perception of differences in principle is distorted by the fact that nineteenth-century economists tended to overgeneralize:[28] Ricardo and Malthus in Britain made specific observations but attempted to report universal truths, as did Henry Carey and Henry Vethake in America. The resulting differences left far less room for the interventionist state in America than they did in Britain.

The Scottish Enlightenment and Political Economy in America

Liberty of contract and other rights recognized under the fourteenth amendment were not merely economic rights but moral and religious rights as well. Laissez-faire ideology was an important part of the religious individualism and self-determination that developed in America during the early nineteenth century. It dominated the thought of the leading democratic political economist of the Jacksonian period, Francis Wayland, president of Brown University. Wayland was raised a New York Baptist, but learned Scottish Realism at the Congregational Andover Seminary in Massachusetts.

When Scottish Realism obtained a foothold in America during the 1760's and 1770's, it imported two ideas about value formation. The first was a unique kind of empiricism that claimed to despise speculation and abstraction. The second was a rationale for individual self-determination that Scottish Realists called the "moral sense." The moral sense enabled a person to know instinctively the difference between right and wrong. "Moral science" was the discipline that used the moral sense to discover the principles of ethical conduct, just as the physical sciences relied on the other five senses to discover the natural principles of the universe. Scottish Realists believed that moral laws are fixed and absolute. They "can never be varied by the institution of man any more than the physical laws," Wayland wrote in 1835.[29] However, these laws are discoverable, so that someone well educated in moral science will be able to make the right decision when he is confronted with an ethical problem. Most of these ideas came straight out of Adam Smith's book on moral science, *The Theory of Moral Sentiments*,[30] published seventeen years before the *Wealth of Nations* and all but forgotten by later figures in the British classical tradition. Like Smith, Wayland wrote books on both the moral sense and the foundations of political economy. "The principles of Political Economy are so closely analogous to those of Moral Philosophy, that almost every question in the one, may be argued on grounds belonging to the other."[31] Wayland's position on the relationship between moral science and political economy was fundamentally Adam Smith's position—but Wayland was writing fifty years later.

For Wayland as for Smith the individual right to property and the profits earned from it was grounded in morality as well as in economics. "[W]e are taught, by Moral Philosophy, that by labor exerted upon any substance, in such manner as to give it value, we establish over that value, either in whole or in part, the right of property." The same applies to invested capital. "If, by labor upon the capital of another, we have raised its value, we establish a right to a portion of it, to be estimated by the respective values of the labor and capital employed."

The moral sense provided a broad rationale for individual self-determination in every aspect of human activity. In the eighteenth century, the idea of the moral sense was highly controversial. Scottish Realists asserted its existence in response to the great Scottish heretic David Hume. The world is forever unknowable, said Hume, because each person's knowledge of it is limited to his sense impressions, and he has no way to prove that his impressions are accurate. Likewise, "ought" statements can never be verified; so no one can be sure that a certain action is right or wrong. Hume's view implied either anarchy or ethical positivism, the idea that an action is wrong only if someone in authority says it is wrong.

Against Hume's empirical skepticism the Scottish Realists gave a pragmatic answer that encouraged individualism and self-determination. They suggested that no one can think without making certain operative assumptions about the world. We can never prove that our eyes give us reliable information—but our feeling that we really see what we think we see is overwhelming, and any other assumption would make science impossible. We can never prove that time is continuous, but if it is not then we can have neither science nor history. Scottish Realism accepted something that earlier modern philosophers had refused to believe: certain ideas about human understanding seem obvious but can never be proven. They are like the basic postulates of geometry; we either accept them or we cannot think systematically at all.

Furthermore, observed the Scottish Realists, precisely the same argument demonstrates the existence of the moral sense. Consider two statements: "the grass is green" and "thieves should be punished." Neither can be "verified" in the strong sense of the word. At most we can say we have a powerful feeling that we are looking at something called grass, and that it is green. According to the Scottish Realists, we have exactly the same kind of powerful feeling that theft is wrong. Each of us feels "a distinct *impulse* to do that which we conceive to be right and to leave undone what we conceive to be wrong," Wayland wrote.[32] This moral sense is deeply implanted in every person and gives the community a set of shared values from which the state may derive legal rules of conduct. Just as science is impossible unless we trust our senses, guidelines for rational human conduct are impossible if we cannot trust our judgments about right and wrong.

The Scottish Realist tradition persisted in America long after it had given way to utilitarianism in Britain. American political economists and jurists continued to subordinate utilitarian solutions to Protestant moral values. One is struck by Justice George Sutherland's assertion in *Adkins v. Children's Hospital* (1923) that there is a "moral requirement" of "just equivalence" between the value of a worker's labor and the price it commands. "If one goes to the butcher, the baker or grocer to buy food, he is morally entitled to obtain the worth of his money but he is not entitled to more. If what he gets is worth what he pays he is not justified in demanding more simply because he needs more."[33]

The Moral Tradition, Utilitarianism, and the Problem of Democracy

Utilitarianism was fundamentally opposed to the Scottish Realist's moral and economic view of the world. Utilitarianism did not become part of the American intellectual mainstream until the rise of pragmatism and Progressive Era social science in the early twentieth century. The reason was plain enough: utilitarians were willing to subordinate moral concerns to their primary goal of maximizing human satisfaction. Mainstream Americans could not accept that juxtaposition of values, and many regarded it as "atheistic." The individual seemed to count for so little in utilitarian thinking: his interests could always be bargained away for the good of society. In the United States, utilitarianism was viewed not so much as a fundamental assumption of economic theory but as a moral view of the world in competition with Protestant orthodoxy. As a result, it was unacceptable to many political economists, including Wayland, on religious or moral grounds, economic objections notwithstanding.[34]

The response of American political economists to utilitarianism was typical of their response to remote, rather than imminent, heresies. They ignored it. Francis Wayland never discussed Bentham in his *Elements of Political Economy*. Harvard's Scottish Realist political economist Francis Bowen evidently refused to permit his students to read Bentham. Henry Carey's three-volume *Principles of Political Economy* (1837), the most important American economics treatise before the Civil War, never discussed Bentham. Although Carey analyzed John Stuart Mill's views on rent and population, he never mentioned Mill's utilitarianism.[35] Considering the dominance of Mill's utilitarianism in English political economy, the omission is remarkable.

America's conservative judiciary perceived itself as the strongest defender of Smith's and Wayland's moral brand of self-reliance. It often perceived the new interventionist politics of the Progressive Era as the greatest threat to liberty. One of the great liberal myths about Progressive Era social scientists and the legislation they inspired is that they protected democracy—that the decision in *Lochner v. New York* was somehow antidemocratic, while the bakers' hour statute that was struck down represented democracy at work. To be sure, in the minds of reformers the social sciences were designed to give laborers some of the dignity and freedom that only the privileged had enjoyed. However, Progressive Era social sciences were much more paternalistic than democratic. Social scientists became just as elitist as the American judiciary. Economists did not support wage and hour laws because the people wanted them but because the economists believed that the laws were good for the people. Almost from the beginning, social scientists were committed to the view that important public decisions should be made by experts.

More than one Supreme Court justice attacked wage and hour legislation by arguing that the laboring class did not want such laws. Justice Rufus Peckham concluded in *Lochner* that "[t]he employee may desire to earn the extra money, which would arise from his working more than the prescribed time, but this statute forbids the employer from permitting the employee to earn it." Justice Sutherland was presented with a real-life example in *Adkins,* in the case of Mary Lyons. Lyons had been an elevator operator in the Congress Hall Hotel. The contested statute established a minimum wage for all women and children in the District of Columbia substantially above the wages Lyons was receiving. But in light of the statute the Congress Hall Hotel decided that her labor would come at too high a price. It converted its elevators to self-service, and Mary Lyons lost her job. She argued that the Congress Hall Hotel had paid her "the best [wages] she was able to obtain for any work she was capable of performing."[36] Her attorney, Felix Frankfurter, argued to the Court until he was red-faced. He showed the Court two thousand pages of statistics about the cost of living, but the statistics did not convince Sutherland that Lyons was better off without her job than she had been with it.

The orthodox judiciary looked at the past and found justification for their most cherished beliefs and institutions. They considered tradition and history powerful forces in shaping contemporary values. Social scientists, by contrast, looked at the past and found only traditions and "folkways"—the slowly evolving, often irrational products of social and economic conflict or the often unspoken compromises people make in order to achieve prosperity.

CHAPTER 8

The Classical Theory
of Federalism

The Formalization of Dual Federalism

Classical economics was predisposed toward the market and against regulatory intervention. Classical law responded not only by creating absolute barriers to regulation, such as substantive due process, but also by limiting the jurisdictional power of both the federal government and state governments. The developing nineteenth-century concept of "dual federalism" assumed that there were only two kinds of markets, intrastate and interstate, and that neither kind was subject to substantial "spillovers," or the effects of one market felt in the other.[1] The result was that when such spillovers occurred, they were often beyond the reach of either the federal government or the states, or they created opportunities for state free riding.

During the Chief Justiceship of Roger B. Taney (1836–1864) the federal system began to take on a distinctly classical appearance. This occurred more quickly in some areas than in others. For example, the Marshall Court had interpreted federal power under the commerce clause of the Constitution broadly. Further, the Court restricted state regulatory power in areas "affecting" interstate commerce even where Congress had not acted. This notion that the mere existence of congressional power to regulate interstate commerce—the so-called dormant commerce clause—deprived the states of the power to regulate interstate commerce was rejected by the states' rights ideology of the Taney Court.[2] The Waite and Fuller Courts later restored the dormant commerce clause and interpreted both state and federal commerce power very narrowly.

The developing view of the federal commerce power was that Congress had exclusive control over interstate *movement,* but not generally over transactions within a single state that merely "affected" interstate commerce.[3] For this reason members of Congress often balked at passing federal regulatory legislation. For example, the authors of the Cullom Committee Report (1886), which preceded passage of the Interstate Commerce Act, refused to assert any authority over intrastate railroad traffic.[4] The legislative history of the Sherman Act is filled with concern that manufacturing cartels were beyond the reach of federal power. In 1895, the concern proved well founded when the Supreme Court held in the *E. C. Knight* antitrust case that congressional power did not extend to "manufacturing" even if the manufactured goods were intended for interstate shipment.[5]

The Jacksonian federalism that eventually dominated the nineteenth-century law of federal-state relations represented the triumph of classical economic theory in American public law. The great architects of laissez-faire constitutional theory, such as Thomas M. Cooley and John F. Dillon, were Jacksonians trained in a western, expansionist, antistatist tradition which believed that state regulation was often little more than grants of special privilege to the politically favored.[6] Competition was the preferred regulator of commercial markets. Governmental control was the exception rather than the rule, and the common law was not yet thought of as "regulatory." State attempts to regulate transactions outside their borders were *inherently* suspect, and they were the most easily condemned under the United States Constitution.

This classical concept of federalism, with its built-in bias against regulatory intervention, created many regulatory vacuums and undermined comprehensive regulation of interstate markets. Ironically, the much broader interpretations of the commerce clause and of state extraterritorial power that emerged in the twentieth century have turned the federal system into one that chronically overregulates, because so many markets are subject to simultaneous federal and state control. But the developers of classical federalism assumed that substantial government intervention was unnecessary. They ignored the fact that even the nineteenth century economy contained interstate markets, that most markets did not follow state lines, and that transactions in one market could have complex effects in related markets. A good example is child labor. Under the Supreme Court's view developed in *E. C. Knight* (1895) that manufacturing is not commerce, the federal government had no power to regulate child labor in manufacturing industries simply because the products were destined for interstate shipment. At the same time, states lacked the proper incentives to control child labor because they were competing for new capital, and entrepreneurs invested where they found the fewest restrictions. The result was that the federal government lacked the power and the states lacked the incentives to control child labor.[7] As Chapter 20 will argue, the same kind of problem undermined state antitrust policy at the turn of the century.

The classical theory of federalism emerged piecemeal over the entire nineteenth century and reached its apogee during the era of substantive due process. The theory permitted the states to regulate "intrastate" or local transactions, but substantially limited state power over transactions that affected more than one state. Decisions like *Swift v. Tyson* (1842), *Pennoyer v. Neff* (1877), *Wabash Railway* (1886), and *Allgeyer v. Louisiana* (1897)[8] removed almost every opportunity for the state to exercise control outside its own borders. *Swift,* of which more will be said later, limited a state court's power to apply "deviant" law to interstate disputes. With its limits on both personal and legislative jurisdiction, *Pennoyer* forbade state courts from asserting their authority over persons or property outside the state. First, "no State can exercise direct jurisdiction and authority over persons or property without its territory." Second, "the laws of one State have no operation outside of its territory, except so far as allowed by comity." *Wabash Railway,* which is discussed more fully in Chapter 13, forbade the states from regulating interstate transportation. In *Allgeyer* the Court held that although a state might regulate insurance companies that sold insurance within the state, it could not regulate a company that sold its insurance only elsewhere, even though the company insured property located within the state. *Allgeyer* was the first of a series of Supreme Court decisions that applied the Constitution's due process clause, commerce clause, and full faith and credit clause to limit a state's power to apply its substantive law to events that occurred in a different state.[9]

State Regulatory Power and the Common Law

The doctrine that the state could not regulate outside its boundaries contained an important exception for common law rules. The distinction between the jurisdictional reach of state legislation and of the common law grew out of a model in which legislation was seen as law "making," but the application of common law rules was seen as nothing more than recognition of general principles. A state could apply the common law to an interstate transaction even though it had no legislative power over that same transaction. Similarly, a federal court could apply common law rules to a purely intrastate dispute that would have been outside the reach of congressional power under the commerce clause. As the corporate law scholar Frederick H. Cooke noted in his 1908 treatise on the commerce clause, there was a "well-established rule" that the congressional commerce power "does not prevent the application even in the courts of a State, as well as the Federal courts, of merely *common-law* rules, that if statutory might be regarded as an invalid exercise of the authority of the State."[10] For example, even though a state could not legislate against interstate railroad rate discrimination, it could apply the common law of rate discrimination to such a transaction.[11]

Within the classical model, the common law was not "regulatory" but merely the institutional enforcement of the rules of the marketplace. For that reason the Supreme Court rejected Western Union's argument in *Call Publishing* (1901) that it was free of both federal and state regulation. Congress had not legislated on the subject of interstate telegraph rates, and the transaction at issue was interstate commerce. Thus, Western Union argued, "the question of rates is left entirely to the judgment or whim of the telegraph company." The Court acknowledged that the states had no power to legislate concerning interstate transactions. However, the common law is neither state law nor federal law as such, but "those principles, usages, and rules of action applicable to the government and security of person and property, which do not rest for their authority upon any express and positive declaration of the will of the legislature."[12] "Can it be . . . that the great multitude of interstate commercial transactions are freed from the burdens created by the common law, as so defined, and are subject to no rule except that to be found in the statutes of Congress?" The Court concluded that "the principles of the common law are operative upon all interstate commercial transactions, except so far as they are modified by congressional enactment."

The common law was the one kind of law that could be applied by any court to almost any transaction—by state courts to interstate transactions and by federal courts to intrastate transactions. The rules of the common law and those of economics were part of the same invisible hand. This fact rendered it doubly important that the common law be kept pure, uncorrupted by local influence or legislative tampering. This task befell the federal courts, whose removal jurisdiction gave them authority to take from the states most disputes in which the defendant was not a citizen of the plaintiff's state, where most state court actions were filed. As John F. Dillon noted in his innovative 1875 treatise on federal removal, federal judicial power to take cases away from the state courts had been continually expanded throughout the nineteenth century, as local prejudice became increasingly offensive to the developing interstate economy.[13] Thus the great importance of *Swift v. Tyson* in nineteenth-century federalism.

Facilitating Markets without "Regulating"

Swift v. Tyson (1842)[14] and the decisions that followed it developed a federal court bias against state regulation and attempted to maintain uniformity in the one body of legal rules that could consistently be applied to both interstate and intrastate transactions—the common law.

In some ways *Swift* itself was an unlikely candidate for this task. The opinion was written by Justice Story, the leading survivor of the Marshall Court, whose opinions in other areas, such as the protection of monopoly rights, were distinctly preclassical. The decision seems inconsistent with the states' rightism that characterized so much Taney Court jurisprudence. Perhaps the best example of such deference to the states is the decision that made Taney infamous—*Dred Scott,* which upheld the right of states to control slavery free from federal intervention.[15]

But *Swift* did something that the monopoly charter cases and states' rights decisions did not. It addressed the market in the most direct way possible. Whatever his ideas about developmental policy, when it came to legal regulation of the market Story was a classicist. His great treatises on commercial law were generally hostile toward statutory regulation, unless it merely codified rules created by custom. Story practically worshiped the *lex mercatoris,* or law merchant—that body of law developed by merchants themselves to control their transactions.

The Swift Decision and the Uniform Commercial Law

The immediate question in *Swift v. Tyson* was whether the holder of a bill of exchange was a "holder in due course," entitled to collect on the bill in spite of a failure of consideration in the transaction upon which the bill was based. The general commercial law said that he was. New

York decisional law probably said that he was not. Justice Story applied the general commercial law. The principle of negotiability—or the notion that commercial paper should be freely transferable from one merchant to another—unquestionably supported Story's decision.

The bill of exchange was one of the great facilitators of modern commerce, giving the international merchant community its own private credit economy. The bill itself has changed very little in either form or character over the last five hundred years. The modern bank check is its direct descendant. In his treatise on bills of exchange, Justice Story borrowed a definition from Chancellor Kent, which described a bill of exchange at the time of *Swift v. Tyson* about as well as one could be described today: "A Bill of Exchange is a written order or request by one person to another, for the payment of money, absolutely and at all events."[16] The last phrase was critical. The bill entitled the payee or his endorsee to claim payment with no strings attached. Thus it served as a substitute for cash.

Bills of exchange generally involved three persons. One person, the drawer, would make out in writing an order to another person, the drawee, to pay money over to a third person, the payee. The bills greatly facilitated credit transfers and enabled merchants to travel long distances without carrying large amounts of money or other valuable media of exchange. Generally, bills of exchange were dated and had a maturity or payment date before which they could not be collected. The mere drafting of a bill by the drawer did not obligate the drawee until he "accepted" the bill, usually by signing the bill itself. Once accepted, the payee could present the bill at the drawee's bank and payment would be made out of the drawee's account. By the 1840's the bills were almost universally held to be negotiable; that is, the payee could endorse the bill over to a fourth party who could then collect on the bill if it had been properly accepted.[17]

A distinguishing feature of the bill of exchange in the nineteenth century was its international, or multijurisdictional, character. Historically, the bills were used most often between merchants a long distance apart, usually located in different countries. Occasionally, eighteenth-century bills of exchange were used in domestic transactions, and a set of legal distinctions developed between "foreign" bills, used when the drawer and drawee were from different countries, and "inland" bills, used when the drawer and drawee were from the same country. The foreign bills were more common, and most of the law referred implicitly to foreign bills. Justice Story's entire treatise on bills of exchange (1843) concerns foreign bills, with only a short chapter addressing the peculiarities of inland bills. Blackstone himself noted that inland bills had always been regarded as a poor stepchild of the bill of exchange, because foreign bills were much more valuable "in the advancement of trade and commerce." In fact, only by statute did the inland bill come to be recognized as generally negotiable in England.[18]

In order to be treated as an inland bill, it was not enough that the drawer's and drawee's jurisdictions be governed by a single sovereignty; they had to have the same local laws and customs. For example, even though England, Scotland, and Ireland were united under the English throne, they were nevertheless "separate and distinct" in their "local laws and jurisprudence." As a result, a bill of exchange drawn by an Englishman against a Scotsman was a foreign bill. Story concluded that inland bills were entirely a matter of local concern, and subject to purely local statutes or rules. A foreign bill was one that was "not governed throughout by our own municipal jurisprudence," but which was extra-territorial and subject only to the general law. Of course, individual jurisdictions differed in their interpretation or recognition of general commercial principles, and Justice Story devoted part of his treatise on conflict of laws to choice-of-law rules governing bills of exchange. Nevertheless, the general principle was clear: inland bills were governed by local law, foreign bills by the general commercial law.[19]

Early in American national history the question arose whether a bill of exchange drawn by someone in one state upon someone in a different state should be considered an inland or a foreign bill. The question was important not only as a principle of commercial law but also as a doctrine of federal jurisdiction. Section 11 of the Judiciary Act of 1789 provided that "[no federal] district or Circuit Court [shall] have cognizance of any suit to recover the contents of any promissory note, or other chose in action, in favour of an assignee; unless a suit might have been prosecuted in such Court, to recover the said contents, if no assignment had been made; except in cases of foreign bills of exchange."[20]

Today it is relatively easy to infer the rationale for the first part of the provision. The federal courts generally had "diversity" jurisdiction if the plaintiff and defendant were from different states. But Congress did not want parties to commercial paper such as promissory notes to create such jurisdiction by the simple device of endorsing a note over to someone from a different state. If the two original parties to a promissory note were from the same state, then any dispute arising out of that transaction would be restricted to the state courts, even though the note might later be assigned to someone from a different state.

But why an exception for foreign bills of exchange? First, a foreign bill was negotiated between a drawer and drawee from two different jurisdictions, so as a basic premise it would seem that diversity would generally exist between the original drawer and drawee. However, diversity would not necessarily exist between the drawee and the original payee. Section 11 permitted suits on foreign bills of exchange whenever there was sufficient diversity between any plaintiff and defendant, in spite of any lack of diversity between the original parties to the bill. The 1789 Judiciary Act implicitly recognized the commercial importance and the interstate character of the foreign bill of exchange by providing for broader diversity jurisdiction in suits involving such bills.

In 1829, the Supreme Court decided that a bill of exchange drawn by a resident of one state upon a drawee in another state was a foreign, and not an inland, bill.[21] Justice Bushrod Washington noted that virtually all state courts considering the question had treated such bills as foreign. Furthermore, the substantive law of many states differed, depending on whether drawer and drawee were from the same state or from different states. For example, many states provided for interest to be added to delinquently paid bills of exchange. Under the law of many states the interest penalty was higher for interstate than for intrastate bills. To the argument that treating interstate bills of exchange as foreign permitted the same sort of fraudulent creation of diversity that the drafters of section 11 had feared respecting promissory notes, the Court responded that interstate bills of exchange "answer all the purposes of remittances, and of commercial facilities, equally with bills drawn upon other countries, or vice versa; and if a choice of jurisdictions be important to the credit of bills of the latter class, which it undoubtedly is, it must be equally so to that of the former." Justice Washington noted that because of "their commercial character," bills of exchange "might be expected to pass fairly into the hands of persons residing in the different states of the Union." He concluded that "in no point of view ought [interstate bills] be considered otherwise than as foreign bills." The result was to make the bills far more easily negotiable by giving the taker greater assurance that a uniform body of rules—the rules of the general common law, and not the law of any particular state—could be applied to a dispute.

Because the foreign bill of exchange involved parties from different jurisdictions, dispute settlement often raised conflict-of-laws problems. The most common was whether the sovereign could impose its will on bills created in a different jurisdiction. Justice Story Americanized the view that no sovereign could assert its jurisdiction over transactions outside its territory. The power of the courts of a state or nation extended to persons and events within the territory of the sovereignty that created the court, but no further.[22] For all practical purposes, this meant that no single state could govern completely the rights and obligations created by a single foreign bill of exchange. Such a document would invariably fall within the jurisdiction of two or more different sovereigns, or else there must be some general set of legal rules, established by agreement or federal coercion.

Story's clearest statement of this position came in *Van Reimsdyk v. Kane* (1812),[23] which he decided while riding circuit in Rhode Island. Suit was brought under a foreign bill of exchange by a resident of Batavia, Java, against a Rhode Island resident who claimed the bill had been discharged under a Rhode Island insolvency statute. Since the bill had been drawn outside Rhode Island, an important issue was whether the Rhode Island insolvency statute could relieve a debtor from an obligation incurred outside the state. Rhode Island courts appeared to believe that they had that power, but Story refused to apply Rhode Island law. Although he reached the same conclusion as he would thirty years later in *Swift*, his reasoning in *Van Reimsdyk* was somewhat different. Notwithstanding section 34's requirement that the "laws of the several states" be the rule of decision in the federal courts, Story concluded that there must be limits on a state's power to apply its law:

> [S]uch a limitation must arise whenever the subject matter of the suit is extraterritorial. In controversies between citizens of a state, as to rights derived under that statute, and in controversies respecting territorial interests, in which, by the laws of nations, the *lex rei sitae*[24] governs, there can be little doubt, that the regulations of the statute apply. But in controversies affecting citizens of other states, and in no degree arising from local regulations as for instance, foreign contracts of a commercial nature; I think it can hardly be maintained, that the laws of the state, to which they have no reference, however narrow, injudicious and inconvenient they may be, are to be the exclusive guides for judicial decision. Such a construction would defeat nearly all the objects, for which the constitution has provided a national court . . . .

In 1838 Story held once again that a federal judge would be bound by general law and not state law when the issue was whether an insurance policy issued in one state upon property in a different state should be interpreted to insure against injuries caused by negligence: "[U]pon commercial questions of a general nature, the courts of the United States . . . are not bound by local decisions."[25]

Negotiability and the Holder in Due Course

The underlying rationale of the general commercial law was the encouragement, simplification, and economy of commercial transactions. One manifestation of that purpose was the doctrine of the holder in due course. As among the original parties, who presumably had firsthand knowledge of the business transactions underlying a promissory note or bill of exchange, the courts recognized a number of equitable defenses to suits for collection. To borrow an example from the facts of *Swift*, suppose that Keith sold land to Tyson. In order to satisfy part of the debt, Keith drew a bill of exchange upon Tyson, made payable to Norton. But title to the land was discovered to be invalid, and Tyson was left with nothing. If Keith sued Tyson for refusing to accept the bill, Tyson could certainly have defended successfully by showing that the land that Keith sold never belonged to Keith in the first place. Similarly, if Norton sued Tyson for refusing to pay, Tyson could raise the same defense. But what if the bill had been endorsed over to Swift, a bona-fide purchaser of the bill with no knowledge of the fraudulent land transaction? If the note or bill passed to such a "holder in due course," the general commercial law held almost universally that the endorsee had a good cause of action, unqualified by any defense that might have been good against one of the original parties. Any other rule would have obliged the endorsee to investigate the transactions underlying every piece of commercial paper. True negotiability required that commercial paper be freely transferable between merchants and bankers.[26]

The case of *Swift v. Tyson* concerned a foreign bill of exchange. The drawer was from Maine and the drawee from New York. The bill was eventually endorsed over to Swift, a bank cashier in Portland, Maine, who had received the bill of exchange as part of everyday banking business. The routine nature of the transaction was important. As Justice Story observed, the receipt by a bank of such a bill was a common occurrence and "probably more than one-half of all bank transactions in our country, as well as those of other countries, are of this nature."[27] Nevertheless, there was some judicial precedent in New York that an endorsee who had taken a bill of exchange in satisfaction of a preexisting debt was not a holder in due course entitled to assert a claim if the drawee objected that the underlying transaction was invalid.[28]

If New York wanted to create a minority rule limiting negotiability of purely domestic transactions, that was its business. But facilitation of the interstate credit market was much more important than any interest that New York might have in a contrary policy governing foreign bills of exchange. "It is for the benefit and convenience of the commercial world to give as wide an extent as practicable to the credit and circulation of negotiable paper," he concluded. The rule developed in the courts of New York "would strike a fatal blow at all discounts of negotiable securities for preexisting debts."

Federal Jurisdiction and State Statutes

Thirteen years after *Swift* the Supreme Court heard *Watson v. Tarpley* (1855),[29] another diversity case involving a bill of exchange drawn in Louisiana and eventually endorsed over to the plaintiff, who was from Mississippi. The plaintiff had sued in federal court to collect on the bill before its maturity date. The trial judge instructed the jury on his interpretation of a Mississippi statute requiring that "no action or suit shall be sustained or commenced on any bill of exchange, until after the maturity thereof."

The Supreme Court unanimously found that the trial judge had erred by considering the statute at all. While "the laws of the several States are of binding authority upon their domestic tribunals, and upon persons and property within their appropriate jurisdiction," it was "equally clear that those laws cannot affect, either by enlargement or diminution, the jurisdiction of the courts of the United States . . . ." For that proposition Justice Peter Daniel cited *Swift v. Tyson.*

In *Swift* Justice Story had avoided the Constitution and purported to interpret only the Federal Judiciary Act. But *Watson* held for the first time that the Constitution mandates a certain choice-of-law rule in federal diversity jurisdiction cases. Watson, who was not a resident of Mississippi, had a constitutional right that the Mississippi statute not be applied by a federal court so as to defeat his recovery. To the extent that the Mississippi statute at issue would "impair the right of a non-resident holder of a bill of exchange" to sue in federal court upon default, such a statute "must be regarded as wholly without authority and inoperative."

Watson not only constitutionalized *Swift* but also extended its coverage from state common law rules to state statutes. What became important was not whether the state's legal rule had been developed judicially or legislatively, but whether it was "local" or "general," as determined by principles of territoriality and interstate federalism. A legal rule was "general" if it attempted to impose obligations or disabilities upon persons who were not within the territory of the sovereign that created the rule. Once a federal judge had determined that a particular rule was general and not local, he was constitutionally obligated to follow the general law rather than any state's peculiar manipulation of the law. *Watson* established that a federal court was constitutionally required to ignore a state's statute designed to protect its own debtor citizens from out-of-state creditors, if the statute was inconsistent with the general commercial law.

In the framework developed by *Swift* and *Watson,* diversity jurisdiction was designed to ensure that the interstate market economy was free, unencumbered by rules that reflected local prejudices at the expense of national economic development.[30] One of the best illustrations of this principle was *Gelpcke v. City of Dubuque* (1864), which involved the validity of municipal bonds issued to finance railroad construction. In the 1850's, the Iowa legislature passed statutes authorizing many municipalities to issue bonds and to levy local taxes to meet payments of principal and interest. Most of the bond purchasers were from out of state, and the bonds commonly traded in eastern markets. The validity of the state's enabling legislation was litigated, and the Supreme Court of Iowa twice upheld the state legislature's power under the Iowa Constitution to authorize municipal issuance of the bonds. But in the 1860's many of the construction projects lost financial support and municipalities began to default. The State supreme court overruled itself and held that under the state constitution the General Assembly had no authority to permit the municipalities to issue the bonds. The court concluded that the bonds were void and unpayable, and that the creditors should take nothing.[31]

The creditors in *Gelpcke,* all from New York, filed a diversity action in the Iowa federal court. The trial court relied on the state court decision invalidating the bonds to hold for the defendant. The Supreme Court reversed, citing the "uniform" commercial principle that a debtor's liability for principal and interest must be established under the law as it existed when the obligation was incurred, and not as of the time of default. Importantly, no federal constitutional issue was involved other than the question of choice of law in diversity cases. Both substantive due process and the federalization of the takings clause were a generation away. Implicit in the Supreme Court's rule was an important commercial principle: buyers rely on the law as of the time of their purchase. If a state could cancel its debts to out-of-state creditors by simply declaring previously issued bonds uncollectible, investors would lose confidence in the public bond market.

In the three decades following *Gelpcke* some three hundred bond cases came before the Supreme Court. The Court invariably upheld the validity of the bonds, state repudiation notwithstanding, when the creditors were citizens of another state. Occasionally the Court found the bonds invalid as to in-state creditors when the state courts had also found them invalid. In nearly every decision the Court relied not on a substantive federal principle but rather on the general commercial law and the federal judiciary's authority to interpret that law recognized in *Swift* and *Watson*.

After *Gelpcke*, Supreme Court decisions ignoring state law in diversity cases became increasingly offensive to state sovereignty. Justice Story had been careful to limit his opinion in *Swift* to cases involving multistate transactions. One would expect local law to govern most property and tort cases. But during the second half of the nineteenth century *Swift* gradually swept the field.[32]

There are two possible explanations for this development. One is that the instrumental foresight of Justice Story's *Swift* opinion, which did much to encourage the development of an interstate credit market, subsequently decayed into a formalism that gave constitutional status to a set of common law rules that were perceived as fixed.[33] But another possibility is that the nature of the problem was changing. Technology, the transportation revolution, and the rise of the interstate corporation were integrating the American economy and, in the process, creating multistate interests in tort rules and property law.

A case in point is the fellow-servant rule, which held that an employer could not be held liable for an employee's injuries caused by the negligence of a fellow employee. One function of such liability-narrowing rules was to shift certain developmental risks and costs away from large interstate employers, such as railroads, and toward their workers.[34] To the extent that a railroad's stockholders might be located in one state and its employees in another, the rule could also transfer wealth from one state to another. Agricultural states having relatively more railroad employees but few railroad stockholders might find it appropriate to modify or abolish the fellow-servant doctrine.

The landmark case applying *Swift* to torts in interstate commerce was *Baltimore & Ohio Railroad v. Baugh* (1893).[35] Baugh, a fireman, was injured because of the negligence of the engineer, his supervisor. Although Ohio generally followed the fellow-servant rule, it created a special exception for employees injured because of the negligence of a supervisor, who under state law was considered not a "fellow" servant but a superior. The lower federal court applied the state rule and the plaintiff recovered. In reversing, Justice Brewer surveyed the railroad law and determined that it was "general" and not "local." Without purporting to place all tort law in the "general" category, Brewer simply noted that the railroad industry itself was interstate and that the Constitution gave the federal government the exclusive power to regulate interstate commerce. Therefore, federal judges should exercise independent judgment in railroad tort cases and not be bound by state law.

Essential to Justice Brewer's argument was an unstated premise that the Justice himself would almost certainly have rejected: that state tort law is "regulatory," consisting of rules imposed by the sovereign upon a certain activity, not unlike a state law fixing the rates of interstate railway carriage. State tort law as applied to an interstate railroad was not merely a judge's discovery of common law principles; it was state rule making, and in the case of interstate railroads, the Constitution gave rule-making authority to the federal government. On the one hand, the *Baugh* decision can be viewed as an outrageous, formalistic extension of *Swift v. Tyson* into the field of torts; on the other, it was a perfectly appropriate assertion of federal regulatory authority in interstate commerce—although in an area where Congress had not acted.

Swift v. Tyson no less than *Baugh* tacitly recognized that the state itself was an interested party in otherwise private commercial disputes. Even the common law of commercial transactions was a form of state rule making. When *Swift* was decided, a major effort was under way in England and most of Europe to develop a common body of rules governing commercial transactions between parties from different countries.[36] One major hindrance to international trade was the host of parochial rules protecting local people or property at the expense of outsiders. Justice Story believed such rules discouraged trade by increasing uncertainty and risk. He argued in his great commentary on the Constitution that a uniform federal jurisdiction across the country would advantageously "increase the confidence and credit between the commercial and agricultural states."[37] Much of Story's life's work was devoted to developing a uniform body of commercial legal rules that would do two things at the same time. First, they would bind the states into a unified nation; second, they would encourage America's participation in world markets. Justice Story used every scholarly vehicle to support this idea, including his commercial treatises on bills of exchange and promissory notes, his path-breaking treatise on conflict of laws, and his judicial opinions in cases such as *Swift v. Tyson*.

CHAPTER 9

An Economic Interpretation
of the Constitution

The Economic Fourteenth Amendment

The principal purpose of the fourteenth amendment was to give black people born in the United States the same constitutional protections enjoyed by white people.[1] Congress passed the Civil Rights Act of 1866 two years before the fourteenth amendment was ratified. The statute presaged the spirit of the fourteenth. It provided that all persons born in the United States were its citizens, and that all citizens, without regard to race, color, or previous condition of servitude should have the same rights "to make and enforce contracts, to sue, be parties, and give evidence, to inherit, purchase, lease, sell, hold, and convey real and personal property, and to full and equal benefit of all laws and proceedings for the security of person and property, as is enjoyed by white citizens."[2] The fourteenth amendment was designed in part to resolve doubts about this statute's constitutionality.[3]

Many critics of substantive due process have accused the Supreme Court of "misdirecting" the fourteenth amendment. They argue that the amendment was designed to protect the "civil rights" of black freedmen, but that it ended up virtually ignoring black Americans and instead shielded employers from protective labor legislation. The pair of Supreme Court decisions identified with this proposition are *Plessy v. Ferguson* (1896), which held that "separate but equal" public facilities did not violate the equal protection clause, and *Lochner v. New York* (1905),[4] which held that a statute setting the maximum hours that bakers could work violated the due process clause.

But such critiques overlook the fact that in 1868 the concept of "civil rights" included two elements: (1) the right to equality of treatment in court trials and of access to the agencies of the state; and (2) a set of distinctly *economic* civil rights, namely, the right to make contracts and the right to own property.[5] When the same Congress that drafted the amendment legislated under it, the legislation involved contract and property rights, not rights of association, privacy, or the freedoms of speech or religion. Among the rights not recognized was freedom from private racial segregation. Congress did not have segregation in mind when it passed the Civil Rights Act of 1866, when it drafted the fourteenth amendment, or even a decade later when, contemplating the end of Reconstruction, it drafted the Civil Rights Act of 1875, which was subsequently struck down by the Supreme Court.[6] Even Radical Republicans maintained a sharp distinction among "civil" rights, "political" rights, and "social" rights. The fourteenth amendment and the Civil Rights Act of 1866 were designed to protect civil and political rights, but not social rights. And civil rights were fundamentally defined as economic rights—principally, the right of equal access to markets.[7]

The fourteenth amendment was economic by design. The freedmen did not need the freedoms of speech or religion or even the fair administration of the criminal process so much as they needed jobs and security. In 1866 Congress selected contracts and property as the civil rights worthy of protection because, within its classical view of the world, the right to make contracts and the right to own property were the keys to economic success. The hard question is not why economic liberties became the amendment's central concern—Congress had that in mind all along—but why the Court used the fourteenth amendment to create substantive rights, rather than merely to ensure that all Americans had the same set of rights, however defined.

The immediate answer is that the due process clause of the fourteenth amendment was not surplusage. If the purpose of the amendment was merely to give freedmen the same set of rights that white citizens enjoyed, then the equal protection clause would have been sufficient. But Congress intended to provide certain substantive rights, protecting freedmen from some kinds of governmental activity. Liberals and conservatives alike agreed about this proposition, and it forms the foundation not only of substantive due process but also of the "incorporation" debate, concerning whether the due process clause of the fourteenth amendment required the states to honor the Bill of Rights.[8]

That these absolute rights should be identified with economic liberties was uncontroversial. But economic liberties had to be defined. That was the province of political economy. The principal concern of classical political economy was not price theory or industrial organization, or even trade or tariff policy, but rather identification of the ideal economic regime that would maximize both prosperity and individual liberty.

Francis Wharton wrote his *Commentaries on Law* (1884)[9] just as the state courts were beginning to develop the fourteenth amendment doctrine of substantive due process. Wharton, as he almost always did, reflected the conservative consensus. His work contained the most explicit argument in the 1880's legal literature that the fourteenth amendment should be used to protect a general, substantive liberty of contract.

Wharton's interpretation of the fourteenth amendment virtually ignored themes of racial justice in favor of economic and business protections. That the legislative history of the fourteenth amendment expressed substantial concern for the rights of black freedmen, and none for the economic rights of others, did not trouble him. The Constitution was for everyone, not merely one particular group:

> [T]he provisions contained in these amendments, bearing distinctively on the negro race, are comparatively ephemeral in their character, while the clause before us is likely to be permanent, and to permeate the whole business system of the Union. Almost all the adjudications in respect to the amendment have, heretofore, related to negro rights. But these are now finally settled . . . and the real importance of the amendment, in securing the rights of the people as a body, is now becoming disclosed.

For Wharton, the purpose of the fourteenth amendment was to constitutionalize a particular theory of political economy. Wharton believed that the fourteenth amendment cured "what was previously the great defect of our system. It destroys the power which had been assumed by state legislatures of interfering with private business, and of doing by law that which can be far better done by individual enterprise." The "real importance" of the fourteenth amendment for Wharton was that it gave citizens, particularly when engaged in business, a set of rights against state legislatures similar to those that the Bill of Rights had given the states and their citizens against the federal government. Wharton was among the first "incorporationists," writing at a time when the only civil rights other than those pertaining to government access were economic. The Bill of Rights protected people from federal usurpation, but it soon "became evident that the people of the states were in danger at least as much from the aggressions of their own legislatures as from the usurpations of congress." For Wharton, the responsibility for determining when private business can do something better than government can belongs to the courts. Thus judges were invited to adopt a theory about the optimal structure of economic relationships, which is of course what nineteenth century political economy was all about.

Thomas M. Cooley, John Norton Pomeroy, Christopher G. Tiedeman, John Dillon, and Joel Parker[10]—the most prominent writers on constitutional law of the postwar period—agreed with Wharton that once the problem of protecting black access to the economic system had been solved, the remaining purpose of the amendment was to enable the courts to define individual economic liberties against the states.

On Finding Political Economy in the Constitution

The thesis of this book is *not* that economists "caused" a revision of the American law of business regulation by developing economic ideas that were then read into the Constitution by American judges. The evidence does not support such a proposition. In any event, that is much too simplistic an explanation for how legal ideas are created. Rather, American political economists and American judges operated in the same, uniquely American "market" for ideas. Like all market participants, each American maker of ideas selected from available inputs to produce his own original output. For the American political economist, the inputs included not only British classicism but also physical experiences about growth and productivity that were far different for someone living in the nineteenth-century United States than for someone living in the British Isles. The inputs of American classical political economy may even have included the decisions of some judges. They certainly included some jurisprudential propositions, such as those about the sanctity of property rights.

American judges appropriated the ideas that seemed most available and useful, and they perceived American experience as more useful than experience from Britain or anywhere else. Political economy was among the most available and most useful of contemporary ideas, for it explained why such things as minimum wage laws or subsidies or state restrictions on entry were bad; and, importantly, why the market worked much better in America than it did in Britain. Such influence was a two-way street. When the American political economist wrote, he wrote about law as much as about economics. Invariably in this prespecialized age he gave his opinions about the sanctity of contracts, strikes, tariffs, national banks, and regulation of interstate commerce. Most of the great nineteenth-century doctrines of American constitutional law were also doctrines of political economy.

It is not particularly difficult to show that nineteenth-century American judges were exposed to political economy. In fact, it is hard to imagine how they could have avoided it. British classical political economy was not technical, and it was dominated by large, accessible policy questions. British and American writing on political economy did not make widespread use of graphs or complex equations until the final two decades of the nineteenth century. The first specialized journals on economics, such as the *Quarterly Journal of Economics* (founded by Harvard in 1886), the *Journal of Political Economy* (Chicago, 1892) and the *American Economic Review* (American Economic Association, 1911), came then or even later.[11]

Although nineteenth-century American political economists wrote many books, their greatest forum for the exchange of ideas was the general review, such as the *North American Review,* the *Yale Review,* or the *Princeton Review.* Judges and lawyers also contributed to the great reviews, which were filled with a wonderfully eclectic mixture of political economy, constitutional law, private law, history, ethics, and even literature.[12] Anyone who was well read—and that certainly included most of the elite bar—was exposed to this array. In 1912, when the Harvard economist A. N. Holcombe criticized the judicial record in wage and hour cases, he placed blame on "the manning of our courts with a set of judges whose economic training was received mainly from the so-called classical school of political economists." Holcombe concluded that "[t]he effect of such judicial interpretation has been to read into the constitution a doctrine that is nowhere expressed therein, namely, the doctrine of freedom of contract."[13]

The judges who molded the classical Constitution, through their invention of such doctrines as substantive due process, were no more out of date or hostile toward theory and policy than were courts in general. Elite American judges generally absorb the thinking of elite American intellectuals. Classical constitutional doctrine followed after the political economy that prevailed in America's best universities. As a result, understanding constitutional theory during the Gilded Age and

Progressive Era means understanding the political economy that guided it. This was the political economy taught in American universities in the 1870's and 1880's. It is important to note that it was *not* the political economy taught in British universities during that same period. The British were a half century ahead of the Americans, first in economic development and the attendant consequences for the distribution of wealth, second in the resultant theory, and third in legislative incorporation.[14]

One criticism of this historical explanation of American public law is that the works of great political economists, British or American, are almost never cited in nineteenth-century judicial opinions. In a few early twentieth-century decisions the Supreme Court made vague reference to social science data contained in briefs, but did not cite any of it explicitly.[15] Beginning in 1917 Justice Louis Brandeis occasionally made a social science reference, mostly in dissents.[16] But the Supreme Court itself did not begin citing social science data with any regularity until *Brown v. Board of Education* (1954).

But this objection is not a formidable one. *Brown* represents, not the Supreme Court's discovery of social science, but rather a remarkable change in the etiquette of writing judicial opinions. In *Brown* the Court abandoned a longstanding legal tradition of refusing to give explicit credit to intellectual sources from outside jurisprudence. Scholasticism, Protestantism, Romanticism, Darwinism, nationalism, abolitionism, and many other intellectual forces have always shaped the law, even though the seminal works in those areas were never cited by contemporary judges, and only rarely by treatise writers. Political economy was treated no differently. In 1906, the Progressive economist Richard T. Ely complained to Justice Oliver Wendell Holmes that the Supreme Court had adopted his definition of monopoly almost verbatim, but had attributed it only to "another," and had not mentioned the work in which it was contained.[17]

The evidence that the Supreme Court read a particular theory of political economy into the Constitution is necessarily circumstantial. It consists of similarities between the views of the economists and those of the judges, occasional statements in which judges put forward economic theories, and the fact that elite lawyers and political economists read in and wrote for the same journals and were concerned with the same kinds of policy issues. Justice Holmes relied on this sort of evidence in 1905 when he accused the Supreme Court of enacting "Mr. Herbert

Spencer's *Social Statics*."[18] Holmes did not cite earlier references to Spencer's work in judicial opinions; there were none.

Social Darwinism and the Constitution

Darwinism unquestionably had a powerful intellectual influence on American scientific thought at the turn of the century. It also had a powerful influence on American jurisprudence. Ever since Richard Hofstadter's path-breaking book on Social Darwinism, it has become almost commonplace to observe that Social Darwinism guided the United States Supreme Court.[19]

But Social Darwinism is the most overrated of Gilded Age ideologies. Justice Holmes's aphorism that "[t]he Fourteenth Amendment does not enact Mr. Herbert Spencer's *Social Statics*" has been interpreted to mean that the Supreme Court *had* written Herbert Spencer into the United States Constitution. In 1950 Henry Steele Commager concluded facetiously that Holmes was "wrong" and that the Court had in fact "enacted" Spencer.

But the influence of Social Darwinism was much less than we have been led to believe.[20] There is painfully little evidence that any members of the Supreme Court were Social Darwinists or for that matter even Darwinian. Even Holmes's credentials are in dispute. Holmes's public and private writings have been scrutinized as carefully as those of any American public figure, but all the evidence that Social Darwinism was an important intellectual influence on his thought comes down to four or five short personal statements, mainly from his early career.[21] A much more defensible proposition is that Holmes once or twice used evolutionary metaphors when speaking about law because theories of evolution dominated popular dialogue for the entire period of his professional life. It was no easier for Holmes to avoid evolution than it was for an intellectual growing up in the 1940's or 1950's to avoid relativity.

The Social Darwinists developed explanatory models and rhetorics that were easily appropriated and suitably revised by expansionist, moralistic Protestant Americans. The influence of Darwinism on the Supreme Court amounted to little in comparison with the influence of orthodox Protestant Realism. The Court's continuous citation in liberty of contract cases to "just equivalence" and "moral requirements" and "natural" or "inherent" rights in property smacked much more of Common Sense Realism than of Social Darwinist naturalism. The degree to which Darwinism and Social Darwinism *failed* to permeate the thinking of the Supreme Court in any obvious way is most amazing.

In both economics and law, "Social Darwinism" was much more an epithet than an analytic tool. It added little more than rhetoric to economic theory. In fact, the two scholars who used the rhetoric most, Herbert Spencer in England and William Graham Sumner in America, were either second-rate social scientists or popularizers. Social Darwinism ultimately had little to say about the appropriate limits of state regulatory policy, antitrust reform, or poverty relief.

Most problematic was Social Darwinism's inability to see anything but the long run. The true Social Darwinist could look at unemployed masses and proclaim their starvation a good thing, discounting the possibility of short-run solutions, for which policy makers must continually search. The leading conservative economists in Gilded Age and Progressive America were not Social Darwinists. They were neoclassicists, looking, as most social scientists were, for a scientific method. They were deeply involved in building a model that would justify competition and define its limits. The Social Darwinists, by contrast, worshiped competition and believed that it had no limits. For example, Social Darwinism had no "theory" of monopoly. Rather, it blithely explained that monopoly resulted from the survival of the fittest. The best society could hope for was that the monopolist would be benevolent.[22]

For most well-educated but nonscientific American Protestants around the turn of the century, Social Darwinism was nothing more than a cosmological argument. This explains how one could be a Social Darwinist without being a Darwinian. Social Darwinism reinforced deeply ingrained Protestant values. Each person bore responsibility for the most fundamental decisions about religious belief, ethical practice, and economic status. The purpose of the state and the church was not to dictate external values but merely to cultivate and reinforce those values that were confirmed to each person by his own perceptions. Social Darwinism was "background" theory: it enabled people to think that biology tended to confirm the religious ethics that they had already been taught.

The influence of this *moral* theory of laissez-faire in the late nineteenth century cannot be overstated. It explains the immense religiosity in Progressive Era reformers, even political economists such as Richard T. Ely and Charles R. Van Hise. Before theologians, economists, or even lawmakers would abandon their commitment to state noninterference and accept extensive social control, the religious and philosophical roots of laissez-faire had to be exhumed, examined, and eradicated. The Progressive Era social reformers did just that. However, for their efforts they were castigated and belittled for making economics too easy a mixture of science and religion.

To be sure, the economics of Progressives such as Ely contained a good deal of religious moralizing that proved unacceptable to more positivistic economists in the 1930's and after.[23] But Progressive economists understood something that later generations did not. In 1900, it was not enough to show that laissez-faire was not utilitarian or that it did not contain the best economic theory. And it was clearly not enough to show that laissez-faire was not the best application of Darwin's theory to human morality. Any successful critique of liberty of contract had to come to terms with the prevailing belief that laissez-faire was *the* Christian economics—even if it produced inequalities of distribution.[24] Moral arguments were absolutely essential to Ely's case. He had the awesome task of showing that laissez-faire was not merely bad economics, but bad religion as well.

The subsequent generation of American social scientists and historians generally ignored the religious roots of nineteenth-century American economic theory and treated it as a mutated child of natural selection. As a result, they failed to understand the complex philosophy of Gilded Age laissez-faire, which was far too orthodox to be truly Darwinian. Later intellectual historians and constitutional or legal historians likewise emphasized the "Spencerian" or "Social Darwinist" nature of substantive due process.[25] They virtually ignored the much older and deeper religious roots. Thus, the laissez-faire Court has been mischaracterized as a bench full of opportunists who adopted a simple-minded popular philosophy and read it into the Constitution, even as many intellectuals were finding it bigoted and naive. Part of the blame for this historical error lies with none other than Justice Holmes, whose most quoted dissent was as misleading as it was correct. He was precisely right when he told the *Lochner* majority that the fourteenth amendment did not "enact Mr. Herbert Spencer's *Social Statics.*" In fact, it enacted Francis Wayland's *Elements of Political Economy.*

THE RISE OF REGULATED INDUSTRY

CHAPTER 10

Market Failure and Constitutional Classicism: The Slaughter-House Cases

Classical political economy believed that markets were robust and almost always the preferred mechanism for allocating goods and services. Jefferson's famous maxim defining the best government as that which governs least easily became "that government is best which regulates least." For classicists this entailed narrowing the scope of government regulation in two ways. First, government intervention should be applied in as few markets as possible. Second, when regulation is applied, it should be applied as narrowly as possible.

The Progressive theory of regulation, commonly identified with Charles Francis Adams, Jr., in the Gilded Age or Louis Brandeis in the Progressive Era,[1] accepted most of classicism's premises about the goals of regulation and its essential nature. Both classicism and the Progressives advocated a "public interest" theory of regulation. They differed in their degree of confidence in the robustness of the unregulated market and the economic models used to describe market behavior. Although Progressives disputed the strong classical presumption in favor of the unregulated market, they expressed their criticism with varying degrees of enthusiasm. Only the most radical Progressives wished to eliminate the market altogether. Most focused their regulatory energies in a relatively small number of areas: the railroads and other public utilities, labor, corporate disclosure, or pure food and drugs.[2]

The orthodox American political economist trained in the classical tradition was confident about how markets worked. He believed that technological progress, large amounts of capital investment, and corporate consolidation would make Americans better off. Further, these things would happen naturally, provided that the government kept its hands off. To be sure, the railroads were a complex, troublesome exception, but one that he readily set aside. The typical Progressive economist, by contrast, was deeply affected by the Panic of 1893, which inaugurated the most severe depression in memory. It is almost a truism in the history of American economic thought that classicism or neoclassicism triumph in times of great prosperity and government yields more discretion to the market. But in the recession that inevitably follows a new generation of economists brushes classicism aside and substitutes a view far more skeptical about the health and even the morality of the market. The great depression of the 1890's gave us Progressive economics, and molded the minds of Richard T. Ely, Henry Carter Adams, Charles R. Van Hise, John R. Commons, and, to a lesser degree, Thorstein Veblen. The Great Depression of the 1930's gave us imperfect and monopolistic competition, and the mindsets of Edward Chamberlin, Gardiner Means, Thurman Arnold, and Arthur Burns.

Progressive legal reformers like Louis Brandeis, whose economic ideas were formed during the 1890's depression, with its dramatically high rates of unemployment and business insolvencies, unprecedented labor strife, and hundreds of business mergers, found the market a frail and unpredictable social instrument. The premise that the state should look first to the market began to fade in favor of a presumption that government intervention is better. But the basic goal of regulatory policy— protection of the public interest—was unchallenged. Both classicism and Progressivism believed that regulation should be used when the market failed to allocate resources in the best way; they simply disagreed about how often that might happen.

Part III will examine the roots of American regulatory policy in the late nineteenth century. From these roots has stemmed a great, now century-long debate over whether regulation has been or can be in the public interest, or whether it invariably leads to "capture"—that is, control of the regulatory process by some interest group, often the regulated firms themselves.

The regulatory "capture" debate is sometimes said to have originated in the 1960's, but I will argue that it is far older. In addition, I take issue with the New Left's conclusion that capture is inevitable, and state regulatory policy *inherently* nothing more than political—that is, that legislative outcomes reflect nothing more than the lobbying success of various special interest groups. The New Left conclusion rejects any role for economic science in the determination of regulatory policy, and such an ideology leads to irrational extremes. For example, it forces us to believe that even the state policy that the grocery business should be competitive, while electric utilities ought to be price-regulated monopolies, is purely political. For some reason the electric utility lobby or some other interest group has managed to convince state legislatures to give the utilities protection from competition through price regulation, while the grocers have had no such success. However, the influence of politics notwithstanding, one can hold a principled, essentially nonpolitical theory justifying competition in the grocery industry but not among utilities. The economic model of declining fixed costs, or economies of scale, has contributed as much as politics to at least certain instances of state regulatory policy.

Of course the more fundamental decision that a society should have a capitalist system containing both competitive and price-regulated private firms is "political." But many New Left historians of regulation have spent little time addressing this "background" policy decision. For the most part, they have argued that within the free enterprise framework individual instances of regulatory policy are explained by nothing more than politics, with the result that regulatory policy is inevitably captured by the interests that it is supposed to regulate.

Regulatory policy historically has been dictated by a mixture of politics and economic theory. When economic theory in an area is poorly formulated and no clear consensus has emerged within the community of experts, politics naturally dominates regulatory decision making, for political interests are always present. For example, the litigants in the *Charles River Bridge* case (1837) had nothing approaching the modern neoclassical model of natural monopoly, but they had a pretty good idea about who would gain and who would lose if the owners of a toll bridge were given a monopoly right. As economic models become formulated, tested, and—most important—as they force consensus within the relevant community, theory thrusts itself next to politics and accounts for part of the emerging policy. To what extent depends on the strength and general acceptance of the theory and the strength of the political interests opposing it.

If I am correct, then there is room once again for a "public interest" theory of regulatory policy, particularly in the writing of history. Economic theory is designed to show that a particular regulatory policy is better because it enhances the well-being of those who gain from it by a greater amount than it reduces the well-being of those who lose. If the public interest can appropriately be identified with this enlargement of community welfare, distributive questions aside, then we can speak of the "public interest" in regulatory policy. For example, the retail grocery market is competitively structured because of a very powerful consensus that the social cost of price and entry regulation in this market would far exceed its benefits. The retail electric power industry, by contrast, consists of price-regulated monopolies because of a somewhat weaker, though traditionally powerful, economic consensus that the social benefits of price and entry regulation in this market will exceed its social costs.

This chapter and the three that follow explore two of the most widely cited instances of regulatory "capture" in American history and provide alternative explanations. The first instance is the *Slaughter-House Cases* of 1873, widely regarded by historians as a clear instance of regulatory capture. The second is the complicated and vexing problem of railroad regulation in the Gilded Age.

Property, Monopoly, and Regulatory Capture

Property is a function of scarcity. If there were an infinite amount of everything, there would be no need for legal property rules. We place value on something because there is not enough of it to give all of us all that we want; we must bid what we want away from someone who values it less.

Historically, the state was not perceived as a substantial creator of "property." Its power to create valuable things was not obvious. There was little reason to think that the government was better than private enterprise at turning pigment into art or wood and steel into buildings. But the state clearly did better than private enterprise at creating monopolies. The *right* to broadcast (as opposed to a broadcast facility) is valuable only because the sovereign has seen fit to prohibit most people from broadcasting.

During the late nineteenth century the legal concept of property and the economic concept of scarcity began to diverge. This conceptual process has been called the "dephysicalization" of property law or, more recently, the "New Property."[3] The evolving view was that property was not the right to exclude others from a physical object that was valuable because it was scarce.[4] Rather, a property right was a promise by the state to protect a particular position or status. For example, a New York city taxicab medallion and a broadcast license are "property" under this new definition. These things are valuable only to the extent that the state makes them scarce.

Once the state becomes involved in creating value, politics inevitably follows. The principal basis for the "regulatory capture" argument is that regulation is nothing more than the consequence of the state's decision to create scarcity for the benefit of some interest group and to the exclusion of all others. A monopoly grant to the Charles River Bridge would make its owners wealthier, while injuring both those who must pay monopoly tolls and those who wish to build competing bridges but cannot. Within this model there are no "right answers" to questions about the state's allocation of property rights; there are only political choices.

Classical political economy had its own regulatory "capture" thesis, rooted in its great hostility toward monopoly. Classicists believed that virtually every state creation of monopoly was economically indefensible and must be explained by politics. But throughout the nineteenth century orthodox classicists were challenged by two very different but equally principled dissenters. First were preclassicists such as Joseph Story, who argued as late as the 1840's that monopoly was necessary to encourage new investment. Second were postclassicists such as Charles Francis Adams, Jr., who argued as early as the 1870's that competition would not work in some industries, particularly the railroads.

The result was a great debate among economists about the legitimacy and appropriate scope of state-created monopoly. That debate was accompanied by an equally vigorous legal debate that often involved the Constitution and the Supreme Court. The economic importance of this legal debate is underscored by the awesome fungibility of legal doctrine relating to regulatory monopolies. Creative lawyers used every conceivable means to attack them. The state's power to regulate by creating monopoly was challenged under the commerce clause, the contract clause, the privileges and immunities clause of article IV, the fourteenth amendment due process clause, the equal protection clause, the fourteenth amendment privileges and immunities clause, the thirteenth amendment, the patents clause, the general theory that states had a finite "police power," or regulatory authority, and the general theory that no legislative decision creating a monopoly could be binding on subsequent legislatures. Throughout the nineteenth century the state-created regulatory monopoly was an institution in search of a legal doctrine that would predictably justify or condemn it.[5]

Preface to the Capture Debate: The Charles River Bridge Case

Legal uncertainty over the proper scope and method of state regulation of natural monopolies ripened in the United States in the *Charles River Bridge* case (1837), in which the Supreme Court considered whether a state's grant to a private company of the right to build a bridge and operate it for profit implied a monopoly. The case has been presented as a dispute between the representatives of two different interest groups, each of which would profit immensely if its own theory were adopted.[6] On the one side were old-money Federalists, who owned many monopoly franchises and argued that private construction of public improvements required monopoly protection for the investors. On the other side was a new group of entrepreneurs, poised to enter American markets. They believed that all markets should be competitive. The dispute is an old one, common in the law of antitrust and business regulation: those already operating in a market want to make new entry by potential competitors as difficult as possible; those trying to enter the market want to make new entry easy.

The established view of the *Charles River Bridge* case sees little more than a political dispute over the nature of the corporation. A toll bridge was a work of public improvement that was historically a "prerogative of the crown"—that is, it could not be operated unless one first obtained the sovereign's permission. The permission took the form of a corporate charter.[7] The question then became whether the charter, once given, implied an exclusive right or a right that a later sovereign could compromise by forcing the grantee to share with others. Morton J. Horwitz finds "contradictory eighteenth-century assumptions" about whether a legal right to engage in a certain business implied a right to exclude competitors. Blackstone developed both views, arguing at one point that the legal right to operate a ferry or market implied an action for nuisance against a competitor, but arguing elsewhere that competitive entry in the milling industry was *damnum absque injuria*—a wrong without a legal remedy—unless the new entrant interfered with the flow of water to the original mill.[8] These two inconsistent ideologies collided in the *Charles River Bridge* case. Chief Justice Taney, a Jacksonian who favored the new entrepreneurs, sided with the pro-competitive interests. Justice

Story, who represented the interests of the landed Federalists earning the monopoly profits, sided with the incumbents.

The story of the *Charles River Bridge* case too easily becomes a story of politics if one neglects its most important technological element: the bridge itself. For a long time states habitually had given monopoly franchises to operators of tollroads, bridges, and ferries, but not to butchers, farmers, or cobblers. States perceived, admittedly in a non-technical way, that public works such as bridges were natural monopolies. Almost the entire cost of establishing and operating a bridge—acquiring the land, construction, and maintenance—was fixed; it varied little with the amount of traffic. Thus, the cost imposed on the bridge operator by one additional user was nearly zero. Furthermore, in most instances a single bridge across a certain part of a river was sufficient for all the traffic at that point. If a second bridge were built nearby, the result in a competitive market would be that each bridge would attempt to increase its traffic by lowering its price to a level approaching marginal costs and not allowing enough to cover fixed costs.[9]

Perhaps the *Charles River Bridge* case was a dispute between two great political interests and ideologies—preclassical vested rights on the one side and classical competition on the other. Much more fundamentally, it was a dispute about the best way for the state to encourage the construction and operation of bridges. The issue was whether a corporate charter giving the plaintiff the right to build and operate a toll bridge implied the power, protected by the contract clause of the Constitution, to exclude competitors even though the charter did not expressly grant such power. The plaintiffs' argument made sense only if they could show a reasonable expectation that the grant of the right to operate a bridge implied monopoly status. This argument concerning reasonable expectations forced the parties to consider economics: would a reasonable grantee have accepted the offer to build a bridge without legal protection from competition? Justice Story was flabbergasted that anyone would even ask the question: "[T]he very statement of such propositions is so startling to my mind . . . that I should always doubt the soundness of any reasoning which should conduct me to such results."[10]

Story had the advantage of perfect hindsight, and he was right. When the competing Warren Bridge opened, the Charles River Bridge lost three-fourths of its tolls.[11] The new bridge probably received the vast majority of fares because local people knew that the Warren Bridge was obligated by law to become free as soon as its proprietors recouped

their investment plus a stipulated return. By the time the case reached
the Supreme Court, the Charles River Bridge—one of the most profitable private corporations in American history to that time—had already
closed. It did not reopen until 1841, when the Commonwealth acquired
it and began to operate it as a free bridge.[12]

The real cause of the Charles River Bridge dispute was that both
sides had miscalculated. The state originally should have granted a
charter that permitted the private company to collect tolls until it recovered its costs plus profits, when the bridge would become the state's.
The proprietors should have negotiated for an express monopoly term
in their charter. By 1820 charters for toll bridges and turnpikes generally provided for automatic transfer to the state once the corporation
had recovered its full costs plus a specified return on its investment
(generally 9 to 12 percent per annum).

Although much has been written about the *Charles River Bridge* case,
its holding is very narrow. There is some evidence that Chief Justice
Taney believed that no state had the right to create a monopoly by
special charter in any area of economic activity. In order to gain a
majority on the Court, however, he accepted a much weaker rule that
"in grants by the public, nothing passes by implication." The real effect
of the *Charles River Bridge* case was to give entrepreneurs what they
bargained for. If a charter to a private company contained no explicit
monopoly grant, none would be implied. If a charter contained a
monopoly provision, most states enforced the provision. Many
monopoly charters continued to be written, even during the height of
the antimonopoly movement in the 1880s.[13]

The ideological differences between Federalists and Jacksonians on
the monopoly question are easily exaggerated. For those who see the
controversy as merely political—a fight between those who controlled
American enterprise and those trying to enter—the preclassicist's enthusiasm for monopoly seems boundless. It was no such thing. Consider
the viewpoints of two of the most intellectually powerful of the antag-
onists. The Federalist Joseph Story represented New England's old
wealth and sided with the monopolists in the *Charles River Bridge* case.
Justice Stephen J. Field, a westerner and a Lincoln appointee, was a
supporter of the new entrepreneurialism, free labor, and a staunch
opponent of state-created monopolies. Justice Field is famous for his
dissents in the *Slaughter-House Cases* and *Munn v. Illinois*,[14] where he
developed the view that business has the right to be free of interference
from the state.

In his *Charles River Bridge* dissent, Justice Story responded to the argument that implying a monopoly in a bridge charter effectively would give a monopoly to all chartered businesses. By the 1830's many manufacturing companies were incorporated and would fall into this group. Story noted the common law distinction between "monopolies" and "franchises." A monopoly was "an exclusive right granted to a few, of something which was before of common right, such as the right to manufacture a certain commodity." Story cited the English Statute against Monopolies as evidence that such "common rights" could not be made the subject of monopoly grants. Among such common rights, Story included manufacturing, banks, and insurance companies.[15]

In contrast, a "franchise" was a permit from the sovereign to engage in an activity that had never been a common right. Story cited ferries, canals, turnpikes, and bridges as examples of franchises. For Story, the chief difference between common rights and franchises was that every citizen had a natural right to exercise the former, but a franchise could be secured only by legislative grant. A franchise was created for the "public good," and its manager was required by law to offer services to the entire public in a nondiscriminatory manner.[16] Because competition creates alternative suppliers, anyone engaging in a common right could serve or refuse to serve a customer as he chose.[17] Here lay the seeds of the modern distinction between regulated and competitive industry, which was to become prominent in the final three decades of the century.

Justice Field has been characterized as the great opponent of state-authorized monopoly.[18] In the *Slaughter-House Cases* he championed substantive due process with his view that private business has the right to be free from state regulation. In *Munn v. Illinois* (1876), discussed in Chapter 12, Field dissented from a decision upholding an Illinois statute that turned the grain storage industry into a price-regulated utility. He addressed the argument that certain monopolists would have a right to gouge the public if they were not price-regulated by the government. Certain businesses were by their nature "dedicated by the owner to public uses." In these, both state monopoly and price regulation were permissible. Field's list of such businesses included "public ferries, bridges, and turnpikes . . . wharfingers, hackneys, and draymen, and . . . interest on money."[19]

The views of Story and Field are much closer than the historical writing on law and American economic development suggests. The appearance of great ideological difference results mainly from the differing situations their opinions addressed. Story presented his views in a dissent from a holding that a bridge corporation was not entitled to a monopoly by implication. Field's views came in dissents from decisions approving a slaughterhouse monopoly and a statute that regulated prices in an industry that had always been competitive. Both butchering and the storage of grain were, in common law parlance, "common rights." The confusion appears because the two Justices had no coherent economic model to support their theories of business regulation. That is why the most important fact of the *Charles River Bridge* case is that it was a case about a bridge. Neither Story nor Field wanted to make farmers into statutory monopolists, and neither wanted as a general matter to encourage the construction of several bridges when one would do. The differences between them lay mostly at the margin—determining precisely where the line between competition and regulated monopoly should be drawn.

The Problem of New Technology

The lack of a usable model for natural monopoly encouraged judges to assess the legality of state-created monopolies by relying on the common law's list of enterprises historically recognized as prerogatives of the crown—bridges, ferries, strategically located seaports, turnpikes, canals, and later steamboat lines and railroads. The apparent incoherence of the list left the policy maker with no rational basis upon which to decide whether a new technology "fit" the model. There was no model.

This absence of theory led to two problems. The first occurred when the states were faced with a new form of technology that could not be characterized easily as either a "common right" or a "prerogative of the crown" entitled to monopoly protection. The second problem arose when a business that had always been competitive—a common right—changed because technology and the market changed.

An example of the first problem is the development of the gas lighting industry during the second, third, and fourth decades of the nineteenth century. Judges were not immediately certain whether the new industry, which delivered gas to urban homes by underground pipelines, was a common right, mandating competition, or a prerogative of the crown, which would permit monopoly. Part of the problem was that the first companies used manufactured coal gas rather than natural gas. As a result, the companies had the attributes of both a common manufacturer (they made the gas in a factory) and a utility (they delivered it to individual subscribers by underground pipeline).[20]

In fact, the industry was an orthodox natural monopoly. An entire community could be served by a single set of underground gas pipes. Competition among incumbents would have necessitated multiple pipes and would have given each company higher fixed costs per unit of gas sold. As a result the cheapest method of delivery was by a monopoly provider. John Stuart Mill recognized this in his *Principles of Political Economy* (1848). He concluded that London would be better served by single water and gas companies rather than the existing plurality, because the cost of operating multiple, parallel lines was so large. "Were there only one establishment, it could make lower charges consistently with obtaining the rate of profit now realized."[21]

But in *Norwich Gas Light Co. v. Norwich City Gas Co.* (1856),[22] the Connecticut Supreme Court refused to enjoin a second gas company from laying competing pipes. The first company's charter from the state originally contained no explicit monopoly provision, but was later amended to include one. In addition, the first company had a grant from the city permitting it to dig up the streets to lay pipes and denying that right to anyone else for a period of fifteen years. The court invalidated both monopoly grants: "[W]e do not see how the plaintiffs' case can be made to differ from the chartered powers of any trading corporation . . . . Two or more companies may consistently use the same streets, for the purpose of laying down their pipes." In distinguishing the bridge cases, the court recognized the state's duty to provide roads and necessary bridges, historically prerogatives of the sovereign; but the government had no duty to provide lighting. Since the company's activity was an "ordinary business . . . in respect to which the government has no exclusive prerogative," the grant was a simple, unjustifiable monopoly. "[A]lthough we have no direct constitutional provision against a monopoly, the whole theory of a free government is opposed to such grants . . . ." The fact that the Connecticut Constitution contained no provision forbidding monopolies makes the decision one of the earliest instances of state substantive due process.

Two years later in *Shepard v. Milwaukee Gas Light Co.* (1858),[23] the Supreme Court of Wisconsin took a much more regulatory approach to gas lighting companies. The defendant gas company's charter gave it the exclusive right to manufacture gas and lay pipes to light the city of Milwaukee. The plaintiff, a Milwaukee merchant, claimed that the company refused to sell him gas, even though his installations were in compliance with the company's regulations. The court concluded that the utility was a franchise obligated to serve all customers capable of paying a nondiscriminatory rate. The court acknowledged that a monopoly utility could make regulations and rules and terminate customers who did not comply, but "these rules and regulations must be reasonable, just, lawful, not capricious, arbitrary, oppressive or unreasonable."

Bruce Wyman, who wrote one of the most influential early treatises on public utility regulation (1911), concluded that at mid-century most state courts followed the logic of the *Norwich* case and refused to recognize any distinctive character of gas or water utilities that might justify monopoly rights. That presumption did not change until late in the century.[24]

The Slaughter-House Cases in American Regulatory History

At mid-century the gaslight industry was new. Whether it should be treated as a common right or a franchise was an open question in an era with no guiding economic model. But the slaughtering of animals for profit had always been a common right undertaken in competitive markets. Thus great hostility attended the creation of the New Orleans slaughterhouse monopoly at issue in the *Slaughter-House Cases* (1873).[25]

The *Slaughter-House* decision is probably the most misunderstood example of circumstances in which new technology and changing markets explain the creation of a price-regulated monopoly. The case has been outrageously misrepresented in a large body of literature, and misperceptions about it had a heavy influence on the antimonopoly movements of the late nineteenth century. The consensus view has been stated many times:[26] in the late 1860's, during Reconstruction, self-interested northerners and illiterate freedmen controlled the Louisiana Legislature. By bribery and corruption, a small group of businessmen convinced this legislature of scoundrels to close all the slaughterhouses in New Orleans and to incorporate the Crescent City Live-Stock Landing and Slaughter-House Company, giving it an exclusive right to slaughter food animals in the city. The statute was special interest legislation of the worst sort, so irrational that it invited the Supreme Court to apply the Civil War constitutional amendments to a business regulation, even though the amendments were designed to apply only to problems of race and slavery.

For this view of the *Slaughter-House Cases,* we are indebted to historians of the Progressive Era, particularly those of the "Dunning School."

William A. Dunning's 1907 history of the Reconstruction was one of the most popular of all time. Dunning and his followers generally depicted postwar blacks as inept and unqualified for self-government and transplanted northern white politicians ("carpetbaggers") as cynical and self-motivated, taking advantage of black ineptness to control southern governments at the expense of the "true" South, which consisted of the former, temporarily disenfranchised white elite. Reconstruction, then, became that awful period when a group of rapacious northern whites and incompetent blacks ruled state legislatures through bribery and corruption. Louisiana was one of the worst victims of this critique, because black political interests were most successful there. For example, Louisiana was the only state to have a black governor during Reconstruction, as well as a black lieutenant governor, treasurer, and superintendent of education. Louisiana's Reconstruction legislature had among the highest percentage of black members.[27]

The Dunning perspective characterized Ella Lonn's *Reconstruction in Louisiana after 1868* (1918),[28] which became an influential account of the *Slaughter-House* controversy. Lonn surveyed the mixed newspaper accounts—the generally pro-Union *New Orleans Times* supporting the monopoly statute, and the *Commercial Bulletin*, *Picayune*, and *Republican*, voices of the Old South, opposing it and creating the "corruption" thesis. Four years later, Charles Warren, who sympathized with the Dunning School, incorporated Lonn's account into his famous work, *The Supreme Court in United States History* (1922).[29] Since that time, Lonn's view has been accepted in American legal literature, notwithstanding its racist overtones.

In fact, the statute that created the Crescent City slaughterhouse monopoly was a work of great genius. In the late 1860's New Orleans was the beef capital of the United States. Eventually, the development of north-south railroads would erode New Orleans' position. Thanks largely to the efforts of Gustavus Swift, rail transport of live beef became common, and in the 1880's Chicago would steal the position of America's butchering capital.[30] But in the 1860's and early 1870's New Orleans' strategic location at the mouth of the Mississippi River made it accessible from both the Gulf and northern river ports. The Civil War had created an extreme imbalance in the distribution of cattle, as there was virtually no movement from the South to the Northeast and the southern market had collapsed. By 1865, there was probably a surplus of three and a half million cattle in Texas and extreme shortages in the northeastern states.[31]

The technology available for shipping beef had changed markedly within the span of a few years. Through the first half of the century, beef destined for the Northeast generally had to be driven alive to remote railroad terminals or slaughterhouses, an expensive and risky enterprise. The development of southwestern railroads and their increasing proximity to ranchers made it commercially feasible to ship live cattle by rail or steamer to New Orleans for butchering, loading, and shipping in large lots. The result was rapid growth of the New Orleans butchering industry, which was crucial to the city's economic recovery from the Civil War. During Reconstruction, the economy of New Orleans recovered more quickly than other southern economies, even to the point of encouraging black migration to Louisiana from other states.

The one impediment to year-round long distance shipment of beef was the lack of a suitable refrigeration process. During the 1840's and 1850's, most shipped beef was iced. It could be reliably transported a long distance only in the winter. In the late 1860's, the Bray refrigeration process made year-round shipment of beef from New Orleans to New York, Philadelphia, and Boston technologically feasible. The Bray process was subject to substantial economies of scale and a large initial cost. For example, an efficient slaughterhouse required its own railroad siding, so that meat could be loaded directly into the refrigerated cars.

The story of the *Slaughter-House Cases* is set against this background. Immediately after the Civil War, New Orleans became overrun with small, economically marginal, grossly unsanitary slaughterhouses. Emancipation and the economic ravages of war had combined to throw thousands of unskilled workers, mostly black, into southern labor markets. Although many of these workers moved north,[32] others remained behind. Former slaves often knew how to butcher cattle. The New Orleans beef boom and the pro-black politics of Louisiana's Reconstruction government gave freedmen the unprecedented opportunity to go into business for themselves. One needed little more than a few hand tools and a place along the river to hang carcasses. It is impossible to say how many people entered the business; the litigants in the *Slaughter-House Cases* estimated that daily operations employed nearly one thousand people.[33]

Nearly all of these slaughterhouses were located along the Mississippi River north of New Orleans. Cattle were loaded and unloaded on the river. The slaughtering operation required great quantities of constantly moving water to flush carcasses, to keep off insects and other vermin, and to dispose of waste materials. In the best-run slaughterhouses a stream of water pumped from the river constantly flowed across the killing floor and swept all waste material back into the current.[34]

One thousand butchers dumping animal waste into the Mississippi River upstream from New Orleans gave the city a monumental health problem. The city's drinking water came from the Mississippi and was unfiltered. The slaughterhouses could not locate south of the city, where the river would have carried their refuse into the Gulf of Mexico. Virtually all the river frontage south of the population line was useless for loading and unloading cattle or for the operation of small-scale slaughterhouses, although the land was suitable for large developments supported on piles driven deep into the ground. The French traveler Berquin-Duvallon described the lower Mississippi as a "low and swampy shore, in many parts drowned by the river, uninhabited and uninhabitable where only a wild and misshapen vegetation subsists." At the beginning of the nineteenth century, when New Orleans was much smaller, slaughtering of animals had been legally confined to the city's south side. But population growth drove the southern edge of the city down the river so that no room remained for the slaughterhouses. In the late 1870's, under the direction of James Eads, Louisiana would undertake a giant engineering project that drained many lower swamps and made the lowest part of the Mississippi more hospitable. But at the time of *Slaughter-House Cases* the city was located as far south as the geography permitted the population to extend.[35]

New Orleans always had contended with various subtropical diseases common in nineteenth-century southern cities. The greatest scourge was yellow fever. In the 1860's the cause of the disease was unknown, although widespread medical opinion related it to sanitation and drinking water. The city experienced yellow fever epidemics every summer between 1812 and 1861. In each of twelve years more than 1,000 people died. In the 1853 epidemic between 30,000 and 40,000 contracted the disease and as many as 9,000 may have died.

In 1863 the Union Army, commanded by General Benjamin Franklin Butler, occupied New Orleans. Butler was determined to rid the city of its annual summer plague. It was widely believed that residents, but not Union soldiers, had built up at least a limited immunity. Locals expected Butler's army to fall dead during the first summer of occupation: the disease would perform the job that the Confederate Army had been unable to do. But immediately after his installation as military governor, Butler ordered a cleanup of the entire city and river bank. He put thousands of unemployed Louisianans to work removing garbage, patrolling the river, and closing the slaughterhouses north of the city. The summer plagues stopped, and during Butler's four-year tenure only one or two cases of yellow fever were reported annually.[36]

New Orleans citizens were not inclined to give the "Beast Butler" credit for his accomplishment. Butler, who later became a Radical Republican, was an aggressive champion of black civil rights—a fact that the southern elite found intolerable. Their ingratitude was exacerbated by the fact that Butler's board of medical advisors was composed entirely of northern doctors. One brave southerner, Erasmus Darwin Fenner, applauded Butler's work, but predicted that the epidemics would resume if the cleanup efforts stopped after the war ended. Unfortunately, because of strong public hostility toward Butler and his efforts, the cleanup program was abandoned the day Butler pulled out. In the summer of 1866 the epidemics returned. The 1867 epidemic killed 3,000 people.[37]

The return of the pestilence placed New Orleans in a difficult position. Butler's experience had convinced the city that, whatever the cause of the epidemics,[38] there was a strong correlation between the disease and the filth of the local water. Cleaning up the water entailed drastic measures against the slaughtering industry that was growing rapidly just to the north. But the city's economic recovery depended on that industry. New Orleans convened a grand jury in 1866 to study the relationship between the plague and the slaughtering industry. Its report recommended the removal of the slaughterhouses to the lower part of the city.[39] The city itself had no authority to close or regulate the operation of slaughterhouses north of its limits, but it petitioned the legislature for relief. In 1867 the legislature responded with "An Act to prevent offal and nuisances from being thrown in the Mississippi river, within the limits of the cities of New Orleans and Jefferson." The new law was unenforceable, however, because putrefying intestinal matter could seldom be traced to its source.

Two years later the legislature held extensive hearings on the health problem once again. The 1868 *Journal* of the Louisiana House tells of the "immense quantity of filth and offal" being dumped into the Mississippi River, "which, if not prejudicial to health, is certainly very revolting." The report noted that "[w]hen the river is low, it is not uncommon to see intestines and portions of putrefied animal matter lodged immediately around the [water] pipes" and being "sucked into the reservoir."[40]

The city's older, better-established butchers—all surviving remnants of the Old South economy—had predicted that the legislature would close all slaughterhouses north of the city. In 1867, four hundred of them organized the Butchers' Benevolent Association, eventually the plaintiff in one of the *Slaughter-House* cases. The association raised a large amount of capital and bought a tract of land on the southern edge of New Orleans along the east bank of the river. It began building its own "super slaughterhouse," modeled after the abattoirs of England and Napoleonic France:[41] a giant structure with a wharf, railroad siding, loading docks, water-sweeping technology, and pens for sheltering and feeding cattle.

But the Louisiana Legislature came up with a more creative solution, not so calculated to give a small group of entrepreneurs a de facto monopoly of the slaughtering industry. It turned the industry into a price-regulated utility. The legislature issued a charter creating the Crescent City Live-Stock Landing and Slaughter-House Company, established a location along the river south of the city where the new corporation could build a "Grand Slaughterhouse," and imposed on the company a set of rules and regulations that permitted all butchers in the city to use the facility by paying prices set in the charter itself. The charter gave the Crescent City Company authority to construct its own railroad and establish its own steam ferries to create links with transportation networks.[42]

The slaughterhouse statute has been popularly characterized as creating a "monopoly" that forced a thousand competing butchers out of business,[43] but the allegation makes no sense. Although the charter allowed only the Crescent City Company to operate a slaughterhouse, the slaughterhouse itself was a public facility, open to every butcher. Users could do their own work on the slaughterhouse floor or have it done for them at rates that the charter established—ten cents per animal per day for pen storage, and slaughtering fees of one dollar per head for cattle, fifty cents for hogs, and thirty cents for sheep, goats, and lambs. Like most public utilities, the company was required to serve any paying customer without discrimination. Even critics of the statute conceded that its immediate effects were to ameliorate the yellow fever problem and to reduce the cost of processing beef.[44]

Regulated monopoly slaughterhouses were not new in the United States. New York operated a public slaughterhouse in the eighteenth century and at times confined all slaughtering to that location. In 1866 Milwaukee passed an ordinance "to establish a city slaughterhouse, and to regulate the management of slaughterhouses and packing houses in the city of Milwaukee, and to prohibit the sale of diseased meat."[45] The city negotiated with W. G. Benedict & Co. to designate its slaughterhouse as the public slaughterhouse and to permit all butchers to slaughter there free of charge. The Wisconsin Supreme Court upheld the ordinance against a charge that it was an unreasonable restraint of trade at common law.

Was the Louisiana Legislature Bribed?

Ella Lonn and most constitutional historians who have written about the *Slaughter-House Cases* have assumed that the legislators who voted for the statute were bribed, with either cash or a promise of stock in the Crescent City Company.[46] Given the apparent irrationality of a statute turning the competitive butchering industry into a private monopoly, the bribery thesis has served a useful explanatory function: no legislature would have passed such a statute had it not been corrupted.

Even assuming that the Louisiana Legislature had proper motives for deciding that New Orleans butchering should become a price-regulated utility, the selection of recipients of the monopoly charter presented an opportunity for corruption. We know little about how legislators in nineteenth-century America designated groups of private investors to receive franchises. Even the granting of the charter for the Charles River Bridge was attended by charges of legislative corruption.[47]

But the allegations of bribery and corruption in the *Slaughter-House Cases* have little evidence to support them. Judge Charles Leaumont of the Fifth District Court of Louisiana, who entertained some of the opening slaughterhouse litigation, found the plaintiff's evidence of legislative corruption inadmissible, because it was "general, loose, and of a railing character, without certainty of detail or specification."[48] He did not elaborate. No one has uncovered credible evidence that any particular member of the Louisiana Legislature was bribed.

The slaughterhouse dispute clearly divided the Old South from the new powers of the Reconstruction era. The victims of the monopoly statute were the city's established wholesale meat companies, whose plants were closed by the creation of the monopoly. These businesses, owned primarily by old southern families, had the most invested and the most to lose. The immediate beneficiaries were new entrants into the business—those whose businesses were in poor financial condition or who had no plants at all. As Charles Allen observed to the Supreme Court in his brief for the defendants:

> If under [the charter's] provisions certain persons cannot carry on the business of butchering as advantageously to themselves as they did before, other persons can carry on the business more advantageously to themselves than they did before. There is no longer any necessity of a butcher providing a slaughter-house for himself. Any man with capital or credit enough to procure the necessary animals may now be a butcher. This charter, therefore, is not a monopoly, in the sense that it prevents anybody from being a butcher; instead of that, it makes it easier to be a butcher than it was before.[49]

Among the statute's beneficiaries were countless freedmen.

The New Orleans press, most of which represented the interests of the Old South, was responsible for the allegations of bribery and corruption, and historians have taken most of their facts at face value from these editorials. Why did the newspapers speak so freely of corruption with so little evidence? Part of the answer is in the 1870's understanding of legislative "corruption." At the time of the *Slaughter-House Cases* the lobbying of legislators was itself considered to be a corrupt, immoral practice. As Charles Fisk Beach noted in his *Treatise on the Law of Monopolies and Industrial Trusts* (1898), the use of lobbyists "is in contravention of public policy and will not be upheld by the courts." Both public policy and "considerations of sound morality require that legislators should act freely and from sole regard to the interests of their constituents."[50] In *Marshall v. Baltimore & Ohio Railroad Co.* (1853),[51] the Supreme Court concluded that the use of lobbyists would "subject the State government to the combined capital of wealthy corporations, and produce universal corruption . . . ." "Speculators in legislation" would "infest the capital of the Union and of every State, till corruption shall become the normal condition of the body politic . . . ."

Not all attempts to convince the legislature to support one's position were wrong. But what paid lobbyists did was perceived as qualitatively different from the ordinary citizen's petitioning his assemblyman. As Justice Reuben A. Chapman of the Supreme Judicial Court of Massachusetts noted in 1863:

> The business of "lobby members" is not to go fairly and openly before the committees and present statements, proofs and arguments that the other side has an opportunity to meet and refute, if they are wrong, but to go secretly to the members and ply them with statements and arguments that the other side cannot openly meet, however erroneous they may be, and

to bring illegitimate influences to bear upon them . . . . The practice of procuring members of the legislature to act under the influence of what they have eaten and drunk at houses of entertainment, tends to render those of them who yield to such influences wholly unfit to act in such cases . . . . The tendency and object of these influences are to obtain by corruption what it is supposed cannot be obtained fairly.[52]

The "corruption" in the *Slaughter-House Cases* appears to have been nothing more than skillful lobbying. The only specific evidence of "corruption" that appears in the long record of this litigation is a suggestion that the slaughterhouse incorporators plied the legislators with "sandwiches, whiskey, brandy . . . and that kind of thing."[53] For those sympathetic with the cause of the Old South, "corruption" was easily found.

The End of the Slaughterhouse Monopoly?

When Reconstruction ended and southern power was restored, the Old South reacted quickly. In 1879 Louisiana, riding the crest of a general antimonopoly movement that was beginning to sweep America, adopted a new constitution with a provision abolishing all de jure monopolies, including those in existing charters. The same constitution gave individual parishes and incorporated municipalities the power to regulate slaughterhouses within their limits.[54] New Orleans immediately passed an ordinance that made slaughtering competitive, and the Butchers' Union, one of the losing parties in the original *Slaughter-House Case,* prepared to reenter the industry. The Crescent City Company sought an injunction, citing the monopoly provision in its charter. But the Supreme Court sided with the new entrants, holding that the legislature that granted the slaughterhouse monopoly did not have the authority to inhibit a future legislature's attempt to control a problem of public health or morals.[55] For a time the slaughtering industry in New Orleans was again competitive.

The city's health problems immediately reappeared. It responded by creating a *de facto* slaughterhouse monopoly. It zoned a three-mile area on the south side as the only region in which slaughterhouses could be established. Then it licensed a single slaughterhouse, the People's Slaughterhouse, to operate in the zone. The Louisiana Supreme Court, now controlled by an all-white southern majority, upheld the statute against the claim that it violated the state constitution's prohibition of monopolies. The personnel operating the slaughterhouse changed, but the monopoly persisted.[56]

CHAPTER 11

Regulation and Incorporation

Mercantile political economy mistrusted the market to allocate resources and believed that government controls of price and entry were frequently necessary.[1] Classicism, by contrast, believed that the market was the best determinant of price and output. Although Adam Smith himself distinguished between a "natural" and a "market" price, his successors quickly secularized that view until by the time of John Stuart Mill the "just" price was nothing other than the price set by the market.[2] Further, although classicism gradually developed a concept of "market failure" that justified price regulation in certain markets, the number of such markets was much smaller than it was perceived to be during the preclassical period.

Until the mid-nineteenth century, regulation was the exception rather than the rule. The principal institutional mechanism for governmental regulation was the corporate charter. In the preclassical era the charter had become a contractual method by which the sovereign engaged a private entrepreneur to carry out some special enterprise. According to Lord Hale's treatise "De Portibus Maris,"[3] written in the 1670's but first published a century later, only industries that were "affected with a publick interest" could be subjected to price regulation. Blackstone likewise believed that regulation was appropriate only for "prerogatives of the Crown"—that is, activities one could perform only with a charter.[4] By the eighteenth century the domains of price-regulated markets and of industries for which one needed a corporate charter in order to do business were nearly identical. The regulatory charter itself, which was a contract with the state, was a convenient and unquestionably legal way for the state to regulate a firm's rates. In exchange for the right to engage in a certain profitable activity, the firm consented in advance to charge a specified price.

Regulation by charter was common well into the nineteenth century, long after general incorporation acts had been developed for ordinary firms. The charters in the *Charles River Bridge* case, which had been granted in 1785, and in the *Slaughter-House Cases*, granted in 1869, both explicitly set the rates that the corporation could charge. In these charters as well as in most others, the regulatory schemes were elaborate, imposing different rates for different classes of customers. The charters also required the standard public utility obligation of universal service. Unlike the ordinary businessperson, who could turn away anyone for any reason, the regulated firm was obligated to serve all paying customers. Most price regulation by states from the Federalist period until the Civil War was contained in corporate charters.

Modern regulation by statute applies more or less equally to all similar firms in a sovereign's jurisdiction—for example, to all common carriers within the state. But regulation by charter was specific to the firm. Two different ferries or toll roads chartered by the same state might be entitled to collect different rates. One might have explicit monopoly protection while the other did not. Corporate charters were individually negotiated with legislatures, and each regulated firm obtained the best deal it could. This approach was generally consistent with classical theory, which regarded regulation as rare and not to be presumed. As late as the 1860's and 1870's railroads were chartered with no price regulation whatsoever. Thus they were entitled to set their own freight rates, even though they might have *de facto* monopoly status. As chapters 12 and 13 discuss, policy makers "regulated" rates by chartering competing railroads rather than by trying to control the rates of existing railroads.

As late as 1877, when *Munn v. Illinois* affirmed the constitutionality of rate regulation of an unincorporated enterprise, many believed price regulation was beyond state power unless the firm operated under a charter authorizing the regulation. Justice Field dissented from the *Munn* majority's conclusion that rate regulation was appropriate whenever an industry was "affected with the public interest." Rather, the concept of "affected with the public interest" applied only to chartered business corporations, and only they could be made subject to rate regulation. When "Sir Matthew Hale . . . spoke of property as affected by a public interest," he "referred to property dedicated by the owner to public uses, or to property the use of which was granted by the government, or in connection with which special privileges were conferred." Counsel for the state had noted several cases upholding rate regulation. But Field responded that these were "mostly cases of public ferries, bridges, and turnpikes, of wharfingers, hackmen, and draymen, and of interest on money." In all of these except interest on money "some special privilege" had been granted by the state, and "[t]he conditions upon which the privilege shall be enjoyed being stated or implied in the legislation authorizing its grant, no right is, of course, impaired by their enforcement. The recipient of the privilege, in effect, stipulates to comply with the conditions. It matters not how limited the privilege conferred, its acceptance implies an assent to the regulation of its use and the compensation for it."

Classical political economists were not anxious to expand the province of rate regulation. No American classicist before the Civil War argued that rate regulation should be administered by general statute rather than by special charter. With the rise of the railroad, however, even many classicists began to realize that competition was not the best way to determine price and output in every market. Further, regulation by charter would not always work. The railroads had higher operating costs than those of earlier price-regulated utilities such as turnpikes and toll bridges. The cost of shipping freight by rail was determined in large part by current expenses for fuel and labor. The cost of operating a toll bridge or turnpike was almost exclusively a function of historical capital costs, since operating costs were extremely small. As a result a corporate charter permanently setting maximum railroad rates was too inflexible. Rates set by a legislature or commission, however, could be changed from time to time as operating costs changed.

In the 1870's and 1880's American political economists began developing a theory of rate regulation to account for markets, particularly the railroads, in which competitive pricing did not appear to work. The classical regulatory theory that emerged was market-based rather than firm-based. The older theory of rate regulation had been that, since a monopoly privilege was necessary to encourage firms to enter certain industries, they would be free from competition once entry had occurred. The same contract that gave them a monopoly privilege should also set maximum rates, for competition would not be available to control them. As classicism matured in the nineteenth century, however, the nature of the enterprise rather than the charter status of particular firms became the determinant of when price regulation was appropriate. The railroads should be price-regulated not because they had charters or because their charters gave them explicit monopoly privileges—most railroad charters did not confer monopoly rights — but because high fixed costs, low variable costs, imperfect competition, and price discrimination seemed inherent in the structure of the industry as a whole.

The resulting switch in state policy from "contractual" to statutory rate regulation occurred quickly following the Supreme Court's approval in the *Granger* cases of statutory rate regulation of both incorporated and unincorporated firms. This movement effectively "de-privatized" rate regulation—it was no longer based on a contract between the sovereign and the regulated firm—and paved the way for modern regulatory theory. The result was the emergence of distinctive legal rules for "franchise," or public utility, corporations.

The *Granger* cases, of which *Munn*[5] received the longest opinion, determined the constitutionality of various Illinois, Wisconsin, Minnesota, and Iowa statutes imposing rate regulation on private firms. The cases were so named because of the influence of the Grange, a lobbying organization of farmers, in obtaining the regulatory legislation. All the cases except *Munn* involved incorporated railroads. *Munn* involved price regulation of an unincorporated elevator company, the partnership of Munn & Scott.

In 1886, almost a decade after *Munn*, Justice Samuel F. Miller revealed that *Munn* had been selected among the *Granger* cases for the most fully developed opinion on state regulatory power because the plaintiff was unincorporated. The case "presented the question of a private citizen, or unincorporated partnership, engaged in the warehousing business in Chicago, free from any claim of right or contract under an act of incorporation of any State whatever . . . ." Justice Miller went on to note that the railroad companies in the companion cases had raised an argument unavailable to Munn & Scott—"namely, that in their charters from the States they each had a contract, express or implied, that they might regulate and establish their own fares and rates of transportation."[6] As noted in Chapter 2, by 1877 the contract clause offered little protection to private corporations. Further, the Granger states had reserved the right to amend corporate charters. However, the railroads argued, price regulation unilaterally imposed by the state was warranted only if it was authorized in the original charter. Surely the Court could not imply the power to impose price regulation from the state's power to amend a corporate charter. At most, state reservation clauses were intended "to leave the stockholders in corporations in such a position that the Legislature could place them on the same footing with natural persons before the law."[7] This argument, based on a distinctly "associational" view of the business corporation, was that a corporation should have the same rights as anyone to be free of unbargained-for rate regulation. It turned out to be a two-edged sword. Counsel for the railroads had made the argument on the theory that rate regulation had always been a two-way, "contractual" arrangement between the corporation and the state. Certainly the Wisconsin Legislature could not use its power to amend a corporate charter to impose rate regulation on a corporation unilaterally, because in the absence of a contract the corporation deserved to be treated just as any unincorporated association. The charter amendment "does, without any doubt, have that effect," Chief Justice Morrison R. Waite conceded. But the argument backfired; the Court had held the same day in *Munn* that rate regulation of unincorporated firms was legal, provided the regulated *market* was "affected with the public interest," as the railroads were.

Clearly it "was within the power of the company to call upon the legislature to fix permanently" a limit beyond which price regulation could not go at the time the charter had been negotiated, Chief Justice Waite noted in another *Granger* decision, thus suggesting that state power to amend corporate charters unilaterally was not infinite.[8] "If that had been done, the charter might have presented a contract against future legislative interference. But it was not . . . ." Without such a promise, the railroad had the same freedom respecting rates as any other common carrier.

The effect of *Munn v. Illinois,* coupled with the Supreme Court's emasculation of the contract clause, was to make corporate status irrelevant to questions about state power to regulate rates. The Court went to extraordinary lengths to hold that the states could regulate rates even in the face of corporate charters that appeared to give the firms the power to set their own rates. For example, in the *Railroad Commission Cases* (1886), discussed in Chapter 2, the Supreme Court held that a charter giving a railroad the power to fix reasonable rates nevertheless reserved to the legislature the power to determine which rates were reasonable.[9]

In analyzing state power to regulate rates after *Munn,* the principal distinction to be made was between firms affected with a public interest and those that were not. Writing in 1900, Christopher Tiedeman argued that rate regulation of franchise corporations such as railroads and utilities could be constitutionally justified much more easily than could rate regulation of unincorporated firms or general manufacturing firms. In fact, the power to regulate rates was inherent in the monopoly grants or privileges extended to such utilities, together with any reserved legislative right to amend a corporate charter. However, general business corporations that receive "no franchise or privilege from the government" could generally be price regulated only if they fell into the "affected with the public interest" category defined in *Munn*.[10]

Tiedeman's distinction between general manufacturing corporations and "franchise," or "quasi-public," corporations stuck. The result was the emergence of a new area of law quite distinct from general corporation law. In the third edition (1894) of his treatise on corporations, William W. Cook first included a large section on "quasi-public" corporations, which he characterized as not quite public, but not quite private either. Early in the twentieth century an entire treatise literature grew up on these quasi-public, or "public service," companies. These treatises differed from earlier, single-industry treatises such as Isaac Redfield's book on railroad law, which was largely on tort and general corporate law. The new genre was concerned almost exclusively with the "regulatory" aspects of public service corporations. These included the public service corporation's duty to provide universal service and its obligation to provide adequate facilities as contemplated by its charter or state law, the legality of rate discrimination, and rate regulation.[11]

The move from charter-based to statute-based rate regulation made application of the due process clause to price regulation all but inevitable. Rates established by charter were the product of an agreement between the state and the stockholders of a particular firm, and the stockholders were free to reject unacceptable offers. But rate regulation by statute was "unilateral." It came from the legislature alone, which might impose "confiscatory" rates, or rates that failed to give the regulated firm a fair rate of return. The Supreme Court first suggested in *Spring Valley Water Works v. Schottler* (1884) that it might apply the due process clause to review the substance of rates if the "authorities do not exercise an honest judgment, or if they fix upon a price which is manifestly unreasonable . . . ." Ultimately in *Smyth v. Ames* (1898),[12] the Court condemned a state statute for failing to give the regulated firms a fair rate of return. This transformation from charter-based to statute-based regulation took only two decades. It effectively de-privatized the law of regulated industry by segregating the public utility from the general corporation.

CHAPTER 12

The Railroads and
the Development of
Regulatory Policy

Understanding Regulation in History

No regulatory issue in the nineteenth century was as controversial or aroused as many levels and branches of government as the proper relation between the sovereign and the railroads. The reasons are clear. Both the economics and the politics of business regulation were going through a period of convulsive change. This was particularly true of those businesses identified by the Supreme Court as "affected with the public interest"—common carriers and public utilities, such as gas lighting, the telegraph, and later electricity and the telephone. The modern economic theory of natural monopoly utility regulation had not yet emerged. But political economists were becoming aware that certain industries were subject to market failures that kept the competitive processes from operating efficiently.[1] Railroads were the most important of these markets. The controversy was sharp because the stakes were so large: in the 1880's the railroads were one of the largest areas of American economic activity, and railroad assets accounted for about 10 percent of American wealth.[2]

Historical studies of Gilded Age railroad regulation have focused so heavily on politics that they have overlooked the fact that even nineteenth-century political economy developed a sophisticated regulatory theory. This myopic treatment of economics in historical writing about railroad regulation carries a certain irony, for two important theories of economic regulation that find subscribers today were developed in writing about the railroads. The "public interest" theory that regulatory policy's purpose is to control monopoly pricing or other abuses of consumers or labor was developed by Progressives such as Charles Francis Adams, Jr., and Louis Brandeis, in writing directed largely at the railroads. The heyday of the public interest theory of regulation— from the Progressive Era until well after the New Deal—was also the age in which the railroads were the dominant regulated industry. The Progressive critique of federal railroad regulation was that regulation was necessary to protect the general public from powerful railroad monopolies too large to be reached by state legislation, that Congress had exactly this in mind when it passed the Interstate Commerce Act in 1887, and that the act would have done what was intended except for its evisceration in a series of Supreme Court decisions that undermined the Interstate Commerce Commission's powers.[3]

But many of the advocates of the public interest theory as well as the liberal historians who have adopted it have never tried to understand the economics of railroad operation or of Gilded Age regulatory policy. For example, they tended to regard practices like rate discrimination as "unjust" per se, and as contrary to the best interests of society. The economic theory suggested that, although particular groups of shippers might be injured by rate discrimination, the discrimination favored shippers as a group because it increased the total amount of cargo that the railroads could carry and reduced overall shipping costs in the process. As the volume of shipping increased, the amount of fixed costs that had to be allocated per unit decreased. Without knowing it, the advocates and historians of the public interest theory often became the spokespersons for particular interest groups, such as farmers shipping short hauls, and thus facilitated regulatory "capture" by particular classes of consumers rather than by the carriers.

Since the earliest days of federal railroad regulation writers have noted the threat of regulatory capture: the possibility that the legislature or regulatory agency would come to represent the interests of one particular group of people, rather than of the public in general. The captors might be the railroads themselves, but they might also be farmers or other shippers who would use government control of railroads as a device to enhance their own welfare at the railroads' expense, or one particular group of shippers seeking favorable treatment at the expense of other groups. In any event, public interest regulation could deteriorate into special interest politics.[4]

The principal difference between the public interest and capture theories of regulation is that the public interest theory believes that regulation is generally efficient: it makes society as a whole better off. Historically, advocates of the public interest theory have not used an economic word like "efficient" to describe regulation's purpose. They would be more inclined to use words like "just" or "fair." Nevertheless, what they had in mind was a regulatory policy in the "public interest," which was identified as the interest of the community as a whole.

By contrast, capture theories argue that regulation ends up serving some particular interest group that has managed to make its case to the legislative body or regulatory agency. Incidentally, the regulation may be efficient, but often it is not. The first generation of post-Progressive revisionist historians who wrote about railroads rejected the public interest theory in favor of a "capture" theory. But those doing the capturing were shippers or farmers rather than the railroads themselves. For example, George Miller argued that the impetus for state railroad regulation in the Midwest came from merchants dependent on river traffic and concerned about their own interests, or midwestern farmers seeking local rates as low as the trunk-line rates to eastern markets. Lee Benson argued that the drive for regulation came from New York City merchants whose favored position at the gateway of America's east-west water routes, primarily the Erie Canal, was being challenged by the railroads, and from New York farmers injured by short-haul/long-haul discrimination. It cost the latter about as much to ship their grain to New York City as it cost midwestern farmers four or five times as far away.[5]

The revisionism contained in the books by Miller and Benson is relatively modest in one respect: both the Progressive public interest theory and Miller/Benson believed that the underlying purpose of railroad regulation was to control the railroads for the benefit of shippers. Likewise, both believed that the railroads were guilty of abuses and that regulatory legislation was designed to force the railroads to be fair.

The work of Miller and Benson is subject to two criticisms. First, interest group politics standing alone fails to establish regulatory capture. Iowa farmers, midwestern shippers, New York merchants, and the railroads may independently have wanted regulation for their own personal benefit. But that observation is as consistent with the traditional theory of regulation in the public interest as with any theory of regulatory capture. In fact, efficient regulation ought to claim more widespread, diverse support than does inefficient regulation for the simple reason that efficient regulation creates greater net benefits. Any convincing theory of regulatory capture must show that an interest group obtained a particular regulatory regime even though the damage to others exceeded benefits to the supporters. Neither Benson nor Miller tried to do this.

Second, neither Benson nor Miller addressed the economic content of nineteenth-century regulatory policy. Gilded Age railroad economists mostly defended widespread rate discrimination, the object of the intensive campaigns described in Benson's and Miller's books, as economically efficient—that is, in the public interest. These late nineteenth-century economic notions have been surprisingly robust, and they continue to form an important part of regulatory policy, subject only to technical revision.

The disdain for economic theory in the history of regulation reached its apogee in the New Left "capture" hypothesis, championed principally by Gabriel Kolko.[6] According to that theory regulatory policy, no matter what its initial motive, inevitably falls under the control of the regulated firms themselves. Regulation protects firms from competition, either by controlling rates or restricting new entry. Further, it guarantees the regulated firms' profit margins, no matter how inefficient their investments or operations. Kolko examined forty years of the legislative and political history of federal railroad regulation and showed that, far from opposing each marginal increase in federal regulatory authority, the railroads were among the strongest supporters. They supported many of the provisions of the original Interstate Commerce Act, as well as most subsequent amendments that broadened federal power and eventually preempted state control. In many cases the railroads received almost exactly what they wanted. Kolko's book presented incontrovertible evidence that principal beneficiaries of federal policy toward the railroads during this period were the railroads themselves.

Kolko's study encouraged a broad-based, New Left cynicism about government regulation.[7] The gist of the argument is that, good intentions notwithstanding, regulation is almost always passed for the benefit of the regulated, mainly in order to protect regulated firms from competition. Consumers are inevitably regulation's victims rather than its beneficiaries. Ironically, this argument is popular not only with the New Left but also with some on the right, who have their own theory of regulatory capture.[8] Only a few liberals have been left to defend the traditional public interest theory, which today is widely characterized as naive, out of date, inefficient, or—perhaps most painful of all—anticonsumer.

But Kolko overstated his case. He minimized or ignored the role that state regulation played in the overall structure of railroad regulation. He also made no attempt to explain how the politics and the economics of the railroad industry engaged each other. *Railroads and Regulation* is a book about railroad lobbying, not about railroad economics. Kolko's anticapitalist biases may have prevented him from seeing that in a market economy that includes privately owned regulated firms the public also has an interest in the long run. The long run in this case included federal protection from aggressive state regulatory policies that were driving the railroads to ruin.

In the absence of a coherent model for natural monopoly, one would be inclined to view the situation as the historians of the Left saw it. The nineteenth-century debate was excessively politicized, because it was not guided by a consensus economic model that explained railroad behavior in any robust way. However, as an economic explanation emerged, regulatory alternatives appeared that might work to the best interest of both railroads and consumers. The revisionists wrote as if Gilded Age regulatory economics had nothing to contribute to Gilded Age railroad practice or policy. As a result, although many of the facts they cited were correct—for example, that by 1887 the railroads were in deep trouble and wanted federal legislation to bail them out—they missed the point.

The point, once again, is that not every regulation that is supported by the regulated interests constitutes regulatory capture. In the revisionist historians' highly politicized view of the world, the railroads and the shippers were playing a zero-sum game. Anytime the railroads won a point the consumers or shippers necessarily lost. But if *both* political and economic considerations were relevant, then the railroads and the shippers were not playing a zero-sum game at all. Within the Progressive model some regulatory solutions seemed better for the community as a whole, even though they injured certain interests. The Progressives may have been mistaken to assume that the optimal theory of regulation would always emerge from the political process, or even that it ever would. But if economics has any role in regulatory policy, it is to develop models that are better than the alternatives. The Progressives were willing to assume that such approaches existed and that right-minded public officials could sometimes find them.

The Right's regulatory "capture" thesis, unlike that of the Left, has been dominated by economic theory.[9] For the Right capture is a likely, but not inevitable, consequence of regulation. The New Right, like the New Left, begins with a powerful suspicion of governmental regulation, although the nature of the suspicion is different. Unlike the New Left, which finds the market just as unscrupulous as explicit regulation, intellectuals of the New Right believe that markets are efficient, robust, and that regulation of entry or pricing is in the public interest much less often than most protagonists of the public interest theory believed. Furthermore, regulation is expensive and yields only the poorest approximations of market behavior.

But regulation in society is pervasive, and there must be some explanation why it exists where it is not economically justified. The answer, says the New Right, is "rent seeking" by special interest groups. Various interests petition legislative bodies for regulation that closes their market to new entry or guarantees their profit margins. A sound regulatory policy must distinguish these self-serving requests for protection from competition from those occasions when bona-fide market failures make regulation necessary. The mere fact that the proposed regulation benefits the regulated firm does not divide the territory. Often the burden of market failure falls on the firms themselves. In such cases the firms may clamor for regulation *and* the regulation may serve the public interest well.

Failure to appreciate the complexity of Gilded Age regulatory policy in a federalist system has led historians to easy oversimplifications about the nature of regulation. Most studies have focused exclusively on either federal regulation or state regulation.[10] Both approaches make identification of the public interest or proof of regulatory capture all too easy. One must view the great debates over railroad control as a controversy about sovereign power, for the American railroad system was a network that simultaneously operated in two "markets" and created two quite different sets of problems. One market was the short-haul, generally intrastate market; the other was the long-haul, or trunk-line market, which was generally interstate. Although the federal government responded to a constituency that was concerned about both sets of problems, until the 1910's prevailing commerce clause doctrine permitted it to address only the long-haul problem in any comprehensive way. Individual states, by contrast, were constitutionally incapable of regulating long-haul traffic directly; after 1886 they had no jurisdiction over shipments that did not begin and end within the same state. However, until 1920 the states had final authority over most short-haul traffic. What the historical record shows is rather consistent lobbying and litigation by the railroads *against* state regulations, but substantial railroad support for federal regulation.

By looking at railroad regulation as a problem of federalism one can see more clearly the relationship between economics and politics in Gilded Age regulatory policy. The Interstate Commerce Act of 1887 was the first comprehensive regulatory measure passed by Congress, but the states had been regulating railroads for a half century. State regulation had contributed significantly to the railroads' financial troubles. The railroads' worst problem in the Gilded Age was that they were an industry subject to substantial market failure, but regulation by a sovereign with the jurisdiction to control the entire system comprehensively had not yet emerged. The inevitable process of federal regulation was to take regulatory authority away from the individual states.

Writing during the Gilded Age, Thomas M. Cooley, both a scholarly observer and an eventual railroad regulator, understood the most fundamental problem of railroad rate regulation far better than many of the historians who have written about it since:

> What is a fatal impediment to its control by law is, that the States and the nation have, in respect to it, a divided power; and while it is for the interest of the nation at large to encourage the competition which favors long hauls, it is for the interest of localities to make competition most active in short hauls. A State is therefore likely to favor legislation which compels proportional charges, or something near such charges, for all distances; but this, if it should be adopted and enforced, would preclude the great through lines of New York and Pennsylvania from competing at Chicago, St. Paul, and St. Louis in the grain-carrying trade of the Northwest, and would reduce such links as are wholly within a State, to the condition of mere local roads, compelled to make high charges or go into bankruptcy.[11]

Understanding Gilded Age railroad regulation as a problem of federalism, as Cooley did, provides important perspective on the regulatory capture debate. In the 1880's states had jurisdiction only over local, intrastate routes, where rates tended to be very high. The federal government had jurisdiction only over interstate routes, and on most of them competition had driven rates so low that they were unremunerative. As a result the problem Congress faced in the final decades of the nineteenth century was not high railroad rates but rather the potential collapse of the national railroad system as a result of rate wars or overzealous state regulation. No case for capture by the railroad interests could be made by looking at, say, the Granger laws or the state maximum rate regulations, struck down by the Supreme Court in *Smyth v. Ames* (1898) but approved in the *Minnesota Rate Cases* (1913).[12]

The Problem of Legislative Intent

Much has been written about the intent of Congress in passing statutes designed to control the railroads, such as the Interstate Commerce Act of 1887, the Sherman Antitrust Act of 1890, and their successors.[13] Much too has been written about state legislative intent in passing various regulatory statutes such as the Granger laws or the New York scheme of railroad regulation.[14] In almost every case the word "intent" means subjective intent, gleaned from statements made by participants in the legislative process. There are the usual questions about whether statements made by those opposing legislation should be counted as statutory "intent." Those opposing legislation are likely to exaggerate a proposed statute's weaknesses and underemphasize or perhaps even mischaracterize its strengths. People speaking in support of a statute may do the opposite.

To ascribe a "motive" to Congress or a state legislature when looking at thirty or so years of regulatory legislation is to apply an individual psychological metaphor to a diverse set of interests, and the metaphor does not work well. Legislators considering railroad legislation had widely different constituencies—those that benefited from low rates for long hauls, such as midwestern shippers, and those that were injured by them, such as New York shippers; those that benefited from price discrimination and those that were injured by it; farmers; easterners; westerners; and the railroads themselves. The political process that yielded the antipooling and antidiscrimination provisions of the Interstate Commerce Act cannot be reduced to something as simple and unified as a particular congressional intent.

The problem of intent in the state legislatures may be simpler, even though state legislative histories are much thinner. States tended to have less complex interests than the federal government had. This was particularly true of rural midwestern states that had undiversified economies. For example, Iowa, Minnesota and Wisconsin, three of the four Granger states, had overwhelmingly agricultural economies and relatively few railroad interests. One can say with some confidence that the purpose of the Granger laws was to improve the economic welfare of resident farmers.[15]

"Objective" rather than "subjective" studies of legislative history are often more reliable indicators about legislative policy or even motive. In order to understand why a legislative body acted it is often more important to know something about the economic, psychological, and intellectual pressures being placed on it than what its individual members said. They are playing to the gallery far too often. The historian trying to understand regulatory legislation should pay more attention to the prevailing economic views and political pressures of the day, and less to the manifold, inconsistent statements of subjective intent. Intellectual history and economic history can be more valuable as explanation devices than legislative history is.

The Politics and Economics of Gilded Age Railroad Policy

The relative weight of distributive and efficiency concerns in legislative policy depends on the state of science in the area affected by the policy. Distributive concerns are always present, and they are generally well known to participants even if the scientific formulation of a problem is relatively primitive. Without a model that describes a social problem and makes reliable predictions, legislative regulation will be highly susceptible to politics, for every legislative proposal produces gainers and losers, whether the resulting regulation is efficient or even coherent. As a robust model develops, consensus builds and legislative policy becomes more coherent. The less controversial the model, the more isolated and impotent its opponents. When a particular scientific explanation becomes widely accepted, the state will more likely be able to conform to the dictates of the model in spite of the objections of losers.

No argument is made here that the legislative process, or even the process of molding scientific models, can transcend politics. On the contrary, science is as political as any discipline, and a scientific model is nothing more than a kind of argument that the world should be viewed in a certain way. Nowhere is this clearer than in the formation of American regulatory policy during the nineteenth century. When the first American railroads were built in the 1820's, the dominant American theory of political economy was classicism, although many American jurists were still educated in a preclassicist, mercantilist theory. Both mercantilism and classicism had poorly articulated theories of natural monopoly. Mercantilists such as Sir William Blackstone and Justice Story believed that the granting of monopoly rights was an important mechanism for encouraging investment. Monopoly rights were generally justified if the investment required to enter a particular market was relatively large.

At the other extreme, classical political economy was an essentially political reaction to the guilds, the Corn Laws and other state-created monopoly interests produced by the crown during the Elizabethan period.[16] Classical political economy was antimonopolistic with a vengeance and developed elaborate theories showing it to be bad. Most classical political economists—who dominated both economic and judicial thinking in America by the 1850's—believed that in every market competition among incumbent sellers was the optimal way for goods and services to be delivered. For the relatively few exceptions, such as the provision of streets or lighthouses or poor relief, there should be no competition at all, but the government or its designated franchisees should be the only supplier.[17]

Classical political and economic theory were in their ascendancy when America undertook a fundamentally irrational plan that, on the whole, proved successful: to develop an essentially unregulated interstate railroad system largely by means of state initiative and almost exclusively under state control. As late as the 1880's, when the collapse of the unregulated railroad system was clearly on the horizon, some diehards continued to assert the classical model against all the evidence. In 1884 Gerrit Lansing argued that rate regulation of railroads was completely unnecessary, because competition was quite adequate to control the problem.[18] Lansing believed that in the long run the railroads could not earn a higher return on their capital than other industries earned, for capital always flows where the return is the highest. As a result, new investment in railroads would continue until the resulting competition drove returns in the railroad industry down to the level prevailing in other industries. This attitude undoubtedly contributed a great deal to the railroad overdevelopment that was already ruining the industry by the time Lansing wrote. Lansing failed to perceive the difficulty of his distinctly classical argument in a market in which the classical model had fallen apart.[19] If railroads were indeed a natural monopoly, monopoly railroads would earn monopoly returns, while competitive railroads would earn negative returns. There was no unregulated equilibrium in which they would perform competitively.

The Railroads and the Growth of Interstate Markets

Although the development of railroads in the United States left behind its share of individual victims, virtually every major interest group as a whole—farmers and other shippers, certainly consumers, and investors—profited immensely. Railroads made more goods available to more people at a lower price. They made economic development of the

Midwest possible, and greatly hastened the pace of development on the eastern seaboard and in the South and the West.[20]

To be sure, railroads often earned monopoly returns, particularly in the earlier period of their development. But they earned them because they were so much better than the available alternatives. Even the most monopolistic railroad freight rates were lower than the prevailing rates under older forms of transportation. As the Yale political economist Arthur Twining Hadley wrote in 1885, before the coming of the railroad wheat could be economically shipped only about two hundred miles from its place of origin. But the railroad made nationwide and eventually even worldwide shipping of wheat and other foodstuffs commonplace.[21] This was a mixed blessing for farmers and other shippers. On the one hand, they could market their products over a much wider area. On the other hand, so could everyone else, and thus many products became much more competitive. Ironically, although many of the railroads were monopolies, their effect was undoubtedly to destroy many more local monopolies than they created by facilitating interregional competition. In fact, one of the greatest complaints of eastern shippers, particularly New York merchants, was that the railroads tended to undermine the merchants' favored position by giving other cities the same access to worldwide markets.[22]

But the railroads did not only create interstate markets for many of the products that they shipped; they themselves became a large, interstate market—the market for interstate transportation services. Competition, cooperation, and regulation all had interstate effects. Although states had to deal with other natural monopolies, such as toll bridges, gaslights, and waterworks, these generally operated in discrete, intrastate markets. This explains why the problem of railroad regulation so quickly became a problem of federalism as well.

The "Railway Problem"

From about the end of the Civil War until well after the passage of the Interstate Commerce Act in 1887, a number of interrelated concerns about railroad governance developed into the "railway problem," as many called it.[23] At the root was one fundamental observation: the laws of competition developed in classical economic theory did not appear to be working for the railroads. This economic problem quickly became a constitutional problem, for it meant that *some* sort of sovereign intervention might be required—precisely the kind of intervention that the classical theory of federalism made so difficult. The railway problem contained two broad, very different issues: how should the railroads be regulated, and which sovereign, state or federal, was the optimal regulator?

The Economics of Railroad Rates

Both the difficult economic problem of railroad regulation and the closely related problem of federalism result from the same fact: narrowly considered, a railroad line between two given points is a "natural monopoly." A single line is generally capable of handling all the traffic, and the acquisition of land and construction and maintenance of the track is one of the largest costs of operating a railroad. Furthermore, even on a single line the cost of shipping tends to decline as volume increases. For example, larger trains carry cargo at a lower cost per unit than smaller trains. As additional cars are added the cost per car decreases. Thus both the building of tracks and the operation of trains are subject to substantial economies of scale. In most cases the total fixed and variable costs of operating one railroad are significantly lower than the total costs of operating two railroads between the same two points, which in turn are lower than the total costs of operating three railroads, and so on. The optimal system would have a single railroad operating between two given points and earning only a competitive return. But since a privately owned railroad seeks to maximize its profits just as much as any other private firm does, monopoly railroads can be expected to charge monopoly prices.

Nothing is deadlier for a natural monopoly firm than to be thrown into "unnatural" competition. Within the neoclassical economic model, there is no equilibrium, or stable situation, in which two or more natural monopoly competitors can both behave competitively and earn positive rates of return. Total costs of operating railroads rise as the number of railroads between two given points increases from one, for the large capital costs of building the additional lines must be incurred multiple times. However, prices are likely to go down as the railroads compete with each other for business. Although railroads have very high fixed costs (acquisition of land, assuming they have to pay for it,[24] construction of tracks, and acquisition of trains), they have relatively low variable costs (fuel and wages). As a result, a price equal to short-run marginal cost—the cost of accepting an additional package for shipment on a train that is already scheduled—is much less than the total cost that shipping the package imposes on the railroad. Under competition prices will be driven down to a level sufficient to cover operating costs but insufficient to cover the fixed costs, and the railroad will be unable to service its long-term debts.

To take a very simple example, assume that a railroad must pay $100,000 monthly in order to amortize its fixed costs on a certain route. Once the land has been acquired and the tracks built, this amount must be paid whether or not the trains run, and it does not vary with the amount of freight the trains carry. The railroad makes 100 runs per month on this route, with trains capable of carrying 1,000 units of cargo each. In order to cover fixed costs alone, the railroad must receive $1.00 per unit. But the cost of accepting an additional unit of cargo on such a train is small—perhaps 40¢ per unit.[25] Assuming that the variable costs of shipping (that is, fuel and labor) are constant, the railroad would make a reasonable rate of profit at a rate of $1.40: enough to pay both fixed and variable costs, which are defined to include a sufficient profit to maintain investment in the industry.

The unregulated monopoly railroad cannot be expected to charge $1.40. It will charge what it estimates the traffic will bear, and this price may very well be much higher than $1.40. A state policy maker witnessing such profits would be disturbed. If this policy maker were a classicist, the first solution that would come to mind would be not rate regulation but competition. But suppose that a second railroad line were chartered and built between the same two points. The first thing that would happen is that fixed costs would double. Now there are two lines, *each* of which must pay $100,000 monthly in order to retire its investment in land, tracks, and equipment. If the volume of shipping were to remain constant at 1,000 units between the two points, the fixed cost component of the freight rate would have to be doubled to $2.00 per unit, for each railroad would carry only one-half the traffic. This is why the market is characterized as a natural monopoly. Variable costs would remain constant at 40¢ per unit.

If the two railroads behave competitively, however, they will begin cutting prices in order to steal business from one another. Any price above operating costs is "profitable" in the sense that it covers the direct costs of shipping and contributes *something* to the amortization of fixed costs. That is, the railroad would be better off accepting a package for 55¢, which would cover its direct costs and contribute 15¢ to fixed costs, than it would be not carrying the package at all, even though 55¢ is not nearly enough to cover all its costs. Such competition would drive prices to operating costs, which are much lower than total costs. Both railroads would lose money until they formed a cartel and set a very high price, sufficient to cover their *joint* fixed costs and variable costs, which would be at least $2.40 per unit. Otherwise, one of the railroads would be driven out of business and the monopoly situation would be restored. Because of the doubling of fixed costs caused by railroad "competition," the price of shipping a package could actually rise while both railroads lost money. In the short run consumers may benefit from very low rates; but in the long run they will end up bearing the cost of needless additional capacity. Once the two railroads are built, not even government price regulation will help the consumers much, because the regulator must set a rate sufficient to guarantee each railroad a reasonable return, and that rate will be much higher if there are two railroads rather than only one.

Responses

The model described above explains virtually every important phenomenon in the regulatory history of American railroads in the late nineteenth century.

1. The states tried to charter multiple railroads. Monopoly railroads charge monopoly rates. In a few early cases states made the expensive mistake of granting railroads exclusive rights to carry cargo or passengers between two named points.[26] But states learned their lessons quickly, and by the mid-nineteenth century the vast majority of railroad charters contained no monopoly provisions. State legislatures generally attempted to solve the problem of high railroad rates by creating more railroads, with the result that railroad routes, particularly along longer hauls, became increasingly competitive between 1860 and the 1890's. The Senate's Cullom Committee Report, urging passage of what was to become the Interstate Commerce Act of 1887, believed that a principal cause of the railroads' financial woes was overdevelopment brought on by state subsidy.[27] The eventual consequences for the railroads were disastrous, as suggested by the simple model above.

2. Subsidies were necessary for multiple railroads. An experienced railroad manager did not need an economic model to know that competition was bad for the railroad business. For this reason, railroads needed to be encouraged to build new lines, particularly if there were other railroads nearby.[28] This explains many of the government subsidies to encourage railroad development in the mid-nineteenth century. The subsidies included free land, subsidized loans often financed by municipal bonds, or sometimes outright grants of cash. State courts frequently considered the constitutionality of such subsidies. The United States Supreme Court and most states approved them, although a few states did not.[29]

3. The states regulated first. States began to regulate railroad rates some forty years before the federal government did—once again, for the reasons noted in the simple model above. Most of the high rates were being charged for short hauls, which were predominantly intrastate, and where the railroads were more likely to have a monopoly. But the greater the distance between two points, the more alternative routes there were. As a result, most long hauls were much more competitive, and interstate rates were quite low. From the viewpoint of the federal government, which had jurisdiction only over interstate shipments, rates seemed competitive or even so low that they were unremunerative.

4. The railroads sought repeatedly to cartelize the interstate freight market, but the cartels did not work very well. Multiple railroads operating between the same two points could not make a profit if they behaved competitively. Many argued that railroad competition made cartelization inevitable.[30] In no American industry have attempts at both legal and illegal cartelization been so persistent, widespread, systematic, or—ultimately— doomed to failure. For thirty years a great debate waged among railroad economists and policy makers over whether "pooling"—a form of cartelization in which traffic and income were divided among participating railroads—should be legal. Many prominent economists and some lawyers and others informed about railroad problems made the case for legal pooling, arguing that it was essential to the survival of the railroads. Some went so far as to argue that "ruinous competition" would destroy the railroads, and that member railroads who cheated on their pooling agreements should be punished.[31]

Shippers were understandably opposed to pooling, and they generally prevailed in Congress, which wrote an antipooling provision into the Interstate Commerce Act of 1887, and an even stronger provision into the Mann-Elkins Act of 1910. The Interstate Commerce Commission itself was more sympathetic with the plight of the railroads, and advocated a certain amount of controlled pooling throughout the 1890's. But the economic arguments for pooling became largely academic after 1897, when the Supreme Court condemned railroad cartels and pools under the antitrust laws.[32] Pooling remained strictly forbidden until it was legalized, subject to Interstate Commerce Commission (ICC) control, in the Transportation Act of 1920.

The complexity of the pooling issue underscores an important difference between the railroads and most other businesses. The *Trans-Missouri* case (1897) condemning railroad cartels has been characterized as a reasonable application of the per se rule in antitrust to a "naked" price-fixing agreement—that is, an agreement that has no purpose except to exact monopoly prices from consumers.[33] Nothing could be further from the truth. In the 1890's the Interstate Commerce Commission had already realized that without minimum and maximum rate regulation, pooling was necessary to preserve the financial integrity of the roads. Further, the railroads were engaged in a joint venture whose scope included much more than joint setting of rates. The railroads themselves had effectively coordinated the first national railroad system, facilitating the handling of through traffic that required the use of multiple roads. In upholding the arrangement eventually struck down by the Supreme Court in *Trans-Missouri,* the circuit court relied on the ICC's conclusion that the railroads needed "common authority" to "fix rates, and to provide for their steady maintenance." In addition, Judge Walter H. Sanborn noted in the circuit court's opinion approving the cartel that merchandise traveling interstate often had to be handled by several different railroads. One agent, at either the beginning or end of the multiline shipment, had to collect the charges, and this required some formula for dividing the fare among carriers. Regulation of the transfer of freight and computation of rates on interstate shipments was "obviously beyond the reach of compulsory [state] legislation . . . ."[34] The judge concluded:

> The fact that the business of railway companies is irretrievably interwoven, that they interchange cars and traffic, that they act as agents for each other in the delivery and receipt of freight and in paying and collecting freight charges, and that commodities received for transportation generally pass through the hands of several carriers, renders it of vital importance to the public that uniform rules and regulations governing railway traffic should be framed by those who have a practical acquaintance with the subject, and that they should be promulgated and faithfully observed.

Just as the economics of the railroad industry explains why the industry was prone to cartelization, however, it also explains why the cartels worked so poorly, particularly in areas of railroad overdevelopment. The cartel rate, which was designed to cover both fixed and variable costs, was so large when compared with variable costs alone that railroads were tempted to shave prices in order to obtain more business. If a railroad could secretly obtain a large shipment at any price higher than its direct operating costs, it could pay the balance to its creditors and stockholders. Cheating by cartel members was wide-spread. The two most common mechanisms were secret rebates given to large shippers, discussed in the following chapter, and intentional misclassification of freight. For example, if the first-class rate, reserved for fine products such as finished textiles or furniture, was 25 cents per unit, while the fourth-class rate for unfinished lumber was 12 cents per unit, the railroad and a large shipper might enter into an agreement under which the furniture would be intentionally misclassified as "lumber," thus qualifying for the lower rate. The Hepburn Act of 1906 made it illegal for a railroad to grant a rebate or for a shipper to receive one. However, there was no federal legislation controlling freight classifications. As a result, after 1906 freight misclassification became the preferred mechanism for giving individual rate preferences to large shippers.[35] Large shippers were much more likely to obtain the benefit of such cheating than smaller shippers because the trade-offs to the railroad were more attractive: the chances of getting caught by other cartel members were no greater for the large shipper, but the rewards were much larger.

The effect of widespread cheating was that "real" freight rates system wide were substantially lower than posted freight rates. Frequently, cheating scandals would erupt, railroads would publicly defect from a cartel or pooling arrangement, and there would be a protracted "rate war" in which all the railroads lost money until the cartel was once again restored. Overall, cartelization of the American railroad industry proved not to be a very successful way of controlling rates.[36]

5. *The great consolidation movement.* The most efficient way to eliminate competition among railroads was to eliminate competition for profits altogether and to destroy all incentives for cheating. This explains the great railroad merger movement that began in the 1890's, transforming America's network of hundreds of small railroads into a half-dozen great systems. The tendency of competing railroads to merge was understood by railway economists as early as 1871, when Charles Francis Adams, Jr., argued that consolidation was inevitable in the presence of competition, but that government control was necessary to prevent monopoly pricing.[37]

A great deal has been made of the impact of the American antitrust laws in causing this merger movement.[38] The argument is that since elimination of competition was essential to survival, but the Supreme Court made all forms of cartelization illegal under the Sherman Act, the only alternative left was merger. In the case of the railroads, however, it seems relatively clear that the loose combinations, or cartels, were not working. Railroad managers would have taken advantage of tighter forms of organization whether or not the Sherman Act was applied to them.

6. *The sorry state of railroads in the 1890's.* The simple economics of railroads explains why by 1895, when overdevelopment of United States railroads in relation to demand was at its worst, one-fourth of American railroads were in receivership,[39] and why the great railroad consolidations probably would have occurred whether or not the Supreme Court had used the Sherman Act to kill the railroad pools.

By the 1870's or 1880's many of the unique features of railroad economics described above were well known to economists.[40] By the 1890's they were known much more broadly. Even the "Great Commoner," William Jennings Bryan, understood them. In his 1898 argument to the Supreme Court defending a Nebraska rate regulation statute he described the peculiar economics of the railroad industry, explaining why the construction of competing lines was not a suitable alternative to rate regulation for determining reasonable rates.[41]

The question was what to do about these problems. If the railroads were permitted to have unregulated monopolies, rate gouging and large monopoly profits at the expense of shippers were sure to result. If the railroads were forced to compete with each other and pooling or other forms of cartelization were strictly forbidden, railroad rates would almost certainly be driven to a level too low to cover fixed costs, forcing the railroads into bankruptcy. The railroads seemed destined to be either filthy rich or perpetually broke.

Finally, and most important, the economic model explains the origin of the most controversial problem of railroad regulatory policy in the Gilded Age—rate discrimination—and the rationales for different and ultimately inconsistent state and federal responses.

CHAPTER 13

Federalism and
Rate Discrimination

The Rationale

Rate discrimination is a difference in rates between two shipments disproportionate to differences in the cost of service. If the same carrier charges three cents per mile for a certain amount of freight between points A and B, but only two cents per mile between points A and C, it discriminates, as it does if it charges different rates for different types of freight or to different shippers of the same freight along the same route. During the Gilded Age rate discrimination was widespread and considered by the railroads to be inherent in the rate-making process. It was widely condemned by critics.

The common law subjected common carrier rates to the general requirement that they be "reasonable," and the presence of discrimination could be a factor in determining reasonableness. As early as the seventeenth century the common law derived the duty to charge reasonable rates from the common carrier's obligation to serve everyone; one could not escape the duty by quoting an undesired shipper a rate higher than the rate offered to others.[1]

At first glance the common law would seem to be an important weapon against rate discrimination. Within the classical theory of federalism it had one distinct advantage over state legislation: extraterritorial reach. Although the commerce clause prevented states from regulating outside their boundaries by statute, it imposed no such limit on the common law. In an important decision involving the telegraph industry the Supreme Court held that a state could apply its common law to an interstate rate because, quoting Chancellor James Kent, "The common law includes those principles . . . which do not rest for their authority upon any express and positive declaration of the will of the legislature."[2] To hold otherwise, Justice David J. Brewer reasoned, would effectively exempt interstate transactions from any regulation whatsoever unless the federal government had passed a statute on the subject.

But the common law was not consistently applied and most often its strictures on rates were insubstantial. The only rule applied with anything approaching uniformity was that a railroad could not charge two different rates to two different shippers for precisely the same shipment—that is, the same quantity of the same cargo between the same two points. Many courts also held that even when the two shipments were identical, the fact that the plaintiff was charged more than someone else could be used only as evidence that the higher rate was unreasonable; it did not conclusively establish unreasonableness. Further, if there was even a slight difference in the articles, the amount shipped, or the route, the common law generally permitted the discrimination. As a result of these limitations, the common law was never effectively applied to short-haul/long-haul discrimination.[3]

Nearly every person who wrote about railroads in the nineteenth and early twentieth century, from Progressive muckrakers like Ida Tarbell and Frank Norris to stuffy formalists like the Harvard law professor Joseph Beale, railed at the widespread practice of rate discrimination.[4] That the railroads could persist in the practice in spite of such criticism seems quite extraordinary, but nevertheless they did. Their rate discrimination, in fact, took three different forms.

Preferred Customers

Most scorned and least defended were preferential rates for large, favored customers, the most notorious being John D. Rockefeller's Standard Oil Company. The reformer Henry Demarest Lloyd became famous through his account of how the Standard Oil drove its competitors out of business by means of secret agreements with the railroads, giving it lower rates than its competitors. Even conservative, pro-railroad economists such as Arthur Twining Hadley abhorred such "personal discrimination."[5] Three factors may explain it. First, lower rates for very large shippers may not have been discriminatory at all, but merely reflective of the lower cost of selling in volume. For example, carload lots could be handled much more cheaply than smaller lots, wh ch required the railroads to "break bulk," and carload lots accordingly received a lower rate. But the record of discriminatory pricing in favor of Standard Oil and other large shippers is substantial[6] and reveals far more than economies of scale in shipping.

Second, preferred rates for certain shippers may have reflected the fact that many of the railroads were vertically integrated firms, with interests in coal, timber, or other commodities. They often gave their own parent or subsidiary firms preferred rates. Section 1 of the Hepburn Act of 1906 attempted to solve this problem, with some overkill to spare, by forbidding vertically integrated railroads from transporting commodities in which they had an interest, with the exception of lumber.[7]

But undoubtedly the most important cause of discrimination in favor of preferred customers was "secret rebates" or improper freight classifications, which resulted when a member of a railroad pool or other cartel cheated on its fellow cartel members by shaving the cartel price in order to capture a large sale.[8] Such cheating made the cartels particularly unstable and thus probably increased competition. Nevertheless, secret rebates were widely condemned by Progressives for enhancing the economic power of large shippers.

Preferred Products

Another form of discrimination, widely practiced but less widely criticized, was rate differentials between different products, such as finished cotton fabrics, which were sent in the highest rate classification, and lumber or coal, which were sent in the lowest. The differences in rates between these classes were substantial, and often the lowest rates were not sufficient to pay the average total costs of operation—that is, the sum of variable costs and a pro rata share of capital costs. As a result, the railroads were sometimes accused of using artificially high rates on the first-class goods to "subsidize" low rates on the cheaper goods. But by 1885 Arthur Twining Hadley had pointed out the fallacy in this reasoning in his famous oyster example, discussed below. Any rate higher than average variable cost contributed to the fund needed to pay fixed costs, and thus tended to reduce rates for other products. Shippers of first-class goods were better off if the railroads shipped fourth-class goods at any rate higher than the railroads' direct operating costs (as opposed to the railroads' not shipping them at all), even if the difference in rate was not justified by differences in cost of service. As Hadley observed, the discrimination worked to everyone's benefit. The railroads could not give everyone the same low rate, because then they would not recover fixed as well as variable costs. They could not charge the lumber and coal dealers the higher rate, because the dealers would not pay it. Bona-fide discrimination on the basis of freight classification, based on shippers' ability to pay, was the least controversial form of rate discrimination, although it was criticized by those who defended "cost of service" rather than "value of service" rate making. Even Congress recognized that such discrimination was sometimes essential.[9]

Short-Haul/Long-Haul Discrimination

In *The Octopus*, Frank Norris's muckraking antirailroad novel of 1901, Harran Derrick, a rancher from Bonneville, California, in the San Joaquin Valley, orders a set of plows from the East. One day, talking casually to the Bonneville railroad freight agent, Harran discovers that his plows are aboard a train standing in the station. At first Harran is pleased, because he can begin plowing immediately. But the agent tells Harran he cannot have the plows, for "the cars are going north, not, as you thought, coming *from* the north. They have not been to San Francisco yet." The agent then patiently explains—undoubtedly for the thousandth time that year—that the plows must be shipped from the East to San Francisco and then *back* to Bonneville, even though the train bound for San Francisco passes through Bonneville. Further, it costs more to ship the plows back the short distance from San Francisco to Bonneville than to ship them all the way across the country, and Harran must pay the sum of the two rates. When Harran expresses his disgust about the "whole dirty business," the agent shrugs. "I am willing to do what I can for you. I'll hurry the plows through, but I can't change the freight regulation of the road."[10]

For Frank Norris this little story about railroad rates was part of a much larger point—that the railroad was impersonal, that it gobbled up fortunes and destroyed the lives of one group of people while it enriched others, all apparently without reason. These things may have been true, but there probably *was* a very good reason for the railroad's rate policy. It was designed to take advantage of the fact that San Francisco was a competitive railroad shipping point, while Bonneville was a monopoly point.

Short-haul/long-haul discrimination occurred when a railroad charged a higher price per mile for a short haul than it did for a long one. Some difference in pricing between short and long hauls was nondiscriminatory. For example, loading and unloading of cars must be done once for both short and long hauls, and generally costs the same whether the cars have traveled ten miles or one thousand. But more often than not the rate differentials between long and short hauls were far out of proportion to actual direct costs. They were outrageously different. Further, if short hauls had merely cost *proportionately* more than long hauls, the voices of complaint in the Gilded Age would undoubtedly have been more muted. But the biggest protest against short-haul/long-haul discrimination arose from the fact that short hauls frequently cost *absolutely* more than long hauls, even though the short haul was contained completely within the long haul route. For example, a shipment from Denver, Colorado, to Peoria, Illinois, might cost absolutely more than a shipment from San Francisco to New York, even though the cargo bound from San Francisco to New York passed through both Denver and Peoria on the way. Such discrimination was considered appalling by both liberal critics and conservative law writers, and nearly every late nineteenth-century legal scholar who wrote on the subject castigated the practice of "unjust" short-haul/long-haul discrimination.[11] A few political economists, such as Arthur Twining Hadley, attempted to defend the principle, but for their trouble they were identified as nothing more than mouthpieces for the railroad interests. Even later historians in the Progressive tradition found such rate discrimination to be abusive, and castigated both the railroads and those who defended it.[12]

The Economics of Short-Haul/Long-Haul Discrimination

Today most of us accept that a flight from San Francisco to New York costs $119, while a flight from Ogden, Utah, to Cedar Rapids, Iowa— one-fourth the distance—costs twice as much. Competition rather than cost determines the rate. By the late 1860's railroad economists were beginning to discern an economic basis for short-haul/long-haul rate discrimination. In a paper presented to the newly founded American Social Science Association in 1869,[13] Joseph Potts, president of the Empire Transportation Company, observed that railroad lines between distant points were far more competitive than people had once thought, because variable costs were so small. Since the competing lines connected the same commercial "centres of commerce" but passed through mutually exclusive points en route, competition for traffic between the centers was far greater than competition for points along the way.

It cost only a little more to ship a package from points A to B by an indirect 600-mile route than by a 300-mile straight line. If one should trace out the possible rail routes from, say, St. Louis to Chicago, one might find as many as sixty possibilities. This simple observation—that lines did not have to be substantially "parallel" in order to compete, because they did not have to be equal in length—lay at the crux of the short-haul/long-haul problem. It also helped explain why railroad pooling worked so badly. Most shippers did not care if their traffic from St. Louis to Chicago went by way of Peoria or even St. Paul; they cared only about what they paid. As a result, in the absence of cartelization a railroad making a rate from St. Louis to Chicago operated in as close to a perfectly competitive market as one could find anywhere.[14] For this reason the rates between major terminal points were generally insufficient to permit the railroad to amortize its capital costs. The champion railroad regulator Charles Francis Adams, Jr., conceded in 1870 that competition among railroads was a "dangerous evil . . . . It disturbs every calculation, vitiates every result, puts a stop to all experiment, destroys all system."[15]

Where there was no competition, railroads set a rate sufficient to cover both their variable and their fixed costs—and those fixed costs that were not covered by the rates on long-haul traffic were covered by the short-haul rates. This created in some minds the notion that the high short-haul rates somehow "subsidized" the long-haul rates. Even the railroad manager Joseph Potts characterized the high short-haul rates as an "oppressive tax" designed to "restore the revenue depletions" that accrued from excessive competition on long hauls.

In fact there was no subsidy, provided that long-haul rates exceeded direct operating costs, which they almost always did. As Arthur Twining Hadley explained in 1885, even the shippers who paid the high local freight rates actually benefited from short-haul/long-haul discrimination. Hadley's argument, which was well known to later railroad economists,[16] was essentially correct. Suppose that suppliers of oysters at point X on the Delaware coast wanted to enlarge their market by shipping oysters to Philadelphia. The market price in Philadelphia was such that the oysters could not profitably be shipped if shipping costs exceeded $1 per hundred pounds. The only railroad between point X and Philadelphia initially agreed to ship the oysters at that rate, provided that the shippers could fill a car on a regular basis. However, the shippers were able to supply only a half carload at a time. The railroad could not profitably ship a half carload at that $1 price, and the shippers could not afford to pay more. It initially appeared that the railroad and the shippers would be unable to do business. However, another possibility appeared:

> At some distance beyond X, the terminus of this railroad, was another oyster-growing place, Y, which sent its oysters to market by another route. The supply at Y was very much greater than at X. The people at Y were paying a dollar a hundred to send their oysters to market. It would hardly cost twenty-five cents to send them from Y to X. If, then, the railroad from X to Philadelphia charged but seventy-five cents a hundred on oysters which came from Y, it could easily fill its car full.[17]

Immediately, of course, the shippers from X complained that oysters originating at Y were charged a lower rate for a greater distance than the rate for oysters originating at X, but Hadley gave the obvious response: the lower rate for the shippers from Y made the rate for shippers from X possible. If the railroad attempted to charge more to the Y shippers, they would not ship, for they had a competitive alternative. If the Y shippers did not ship, the rate from X would become unprofitable, because even the lower rate from Y was contributing enough to operating costs to make the addition of the oyster car profitable. The shippers at X were actually better off with this "adverse" rate discrimination than without it.

In a seminal contribution to the development of regulatory economics in 1891, the Harvard economist Frank W. Taussig explained in more technical terms why price discrimination was important for natural monopoly industries with high fixed costs. Taussig began with the observation, already well known in the economics literature on railroads,[18] that rates under competition were a function of variable, or operating, costs, not of fixed costs. Nevertheless, fixed costs must be paid. As a result, the railroads were an industry subject to "joint" costs, only one of which would be calculated into the price in a competitive situation. If fixed costs were not accounted for, the railroads would be unprofitable and there would be no new investment in them. But since the competitive pricing mechanism did not allocate anything to fixed costs, how should they be accounted for in rate making?

Taussig concluded that the notion of "cost of service" had no meaning apart from the variable costs incurred in performing that particular service. There was no cost-based mechanism for determining how fixed costs should be allocated in railroad rates. Taussig concluded that *value* of service rather than cost would be the most efficient mechanism for allocating fixed costs, because it would maximize the amount of traffic on the railroads. Those who are able to pay more should pay more. Taussig argued that price discrimination based on freight classifications was economically sound, as was geographic discrimination based on the amount of competition along a particular route. Such discrimination was efficient when it permitted items to be shipped that would not be shipped otherwise. In short, the most efficient policy was to encourage the greatest amount of shipping of all kinds of products, even if they had to be shipped at widely disparate rates. This would permit fixed costs to be amortized over the largest possible amount of cargo, and thus would tend to lower freight rates overall. Taussig concluded that the railroads' existing rate-making practices were generally efficient, for precisely this reason.[19]

According to the Taussig formulation, in an efficient railroad system intrastate, short-haul rates would always be higher than interstate trunk-line rates. But state legislators were generally more interested in the relative size of the intrastate rates paid by their shipper constituencies than in the efficiency of the national railroad system. State and federal concerns were inherently inimical to one another. Although Taussig himself did not address the issue, within his model the efficient regulatory scheme would give all authority over railroad rates to the federal government or leave it to the railroads themselves.

State and Federal Responses to Short-Haul/Long-Haul Discrimination

The most important problem of federalism posed by market failure in the railroad industry is illustrated by the accompanying figure, which shows part of a railroad traveler's map in 1879. By the late 1870's the United States had a large, impressive network of railroads. By the 1880's many people, particularly those within the industry, believed that there was severe overbuilding of railroad trackage.[20] However, the impact of this overbuilding on a particular shipment depended very much on two factors: the relationship between the departure and destination points and a large commercial center, and the distance that the shipment was to be sent. Railroad competition for large commercial centers was keen, but for small, isolated towns it was frequently nonexistent. Furthermore, the longer the route, the more alternatives there were. For example, someone shipping from St. Louis to Chicago had a choice of many different routes. Even someone shipping to Chicago from Omaha had a wide variety of alternative routes, notwithstanding that Nebraska was relatively underdeveloped. But someone shipping from one small town to another—for example, from Galesburg, Illinois, to Quincy, Illinois, or from Hopkins, Missouri, to Creston, Iowa—would have only a single alternative. Likewise, someone shipping even to Chicago from a nearby smaller town, such as Joliet or Aurora, would have only one or two alternatives, while towns farther away had several. Within a particular state, many rates were noncompetitive. Interstate traffic, by contrast, was generally quite competitive except in large isolated areas.

When the railroads were forced to compete they slashed prices and lost money on the competitive longer hauls. In 1886 the railroad bank-

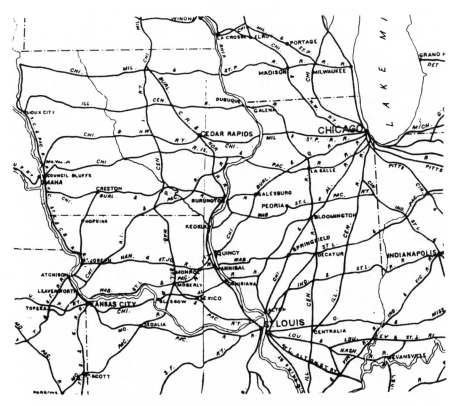

Detail of Rand, McNally & Company's Railroad Travelers' Map (1879).

ruptcy lawyer William P. Shinn observed that "[t]he rate wars which have of late years so devastated the finances of railroad companies, are all inaugurated and carried on upon *inter-state* traffic."[21] But the railroads refused to make equivalent price cuts for short hauls between points where they had a monopoly. On the contrary, they charged a monopoly price for traffic on those routes and were commonly thought to be subsidizing their low rates on the longer routes by charging higher rates on the shorter routes.

One result of this situation was that the federal problem of railroad regulation was perceived quite differently from the state problem. The federal government's authority to regulate interstate commerce gave it jurisdiction over interstate railroad rates. Until well into the twentieth century the prevailing understanding was that the federal government had no jurisdiction over rates on intrastate shipments—those where the bill of lading showed departure and destination points in the same state.[22] The interstate shipping market, which consisted of longer hauls, tended to be very competitive. By looking exclusively at federal railroad regulation, writers such as Gabriel Kolko have concluded that the principal purpose and effect of rate regulation in the United States was the protection of the railroads from competition.[23] But such protection was necessary for the continued viability of a national railroad system, particularly given the fact of state regulation that did not take the existence of interstate competition into account.

The problem of state regulation was very much different. The state's jurisdictional power was roughly the mirror image of the federal government's: a state could regulate shipments that commenced and terminated within the state, but it had no power over interstate shipments. Indeed, in 1886 the Supreme Court made clear that a state did not even have the power to regulate the intrastate portion of an interstate shipment.[24]

The perceived intrastate regulation problem was not to save railroads from bankruptcy resulting from ruinous competition but rather to prevent price gouging on short hauls. The seriousness of the problem varied from state to state with the degree of railroad development. This explains why states began regulating maximum railroad rates nearly a half century before the federal government did, and why rate regulation first became prominent in relatively rural states. When the Granger laws regulating maximum railroad rates were first passed by midwestern states in the late 1860's and early 1870's, Minnesota, Wisconsin, Illinois, and Iowa were in the relatively early stages of railroad development and there were many monopoly routes, on which freight rates were very high. But even then interstate freight rates to the east were so low that farmers and merchants from upstate New York were complaining that midwestern farmers could make an interstate shipment to the port of New York City as cheaply as they could make an intrastate shipment only one-fifth the distance.[25]

When Congress was in the same position as the states, it too legislated rates. For example, in 1886, more than two decades before Congress first authorized federal rate setting, it passed a statute authorizing the construction of railroads in federal Indian territory. The statute, which authorized the Kansas City, Fort Scott, and Gulf Railroad Company to build a railroad, specifically provided that the railroad could not set higher rates than those currently authorized by statute in the state of Arkansas, and that passenger rates could not exceed three cents per mile. Likewise, when Congress first incorporated the Washington and Western Maryland Railroad Company to operate in the District of Columbia, it set the maximum rates at six cents per ton per mile for freight, and three cents per mile per passenger.[26] Congress, just as much as the most radical Granger states, did not want local railroads that were subject to its direct control to charge monopoly prices.

Extraterritorial Effects of State Regulation

State free-riding and federal judicial review of rates. States could respond to the problem of high rates for intrastate hauls in two quite different ways. First, they might adopt an antidiscrimination provision that either required railroad tariffs to be proportional to distance or that forbade rates on short hauls from being higher than rates for long hauls on the same route. At first glance, such responses seem more moderate than direct regulation of maximum rates. In fact they were more radical, because competition had forced long-haul rates too low to cover fixed costs. Antidiscrimination provisions imposed the same below-cost rates for intrastate traffic that the railroads were obtaining on interstate traffic.

Effective state legislation against most short-haul/long-haul discrimination became impossible in 1886 when the Supreme Court decided that a state could control such discrimination only if both terminal points of *both* the long and the short haul were within the state.[27] Since short-haul/long-haul discrimination was fundamentally an interstate problem, the states lost most of the power to control it.

The alternative was direct maximum rate regulation, which was designed to keep local rates closer to long-haul rates. By the late 1870's many states were engaging in direct rate regulation. Although in *Munn* the Court appeared to permit such regulation without qualification, it concluded in 1884 and again in 1890 that the federal courts must review the substantive reasonableness of the rates set. Finally in 1898, in *Smyth v. Ames*, it condemned a maximum rate too low for the railroad to recover its operating costs plus a reasonable return on its property located within the regulating state. The federal courts were immediately embedded in a quicksand of substantive rate cases.[28]

The Supreme Court of the Gilded Age and the Progressive Era has often been criticized for giving the federal courts so much authority to review the substance of rates set by state statute or commission. But the potential for state free-riding was substantial, and federal intervention was necessary. Congress was perceived to have no power over intrastate rates; so the job fell to the courts. The Progressive critique, which criticizes the Supreme Court for usurping state administrative prerogatives,[29] misses the point. The point was not that the federal courts were better fact finders than state agencies, but that the agencies represented the state and its parochial interests. The federal courts were the only competent federal arm to control state free-riding and protect the integrity of the national railroad system.

Before the Granger statutes regulating maximum railroad rates were upheld in *Munn,* most rate regulation imposed by states was written into corporate charters, which often stipulated the maximum amount that the chartered firm could charge.[30] Rates set by charter and rates set by statute differ in two important respects, however. First, a charter is issued before a corporation has made its investment; statutory regulation is generally imposed after the fact. Once a bridge or railroad tracks are installed, those costs become "sunk" and cannot generally be recovered, whether or not the facility goes into operation. As a result, a state could set a statutory rate slightly higher than direct operating costs, but not large enough to retire the indebtedness for the capital expenditure. As long as operating costs were covered, the corporation would be better off operating than shutting down.

Second, a charter was a contract with the state, and no one was forced to accept a charter unless its terms were agreeable. For that reason even laissez-faire constitutional scholars such as Thomas M. Cooley and Isaac Redfield[31] approved enforcement of charter provisions stipulating maximum rates. The corporation had voluntarily agreed to be bound by such rates at the time the charter had been negotiated. But statutory rate regulation of a firm whose charter said nothing about state power to set rates smacked of "retroactive legislation," or a state's reneging on its original grant, as Francis Wharton argued in a critique of the Granger statutes.[32] By regulating rates on railroads that had been chartered under the assumption that the proprietors could set their own rates, the state was effectively changing the terms of a binding contract.

The problem of state opportunism was exacerbated in the case of the railroads because most railroads were fundamentally interstate enterprises, even if they operated under state charters. By the 1870's many railroads were chartered in multiple states and operated continuously through them. State incentive to impose unremunerative rates on railroads became much larger when the railroad was an interstate enterprise. Since the railroads were common carriers, they were required by law to accept in the ordinary course of business all those willing to pay.[33] The states had jurisdiction only over purely intrastate traffic, and this was typically less than 15 percent of the total.[34] As a result, a very low rate on local traffic in any particular state would not have a substantial impact on the railroad's total revenue, and the railroad would continue to operate within the state even if the maximum permissible rates on the relatively small amount of intrastate cargo were very low.

In *Smyth v. Ames* (1898) the Supreme Court decided that state rates too low to permit the railroads a reasonable return on that part of their investment dedicated to local traffic amounted to an unconstitutional taking of private property without due process of law. The Court rejected the obvious argument, raised by the states, that if a railroad's overall business within the state was profitable it should not matter what the rates were on intrastate traffic. It also rejected the argument that a state could constitutionally reduce rates to a level sufficient to cover only direct operating costs. Either of these rules would have shifted to interstate traffic the burden of amortizing the railroads' fixed costs.[35]

State power to regulate the interstate system. In the *Granger* cases (1877)[36] the Supreme Court appeared to approve state regulation of railroad rates if *either* the origin or the destination were within the state. But in *Wabash Railway* (1886) the Supreme Court severely qualified the *Granger* cases by strictly limiting the state's regulatory power to shipments that both commenced and terminated within the regulating state. The Court struck down application by Illinois of a short-haul/long-haul antidiscrimination provision to a rate from two different points in Illinois to New York City. The Wabash, St. Louis, & Pacific Railway had carried

162 · THE RISE OF REGULATED INDUSTRY

goods from Peoria, Illinois, to New York for fifteen cents per hundred pounds; and goods of the same classification from Gilman, Illinois, to New York for twenty-five cents per hundred pounds. The distance from Peoria to New York was eighty-six miles greater than the distance from Gilman, and the route was identical: the goods bound for New York from Peoria passed through Gilman on the way. The discrimination resulted from the fact that Peoria was a highly competitive shipping point, and Gilman was a monopoly point. The Court found that application of the antidiscrimination statute to these transactions was a regulation of interstate commerce forbidden to the states.

In his dissent in *Wabash*, Justice Joseph P. Bradley noted what appeared to be obvious: the extraterritorial part of the route was identical in the two shipments to which the Illinois antidiscrimination statute was being applied. The only difference in the two routes lay entirely within Illinois. As a result the Illinois requirement of proportionality of rates made a difference only within the state.

However, Justice Samuel F. Miller's opinion for the Court noted something else: application of the Illinois statute to shipments between Illinois and other states could have a substantial effect on interstate rate making. For example, Miller suggested, interstate competition might indicate a rate of fifteen cents per hundred pounds from New York City to Peoria, but the railroad would be forbidden from charging this low rate because it was already charging higher rates on the noncompetitive parts of its lines. The statute required it to charge the higher rate on the interstate shipment as well. Likewise, the rate charged by a railroad for a very short local haul—from Gilman to Sheldon, Illinois, a distance of twenty-three miles—would end up dictating the minimum rate that the railroad could charge on interstate shipments, even though the cost of loading and unloading accounted for almost the entire expense of the short haul, but only a small percentage of the expense of the long haul.[37]

Justice Miller's illustrations were more rhetorical than realistic: he assumed in all of them that the effect of the antidiscrimination provision would be that the railroads would *raise* the rates for interstate shipments rather than lower the rates for local shipments. The state legislature had of course predicted the contrary, and the legislature was almost certainly correct, for the interstate rates were set by competition. The Wabash railway could comply with the statute only by lowering its local rates.

But Justice Miller's basic observation was nonetheless valid. By prohibiting short-haul/long-haul discrimination on interstate routes a state could quite effectively depress interstate freight rates along competitive trunk lines. By the late 1880's railroad scholars began to note that state regulation was affecting interstate operations.[38] The Supreme Court's stubborn distinction between "direct" and "indirect" effects on interstate commerce prevented it from dealing effectively with this important state power over interstate rates. For example, in *Smyth v. Ames* in 1898, then Judge David Brewer refused to hold that a Nebraska maximum rate statute unduly burdened interstate commerce, because the resulting maximum intrastate rate forced a readjustment of interstate rates on traffic through surrounding states as well.[39] Likewise, in the *Louisville & Nashville* case (1902) the Supreme Court rejected an argument that a short-haul/long-haul antidiscrimination provision applied entirely within the state was unconstitutional because the long-haul rate was determined by competition with routes outside the state, and application of the Kentucky statute would force a change in those rates. The court conceded that intrastate rate regulation "may somewhat affect commerce generally"; however, "such a result is too remote and indirect to be regarded as an interference with interstate commerce . . . ."[40]

During the decade after *Smyth v. Ames* state power over interstate rates became more fully understood. In approving the *Smyth* decision, Harry Robinson, editor of *The Railway Age,* noted that individual states were too small to regulate the rates of an essentially national railroad system.[41] The result was self dealing, as each state tried to ensure that its rates were no higher than the rates of its neighbors. But no one was concerned for the integrity of the system as a whole. "It would be an incalculable blessing, both to the people and the companies," Robinson argued, "if the railway system of the United States could be treated as a national unit under federal control only."

In a seminal article in 1908 entitled "How the States Make Interstate Rates,"[42] Robert Mather, president of the Rock Island Railroad, showed how state regulation of purely intrastate rates effectively controlled a broad range of interstate rates. The largest force in setting interstate rates was competition. The effect of a maximum intrastate rate from one state border to another was that competitive lines outside the state were forced to match the legislated rate or lose their business. This created an effect that could be felt all the way up and down the line, and over routes that crossed several states. What was more ominous, argued Mather, was that the states were interested only in protecting their own constituencies. Unlike the Interstate Commerce Commission, which had jurisdiction over interstate rate making, the states had no regard for the integrity of the system as a whole or for the effects of interstate competition in controlling through rates. "The carrier makes no rates that are not effectively molded by these conditions, and the rate-making power of the Interstate Commerce Commission itself cannot ignore them," Mather noted. "The only rate-regulating body that makes rates without reference to these commercial conditions is the legislature or the railroad commission of a single state."

But in the *Minnesota Rate Cases* (1913) the Supreme Court reaffirmed Judge Brewer's ruling in *Smyth*. It conceded that the states had substantial practical power over interstate rates, but once again classified this as merely an "indirect" burden on interstate commerce. Additionally, the Court held that in determining whether a state maximum rate was so low as to be unconstitutionally confiscatory, the courts must look at operating costs plus the return on that portion of the tonnage carried within the state devoted entirely to intrastate traffic. Under the Court's analysis, if a railroad had property worth $1,000,000 within the state and 12 percent of the traffic measured by ton miles was intrastate, the rate must be high enough to give the railroad its operating expenses and a reasonable return on $120,000.[43] Finally, the court placed on the railroads the considerable burden of showing that the rates legislated by the states were confiscatory.

Under this rule, if a state set its rates at the constitutional minimum, the railroad would have to amortize its fixed costs evenly over intrastate and interstate traffic or else it would fail to break even. Given that competition tended to force rates on interstate routes to variable costs, the rule in the *Minnesota Rate Cases* effectively permitted states to impose negative returns overall. This is the best explanation why, Supreme Court intervention notwithstanding, Congress eventually preempted most state rate-making power. The Supreme Court should be faulted, not for interfering in the state rate-making process, but for setting a constitutional minimum that was too low to prevent the state free-riding that undermined the integrity of the national railroad system.

The Development of Federal Supremacy

In the early twentieth century the rapid growth of federal supremacy over the American economy was controversial but appeared inevitable. Woodrow Wilson found himself caught in a quandary, wishing to protect the federal system and the state's right to regulate, but recognizing that the economy was national, that inconsistent state laws were imposing enormous costs on business, and that there was no realistic hope for uniform state law making. Henry Wade Rogers, dean of Yale Law School, also admitted the problem, but believed that the states' authority to regulate their own business was essential to the preservation of the federal system.[44] The railroads stood at the crossroads of this conflict of sovereignties. State prerogatives notwithstanding, expanded federal control clearly lay on the horizon.

Congress gradually increased the authority of the Interstate Commerce Commission over interstate rates. The Elkins Act of 1903 forbade rebating and required the railroads to file their rates with the commission. Once filed, these rates became mandatory, and railroads were forbidden to deviate from them. Since joint rate making was legal under the act, its overall effect was to make cartel cheating more difficult. Thus the statute tended to shore up secret pools and price-fixing arrangements, and may have made interstate rates more profitable. The Hepburn Act of 1906 additionally empowered the commission, upon complaint, to declare an existing rate unreasonable and prescribe a new one, thus giving the commission its first real rate-making powers. The Mann-Elkins Act of 1910 carried the commission's power one step further by authorizing it to suspend proposed changes in interstate rates pending an investigation and to condemn short-haul/long-haul discrimination without the need for a complaint. The Mann-Elkins Act effectively gave the commission full control over interstate rates, subject to judicial review of their reasonableness.[45]

In 1889 the Interstate Commerce Commission had already begun to advocate broader federal control over *intra*state railroad rates. Congress would not assert such authority for another thirty years. On the contrary, it had explicitly exempted intrastate shipments from the Interstate Commerce Act in 1887 and did so once again in the Hepburn Act in 1906.[46] Congress probably continued to believe that it had no authority to legislate intrastate rates, and thus refused to give that power to the commission.

But the commission received some encouragement in 1913 in the *Minnesota Rate Cases.* The Court suggested that where the extraterritorial effects of intrastate rate making were clear because of the "interblending of the interstate and intrastate operations of interstate carriers," Congress might have the power to preempt state rate control. Such preemption would require a showing that "adequate regulation of . . . interstate rates cannot be maintained without imposing requirements with respect to . . . intrastate rates which substantially affect the former . . . ."[47]

The Supreme Court made its position clearer a year later in the

Shreveport Rate Case,[48] when it held that even the existing legislation gave the Interstate Commerce Commission power over purely intrastate rates if they could be shown actually to burden interstate traffic. Shreveport, Louisiana, was an important port city on the Red River, a large tributary of the Mississippi, with direct access to all Mississippi River traffic. This substantial competition with water routes forced railroads to make very low rates into and out of Shreveport.

The Texas Railroad Commission, which set Texas rates, followed its own policy of encouraging the economic growth of Texas cities.[49] It attempted to compensate for the low interstate rates to and from Shreveport by making rates within Texas much lower than the interstate rates between Shreveport and the same Texas points. For example, the rate from Houston to Lufkin, Texas, a distance of 118.2 miles, was 50 cents per hundred pounds. The rate from Shreveport to Lufkin, a distance of 112.5 miles, was 69 cents. The effect of this scheme was to undermine Shreveport's advantage in favor of Houston and Dallas with respect to shipments originating in or destined for other Texas points.

The Interstate Commerce Commission responded with an order that was the obverse of the statute struck down in the *Wabash Railway* case: it ordered the carriers to make intrastate rates proportional to the prevailing interstate rates. The classical theory of commerce clause power would have suggested that just as the state could not apply its antidiscrimination provision to interstate traffic, neither could Congress apply its antidiscrimination law to intrastate traffic. The Court noted the lack of symmetry between its decisions condemning state power and approving federal power over interstate/intrastate discrimination, but concluded that it was "for Congress to supply the needed correction where the relation between intrastate and interstate rates presents the evil to be corrected . . . ."

The *Shreveport Rate* case made Congress aware of the harmful potential of simultaneous state and federal rate making. Its eventual response was the Transportation Act of 1920, which rewrote railroad regulatory policy and for the first time created a single, national railroad system. The Transportation Act gave the Interstate Commerce Commission substantial power to set intrastate as well as interstate rates and to set minimum as well as maximum rates. The immediate result was a number of commission actions challenging unduly low state-imposed rates, on the theory that they discriminated against interstate commerce. In upholding the commission's power over intrastate rates the Supreme Court expressly relied on the interstate effects of low intrastate rates, concluding that "[i]f the railways are to earn a fixed net percentage of income, the lower the intrastate rates, the higher the interstate rates may have to be." Effective ICC administration of the Transportation Act "will reasonably and justly require that the intrastate traffic should pay a fair and proportionate share of the cost of maintaining an adequate railway system."[50]

Federalism and Regulatory Capture

An important part of any theory of regulation is the identification of the optimal regulatory sovereign. Who should regulate? The most serious problem the railroads faced in the late nineteenth century was not that no one understood the simple economics of running railroads, for many did. Far more serious was that for half a century the primary task of controlling an essentially national railroad system had been left to the states with their parochial interests. The railroads looked to the federal government for salvation because they wanted some order in a national system that was falling apart.

The fact that American railroads were going bankrupt, that they petitioned Congress for relief, and that Congress responded with legislation may be consistent with a capture theory of regulation, but it falls far short of establishing capture. Americans had made a policy choice in favor of private rather than state-owned railroads. Given the assumption of private railroads, any examination of the historical development of railroad regulation must include the premise that the investor-owned railroad company is entitled to earn a profit. Protection of railroad profits is as important a part of government regulatory policy as is consumer protection, for without profits no new investment can be expected.

The record of congressional railroad activity in the late nineteenth and early twentieth centuries is probably as consistent with the traditional Progressive "public interest" theory of regulation as it is with revisionist alternatives. The alternative that makes the most sense is that, beginning with the Interstate Commerce Act in 1887, the national railroad system first became a regulated "market"—that is, an industry regulated by a sovereign large enough to encompass all its operations. The resulting regulatory policy was not perfect; on the contrary, it was highly experimental and filled with flaws. But the flaws were not ones of motive or of extreme naiveté. They were flaws that derived from two factors—first, an economic model that was incomplete and only imperfectly understood; second, a set of constitutional rules and historical precedents that continually forced Congress to pay excessive deference to state interests until the Supreme Court finally relaxed its views about congressional power over intrastate rates. Such a record makes a poor case for congressional philandering with the regulated.

PART IV

THE POLITICAL ECONOMY
OF SUBSTANTIVE DUE PROCESS

CHAPTER 14

Historical Explanation
and Substantive Due Process

"Substantive due process" is a doctrine that the United States Supreme Court and other American courts used from around 1885[1] until the Roosevelt court-packing crisis of 1937 to determine the constitutionality of regulatory legislation. The courts derived a test from the due process clause of the fourteenth amendment for evaluating the substantive effect of economic regulations such as wage and hour laws, product quality laws, licensing restrictions, restrictions on entry into business, and price regulation. The language of substantive due process spoke not of substantive regulatory standards but rather of individual constitutional right. Individuals were said to possess a "liberty of contract" that gave them freedom from governmental interference—in this case, freedom to make choices affecting individual economic status. As Justice Sutherland wrote in *Adkins v. Children's Hospital,* "the right to contract about one's affairs is a part of the liberty of the individual protected by [the due process] clause."[2]

Two aspects of this age of "liberty of contract" stand out. First, it was an unprecedented period of judicial activism and creativity. The United States Supreme Court and many state courts reversed a long-standing policy of judicial deference to legislation and began second-guessing the wisdom of lawmakers on a large scale. In the process, courts often created substantive doctrines unsupported by the language or legislative history of any constitutional provision. Second, the economic doctrine of substantive due process was not only revisionist but seemed peculiarly out of step with the dominant political values of the day. The Supreme

Court appeared determined to prevent the emergence of the regulatory state, despite substantial support for such change by a variety of interests, including both business and labor, the wealthy and the impoverished.[3]

Historians have developed a number of hypotheses to explain substantive due process. The hypotheses are inconsistent with each other, and to one degree or another, all are inconsistent with the hypothesis offered here.

Legal Formalism

Critics of substantive due process observed that those responsible for constitutionalizing the doctrine were out of step with their time.[4] In a world dominated by Darwin and the social sciences, how could anyone believe that people had a right to be free of governmental economic regulation?

One of the most important intellectual events of the 1880's and 1890's was the rise of the modern social sciences—economics, psychology and psychiatry, sociology, and political science.[5] By the turn of the century, social scientists in America were developing a rather high view of themselves: their self-professed job was to identify social problems and to formulate policies for solving them. Social scientists thought these policies should be implemented by legislation,.executive orders, or judicial rules. They believed the state should adopt these policies because they were scientifically formulated. No one could verify the statement of a right, such as "an employer has a right to pay any wage he and his employees agree upon." But Progressive Era social scientists such as Charles R. Van Hise, Richard T. Ely, Edward A. Ross, and jurisprudent Roscoe Pound believed that statements such as "minimum wage laws provide more efficient use of economic resources" had a scientific, or empirical, meaning that made them more plausible than doctrines like liberty of contract. State legislatures appeared to agree. They passed a wide variety of statutes regulating wages, hours, working conditions, and product quality.[6]

The result was a great tension between the legislative process and the common law. The great economic and industrial expansion of the nineteenth century, the massive growth in the political power of the lower economic classes, and the great increase in state legislation, much of which abrogated the common law, threatened the common law's traditional role as primary economic regulator. One widely accepted explanation of the substantive due process era is that judges responded to this threat by looking within. They became obsessed with deriving from the common law its own set of values, which required protection of certain abstractly defined property rights. This critique accuses substantive due process judges of being "formalist."[7]

Formalism is law without a policy—except perhaps for the policy that the law must be internally consistent and self-contained, and must not draw its wisdom from outside. Legal Progressives such as Roscoe Pound, who were contemporaries of the substantive due process courts, attacked legal formalism as judicial decision making detached from any policy considerations. Some later historians have also described the period of substantive due process as the age of formalism.[8]

But even formalistic law contains a policy, although it may be the policy of the judges themselves and not the perceived policy of the legislature. For example, when Holmes attacked the majority's substantive due process decision in *Lochner v. New York* (1905), he did not accuse the Court of creating a legal rule without a policy. He accused it of enacting "Mr. Herbert Spencer's *Social Statics*," and of deciding the case "upon an economic theory which a large part of the country does not entertain."[9] The policy encased in judicial formalism might be that judges should protect the propertied class from the tyranny of the masses, or simply that one economic or social theory is better than another one. Nevertheless, even the most formalistic judge has an idea that his decision will somehow be best for the community. The Supreme Court that decided *Lochner* in 1905 was "formalistic" only because it preferred one economic theory to another, or perhaps because it believed that the prerogative of selecting economic theories belongs to judges rather than to legislators.

Another objection to the formalist thesis is that it hypothesizes a law that is both static and uncreative.[10] Substantive due process was neither. The law changed very rapidly during the period in which substantive due process dominated constitutional adjudication. Further, judges who used substantive due process also produced some of the most creative, noninterpretivist decisions ever known. One example is *In re Debs* (1895), where the Court cut from new cloth the doctrine that the executive branch has the power to protect interstate commerce from labor disputes, even though Congress had not passed a statute authorizing the executive's action.[11] Another is *Ex parte Young* (1908), where Justice Peckham held that the sovereign immunity provision of the eleventh amendment does not apply when a private party seeks to enjoin a state official from enforcing an unconstitutional statute, because the official is "stripped of his official or representative character."[12] The statute at issue in *Young* was a railroad rate regulation alleged to interfere with the free market.

But more important than these novel assertions of judicial prerogative to make policy is the fact that substantive due process was highly creative at its core. It devised a set of economic rules from a constitutional provision in which they were nowhere to be found. Neither the language nor the legislative history of the fourteenth amendment suggested a congressional concern with minimum wage laws, rate regulation, or business licensing. Indeed, the legislative history of the fourteenth amendment was all but irrelevant in substantive due process cases. The judges practiced aggressive, loose constructionism equal to anything known in the 1960's and after. One of the great jurisprudential documents of substantive due process was a book written in 1890, with a peculiarly modern sounding title—Christopher Tiedeman's *Unwritten Constitution of United States*.[13] Tiedeman argued that an "unwritten constitution" condemned state attempts to "protect the weak against the shrewdness of the stronger, to determine what wages a workman shall receive for his labor, and how many hours he shall labor." And the unwritten constitution should be called upon whenever the state tried to make a monopoly out of an ordinary calling. This "unwritten" constitution was the one that substantive due process courts applied.

The language of legal formalism belonged largely to private law. The paradigm example of formalism in private law is undoubtedly Christopher Columbus Langdell's 1871 casebook on contracts,[14] which probably did more than any other document to convince two generations of lawyers that legal rules should be derived only from earlier decisions. But Langdell's work had little analogue in public law. On the contrary, constitutional scholarship was about to embark on one of its most fertile, interdisciplinary periods. It would aggressively incorporate another discipline—economics—on a large scale. The economic theory employed by the courts, whether right or wrong, was an *economic* theory, not the product of legal formalism.

Formalism was the *rhetoric* of law in the late nineteenth century, particularly of private law. Lawyers beginning with Langdell or perhaps even earlier wanted the law to be seen as a self-contained system—a science whose "data" consisted entirely of earlier legal decisions—because they were obsessed with placing law on the same epistemological plane as the other sciences.[15] But Langdell's formalism was only a vision, never reality, and even formalism at its best (or worst) never did what it said. The Harvard professor Joseph Beale, who has come to be identified with formalism run amok, often incorporated policy concerns into his legal reasoning, and these policies often drew on the wisdom of other disciplines.[16] Substantive due process was a system of law based on an economic theory.

Economic Hypotheses

Historians often use the word "economic" in a different sense than do economists. Many economists, particularly modern neoclassicists, believe that economics is a science concerned with the efficient allocation of resources, but not with their distribution.[17] An "economic" question to them is a question about how resources can most efficiently be assigned, regardless of who might be richer and who poorer. Questions about how resources should be divided among conflicting claimants are "political."

When historians, particularly those of the Left, use the word "economic," they generally mean "political" in this sense. For example, Charles Beard's *Economic Interpretation of the Constitution* (1913)[18] does not develop a theory that the Constitution's framers set out to devise a document that would maximize American wealth or welfare. On the contrary, Beard argues that the framers represented various special interest groups, each of which wished to maximize its own personal wealth. Beard's "economic" interpretation is really a "political" interpretation.

Many legal historians use economic theories to explain the development of the law.[19] This does not necessarily mean, of course, that they are economic determinists. Economic determinists generally believe that legal rights are nothing more than the consequence of struggles over scarce resources. Karl Marx and William Graham Sumner[20]—who held extraordinarily different political views—agreed about that. But historians who are not economic determinists believe that people make some decisions that are not dictated by resource scarcity. They do not believe that politics, science, or even religion and the arts developed out of conflicts between economic interests. Although many legal historians have justified their broad use of economic explanations for the development of law, most of them would probably say that the law has a special quality that makes economic explanation more appropriate there than in other areas of human expression.

This special quality is the law's own economic consciousness. Law is a cultural activity. The weight of institutional practice, tradition, and force of habit notwithstanding, law consists of the things people think about, and people frequently perceive legal conflicts as economic conflicts. When in a hard case an appellate judge is asked to make a certain rule— perhaps that railroad operators should be liable only for the foreseeable consequences of their negligent acts—the judge understands that she is encouraging or discouraging certain activities by applying economic sanctions. The accumulated weight of a large number of such rules will form a policy about railroads—about how much it should cost to operate them and how the members of society should share this cost. Of course, not every judge has enough vision to consider what role the railroad plays in the American economy and how a particular rule will affect that role.[21] But even the most rule-bound judge asks herself simple economic questions, such as which party ought to be on guard at railroad crossings and who should pay the consequences. Invariably, the judge makes an economic decision.

This book argues that American judges had an economic point of view that the treatise writer Theodore Sedgwick offered as early as 1836.[22] This view holds that good law and good political economy are the same, except that law is positive while political economy is normative. Law "teaches what the law is, which it is the business of the lawyer to learn." Political economy "teaches what law should be, which is the business of the public economist, or legislator to learn."

But the judges who developed substantive due process behaved more like Sedgwick's political economists, separating those laws that they saw as tending to the production of wealth from those that did not. In the process these judges hid, suppressed, or trivialized underlying conflicts about how wealth should be distributed. Their political economy convinced them that questions about economic regulation should be treated as nothing more than questions about economic efficiency. Within the classical model these questions had right answers that legislators had failed to discover.

The importance of this argument is not to show that the judges were right, but that political economy helped them think they were right. Substantive due process was another of many failed nineteenth-century quests for a "rule of law"—a set of legal rights that could be considered just or fair without regard to the way they distributed wealth among conflicting claimants. In the end, of course, classical political economy was as temporal and mortal as substantive due process itself. Judicial attitudes toward substantive due process changed when the prevailing economic doctrine changed.

In the late nineteenth century most judges were reluctant to recognize economic conflict explicitly as a justification for changing legal rules. This was not the case with the legislatures. By the turn of the century, a large gap had developed between judicial and legislative perceptions about the role of the law as a wealth distribution device. Many states had enacted legislation that intervened in the market on behalf of labor, regulating child labor, women's maximum work hours, and hours or working conditions in certain industries. They had also enacted a host of licensing and regulatory restrictions that benefited established businesses at the expense of prospective entrants, although some of these regulations had health or safety justifications as well. Fierce attacks on classical laissez-faire economic theory by economists such as Charles Francis Adams, Jr., Richard T. Ely, Edwin R. A. Seligman, and John R. Commons provided intellectual support for this legislative reform.[23] But the Supreme Court continued to rely on classical economic theories developed in the late eighteenth and early nineteenth centuries. Why it was so sternly committed to an obsolete economic theory is a perplexing question.

The economic explanation that seems least reasonable, although even Holmes appeared to believe it, is that substantive due process judges were protecting the interests of America's "solid" classes—who just happened to be the classes who had worked to secure the judges' appointment to the bench. According to this argument, many of the substantive due process cases presented a conflict between property holders and unpropertied wage earners. In 1897, Holmes, not yet appointed to the United States Supreme Court, wrote:

> when socialism first began to be talked about, the comfortable classes of the community were a good deal frightened. I suspect that this fear has influenced judicial action both here and in England . . . . I think that something similar has led people who no longer hope to control the legislatures to look to the courts as expounders of the Constitution, and that in some courts new principles have been discovered outside the bodies of those instruments, which may be generalized into acceptance of the economic doctrines which prevailed about fifty years ago . . . .[24]

The Justices of the Supreme Court, most of whom came from the ranks of the propertied minority, consciously or unconsciously voted for "their side" in cases presenting important social conflicts. This rationale may also explain why the Court upheld comprehensive land-use planning, which seemed to interfere with liberty of contract at least as much as did the wage and hour regulations that the Court struck down.[25] The land-use cases were not conflicts between the propertied and the penniless but conflicts between competing landowners over how land should be used. Wealthy developers who wanted to use their land for industry often challenged zoning ordinances, while affluent businessmen or professionals who wanted to preserve the integrity of their residential or retail neighborhoods often defended them. The Court was willing to allow legislative regulation in these cases, the argument goes, because the statutes produced no clear benefit to wage earners at the expense of the wealthy.

Although it explains some hard cases, this economic interest argument ultimately fails. First, it makes casual assumptions that impeach the integrity of the Justices on the basis of little or no extrinsic evidence. Second, it gives substantive due process a rather odd pedigree. The Court first entertained the doctrine in 1873 in the *Slaughter-House Cases,* in which four Justices were ready to condemn a state statute that they believed gave a monopoly to a group of legislatively favored butchers at the expense of those not so favored.[26] But whatever the statute in the *Slaughter-House Cases* may have been, it was *not* a legislative attempt to transfer money from property owners to the working class. The Supreme Court finally adopted a substantive due process argument in *Allgeyer v. Louisiana* to strike down a statute restricting the sale of insurance within the state by out-of-state insurance companies. The legislature probably enacted the statute in *Allgeyer* to protect in-state insurance companies from out-of-state competitors.[27] In any event, only people with some property purchased insurance. Neither the *Slaughter-House Cases* nor *Allgeyer* can be characterized as cases in which the Supreme Court sided with the propertied at the expense of the penniless.

Neither is the hypothesis of vested judicial interest consistent with the later judicial record of substantive due process. Most of the critics of substantive due process were Progressives or else strong supporters of the ideology of the New Deal. They often drew a distorted picture of the economic impact of substantive due process decisions. For example, in discussing cases that struck down wage and hour legislation, they suggested that the substantive due process Court was "antilabor." In fact, the Court sometimes upheld statutes that interfered quite substantially with the contractual relationship between employers and employees. Further, although some of the better known substantive due process decisions involved conflicts between industry and labor, most cases cannot be so characterized. For example, many statutes creating entry or licensing restrictions for various occupations or professions were overturned.[28]

State courts also struck down legislative attempts to impose licensing on blacksmiths, undertakers, ticket agents, druggists, and plumbers. As Thomas M. Cooley noted, such licensing restrictions almost always protected established businesses from potential competitors. Many of the courts that struck down such statutes made express findings to this effect and condemned the statutes as monopolistic. For example, in 1910 when the New York Court of Appeals struck down a statute setting conditions on the licensing of embalmers and undertakers, the court found the "public health" justification offered by the state inadequate. Rather, "[w]e cannot refrain from the thought that the act in question was conceived and promulgated in the interests of those then engaged in the undertaking business, and that the relation which the business bears to the general health, morals, and welfare of the state had much less influence upon its originators than the prospective monopoly that could be exercised with the aid of its provisions." In 1906 a Washington court complained that "every legislative session brings forth some new act in the interest of some new trade or occupation." The "doctor, the lawyer, the druggist, the dentist, the barber, the horseshoer, and the plumber have already received favorable consideration" from the legislature, and "the nurse and the undertaker are knocking at the door." Similar sentiments were voiced in decisions employing either substantive due process or the public purpose doctrine to strike down legislative subsidies for private business.[29]

These decisions cannot be characterized as a judicial choice to side with business against labor, immigrants, and the poor. On the contrary, they permitted such groups increased entry in the face of legislation designed to protect established firms from competition. Business, just as much as labor, was required to survive the test of the marketplace. Even Supreme Court decisions striking down legislative price regulations must be characterized as ambiguous. Under the "public interest" view of regulation that dominated the Progressive critique of substantive due process, these statutes were passed for the benefit of consumers in order to control monopoly pricing by various industries. The record suggests just as strongly, however, that the businesses themselves wanted the relief from competition that price regulation can bring, and that they were often its beneficiaries.[30]

A more recent economic argument,[31] which gives judges more credit for having a social vision, is built on the observation that laissez-faire legal theory greatly aided American commercial development in the early nineteenth century. According to this theory, business counsel and judges with a vision of American expansion developed an instrumental law that encouraged such development. By the middle of the century, however, the commercial class had succeeded in obtaining legal rules that protected their interests. When conflicting political interests began to emerge, the legal rules failed to respond. They continued to protect business from external control long after some kinds of regulation and redistribution had become appropriate. The same legal rules that had been novel and instrumental when they were first created became formalistic and outdated, because they no longer agreed with the dominant legislative policy. The old rules were perpetuated largely because the wealthy commercial interests, which commanded the best legal talent, gained enormously from their continuation.

This argument is appealing, but it does not answer every question. Most important, it does not account for the fact that, when substantive due process first appeared in the state courts, by far the greater number of cases struck down professional licensing statutes or more direct business subsidies rather than wage and hour regulations. Since the principal beneficiaries of the licensing statutes were established businesses and the victims were newcomers, substantive due process in this area had an effect precisely the opposite of the one suggested.

Further, this argument finds little support in the record of judicial "behavior," in a sense larger than opinion writing. Why were the judges in the 1830's so open to the idea that business needed freedom to expand, but so blind at the end of the century to the equally obvious need for protection of the competing rights of laborers and consumers? Why was it relatively easy for judges like Lemuel Shaw and Roger Brooke Taney to find compelling policy reasons for rejecting established rules in the first half of the nineteenth century, but so hard for judges like Rufus Peckham and George Sutherland to do so later? The intellectual stature of the judges themselves may account for these discrepancies, although, as noted above, the substantive due process era was a period of great judicial creativity. The influence of political interests in the appointments of Supreme Court justices might also explain the differences.[32] However, political conflict alone cannot explain the judicial record.

Yet another economic argument is that judges developed substantive due process as a device for combating special privilege—instances when

a legislature displayed favoritism or unreasonably rewarded one constituency at the expense of another.[33] This argument begins with the
observation that one of the earliest concerns expressed in the literature
of substantive due process was that "due process" meant fair treatment
by the government, whether legislature, executive, or judiciary. It was
not fair for the government to "take the property of A. and give it to
B.," as Chief Justice Salmon P. Chase said in 1871.[34] Under the commonwealth principle, developed first in England and later in America,
the state could intervene in the market in order to make *everyone* better
off; but it could not intervene in order to benefit some people at the
expense of others.[35]

This argument is good as far as it goes, but ultimately it begs the
question unless it is accompanied by some sort of conspiracy theory
concerning the legislative process. It does not answer *why* it is bad to
take the property of *A* and give it to *B*—or, to cast the problem into
economic terms, why the courts believed that wealth redistribution
forced by the state was a bad thing. Substantive due process would have
been a trivial doctrine had it stood only for the proposition that legislatively forced wealth transfers caused by bribery or corruption were
void.

One possibility, of course, is that the courts viewed all such legislative
transfers as a form of corruption, as in the *Slaughter-House Cases*. In
Lochner, Justice Peckham voiced his suspicion that many wage and hour
laws were passed for "other motives" than the ones articulated by the
legislative body.[36] More realistically, however, in the great majority of
substantive due process cases there was simply no evidence of corruption, or even of inappropriate "special privilege." In any event, the
courts did not insist on any. If the special privilege argument is to
survive, it must stand for the proposition that the mere legislative
transfer of wealth through certain devices, such as price regulation,
licensing restrictions, and wage and hour laws, is an impermissible special privilege. But such a statement is supportable only if there is a
theory behind it. Practically every act of government injures one group
of people and benefits another, but the great majority of these acts are
and have been constitutionally valid.

Substantive due process judges believed that certain forced wealth
transfers were economically irrational and harmful, and that corruption
or special privilege might explain why legislatures would pass such
statutes. When courts found explicit evidence that a statute was tainted
by such corruption or privilege, substantive due process permitted them

to strike it down.[37] But the important question for understanding substantive due process is not why the legislatures passed such statutes, but rather why the judiciaries so widely believed legislative wealth transfers in general to be harmful. This question is fundamentally about economic theory, and not merely about imperfections in the legislative process.

Judges of the substantive due process era were neither more "formalist" nor more socially biased than judges are today. Like judges of every era, they drew their wisdom—particularly the wisdom they applied to public law—from outside. To be sure, they operated under rules of form that prevented them from citing this outside wisdom expressly, as judges frequently do today. They simply accepted, and asserted as obvious, doctrine that had become part of the well-established consensus models of other disciplines. In the case of substantive due process, the judges wrote into the Constitution a unique American perspective on economics.

Holmes was right in *Lochner* when he accused the majority of basing its decision on "an economic theory which a large part of the country does not entertain." *Lochner* was supported by American classical political economists, although by 1905 classical political economy was rapidly losing ground to institutional economics and marginal utility theory. More important, classical economics had become largely irrelevant, given the political pressures of the day. The Progressives' rejection of classicism provided the excuse, not the reason, for the passage of reform legislation. But Holmes's accusation that the majority relied on an *obsolete* economic theory is not nearly as important or as interesting as his recognition that it relied on an *economic* theory, whether right or wrong, obsolete or current.

CHAPTER 15

The American School
of Political Economy

Two phenomena distinguished nineteenth-century American political economy from that of Britain. One was the persistence of Scottish Realism, which dominated American intellectual life long after the majority factions in Britain had discarded it in favor of more liberal alternatives. Nineteenth-century American political economists clung to a set of explicitly moral, orthodox Protestant values that the British purported to reject.[1]

The second phenomenon was the premise of unlimited, rapid economic growth, which Malthus, Ricardo, and their successors had abandoned in Britain early in the nineteenth century. It survived in America for another century. Beginning with Malthus in the 1790's, British economists assumed that future economic growth would be slow and painful, particularly in agriculture, that there would be a surplus of labor, and that limitations on the amount of land would permit a small number of people to become wealthy at the expense of the laboring masses. British labor unrest confirmed these fears. By the 1830's England faced a restive labor force and the threat of organized revolt. Real wages in England were widely perceived as falling during the first half of the nineteenth century, even as they were perceived as rising in America. In reaction to these conditions, British political economists came to believe that a certain amount of wealth redistribution, along the lines of the Poor Laws and perhaps even the Factory Acts, would increase social welfare by reducing the threat of costly revolution. Distribution became a major concern in nineteenth-century British political economy.[2]

But in America, even as Malthus was writing, the economy was poised to take off. The new nation's growth potential seemed unlimited. Room for entry into new business was abundant, provided that the sovereign did not create artificial restrictions on entry, such as monopoly franchises or business licensing. Labor was generally perceived to be in short supply. The early American political economist Willard Phillips noted that labor was sufficiently scarce in the United States that apprentices received wages from their masters, while in England they paid their masters.[3] This expansionist view was institutionalized into an "American school" of political economy in the writings of Henry C. Carey,[4] America's greatest antebellum political economist, just as British political economists were beginning to justify radical departures from laissez-faire policy. Carey's view predominated until well into the twentieth century in America. For example, in *Adkins v. Children's Hospital* (1923) Justice Sutherland took judicial notice of the fact that wages in the United States were increasing; as a result, minimum wages laws were bad policy.[5]

The Perception of Unlimited Growth

Many American economists believed that the United States was a superior laboratory for the study of the principles of political economy. As the political economist Jacob Cardozo observed in 1826, America was much closer than Britain to the state of nature. A "country whose institutions and laws have done less to derange the natural order of things than where a vicious social organization has resulted either from military violence or a selfish policy, will present the fairest field for analysis and speculation into the causes of wealth."[6]

Clearly, American and British political economists made widely different assumptions about the nature of things, and these yielded profoundly different views of state polity. The assumptions worked their way into the law. For example, in his small but influential treatise on contracts (1825), Gulian Verplanck argued that Ricardo's observations concerning rents on land created a perception of unequal bargaining position sufficient to justify English judicial interference with private agreements. However, Verplanck opined, in America, with its open, cheap land and easy entry into business, unequal bargaining power almost never existed, and thus seldom relieved parties from the consequences of their agreements. Differences in environment justified a stronger liberty of contract doctrine in America than in England.[7]

Malthus in America

As noted in Chapter 7, Malthus's "iron law" of population supported a very strong version of laissez-faire. Any attempt to interfere with the free market to ease the lot of the poor would only increase the ratio of poor persons to the food supply and productive capital; eventually even more poor people would starve. But most British political economists never took the strictest implications of Malthus's iron law very seriously. The weaker version of his theory, adopted rather early in the nineteenth century, tended to undermine the laissez-faire element in British political economy.

Many Americans accepted the stronger implications of Malthus's theory. At the same time, however, they tended to regard it as inapplicable to America's poor.[8] America's capacity to produce food seemed far greater than any population growth anticipated in the immediate future. Even later in the century, after population growth had outrun most earlier expectations, many American political economists continued to accept the stronger version of Malthus's principle of population, but did not foresee mass starvation. Malthus enjoyed special popularity among America's Social Darwinists, such as the Yale professor William Graham Sumner.[9]

John McVikar, a Federalist follower of Hamilton, was the earliest American political economist who wrote extensively on Malthus. He accepted the stronger version of Malthus's principle in theory, but argued that its applicability to America was several centuries premature, because of the abundance of undeveloped resources. McVikar correctly predicted that there would be labor shortages rather than surpluses for many years to come and argued that anticipated production was much larger than anticipated consumption.[10]

Thomas Cooper, a Jeffersonian Democrat, agreed with McVikar about Malthus, if not about much else. Cooper believed that some prudence was important if food shortages were to be avoided in the future, although he thought the problem was far worse in England than in America. His 1826 *Lectures on the Elements of Political Economy* argued that the "iron law" of Malthus clearly established that the English Poor Laws should be repealed. He would even have abolished public education, except at the elementary level.[11]

American critics of Malthus generally made assumptions about economic growth that far exceeded any made by British classical economists.[12] For example, Jacob Cardozo argued that Malthus had overlooked "the effect of improvements in Agriculture," which tended to undermine his principle of population. Alexander Everett, one of Malthus's most outspoken American critics, argued that when population growth approached the hiring capacity of industry, laborers moved elsewhere, thus spreading economic growth more widely. Everett explained the settlement of the American West in this manner. These observations were of course only relevant in a country with plenty of room for such expansion and where movement was easy. Thomas Jefferson himself had been concerned about the implications of Malthus's theory for America. However, the Louisiana Purchase removed his doubts—the supply of land appeared virtually unlimited.[13]

Henry Carey was one of the few nineteenth-century Americans to observe that the theory of Malthus that population grew geometrically while the food supply grew only arithmetically must be based on empirical observation if on anything at all. Carey's argument displayed a common theme: the contrast of British "speculation" with American "facts," or British "deduction" with the American "Baconian" or inductive method. Carey's "facts" were based on rather casual observations as well. But even in densely populated New England, agricultural productivity had appeared to keep up with or even to surpass population growth. This view that Malthus had simply gotten his numbers wrong prevailed in the United States for the next half century. Even in the 1880's, a few quick calculations by the American Van Buren Denslow revealed that mankind's entire food supply tended to multiply much faster than mankind itself. In all the "bulky volumes written in support" of Malthus, Denslow scoffed, "never has the actual fecundity of a human couple been compared with that of a grain of wheat, a potato, a couple of swine, or a pair of beeves."[14]

The principal difference between Malthus and Carey was context. Malthus looked at London's impoverished masses and saw population constantly pushing against the ability of agriculture and capital to support it. Carey, by contrast, believed that the growth of capital permitted the growth of population. He observed that many parts of the world, such as India and South America, experienced horrible starvation in spite of the fact that plenty of idle, fertile land was available for production. The problem was not lack of land but lack of investment. Free movement of capital permitted population to grow, but it permitted agricultural productivity to grow even faster. As a result, the most developed countries tended to have the must abundant food, regardless of the relation between population and land.[15]

Carey represents unbridled American optimism about the capacity for future growth, against Malthus's dark English pessimism. Both views were inspired by the environments in which these individuals found themselves. Malthus lived in a country where the amount of investment was seen as relatively high, and the amount of available land very low. Carey lived in a country where land was abundant, but which had experienced chronic underinvestment. The solution to the American problem was therefore simple: encourage investment and eliminate all artificial constraints on it. The theory of Carey, Wayland, and other Americans that capital investment permits population growth was optimistic simply because both undeveloped land and the potential for capital investment seemed almost infinite. Such views persisted in America virtually unchanged until the 1880's and 1890's.[16]

Ricardo in America

Ricardo's theory of rents, discussed in Chapter 7, spawned a strenuous reaction to classical laissez-faire political economy in Britain. The theory was that as increasingly marginal land was placed into production, a higher percentage of the price of commodities would go to monopoly profits for landlords, and wages would decline to subsistence levels. In the United States, Ricardo's theory would become the basis of Henry George's "single tax" movement, espoused by some Progressive and socialist politicians at the end of the century.[17] But among Americans, George's application of Ricardo was the exception rather than the rule.

The doctrine of rents in the American "classical" tradition. Ricardo's theory had no significant effect on classical American political economy. Some Americans suggested about Ricardo, as they did about Malthus, that perhaps in some distant future the problem of rents would become significant in the United States. But any American who looked west after 1803 saw a seemingly endless expanse of fertile, untilled land. Its great abundance would keep land prices low for a long time. Rents were not a problem, because land currently brought into production was just as fertile as older land that had been under cultivation for a long time. Classical economists such as Willard Phillips argued that, whatever validity Ricardo's theory might have in Britain, it was of little relevance in the United States, where "a much greater quantity of wheat could be produced . . . without any increase of the expense per bushel in the production."[18]

Other Americans skeptical of Ricardo looked, not at the vast amount of untilled land, but rather at the relative backwardness of American agricultural technology. Increased productivity in the future would certainly undermine the doctrine of rents. In a lengthy attack on Ricardo, Jacob Cardozo argued that rents are much less significant in a world of rapid technological progress than in one where progress has come to an end.[19] Cardozo was optimistic that increased productivity would offset any price increases in food brought about by the employment of less productive land. Ricardo's principal shortcoming, Cardozo argued, was that he neglected to account for government limitations on agricultural production in England, such as the Corn Laws, which reduced incentives for production and led to inflated prices. Only when the *state* prohibits increased production do rents become possible, and then of course the rents on more fertile land will be greater than those on the less fertile.

Henry Carey made the doctrine of rents virtually superfluous in American political economy until the writings of Henry George became popular during the Progressive Era. Carey devoted nearly an entire volume of his *Principles of Political Economy* to the relative value of land, capital, and labor. He believed Ricardo's theory outrageously oversimplified a complicated state of affairs. Carey noted that even identifying the "best" agricultural land is extremely difficult, at least in a developing country. Given equal expenditures of capital and labor, some land will yield more than other land. However, the most productive land may be located far from population centers, may require considerable deforestation, or may lack access to rivers or other forms of transportation. As a result, Carey argued, less fertile land is often placed into production before more fertile land. The choice of which land to place into production at any given time is made by comparing the gain to be produced from that land with the investment that must be made in it. As population centers moved westward, the cost of bringing western land into production would decrease. Francis Wayland agreed, observing that American agricultural efficiency did not increase substantially until the Mississippi Valley was settled in the late eighteenth century. "The result has been, that the western farmers have undersold the farmers of the north and east; and now, but little wheat is raised in any part of New England."[20]

Carey also observed that the productivity of land is a function of the capital invested not only in land but also in labor-saving equipment. As more capital is invested in such equipment, the amount of labor needed to produce a given quantity declines. The relative value of farm land declines as well, for capital investment makes farming possible on a wider variety of land, makes new, more remote land accessible, and increases the amount that can be produced on a given parcel of land. Even Henry Vethake, perhaps Ricardo's most loyal follower among antebellum American political economists, conceded that technological progress tended to reduce rents insofar as it increased agricultural productivity.[21]

Did Ricardo and Carey actually disagree? Perhaps, but for the most part they simply made very different factual assumptions. Both probably would have agreed that capital investment is subject eventually to the law of diminishing returns. Carey assumed, however, that the marginal value of new capital investment was very high. In America, which was relatively undeveloped in the 1830s, Carey's assumption was justified. A new road, canal, or bridge could bring thousands of acres of new land into production.[22] Ricardo assumed a much more developed economy, in which the marginal value of new capital was much lower. He predicted that future increases in productivity would not be substantial.[23] Similarly, Carey assumed the availability of a great deal of land, which would not be significantly less fertile than land already in production once it was cleared and made more accessible. Ricardo, assumed that the best land had all been taken and that any new production must take place on significantly inferior land. Under Carey's assumptions, the optimal state policy was to encourage more development without worrying about distribution, which would take care of itself. Ricardo, placed substantially less value on further development, which he believed would exacerbate the problem of maldistribution of wealth and produce only marginal increases in production.

Rents and the Progressives. Except for the work of Henry George, the orthodox Ricardian doctrine of rents was never influential in the United States, not even in the work of the Progressive Era economists, who rejected much of both the classical and the neoclassical traditions. More conservative turn-of-the-century economists, such as John Bates Clark, generally agreed with the Progressives that Ricardo's theory of land rents had no application in the United States. In *Capital and Its Earnings* (1889),[24] Clark attempted to refute the arguments of the socialist economists by showing that the rents that might be derived from land are in no way different than from those derived from capital in general. For example, the least efficient ship capable of operating in a competitive shipping market will earn no rent, while the more efficient ones will. But new investment will be made only in the more efficient ships—

because capital always goes where the expected rents are the highest. Land, Clark argued, is no exception to this rule. He conceded that land bears certain "natural monopoly" characteristics because it cannot be infinitely reproduced. But these characteristics are insignificant at best, since most of the elements of value in land, such as proximity to transportation, drainage, irrigation, and clearing, are the product of labor and not inherent in the land itself.

A critical difference between the theories of monopoly in the classical tradition and the Progressive Era is that the latter considered capital investment rather than land to be the chief cause of monopoly. American classicists followed the British classical economists in viewing land as the only significant producer of monopoly profits. As a result they tended to believe that monopoly (and the resultant maldistribution of wealth) was not a problem in America because of the abundance of good, available land. "Monopoly" would exist only if the state created it by exclusive franchises or licensing restrictions. Up to the time of the Sherman Antitrust Act in 1890, the word "monopoly" in the United States referred to monopolies created by the sovereign.

When the Progressives began to write, good land was still abundant. Monopoly profits were being earned, not from land, but from railroads, oil, and other forms of industrial development. America's Progressive Era economists, concerned about the effects of monopoly on wages and productivity, focused their attention not on rents in land but rather on industrial monopolies and trusts. For American Progressives, technology, not land, was the producer of subsistence wages and maldistribution of wealth.[25]

For example, Richard T. Ely discussed rents at length in his book on property and contract (1914). The chief rent-producing engine was not land, however, but large concentrations of capital.[26] Ely identified railroads and telegraph companies as the types of property interests that were causing maldistribution of wealth in the United States. Most Progressives shared Ely's view. In the literature of both the populist Granger movement and the Progressive Era, the farmer was the victim, not the cause, of monopoly.[27] The owners of agricultural land were never depicted in American political economy as the rent-stealing monsters that they were in Ricardo's England.

There is an important difference between the British emphasis on monopoly created by land rents and the emerging American concern with monopoly created by capital investment and trusts. Land cannot be reproduced. British neoclassicists such as Alfred Marshall, a contemporary of the American Progressives, continued to assume that the monopoly profits available from land, which was inherently incapable of being increased, were much more problematic than the monopoly profits available from technology, which could be duplicated; they felt the former could only be solved through radical state interference in the market system.[28]

But American Progressives generally believed the "problem of monopoly" created by the trusts could be solved *within* the capitalist system. In fact, the Sherman Antitrust Act of 1890 was dedicated to that proposition. Only the most extreme Progressives proposed the elimination of capitalism as a solution to the trust problem. More moderate Progressives, who were the only ones to achieve substantial political power, sought reform through the antitrust laws. The problem of monopoly created by capital was soluble because it was artificial: Capital itself could be reproduced indefinitely, and only the combinations and conspiracies of investors prevented competition from driving monopoly profits out of the market. American monopoly, when it finally appeared, had a market solution.

Marginalism, Welfare Economics, and the Progressives

The marginalist revolution brought about the end of the classical tradition in British political economy and appeared to undermine most of the classical arguments for laissez-faire as a theory of social welfare. Marginalism, with its much more interventionist view of the state, dominated the thought of the leading political economists in Britain after John Stuart Mill: William Stanley Jevons in the 1870's, Alfred Marshall in the 1890's and after, and Arthur Pigou in the 1920's and 1930's. Each was more interventionist than his predecessor. In 1920, Pigou, professor of political economy at Cambridge, argued that the principal distinction between the wealthy and the working class was that less money had been invested in the productive capacity of the latter. According to the law of diminishing returns, additional investment in development of the poor would produce greater social benefit than would equivalent investment in development of the rich. Pigou's thesis carried an important corollary: a dollar *transferred* from the wealthy to the poor would do more good to the poor transferee than it would do harm to the wealthy transferor. The result was an efficiency argument for graduated income taxes, minimum wage laws, regulation of working conditions and hours, product quality, welfare benefits—in short, for state-enforced wealth transfers.[29]

But the marginalist revolution consisted of two quite distinct parts. One part was the public, or "macro," theory that had the implications for welfare described above. The other was a private, or "micro," theory of individual and firm behavior that employed extraordinarily powerful analytic concepts such as marginal cost and marginal revenue. Marginalism as a theory of firm behavior first appeared in American scholarship shortly before the rise of substantive due process, principally in the work of John Bates Clark. Progressive Era economists such as Ely later adopted the welfare theory of marginalism as a *critique* of the doctrine of substantive due process.

Clark, whose contributions to the theory of marginal utility earned worldwide recognition, was almost as laissez-faire on matters of state policy as were his classical American predecessors. He believed that the concept of marginal cost could teach business firms how to maximize their profits and that, in a competitive market, such profit-maximizing behavior tended to maximize social wealth as well, because each person received an amount precisely equal to his marginal value to someone else. Any state-enforced "adjustment," other than one calculated to eliminate monopoly, would interfere with this goal. Clark's view that each laborer was entitled to his "marginal product" was part of the "free labor" ideology that had dominated American labor policy since the passage of the fourteenth amendment.[30]

The dominant political economy in America in the 1880's and 1890's at the dawn of substantive due process belonged to Clark and the American neoclassicists, not to the much more interventionist British neoclassicists, and certainly not to the Progressives, most of whom had not yet begun to write. Although few of the judges who decided liberty of contract cases were trained as economists, they imbibed the dominant economic thinking of the nineteenth-century American tradition. The judges who developed the doctrine made the unfortunate mistake of attaching themselves to the dominant economic view just as that view was on the verge of falling apart, to be replaced by a more complex, and much more regulatory, economic view of the world.

CHAPTER 16

The Wages Fund

One of the most neglected debates in American intellectual history is the great controversy over the "theory of distribution," or the wage-fund doctrine, that raged in the newly founded academic journals of political economy at the turn of the century. According to the wage-fund doctrine, the aggregate fund available to pay the wages of all laborers in the economy was directly proportional to the aggregate level of capital invested. If wages were larger than the fund, capital would be depleted and eventually become insufficient to pay wages. Further, the amount of capital left for new investment would decline and reduce both output and the demand for labor even further. Most mid-nineteenth-century American classical economists subscribed to the wage-fund theory. When the theory came under attack later in the century, economists entered into an extensive debate over the doctrine.

The implications of the debate were enormous. If the classical wage-fund theory was correct, then there was an absolute limit to the total value of wages that could be paid in any given period. According to the theory, actions designed to increase real wages, such as minimum wage or maximum hours statutes or trade unionism, would undermine economic progress and could only harm the laborers they were designed to benefit. "Liberty of contract"—each wage earner bargaining freely with his employer—was absolutely essential to the welfare, in fact the survival, of both.

The original idea of the wage "fund" is deceptively simple, and explains the attractiveness of the theory to the classicists, who were inclined to see order and pattern in everything. The farmer currently laboring on his plantings must live off that part of last year's crop placed in storage. If he consumes it too early he will not live to bring the new crop to harvest. The moral: the amount available for wages at any given time is a function of that which has already been invested. If the workers take more out than has been put in, they will deplete the amount of invested capital. But if they take less than is put in, the amount invested will grow and the workers will experience increased prosperity. Thus the amount of money available in the economy for the payment of wages at any given time is directly proportional to the amount of capital invested. Also, each worker's share of the fund is inversely proportional to the number in the total working population, because the fund must be divided among them. As William Graham Sumner put it in 1883, "[c]hanges in rates of wages can only be produced by changes in the amount of capital distributable as wages, or by changes in the number of persons competing for wages."[1]

Even though wages in America were relatively high and on the rise, there was a limit beyond which they could not go. Francis Wayland, one of the early American supporters of the doctrine, presented what was to become the standard American perspective:

> The prosperity of a nation does not depend simply upon the *absolute* amount of its capital, but upon the ratio which its capital bears to its population, and the ratio which is maintained between the increase of both. [1] If the increase of capital be so rapid as to allow the simple laborer sufficient wages to support and rear as many children as, under ordinary circumstances, form a human family, there will be no distress in any class . . . . [2] If the increase of capital be more rapid than this, every one will have, beside support and maintenance, many of the conveniences of life; and a large proportion will be continually rising from a lower to a higher grade of employment. [3] When the increase of capital is less rapid than the ordinary increase of the human race, there will be, in the lowest class, continual distress; children will die in great numbers; the average duration of human life will be shortened; and many persons will be sinking from the higher, into the lower grades of employment and comfort.[2]

America, Wayland believed, fell within the second category.

It is not easy for someone trained in the economics of twentieth-century marginalism to picture the wage-fund doctrine, or to appreciate how powerful the idea was during the classical period. The wage-fund idea is distinctively "premarginalist," and could only come out of a model in which average rather than marginal costs and benefits govern production decisions. Average costs and benefits are those that have already been incurred; marginal costs and benefits are those that are currently anticipated. Under the wage-fund doctrine, the amount available for wages is a function of *previously* invested capital, rather than of current productivity. William Graham Sumner, one of the staunchest American supporters of the classical wage-fund doctrine in the late nineteenth century, ridiculed emerging marginalism for suggesting "that a man who was tilling the ground in June could eat the crop he expected to have in September, or that a tailor could be wearing the coat which he was making."[3]

For those who believed in the wage-fund doctrine, "artificial" wage increases above the value of labor—such as might result from minimum wage laws or the bargaining power of labor unions—had disastrous implications. First, since more capital would be invested in wages, less would be left for capital improvements. Second, higher wages would increase the price of goods, reducing demand below the level set by the invisible hand, and ultimately decreasing the demand for labor. Production would decline, and the smaller profit per unit accompanying the higher wages would further reduce investment in capital improvements. This would lead to a vicious cycle: the amount of production would become ever smaller in relation to the population; economic development would grind to a halt or slow dramatically; and the working population would face the prospect of massive unemployment and starvation, until their numbers were reduced substantially or wages were driven back down to a level commensurate with the "fund." A. L. Perry's popular *Elements of Political Economy* (1866) described the wage-fund theory as an inexorable law of nature:

> That which pays for labor in every country, is a certain portion of actually accumulated capital, which cannot be increased by the proposed action of government, nor by the influence of public opinion, nor by combinations among the workmen themselves. There is also in every country a certain number of laborers, and this number cannot be diminished by the proposed action of government, nor by public opinion, nor by combinations among themselves. There is to be a division now among all these laborers of the portion of capital actually there present.[4]

The implications of the wage-fund doctrine cannot be overstated. *Any* forced wealth transfer from capitalists to laborers would upset the equilibrium and spell disaster for the laborer. For those who believed in the wage-fund doctrine, labor unions, minimum wage laws, and graduated income taxes were all bad. More important, the true believer could

196 · SUBSTANTIVE DUE PROCESS

think that they were bad because they were contrary to the laborer's own best interests.

The wage-fund doctrine was popular in Britain in the early nineteenth century.[5] John Stuart Mill repudiated it in 1869 (late in life, however), as did 1870's marginalists such as William Jevons and 1890's neoclassicists such as Alfred Marshall.[6] The doctrine persisted in the United States until much later. Prominent mid-century political economists such as Francis Wayland and A. L. Perry embraced it as an article of faith. It had also been accepted in various forms by earlier American political economists such as Jacob Cardozo, Samuel Newman, Willard Phillips, Henry Vethake, and above all, Henry Carey. Silas M. MacVane, the most influential member of Harvard's economics department in the Gilded Age, adhered to the doctrine in his popular textbook published in 1890. The neoclassicist Frank W. Taussig accepted a version of it in the 1890's, as did William Graham Sumner and the well-known lawyer Henry T. Terry.[7]

That Americans subscribed to the wage-fund theory so long after the British mainstream had rejected it is perplexing. The best answer is that in the United States, where economic growth was rapid and the fund appeared to be growing and making each generation of American laborers better off than the preceding one, the theory was far less brutal than it was in England. One could accept the wage-fund theory in the United States without accepting starvation as a corollary. For example, Henry Carey's version of the wage-fund theory was much more optimistic than the classical wage-fund theory. Carey did believe that the fund that could be set aside for wages was limited at any given time by the amount of invested capital.[8] But he also strongly believed that, when one allowed for economic growth, wages would increase more quickly than capital increased. Assuming rapid economic growth, rapid growth of invested capital, and a relative shortage of laborers— actual conditions in nineteenth-century America—one could have both the wage-fund doctrine and labor prosperity.

No method existed to test the wage-fund doctrine empirically. It was accepted or rejected principally for ideological reasons. Those who accepted the theory regarded it as "proof" of the disastrous consequences that would attend minimum wage laws, maximum hours laws, or effective union organization. A renewed assertion of the wage-fund theory in the United States at the end of the nineteenth century provoked the largest single debate in America's first economics journal, the *Quarterly Journal of Economics,* during its first two decades of publication.

The story actually began in 1875, when the revisionist economist Francis "General" Walker, president of the Massachusetts Institute of Technology, wrote an article attacking the wage-fund theory.[9] Walker suggested that the value of wages is determined not by the amount of previously invested capital but by workers' current productivity. A decade later, Walker began developing his own theory of wages, suggesting that optimal wages should equal the workers' productivity, and that many workers were in fact paid far less than they produced for their employers. This perspective inspired Walker to become a supporter of the growing American labor movement.[10] The theoretical battle between neoclassical and Progressive economists was joined.

The following decade saw an outpouring of scholarship on the "distribution question," or the notion that there was an absolute limit to the workers' share of industrial productivity.[11] Richard T. Ely and other Progressives such as Stuart Wood scoffed at the idea that there was a fixed ratio between capital and wages.[12] The neoclassicist John Bates Clark eventually rejected the wage-fund theory in favor of a marginal productivity standard.[13] But unlike the Progressives, he continued to oppose labor unions and government employment regulation.

One fact not widely appreciated is that even liberal American political economists were not generally supportive of wage and hour legislation until after the turn of the century. For example, even in 1898 Henry George believed that the natural law of wages was so absolute that any attempt to regulate them would be disastrous. In *Progress and Poverty* (1879),[14] George's most popular and most radical work, he devoted two chapters to disproving the wage-fund doctrine. But in its place he substituted his own iron law that the fund for the payment of wages is determined by the "margin of cultivation," or the difference between the cost of cultivation and the market price of the poorest land currently in production. Wages, he said, will tend to be high in new countries where plenty of fertile land is still available. No one will accept low wages "when he can go upon the next quarter section and take up a farm for himself." Only when "land becomes monopolized and these natural opportunities are shut off from labor" are wages reduced to a subsistence level. George's argument had great success and influence in the late nineteenth century. The point seemed straight forward: as long as land was readily available and cheap, wages would have to be at least as high as the return from farming, because any laborer asked to work for less would farm instead.

After the turn of the century nearly every economist of any repute rejected the wage-fund doctrine in favor of some kind of marginal productivity theory of wages. But some judges continued the wage-fund debate until much later. For example, in *Adkins v. Children's Hospital* (1923) Justice Sutherland observed that a statute that raised wages without raising the amount or the productive efficiency of invested capital addressed only half the problem of labor: "[I]n practice the former half without the latter must lead to ultimate failure, in accordance with the inexorable law that no one can continue indefinitely to take out more than he puts in without ultimately exhausting the supply."[15] This was as orthodox a statement of the wage-fund doctrine as could be found in any nineteenth-century manual of political economy.

CHAPTER 17

Market Failure and
the Constitution

The substantive due process courts upheld more regulatory statutes than they struck down.[1] Both the Supreme Court and state courts purported to defer to the wisdom of legislators in most areas of economic regulation. To be sure, critics frequently have accused the Supreme Court of substituting its own judgment for that of legislators.[2] In *Lochner,* Justice Peckham wrote: "This is not a question of substituting the judgment of the court for that of the legislature. If the act be within the power of the State it is valid, although the judgment of the court might be totally opposed to the enactment of such a law."[3] Immediately after, of course, Justice Peckham did appear to substitute the judgment of the Supreme Court for that of the legislature, and found the statute invalid.

But the Court was not as iconoclastic as a first glance suggests. In general, the Court presumed constitutionality. That presumption could be defeated if the legislation at issue appeared to interfere with a right guaranteed by the fourteenth amendment—which encompassed the rights of each seller of property or labor to set his own price, and of each property owner or laborer to receive fair market value in exchange. If a statute was deemed to interfere substantially with one of these marketplace rights, then it would be upheld only if the regulation were justified by a strong public interest. In the words of the Supreme Court, economic regulations would be upheld only if they applied to property "affected with the public interest."[4]

The Court made clear that identifying property "affected with the public interest" was a judicial rather than a legislative prerogative. "[T]he mere declaration by the legislature that a particular kind of property or business is affected with a public interest is not conclusive . . . . The matter is one which is always open to judicial inquiry." Nonetheless, judges had no fixed idea about what to look for. Justice Felix Frankfurter later opined that affectation with the public interest was an "empty formula," and Holmes confessed that he regarded it as "little more than a fiction."[5] Even Thomas M. Cooley, who was as instrumental as anyone in developing substantive due process, admitted that "[w]hat circumstances shall affect property with a public interest is not very clear." The fact that the public is benefited by a business is insufficient; such a rule "would subject the stock of the merchant, and his charges, to public regulation." Cooley urged reliance on classical political economy. His short list of property affected with the public interest included: (1) facilities controlled by the government; (2) monopolies, including strategically located facilities such as the grain elevators in *Munn,* which could take toll from all who pass; (3) businesses traditionally permitted only by franchise from the state; (4) businesses that receive special assistance from the state; (5) businesses subject to exclusive privileges granted by the state; and (6) businesses whose regulation is clearly compelled by public safety. In all other business, most forms of economic regulation should be deemed improper. The Supreme Court eventually adopted a position similar to Cooley's. Economic regulation was legitimate only if the regulated firm operated under a special franchise, was traditionally in a market subject to economic regulation, or had experienced a change in character that compelled public regulation.[6]

The narrow limits of economic regulation under substantive due process analysis are best explained by the narrowness of the concept of market failure in classical political economy. By the time of John Stuart Mill, classicism had already developed a fairly sophisticated doctrine of "externalities," which referred to circumstances in which private bargaining could not be trusted to secure the best interests of society, because the agreements affected people who were not privy to the negotiations. For the British classicists, the scope of the doctrine was narrow. Mill included lighthouses, scientific exploration, and scholarship among the markets in which competition would not yield the proper amount or price of service. Nothing resembling the modern theory of private, regulated industry emerged in his thinking.[7]

The doctrine of externalities was most fully developed by the British marginalists after the turn of the century, principally by Arthur Cecil Pigou of Cambridge. In 1912, Pigou published *Wealth and Welfare,* which he subsequently enlarged and reissued in 1920 as *The Economics of Welfare.* Pigou observed that certain transactions create a "divergence between social and private net product"—something that later generations of economists would call the problem of "social cost." This divergence occurs when "A, in the course of rendering some service, for which payment is made, to a second person B, incidentally also renders services or disservices to other persons . . . of such a sort that payment cannot be exacted from the benefitted parties or compensation enforced on behalf of the injured parties." The problems that result cannot be solved "by a modification of the contractual relation between any two contracting parties, because the [problem] arises out of a . . . disservice rendered to persons other than the contracting parties." The obvious solution was for the state to intervene through regulatory legislation to protect third-party interests.[8]

Both Cooley and the Supreme Court read into substantive due process doctrine a theory of externalities much like Pigou's. The Court approved regulatory legislation if it was convinced that market exchanges produced negative externalities for which the bargaining parties would not account. Justice Stone explained it this way in 1927: "The constitutional theory that prices normally may not be regulated rests upon the assumption that the public interest and private right are both adequately protected when there is "free" competition among buyers and sellers, and that in such a state of economic society, the interference with so important an incident of the ownership of private property as price fixing is not justified and hence is a taking of property without due process of law."[9] In order to justify state regulation, its proponents had to show a substantial divergence between "the public interest and private right"—a legal concept similar to Pigou's "divergence between social and private net product."

This doctrine of externalities led the Supreme Court to its decisions that struck down regulatory legislation as well as those that upheld statutes where qualifying externalities were found. It also explains why the Court generally refused to tolerate inequality of bargaining power as a qualifying public interest. Inequality of bargaining power between capitalists and laborers affected the distribution of wealth *between* the bargaining parties, but the Court saw no effect on anyone else. For example, Justice Peckham held that the bakers' hours statute in *Lochner* (1905) must fall unless the plaintiffs could show a relationship between the number of hours a baker works and the "healthful quality" of the bread he produces. The mere fact that long hours of work were bad for the bakers, who were adults capable of protecting themselves, was insufficient to justify the regulation: "The law must be upheld, if at all, as a law pertaining to the health of the individual engaged in the occupation of a baker. It does not affect any other portion of the public than those who are engaged in that occupation. Clean and wholesome bread does not depend upon whether the baker works but ten hours per day or only sixty hours a week . . . ."[10]

In *Muller v. Oregon* (1908), Louis Brandeis, then an attorney arguing before the Court, convinced the Supreme Court that the labor of women was subject to externalities that did not apply to the labor of men. This argument saved the women's ten-hour statute from almost certain invalidation, given the decision three years earlier in *Lochner*. Muller's famous "Brandeis Brief" of social science data about the legal and employment status of women was designed to convince the Court that the legislature acted reasonably in passing its statute. The brief itself was an odd assortment of information disguising a brilliant rhetorical agenda. The brief quoted from domestic and foreign statutes, tracts, writings of clergymen, and reports of regulatory agencies. Most of this was not "social science" data at all, at least not as we understand that term today. Many of the reports Brandeis quoted were purely anecdotal or polemic. Brandeis himself was careful not to use the term "social science." Rather, the brief contained a record of "the world's experience upon which the legislation limiting the hours of labor for women is based." The "world's experience" turned out to be that women had less endurance than men, that their reproductive systems were more easily damaged, and that they had less capacity than men to enter into sound business agreements that adequately protected their own interests.[11]

Most important, Brandeis suggested that women, in bargaining with their employers, would not protect every interest that society believed needed protection. "'It is well known that like begets like,' and if the parents are feeble in constitution, the children must also inevitably be feeble." Furthermore, young working women could not be trusted to protect society's interests in the reproduction of healthy offspring. "The object of [women's hours legislation] is the protection of the physical well-being of the community by setting a limit to the exploitation of the improvident, unworkmanlike, unorganized women who are yet the mothers, actual or prospective, of the coming generation."[12]

The sentiments were outrageously Spencerian. Brandeis relied on the fact that a woman's reproductive capacity had always given her a special position at common law, justifying substantial regulation of the health of the unborn. This argument probably saved the women's maximum hours statute. It certainly received all the attention of the Supreme Court. A woman, as distinct from a man, "becomes an object of public interest and care in order to preserve the strength and vigor of the race." As a result, a woman may be "properly placed in a class by herself, and legislation designed for her protection may be sustained, even when like legislation is not necessary for men and could not be sustained."[13]

A concept of externalities also explains the Supreme Court's seemingly odd defections from liberty of contract in the land-use cases, where it consistently upheld intensive regulation that interfered with the free market for land. Four years after he wrote the opinion of the Court in *Lochner,* Justice Peckham wrote the majority opinion in *Welch v. Swasey* (1909), which upheld a statute limiting the heights of buildings in Boston. And three years after he wrote the majority opinion in *Adkins,* Justice Sutherland wrote the majority opinion in *Village of Euclid v. Amber Realty Co.* (1926), which upheld comprehensive land-use planning—a far more interventionist form of regulation than anything the Court had encountered before.[14]

The Supreme Court's land-use opinions are filled with citations of possible externalities justifying state intrusion. In *Welch,* Justice Peckham cited evidence that the danger of fire was greater with respect to tall buildings than with respect to shorter ones, but that the commercial area, where taller buildings were permitted, was both closer to a supply of water and less likely to be filled with women and children who would be endangered. In *Euclid,* as well, Justice Sutherland cited a large number of externalities:

> promotion of the health and security from injury of children and others by separating dwelling houses from territory devoted to trade and industry; suppression and prevention of disorder; facilitating the extinguishment of fires, and the enforcement of street traffic regulations and other general welfare ordinances; aiding the health and safety of the community by excluding from residential areas the confusion and danger of fire, contagion and disorder which in greater or less degree attach to the location of stores, shops and factories. Another ground is that the construction and repair of streets may be rendered easier and less expensive by confining the greater part of the heavy traffic to the streets where business is carried on.

All of Sutherland's examples shared one attribute: they were based on the recognition that, because individual parcels are so dependent on the whole, a municipality is composed just as much of "commons" as of individually owned property. A single builder would not consider the costs imposed by the increased risk of fire or the increased traffic caused by his own structure, because he would have to bear only a tiny fraction of those costs. As a result, one could expect more than the optimal amount of construction. Indeed, high density in relation to the risk of fire was an important justification for municipal zoning.[15]

The economic antecedents to the Court's land-use cases are explicit in the work of Pigou, who had recognized land use as presenting a problem of externalities prior to the Court's decision in *Euclid*. Externalities arise, for example, "when the owner of a site in a residential quarter of a city builds a factory there and so destroys a great part of the amenities of the neighboring sites." Pigou concluded that the municipal power to control the density and type of construction was virtually "an axiom of government."[16]

The courts of the substantive due process era were guided by prevailing scientific doctrines much as courts are today. They took the law for what it was, a human creation and an intellectual activity, never able to transcend the worldview in which it was formed. Judges trained in the classical tradition of political economy carried that intellectual baggage into their chambers. In the case of substantive due process, they carried American writers' unique perspective on political economy, which for them defined both the content of the property rights protected by the Constitution and the limits of the state's power to interfere. When the dominant American economic ideology changed—not until the first three decades of the twentieth century—the legal ideology followed close behind.

PART V

THE LABOR COMBINATION
IN AMERICAN LAW

CHAPTER 18

Classical Theory and
the Labor Cartel

The Conspiracy Theory of Labor Organization

One of the most successful union-busting devices in nineteenth-century America was the law of labor combinations, which was often employed to restrain labor strikes, picketing, boycotts, or demands for closed shops. The law held, quite simply, that although labor organizing was not illegal per se, many union activities were illegal under the common law of torts or trade restraints. After 1890 many organized labor activities were declared unlawful under section 1 of the Sherman Antitrust Act, which condemned contracts, combinations, or conspiracies in restraint of trade. Some strikes in the railroad industry were additionally condemned under the Interstate Commerce Act of 1887, and a few were enjoined directly under the commerce clause itself, under the theory that the federal government had the power to keep interstate commerce flowing smoothly.[1] Early in the twentieth century the list of forbidden labor activities grew dramatically larger, until even nonviolent strikes became illegal.

The increased judicial hostility toward organized labor at the turn of the century may have a number of explanations. As Holmes suggested in 1897,[2] socialism appeared to many conservatives to be a more serious threat than it had been before, and that perception may have influenced judicial thinking. The unionization movement was associated with socialist and Marxist ideas. Further, after the Civil War strikes by organized labor became both more frequent and more violent than they had been before. Even Progressives like Jane Addams, the founder of Hull House, were shocked by the extent of labor union violence, and popularizers such as the detective Allan Pinkerton drew colorful pictures of union corruption, violence, and even murder. The development of the unions was symbolic of an increasing restiveness in American society and—perhaps even more threatening —growing pluralism. A common perception was that the unions were filled with foreigners, who were thought to be less committed to American democratic values and more willing to trade them away for a bigger piece of the pie.[3] In addition, several writers have suggested that American public law in general during this age of legal "formalism" had a policy agenda that favored big business. This thesis has been explicitly applied to the judiciary's treatment of organized labor during the same period.[4]

This chapter argues that changing attitudes toward labor law in the late nineteenth century reflected changing views of political economy. Far from being aligned with big business, the courts applied the same stricter standards to business and labor alike, although the consequences for labor were more devastating. During the late nineteenth century American political economy began to develop an increased sensitivity to the dangers of collusion of various kinds. These new economic ideas quickly entered the law of combinations in restraint of trade, both of labor and of capital.

During most of the nineteenth century British law was more tolerant of labor organizing than American law was. This had not always been so. Labor combinations in Britain had once been illegal per se. During the eighteenth and early nineteenth centuries Britain passed a series of Combination Acts, which prohibited two or more employees acting in concert from withholding their labor until they received higher wages. The British Combination Acts, which were substantially repealed in the 1820's, may have done no more than codify a hostility toward labor organizations in the earlier common law, thus justifying a few early American courts in concluding that the combinations were illegal under received common law. Under the Combination Acts, the strikers did not need to engage in some independently unlawful act, such as violence directed against nonparticipants. Nor did it matter that it was perfectly legal for an individual acting alone to refuse to work unless his wages were increased. The mere fact of a "conspiracy" was sufficient to condemn a joint refusal to work.[5]

During the first decades of the nineteenth century American courts toyed with such a "conspiracy" theory of labor organizing. Whether

American courts ever adopted such a conspiracy theory is doubtful. Only a small handful of American antebellum decisions involved the conspiracy doctrine per se—that is, a mere combination and strike for the purpose of raising wages, with no coercive activity directed at others. It appears that no American case before the late nineteenth century condemned laborers for the simple act of combining in order to increase wages.[6]

In *Commonwealth v. Hunt,* certainly the most important American labor combination case of the first half of the nineteenth century, Chief Justice Lemuel Shaw of the Massachusetts Supreme Judicial Court effectively laid to rest the American labor conspiracy doctrine, if there had ever been one. His court held that a combination of laborers was not unlawful unless the thing they were seeking was unlawful or unlawful means were employed in attaining it. The important but unstated corollary was that the conspiracy itself was all but irrelevant. Judicial acceptance of this principle marks the emergence of what one might call the "tort" theory of labor activity. If a striking labor union member should use violence against the employer or against a worker who failed to participate in the strike, the violence itself was an illegal tort whether or not it was carried out as part of a conspiracy. The "conspiracy," or agreement, was not itself illegal, although it might be used to determine who could be held accountable for independently illegal acts. In 1867, twenty years after *Hunt,* the Supreme Judicial Court of Massachusetts held that a plaintiff could not complain about the mere fact of a union "conspiracy" to seek higher wages. It could enjoin the violent, illegal acts of those involved; however, "the averment that [these] acts were done in pursuance of a conspiracy does not change the nature of the action."[7]

The rejection of any conspiracy theory of labor organizing and the adoption of the tort theory made the law of labor activities more consistent with the law of criminal conspiracies in general. Under the common law a conspiracy—an agreement among people to do something—was not illegal unless the planned activity was illegal. The doctrine of conspiracy could be used for two purposes. First, it might enable a court to reach unconsummated illegal activity: conspiring to rob a store was illegal even though the conspiring members had not yet robbed it. Second, it might enable the court to punish people who had not actually performed the illegal act, but who had been part of the conspiracy to commit it. For example, a court might apply common law conspiracy principles to hold union officers answerable even though they themselves had committed no illegal acts of violence.[8]

American courts operating under the tort theory did not often consider that certain activities might become socially or economically threatening merely because they were carried on by groups of people acting in concert. As a British court held in the 1840's, for one patron to heckle an actor and injure him was perfectly legal, but for a group acting in concert to heckle him was far more harmful and deserved condemnation.[9] Likewise, a single railroad worker's threat to quit his job unless his wages were raised would have little impact on the free flow of goods in interstate commerce. But if all the workers on one or more railroads withheld their labor until they received a wage increase, then the injury to interstate commerce might become significant. During the late nineteenth century political economists began rethinking this problem of combinations. One result was the emergence of an economic theory that explained how concerted activity could be harmful, simply because it was carried out by a group that collectively dominated some market. The developing theory of combinations was applied first to manufacturer cartels and other kinds of producer combinations. Soon it was applied to labor combinations as well.

The issue of manufacturer combinations was complicated by the fact that many of them appeared to realize great efficiencies, such as economies of scale, even as they threatened monopoly. For this reason economic and legal policy from about 1890 to about 1920 was ambiguous and dominated by a debate among economists and lawyers over the relative social good and evil caused by business cartels. No one knew precisely when to condemn combinations, for no one knew when the monopolistic effects of price fixing tended to outweigh the advantages of scale economies.

But labor combinations enjoyed the benefit of no such ambiguity. Considered in entrepreneurial terms, combinations of people produced no economies of scale but only instability and inefficiency. Under the developing model of combinations in restraint of trade, labor combinations were perceived simply as anticompetitive, with few offsetting social benefits.

When American law treatise writers and later American courts began to view strikes as a problem of large numbers, or market dominance, rather than merely a threat of extrinsic illegal activities, the conspiracy theory of labor began to find a new place in the law. As Frederick H. Cooke observed in 1909, "[c]omparatively recently has sprung into recognition the doctrine that an act, entirely lawful if done by a single individual, may be unlawful by reason of being done in pursuance of a combination . . . ." The oldest case Cooke cited for that proposition was an 1893 federal decision condemning a train engineer for abandoning his train as part of a labor conspiracy.[10]

Combinations of Labor in the Treatise Tradition

Anyone who reads the labor law literature of the late nineteenth century is struck by the similarity of treatment that the treatise writers accorded combinations of laborers and combinations of producers or sellers. Frederick Cooke observed that "[o]n principle, it is not apparent why the legality of combinations among employees as such, should be subjected to any different test from that applied to combinations among employers as such, or among tradesmen as such." Several treatises were published between 1880 and 1910 with titles similar to that of Cooke's *The Law of Combinations, Monopolies, and Labor Unions*—each suggesting that the law in these areas was similar enough to justify combined treatment.[11]

Some courts drew the same analogy. Around 1890 courts gradually began to adopt the theory that labor was a commodity and that the "labor and skill of the workman" and the "plant of the manufacturer" were all equally "property," to which the same set of legal rules should apply.[12] But the standards that courts applied to combinations of labor were actually much different from those that applied to combinations of capital, and many legal writers at the turn of the century found the differences irrational. Most of the treatise authors believed that the law was unreasonably kind to combinations of labor. Today we think of Gilded Age labor law as hostile toward unions, largely on the basis of historical writing about the labor movement as well as about constitutional doctrines such as substantive due process, under which courts struck down protective wage and hour legislation. Our view of the labor law of the period is reinforced by a Progressive social literature and history that contrasts the fortunes of the great capitalist entrepreneurs with the poverty of urban workers and their slums.[13] The law of the Gilded Age and Progressive Era also appears extremely hostile toward labor when it is contrasted with the labor policy of the New Deal, which laid the groundwork for our modern labor legislation.

But this was hardly the view of the elite bar, as represented in the treatise tradition at the turn of the century. Almost unanimously its members believed that the courts had come to view combinations of labor more favorably than business combinations. Writing in 1901,

Arthur Eddy concluded his two-volume treatise on combinations of labor and capital by observing that the public policy respecting labor combinations ought to be the same as the policy concerning cartels. Prices are based on costs, he argued, and cost consists of "Labor, represented by wages . . . ," and "Capital, represented by the material consumed and depreciation of plant, machinery, tools, etc." Since the "object of decisions and laws against combinations" is "to protect the consumer against maintenance of price at abnormal levels, it would naturally be supposed that both laws and decisions would be directed impartially against combinations of both labor and capital," for "a combination of one may affect prices in exactly the same way as a combination of the other." But, Eddy lamented, the law was not so. On the one hand, "[c]ombinations of labor to restrict production by shortening hours, or to advance wages, are legal." On the other, "[c]ombinations of capital to restrict production in any manner, or control prices, are illegal." In fact, under the developing federal antitrust case law such business combinations were a misdemeanor punishable by fine or imprisonment. "The manifest injustice, not to say absurdity, of this condition of things appeals to every fair-minded man," Eddy concluded.[14] Eddy's sense of justice and fair play would not be violated for long. Even as he was writing the federal courts were beginning to deploy the Sherman Act as a savage weapon against labor combinations.

Eddy never articulated the concern that would become prominent in Progressive Era labor literature and the labor law of the New Deal: the welfare of the worker. Both the rise of the social sciences and the development of substantive due process, widely perceived by Progressives to be antilabor, inspired public-spirited liberals in the 1890's and after to begin assembling data documenting the plight of the American factory worker. State bureaus of labor statistics collected an array of information about working conditions in America. For example, the 1899 report of the New York bureau included 550 pages of data about the economic condition of workers, 55 pages of data about their wages, and more than 600 pages about worker accidents and compensation. Even for Progressives not directly involved in law or legislation, exposing the poverty of the urban working class became a social, religious, and even artistic mission. The result was that most liberals emerged from the Progressive Era with a view of the "balance of power" between labor and capital very different from that held by elite lawyers such as Arthur Eddy at the turn of the century.[15]

The emerging view was that jobs were scarce and laborers were available in virtually unlimited number, so that they even fought one another for the opportunity to work. Employers could get away with paying pitiful wages and forcing workers to put in long hours under unconscionable conditions. Even "good" entrepreneurs were forced to set the same policies, because they had to compete with others who were less solicitous of the conditions of labor.[16] The worker had no bargaining power.

Unions took a number of approaches to this changing situation. First, they looked for ways to limit the supply of labor in their particular areas of enterprise. Trade unions sometimes tried to perpetuate artificial shortages by restricting the number of apprentices. They also lobbied hard for reduction in the number of immigrants coming into the United States. With the advent of the closed shop they looked for ways to limit union membership itself. Race discrimination was one of the most popular, and substantially reduced the participation of Americans of color in many trades.[17] Finally the unions sought special protection, such as statutory controls of hours, working conditions, and minimum wages, from the state.

But the treatise writers of the turn of the century did not see the balance of power as the Progressives saw it. They tended to view capital and labor as more or less equally balanced. In fact, the advantage, if there was one, lay with labor. Historically, they were generally right. Throughout the eighteenth and nineteenth centuries America suffered from chronic, dramatic labor shortages, at least in the West. The shortages were so substantial that they accounted for such phenomena as slavery in the United States, long after other Western nations had abandoned it. They also explain American entrepreneurs' leadership in the development of labor-saving technology,[18] America's open immigration policy, the importation of Chinese workers to build railroads, and the relative quiet of American labor at a time when England was experiencing substantial unrest. The shortages also explain why real wages in the United States were perceived as rising steadily through most of the nineteenth century, why they were higher than wages in Europe, and why working conditions were generally better. All these facts were well known to political economists by the turn of the century.[19]

Equally important was the perception of easy mobility that dominated most of the nineteenth century: any American laborer who wished could save a little money, borrow from others, and become an entrepreneur himself. As Theodore Sedgwick had already observed in 1836, in New England laborers were able to "lay up half their wages" until within a few years they could either "settle as farmers in the new states" or "undertake an independent business in the old." By contrast, "[i]n Europe, the common rule is, once a servant, always a servant; once a mechanic, always a mechanic; once a tenant, always a tenant; . . ." This apparent combination of labor shortage and easy exit created the perception that laborers in the United States had a bargaining position of some strength.[20] They, not the employers, could make "take it or leave it" offers.

The best support for Eddy's position came from the industry in which Gilded Age labor activity was most visible: the railroads. Since the 1870's the railroads had been plagued with a series of strikes, many of them violent, even as railroad executives were complaining about severe labor shortages. In earlier strikes organizational power rather than higher wages had most often been the main issue. In fact, the railroad labor situation was complex. In railway construction, particularly in the West, the labor shortages were severe. But in railway operation, which was far less labor intensive, a more ample supply of workers was available, especially for unskilled jobs, and in parts of the East there was even a surplus. Nonetheless, two stories dominated the public's perception of railway labor at least until the 1890's: first, the railroads were always looking for laborers on the "frontier," where construction was going on; second, the workers were constantly going on strike and threatening to shut down America's largest and most important industrial system.[21]

Competition, Combination, and Labor in the Gilded Age

Combinations in Restraint of Trade

Price fixing was generally legal under both British and American common law during most of the nineteenth century. The general rule of the common law was that agreements to fix prices were in restraint of trade, and as a result they could not be enforced in court. However, neither could they be challenged by third parties or the state.[22] Failure to appreciate the distinction between illegality and unenforceability explains why some scholars incorrectly concluded that price fixing was illegal. For example, in his article "Trade Combinations at Common Law," written to show that the Sherman Act merely enacted the common law, Frank J. Goodnow tried to establish that price fixing had always been illegal. But the cases he cited held only that one party to a price-fixing agreement could not enforce it against another party.[23] Arthur

Eddy found no case in which a combination in restraint of trade that made no attempt to coerce the activities of others was actionable by an outsider. In his well-known *Addyston Pipe* antitrust decision, discussed in Chapter 21, Judge Taft similarly acknowledged that "contracts that were in unreasonable restraint of trade at common law were not unlawful in the sense of being criminal" or tortious. Rather, they "were simply void, and were not enforced by the courts." The Sherman Act made the unenforceable contract in restraint of trade at common law positively illegal and challengeable by the government or third parties.[24] In this important respect, the Sherman Act did much more than merely "enact" the common law of trade restraints.

But the common law distinguished between agreements among sellers to charge higher prices and concerted *pressure* put on unwilling outsiders to participate or not to compete with the cartel. Such "boycotts" were almost uniformly considered not merely unenforceable but tortious or even criminal. As many courts put it, one had a right to control one's own price and output offerings and even to do this by agreement with others. But one did not have a right to exclude others from the market or force them to make decisions that they believed were contrary to their own economic interests. If the combination used its power "to coerce and intimidate third parties," then their actions were tortious against the third parties. Arthur Eddy examined the case law on the distinction between legal and illegal cartelization by considering the nature of the injury suffered by competitors at the hands of the combination. If that injury was caused by otherwise legitimate competition—for example, if the combination was able to charge a lower price or attain more uniformity in marketing—then competitors might certainly be injured but their injuries were not actionable. This conclusion flowed from the general common law proposition accepted in the late nineteenth century that although "competition" per se injures those who must lower their prices or go out of business, such injury is *damnum absque injuria*.[25]

Some kinds of injuries caused by cartels seemed to fall ambiguously between the coercive and the noncoercive. For example, Eddy agreed with the decision in *Bohn Manufacturing Co.* (1893) that an agreement among dealers not to purchase from a manufacturer who dealt directly with the public was legal. In this case the dealers were almost certainly fixing retail prices, and some manufacturers were attempting to avoid this cartel by selling at retail directly. But any person acting alone had the right to purchase or refuse to purchase from whom he pleased; as a result, the fact that they conspired with one another to do so could not make the conduct illegal. The court in *Bohn Manufacturing* observed that "[w]hat one man may lawfully do singly, two or more may lawfully agree to do jointly. The number who united to do the act cannot change its character from lawful to unlawful." A generation later the United States Supreme Court condemned an identical concerted refusal to deal under the antitrust laws, in a clear extension of the Sherman Act beyond the common law.[26]

Labor organizing and even simple strikes for higher wages were also generally legal. Like producer cartels, labor cartels crossed the line into illegality only when they committed some act that would have been illegal even had a single person done it unilaterally—such as forcing an unwilling person to participate in a cartel through intimidation or violence. For example, *People v. Fisher* (1835), sometimes cited for the proposition that agreements among laborers to insist on higher wages were illegal, was in fact an indictment alleging that a group of journeymen shoemakers conspired "to prevent any journeyman boot and shoemaker in the village of Geneva from working his trade and occupation below certain rates and prices prescribed by the defendants." The court condemned the coercion directed at others, not the price-fixing agreement among the defendants. "If the defendants cannot make coarse boots for less than one dollar per pair, let them refuse to do so; but let them not directly or indirectly undertake to say that others shall not work for a less price."[27]

Toward the end of the nineteenth century judicial hostility toward producer or seller cartels grew enormously. Courts also became much more hostile toward labor combinations. The result was the revitalization of the conspiracy doctrine in both areas. But the consequences proved to be much more severe for labor organizations than for combinations of capital.

Combinations and the Theory of Competition

Combinations and the competition model at common law. Classical political economy contained nothing like the modern theory of competition until late in the nineteenth century. "Competition" referred loosely to rivalry. There was little perception of the effect of competition upon price and output in a given market—certainly little perception that classical political economy was capable of formulating in any rigorous way. Alfred Marshall's *Principles of Economics* (1890) was the first economics treatise to incorporate terms such as elasticity of demand and marginal revenue in a way that permitted technical descriptions of price and output under competition and monopoly. After that, the classical model of "perfect competition" developed fairly quickly, coming to maturity in the 1920's.[28]

So the American law of economic relations at the turn of the century did not have the benefit of the modern economic model of "competition." As late as 1888 the M.I.T. economist Francis Walker defined "competition" in his *Political Economy* as "the operation of individual self-interest, among buyers and sellers."[29] He then used the term indiscriminately to refer both to rivalries among sellers and to the rivalry that exists between a buyer and a seller. This view of competition was quite common among writers of legal treatises and jurists as well. For example, in his treatise on combinations Frederick H. Cooke found that "the same test [should be] applicable to the relations of employer and employee as to that of trade competitors," for "the contest between them is only competition on a wide basis."[30] Even Holmes, who understood economics better than most late nineteenth-century judges, argued that the hierarchical relationship between employer and employee must be viewed as competitive. The policy of competition "is not limited to struggles between persons of the same class competing for the same end. It applies to all conflicts of temporal interests."[31]

Entirely missing from the concept as expressed by Walker, Cooke, and Holmes was the notion that competition is *horizontal*—that it refers to relationships between people operating at the same level in the same market, as, for instance, two sellers of shoes in the same city or two prospective employees seeking the same job. Although there might be a "conflict" or "rivalry" between a buyer and a seller of either commodities or labor—the first wishes to give the lowest price possible and the second to obtain the highest price possible—this kind of *vertical* rivalry was not "competition" economically defined.

This failure to distinguish horizontal from vertical rivalry is apparent in Justice Holmes's famous dissent in the *Dr. Miles* case of 1911:

> I think that we greatly exaggerate the value and importance to the public of competition in the production or distribution of an article . . . as fixing a fair price. What really fixes that is the competition of conflicting desires. We, none of us, can have as much as we want of all the things that we want. Therefore, we have to choose. As soon as the price of something that we want goes above the point at which we are willing to give up other things to have that, we cease to buy it and buy something else.[32]

Within Holmes's notion of competition, the presence of multiple suppliers, each trying to obtaining a sale by offering better terms, was not all that important. This was so because consumers themselves were in "competition" with sellers. Largely absent from this model was any notion of a "consumers' surplus"—that is, that consumers were often willing to pay monopoly prices rather than do without.[33] The concept of consumers' surplus entered into the common law only with respect to special rules for staples, or the necessities of life, where price-enhancing practices such as engrossing and regrating were illegal. The theory, discussed in Chapter 21, was that because people could not do without these products, they were at the mercy of the seller.

Simple price fixing, without coercion directed at those unwilling to participate, was not perceived to be particularly harmful. After all, both the individual seller and the group of sellers acting in combination faced precisely the same restraint: if they set the price too high, consumers, with whom they were also in "competition," would purchase something else. Albert Stickney explained in his treatise on *State Control of Trade and Commerce* (1897) that the only possible harm from price fixing "consists in a slight temporary raising or enhancing of prices."[34] His argument lacked any notion that attempts by cartels to raise prices might be more harmful than similar attempts by sellers acting unilaterally, because the cartel is likely to control all or at least most of a market. When the seller acts unilaterally, customers will purchase from a competitor. However, when all the suppliers in a market raise the price in concert, the customer must either pay the higher price or do without.

But the fault for this oversight is not Stickney's. The simple and rather obvious proposition of price theory, that cartels are more harmful than sellers acting alone, had not yet found its way into the legal literature. But this was rapidly changing. Even as Stickney was writing, American federal courts were beginning to use the Sherman Act as a vehicle for reading a much more modern notion of "competition" into the law. With it came greatly increased judicial hostility to combinations of both capital and labor.

Combinations, labor, and efficiency. Economists at the turn of the century remained relatively sanguine about business cartels even though they understood more clearly the relationship between market share and the ability to charge a market price than Stickney did. Their lack of concern resulted from a heightened awareness of the power of economies of scale. George Gunton, an industrial economist and the editor of *Gunton's Magazine,* a sort of turn-of-the-century version of *Fortune,* concluded that the large trusts made production both cheaper and more consistent by reducing costs as well as the threat of work stoppages.[35] Reporting on the Chicago Trust Conference in 1899, H. R. Hatfield concluded that the great majority of American economists believed that industry had become subject to massive scale economies that tended to favor large firms over small ones. Most believed that the great industrial trusts would, on balance, do more good than harm. The Cornell University economist Jeremiah Jenks argued that even though the trusts acquired very large market shares and the power to set monopoly prices, the cost reductions attending large-scale operations would more than offset them. Prominent university economists such as Yale's Irving Fisher, Cornell's Frank Fetter, and Harvard's Frank W. Taussig concluded that the trusts would generally produce lower prices rather than higher ones.[36]

The same economists generally felt that the federal antitrust laws would not merely be useless; they would be positively harmful to the extent they restrained business from obtaining its efficient size, whether by combination or otherwise. Most American political economists in the late nineteenth century, believing that industrial monopoly was both inevitable and socially beneficial, were opposed to the Sherman Act. As Jenks put it in condemning the act, "industrial efficiency tends toward monopoly," for "the genius whose industrial efficiency is greatest tends to overcome his rivals, and to take over a continually increasing proportion of the business."[37]

But labor enjoyed no such advantages of scale economies. By 1890 American neoclassical political economy had developed a theoretical model within which combinations of capital were generally considered to be socially beneficial, while labor combinations were believed to be harmful. The notion that the existence of combinations of capital justifies the existence of labor combinations as well was absurd, argued Albert Bolles, lecturer in law and banking at the University of Pennsylvania. The former is efficient and benefits society; the latter harmful.[38] Progressive economists such as John R. Commons tried to prove the contrary with communitarian arguments that "organized" labor was more efficient in the workplace simply because it was organized—that is, labor unity not only applied to a common position on wages, working conditions, and job security, but also spilled over into the integration of production.[39]

But such arguments did not appeal to the more individualistic bent of the classicist. When a mainstream American political economist around 1900 viewed business combinations he saw increased efficiencies from economies of scale, lower prices, better product quality, and higher profits. The same economist looked at labor combinations and saw only higher product prices. Unions bred inefficiency by insisting on shorter worker hours and better conditions as well as higher wages. The Yale political economist Arthur Twining Hadley criticized the legal attack on combinations of capital. Had the attack been more successful, many of the efficiencies of modern large-scale enterprise would have been lost. But in the same volume Hadley condemned labor combinations for "discourag[ing] industrial efficiency" just as much as the medieval trade guilds had done. In 1915 C. Bertrand Thompson of the Harvard Business School argued that, whether or not unions admitted it, reduction of labor output was a clear goal of the union movement, for only by reducing output could they raise wages. Thompson's colleague Frank W. Taussig, of Harvard's economics department, simultaneously praised the trusts for their great efficiencies in production and damned the labor movement for using inefficiency and restriction of output as the mechanism for raising the union members' standard of living at the expense of society. "They are naturally led to think and say that higher returns for everybody can be secured through limitation of output and restriction of competition," Taussig wrote, though in fact the "basis for a real gain to all the community and the laborers is in a general advance in productive efficiency . . . ." In his view the labor unions' actions were in conflict with their own long-run best interests.[40]

The lawyer and treatise writer Arthur Eddy was quick to pick up on these economic arguments from union inefficiency. In 1914 he produced an apology for business consolidations, entitled *The New Competition,* which simultaneously commended business combinations for their efficiency and condemned the unions for their lack of it. "Partnerships, corporations, trusts are all in the direction of more for less money," he argued, and "labor unions and farmers' organizations are all in the direction of less for more money."[41]

Finally there was labor's opposition to "scientific management," one of the most frequently proposed cures for industrial inefficiency in the first two decades of the twentieth century. By the 1880's George Gunton had already argued that higher wages and better working conditions were an inevitable result of technological progress—everyone, including labor, would benefit from increased business efficiency. After the turn of the century the theory of scientific management came to represent the industrial economist's formal discovery of transaction costs. To its proponents, such as Frederick Winslow Taylor, scientific management promised to reduce the costs of business—even to make small business as efficient as big business—by eliminating waste in production.[42]

Whatever the merits of the scientific management debate among capitalists and regulators, the labor unions were uniformly opposed to the idea. When industrialists inspired by "Taylorism" gave their managers stopwatches and told them to break every task into its simplest components so that the worker could perform it over and over again with maximum speed, the workers themselves rightfully complained. The managers of Henry Ford's assembly line, which had been developed under the principles of scientific management, had "no use for experience" and preferred the untrained, who had nothing to unlearn. Pride in one's work disappeared at the same time. In 1912 the women's and labor activist Josephine Goldmark published a large book detailing the consequences of "efficient" management on workers, now burdened by higher production quotas and more routinized and mechanical tasks. The Harvard economist C. Bertrand Thompson complained that the labor unions did not realize that anything that reduced the cost of production would ultimately make everyone, including labor, better off.[43] But this was a trickle-down theory of prosperity that labor simply could not buy.

Marginalism and Free Labor

As noted in Chapter 16, the marginalist revolution in political economy effectively killed the wage-fund doctrine. For some American political economists, such as Francis Walker, this meant increased sympathy with the labor union. But John Bates Clark, the country's most prominent marginalist at the end of the nineteenth century, remained just as hostile to the unions as any hard-core classicist. Clark argued that welfare is maximized when each person, whether capitalist or laborer, received his "marginal product" in return for his contribution to society. If any worker was earning less than his marginal product—the amount of value he contributed to his employer—someone else would bid him away. "To every man his product, his whole product and nothing but his product" is the "standard of wages" as well as "the standard that society tends to realize" in all other aspects of life. Labor unions should be condemned because their principal purpose was to enable workers to receive more than their social contribution, or marginal product. Such deviations undermined the efficiency of the productive process. Prices would rise, demand would decline, and social wealth would be diminished.[44]

Clark was an economic revisionist who did much of his writing in the publications of the American Economic Association, which had been organized in 1885 as an alternative forum for economists who were critical of the orthodox classicism that dominated American economic thought. But even the post-classical, marginalist revolution left economists such as Clark arguing that wages should be the product of individual bargaining rather than of group pressure.

Clark's "marginal product" rule was the economic expression of the free labor ideology that had dominated discourse about American labor since the abolition of slavery and the passage of the fourteenth amendment. "Free labor" became both a rallying cry and a burden for the American worker in the decades following the Civil War. First of all, "free labor" was the freedman's claim for justice. To liberals such as the Freedmen's Bureau agent John E. Bryant, the term meant "*impartial justice*" for the freedman. With it, "he will work better as a freedman than he did as a slave." Before long the ideology of free labor had spread beyond the freedman to encompass America's entire laboring class.[45]

But the liberating ideology of "free labor" was as hostile toward unionism as it was toward enslavement. The free labor movement was dedicated to the proposition that each laborer deserved to be free, independent, and equal in the eyes of the law, precisely the same as each capitalist and employer. The first great statement of the free labor ideology in the Supreme Court was Justice Field's dissenting opinion in the *Slaughter-House Cases* (1873), arguing that the fourteenth amendment was designed to protect the New Orleans butchers from a law that made it illegal for them to practice their trade. "Free labor" meant for Field that every person has a right to "pursue a calling" and to reap the "fruits of his own labor." Field claimed to take his "free labor" ideology from Adam Smith, whom he quoted in his opinion:

"The property which every man has in his own labor," says Adam Smith, "as it is the original foundation of all other property, so it is the most sacred and inviolable. The patrimony of the poor man lies in the strength and dexterity of his own hands; and to hinder him from employing this strength and dexterity in what manner he thinks proper, without injury to his neighbor, is a plain violation of this most sacred property. It is a manifest encroachment upon the just liberty both of the workman and of those who might be disposed to employ him . . . ."[46]

Within a decade the ideology of free labor began to move erratically in two inconsistent directions. The conservative, or bourgeois, free labor ideology looked back to Field's *Slaughter-House* opinion. It emphasized each person's right to enter into an occupation, exit from it, and declare or bargain for his own terms of employment. Concurrently, it stressed complementary rights in the employer. Union picketing or "coercion" was just as contrary to the principles of bourgeois free labor as was slavery or a statute denying people the right to pursue their callings. The emerging doctrine of liberty of contract in the 1880's was the legal recrudescence of bourgeois "free labor" ideology. Early liberty of contract cases in the state courts treated Justice Field's dissent as ruling law.[47] Bourgeois "free labor" became substantive due process.

The more radical free labor ideology developed within the labor movement itself. The radicals believed that the political and legal systems had always discriminated against labor in favor of capital. They were inclined to see the bourgeois ideology as nothing more than a rationalization for worker oppression. "Free labor" as envisioned by the courts was nothing more than "wage slavery"—a situation in which the worker is compelled to work, because he has no capital, but the capitalist uses his leverage to capture most of the added value that the worker contributes to the production process. Substantive due process was a fraud upon the laborer.[48]

The ideology of free labor permeated emergent neoclassicism, particularly in its rejection of the wage-fund doctrine. The classical doctrine of the wages fund contained an oddly collective element generally inconsistent with classical economic theory. Under the doctrine, labor was a class and the fund was a sum of money to be divided among the members. The more workers, the lower the wages each would receive. Thus a worker's wages depended not merely on the amount he produced, but also on the number of laborers competing for the fund. The rate of wages bore no relationship to the worker's productivity. How could it, George Gunton noted in 1891, since wages were "stipulated" far in advance of sales. No one knew at the time the wage contract was made what the worker's contribution would be.[49]

Both the bourgeois and radical free labor ideologies were hostile toward the wage-fund doctrine. Under the doctrine the individual workers "could secure none of the benefits of social progress and economic improvement" until "they slowly filtered down to him through his sum in long division." How could workers be said to be free when their wages were forever tied to the investment in capital and the laboring population? When Francis Walker rejected the wage-fund theory in the mid-seventies, he opted instead for the view that wages tended toward the "contribution" that the worker makes to the production process. This would happen in a regime of "full and free competition, each man seeking and finding his own best market, unhindered by any cause, whether objective or subjective in its origin." In an 1891 response to Gunton, Walker scoffed at the argument that wages were unrelated to productivity because they were stipulated before profits were known. Of course, Walker said, they are stipulated on the basis of *anticipated* productivity, and our expectations are a function of past experience.[50]

The rise of American marginalism discredited the wages fund and brought an ideological defense of free labor ideology. Initially, however, there was a debate about which free labor ideology, bourgeois or radical, the political economists would embrace. The technical question concerned who, capitalist or laborer, was the "residual claimant" to monopoly rents. Under the developing concepts of marginalism every capitalist and every worker would receive his marginal contribution as a reward. But suppose that revenues were higher than contributions. Would the excess accrue to labor or capital, or would they share it?

What emerged was the view that monopoly in the capital market and monopoly in the labor market were two, quite different things. More important, although monopoly in the capital market might yield monopoly profits to capitalists, these profits would not come out of wages. If anything, monopolists tended to pay higher wages than competitors.[51] Monopoly in the labor market, by contrast, could reduce the short-run returns to capital by increasing the cost of production. Walker concluded that "the economic condition of the laboring class is very largely put into their own hands . . . ." Suppose that the returns in a competitive industry consist of three parts: rent on lands, return on investment in equipment, and labor wages. Now suddenly one group of laborers becomes much more productive than the others, and thus able to do far more at lower cost. Who will reap the benefit of this increased productivity? Clearly, argued Walker, it will be the laborers themselves. If their current employer will not raise their wages, they will seek another employer until they are at the margin that their wages would be increased by their added productivity.[52]

For John Bates Clark even more than Walker, marginalism relieved the theory of value from previous investment and tied it to productivity. "[W]ages conform to the product that is attributable to marginal labor."

In a free market wages will be determined precisely by the laborer's value to the higher bidder—that is, they will be equal, at the margin, to the amount of wealth that the worker's labor contributed to his employer. If "I can add to your previous product exactly what I ask as wages," Clark argued, "you will be indifferent as to whether to hire me. If I can add more you will hire me; if I can add less you will not." At the margin, then, any worker in a society with free movement will earn precisely his contribution to his employer. "Like other vendors, the laborer can get the true value of his product and he can get no more." And, Clark suggested in 1907, under perfect competition wages and capitalists will tend to have the same earnings. As long as the return to capital is higher than prevailing wages, workers will become capitalists, until the two are equalized. The Wharton School economist Simon N. Patten agreed that "free laborers" would continually gravitate toward jobs in which they earned what they contributed to society.[53]

Even American marginalism, when it finally came, gave the labor unions little comfort. Inherent in Clark's theory were some notions that would give the emerging labor movement great difficulty. Most important, Clark believed that skilled workers produce a greater marginal product, and that their wages should be higher in proportion.[54] But the union itself was unnecessary to yield this result; Clark and many of his peers believed it would happen naturally. The unions—insofar as they attempted to give the laborer more than he contributed—were an evil. Elite political economy, just as elite law, had unambiguously chosen the bourgeois ideology of free labor.

CHAPTER 19

Coercion and Its Meaning: Antitrust and the Labor Injunction

When the Sherman Antitrust Act was passed in 1890, the law concerning the right to strike was clear. Workers could not be forced to accept a wage that they did not want, and they had the right to refuse to work either singly or in combination. But they could not coerce other employees to join them, or other businesses to refuse to deal with the struck employer. The common law of business combinations such as cartels was similar: although cartel agreements were not enforceable among participants, they could not be challenged by nonparticipants, provided that cartel members refrained from boycotts, violence, or other forms of intimidation to coerce compliance.

Of course, even a completely voluntary strike can cause substantial public injury. Most obviously, it can force the struck employer to reduce or cease production, and the resulting social impact can range from trivial to devastating. But the common law generally did not count this injury as serious enough to warrant condemnation of the strike, even if the struck employer were a business essential to the public, such as a railroad. Application of the Sherman Act to labor combinations gradually undermined this basic rule. Courts in the late nineteenth and early twentieth centuries began scrutinizing strikes very closely for evidence of "coercion" of unwilling participants. Activities that were not generally considered coercive in the 1870's and 1880's, such as simple picketing, became so after 1900. Some courts eventually held that a simple agreement to strike was illegal and enjoinable under the antitrust laws. Once again, the law of business combinations and that of labor combinations moved in the same direction. Accompanying this increased hostility toward agreements among laborers was a correspondingly higher scrutiny of agreements among competing sellers. These developments will be taken up in Chapter 21.

There are important economic differences between business cartels and labor organizations. Business cartels most frequently succeed in heavy industries that are subject to high fixed costs and fairly substantial economies of scale. These industries are said to have high "barriers to entry," a characteristic that makes cartelization possible. Most of the trusts and virtually all of the early price-fixing antitrust cases arose in such industries: the railroads, steel and pipe manufacturing, bathroom fixture manufacturing, petroleum refining, and the like.

But labor, particularly unskilled labor, is inherently an "easy entry" industry. Laborers can be moved quickly from one spot to another, and unskilled laborers can generally be employed on very short notice. Employers of striking unskilled laborers often produced carloads of scabs within a day or two after a strike began. As the economist J. Laurence Laughlin argued in 1906, as soon as union pressure raised wages the demand for labor would diminish, because employers would seek to use fewer workers and would sell less of higher-priced products. The result would be a steadily increasing supply of nonunion workers and other unemployed, willing to accept jobs at a moment's notice. Laughlin concluded that strikes could not successfully increase general wages for a prolonged period.[1]

The "easy entry" nature of labor makes labor strikes much more difficult to maintain than price-fixing arrangements among sellers of manufactured goods, particularly in capital-intensive industries. For the labor unions, various kinds of "secondary" activities were essential. These secondary activities could include simple picketing, intended to intimidate both customers and nonparticipating employees of the struck employer. They might involve more forceful acts, including boycotts of those unsympathetic to the strike, such as retailers who sold struck goods, and they might even include violence directed at workers who refused to participate. One important but often overlooked fact about some great early labor conspiracy cases, such as *Commonwealth v. Pullis* (1819) and *Commonwealth v. Hunt* (1842),[2] is that the complainants were not employers seeking to discipline unions but rather fellow employees whom union members had attempted to exclude from the labor market because of their willingness to work at too low a wage.

Violence was of course a criminal act, without regard to any underlying conspiracy among laborers and their unions. Nevertheless, striking laborers were inclined to think that it was their right, whether moral or legal, that their strike not be undermined. One federal court observed that "a large number of the laboring class" apparently believed that "if they quit work because of unsatisfactory conditions, those who take the places vacated are doing a wrong, an injustice, to the families and persons of those who quit." Whether or not that proposition had any ethical force, the court concluded, "it has no legal support." Several courts explicitly found union coercion against nonparticipants inconsistent with American principles of democracy. The laborers' redress was to be "through the courts and at the ballot-box,"[3] not through self-help by violence.

Finally, the fact that the "product" whose output was being restrained in a labor strike was human labor contributed greatly to the volatility of strikes. The participants in late nineteenth-century strikes frequently did not have a great deal to lose. They were not society's most highly respected citizens. They were people earning subsistence wages watching others steal their jobs. Individual union members did not have legal counsel looking over their shoulders advising them on every move.

Thus a legal rule that combinations to fix prices or wages were legal only if they did not involve coercion of nonparticipants was inherently a much heavier burden on labor unions than it was on most manufacturers of products. In fact, such a rule permitted many forms of commodity price fixing to continue, while it spelled virtual death for labor strikes. Some writers were quite candid about this. Henry Clews argued in 1886 that the common law rule approving peaceful, noncoercive strikes but condemning coercion drew the line in the proper place, because the strikes were harmless without the coercion. "[T]he places of those who vacate good situations are easily filled by the new-comers."[4] It was the "disturbances," argued Clews, that gave the unions a chance of success in achieving their goals and therefore constituted a greater threat to society. Labor combinations fared even worse under an emerging economic and legal theory that feared even noncoercive combinations of capital and labor. The federal antitrust laws were the principal mechanism by which the new theory entered the law of both kinds of combinations.

Labor Conspiracies and the Antitrust Laws

Beginning in 1897, the Supreme Court and lower courts began condemning simple horizontal price-fixing agreements, which involved no coercion directed at nonparticipants. Under the Sherman Act, unlike the common law, these agreements were not merely unenforceable; they were illegal and actionable by the federal government itself. Likewise, the Court began to hold that certain mergers and concerted refusals to deal, generally legal at common law, were illegal under the antitrust laws, particularly if these activities concentrated large amounts of economic power in a small number of individuals or private firms.[5]

During the period 1890–1895 American labor unions grew at an unprecedented pace.[6] Government paranoia may have grown commensurately. Between 1890 and 1897 lower courts found antitrust violations in thirteen reported decisions. One of those thirteen cases involved a conspiracy of capitalists.[7] The other twelve all involved conspiracies of labor unions.[8] To be sure, these numbers may overstate the antilabor bias of early Sherman Act prosecutions. Ten of the twelve labor conspiracy cases involved a single set of incidents: the great Pullman sleeping-coach strike led by Eugene Debs, which crippled the American railroad network in 1894. Nevertheless, although economists and many statesmen had substantial doubts about the effectiveness of the Sherman Act against industrial combinations and trusts, from the start the new statute was perceived to be a powerful union-busting device.

Union leaders naturally expressed outrage at the judicial decisions applying the Sherman Act to labor combinations and proclaimed that Congress had never intended the act to be used against them.[9] But the union leaders were probably wrong. During the course of the debate on the Sherman Act the subject of unions, farmers' organizations, and other "noncapitalist" combinations came up repeatedly. Several members of Congress offered amendments, including one proposed by Senator John Sherman that "this act shall not be construed to apply to any arrangements, agreements, or combinations between laborers . . . ." Sherman's amendment was adopted by the Senate on a voice vote. But the statute was then referred to the judiciary committee, which struck out Sherman's amendment as well as many others. This suggests that Congress considered whether there should be an exemption for labor and decided that all combinations, whether of capital or labor, should be included. Most of the literature analyzing the legislative history has come to this conclusion, with only a few dissenters.[10] In the *Danbury Hatters* case (1908)[11] the Supreme Court adopted the consensus view and applied the Sherman Act to a labor union.

The more interesting question is not whether the Sherman Act applied to labor organizations but what kinds of labor activities were condemned under the statute. As noted above, a mere agreement among laborers not to work until they should receive higher wages was not an illegal combination at common law. The arrangement had to involve coercion of others. The greatest contemporary scholar of the relationship between the Sherman Act and the common law of trade restraints, Justice William Howard Taft, believed that the same standard should be applied under the Sherman Act. As a result, "mere striking to secure better wages" was not unlawful, since it had been permissible at common law. But when strikers "go further and seek . . . to coerce others who have no normal relation to the fight to assist them in it and injure their employer, they step over the line of lawfulness."[12] However, the *Trans-Missouri* opinion made it clear that some combinations in restraint of trade could be illegal even if they had not been condemned at common law and involved no coercion directed at nonparticipants. The economic theory invited the courts to apply the same standard to combinations of labor.

The earliest Sherman Act labor cases involved strikes that included a fair amount of coercion directed at nonparticipants. This was certainly true of the Pullman strike, which produced a great deal of violence and paralyzed the American railroad industry. The strike would have been condemned under the common law as well. But early on the federal courts opined that such coercion was not essential to a Sherman Act conviction. If a manufacturer was sufficiently involved in interstate commerce a simple, noncoercive strike against him, if successful, literally "restrained" commerce. For example, the mere fact that the employer stopped production or reduced output during the period of the strike might be a qualifying "restraint."[13]

This emerging economic view of anticompetitive behavior was first adopted by courts in decisions enjoining strikes under the Interstate Commerce Act, not the Sherman Act. The theory that the strike itself injured the public, without regard to any secondary coercion, seemed natural there because of the kinds of industries the Interstate Commerce Act regulated. These were common carriers, principally railroads. At common law such carriers operated under a duty of continuous operation. Additionally, the policy of the Interstate Commerce Act was to encourage the free flow of interstate traffic. If one railroad was struck, other railroads could be greatly hindered in transferring cargo. As a result, a strike in the railroad industry was perceived to have a far greater adverse impact on the public than a strike in a general manufacturing industry.[14]

The Progressive economist Richard T. Ely argued that laborers for natural monopoly industries such as railroads should, if anything, be given broader powers to organize, because monopoly power implied the power to monopolize both laborers and consumers.[15] Although Ely's economics were dubious—monopoly firms, if anything, pay higher wages—the general concern he expressed was important. The country had a broad interest in reducing the number of labor disputes among common carriers. The only question was whether to use a carrot or a stick. In 1926 Congress decided on the former and passed the Railway Labor Act,[16] approving collective bargaining in the railroad industry a decade before New Deal legislation gave general labor broader collective bargaining rights.

But in the 1890's Ely was clearly in a minority. Labor troubles among common carriers were viewed as something that needed to be suppressed at all costs. The courts responded accordingly. The federal labor injunction was developed largely in common carrier cases, on the theory that *any* strike in such industries was harmful to the public, whether or not it was accompanied by violence or secondary boycotts.[17] In the *Toledo Railway* case (1893) Judge Taft, who later was to argue that the Sherman Act should not be used against simple strikes, held that a railroad strike within the jurisdiction of the Interstate Commerce Act was virtually illegal per se, and could thus be enjoined. The Supreme Court agreed in the *Debs* case two years later, supporting its injunction by noting the congressional duty of "keeping those highways . . . free from obstruction."[18]

But the Sherman Act placed all business in interstate commerce within its jurisdiction—even ordinary, competitively structured manufacturing. One of the most important questions in early Sherman Act labor cases was whether federal courts should adhere to the traditional common law rule that only strikes involving coercion of nonparticipants should be illegal, or else follow Justice Peckham's view adopted in the *Trans-Missouri* case for combinations of capital, that "every" combination in restraint of trade was condemned by the act.[19] It quickly appeared that, just as the federal courts would not be bound by the common law in Sherman Act business combination cases, they would not be bound in labor cases.

In 1894 Holmes rejected the common law notion that an illegal conspiracy occurs only when a group of people conspires to commit an act that is independently illegal. Rather, he suggested, mere numbers should condemn certain kinds of acts.[20] Among these Holmes included union boycotts. Further, the relative *size* of the combination was important in determining its legality. Under the law of combinations "[i]t is a question of degree at what point the combination becomes large enough to be wrong . . . ." In 1912 James Emery argued that labor boycotts of workers should be condemned just as seller boycotts of other businessmen willing to sell at a lower price had been condemned by the Supreme Court in *Montague v. Lowry* (1904). C. J. Primm argued that strikes by unions with monopoly power should be held inherently illegal. In 1923 the antitrust scholar Albert M. Kales likewise suggested a market dominance standard for both business and labor combinations: "[i]f the collective unit becomes so large as to occupy a predominant position in the market . . . , then the acts which before were lawful, become unlawful." The labor union, like the industrial trust, was suddenly perceived as a force wielding great economic power, which the antitrust laws must bring under control. Conspiracy itself became the law's target.[21]

The closed-shop campaign tended to confirm the perception that the labor movement threatened to monopolize the labor market in the same way that the trusts threatened to become industrial monopolies. Strikes for closed shops were generally viewed as devices by which unions sought to control the labor in a certain plant by denying nonunion workers an opportunity to sell their services. The union organizer John Mitchell argued that workers had a moral right to work in an environment free of nonunion labor,[22] but most elite lawyers and economists did not see it that way. The University of Illinois economist H. E. Hoagland argued that the closed shop indefensibly created an artificial monopoly for the benefit of a few workers at the expense of many others. Howard T. Lewis argued that strikes designed to create closed shops should be illegal because they were motivated by an attempt to monopolize the labor of a particular employer. Frank W. Taussig tried to take a balanced view of the labor movement, but concluded that the "monopolistic" tendencies of the closed shop campaign were dangerous.[23] In 1923 Kales observed that both state common law and the federal antitrust laws had been applied to condemn concerted boycotts of suppliers who did not cooperate with the boycotters' attempts to control commodities markets. So too, Kales argued, strikes for closed shops should be condemned for doing exactly the same thing in the labor market. He applied the same reasoning to "hot cargo" strikes—strikes designed to force employers not to use materials produced by nonunion labor. These too seemed motivated by an illegitimate desire to obtain a monopoly of the labor market.[24]

By the time these economists and legal scholars were writing, the courts had been facing the problem of the closed shop for some decades. *Commonwealth v. Hunt* (1842), which had rejected the conspiracy theory of labor combinations, was a closed-shop case: the union members had agreed not to work for anyone who employed nonunion help. But beginning in 1911 the Supreme Judicial Court of Massachusetts began to hold that, whatever validity strikes had in and of themselves, they could not have the closed shop as their objective. Other state courts agreed, as did the Supreme Court in *Duplex Printing* (1921), decided under the federal antitrust laws. In *Bedford Cut Stone* (1927) the Supreme Court condemned and enjoined a hot cargo strike under the antitrust laws. The Supreme Court relied on a manufacturer boycott case to hold that an agreement not to deal in materials manufactured by nonunion labor restrained trade in such materials just as much as did an agreement of sellers of a product not to deal in the product of some competitor or supplier. Several state courts condemned hot cargo strikes as well.[25]

Along with this heightened awareness of the "monopoly" problem of unionism came much closer scrutiny of labor's coercive activities. Most of the earlier Sherman Act labor cases involved secondary activities that were sufficiently coercive to warrant condemnation even under a common law standard. For example, most courts agreed that violence or intimidation by union members against others, or seizure or physical destruction of plant and equipment warranted condemnation under the Sherman Act.[26]

But some of the antitrust decisions went much further. For example, the circuit court in *Debs* held that mere attempts by strikers to persuade other employees to stop working warranted condemnation, at least if it was reasonable to suspect that the strike would be attended by violence.[27] In the *Danbury Hatters* strike case (1908) the Supreme Court held that "the anti-trust law has a broader application than the prohibition of restraints of trade unlawful at common law." Restraint on interstate trade was all the Sherman Act demanded. In a 1911 decision the Supreme Court, while reversing a contempt citation, approved a lower court injunction against publishing the names of "unfair" employees. In *Duplex Printing* (1921) it held that an absolutely peaceful strike could violate the antitrust laws, if it had a sufficiently adverse impact on interstate commerce. A "restraint produced by peaceable persuasion is as much within the prohibition as one accomplished by force or threats of force." A sufficiently adverse impact, it turned out, was nothing more than a reduction in the output of the struck employer—precisely the goal of any successful strike. The decree in *Duplex Printing* enjoined the defendants from "even persuasion with the object of having the effect of causing any person or persons to decline employment, cease employment, or not seek employment, or to refrain from work . . . ." In the *United Mine Workers* case (1925) the Supreme Court held that a "mere reduction in the supply of an article to be shipped in interstate commerce" violated the antitrust laws, if the reduction was caused by strikers who intended "to restrain or control the supply . . . ." In the eyes of the federal courts the labor union, just as much as the business trust, had become capable of wielding monopoly power to society's detriment. As a result, the mere fact of combination, economic power, and reduction in output was sufficient for condemnation. The very thing that made a strike successful —reduced output by the employer—also made it illegal.[28]

Unions and Incorporation

The law of labor combinations seems even harsher when viewed against the many successes business enjoyed in evading both the federal antitrust laws and the state law of trade restraints. Although the law came down hard on naked price fixing agreements, entrepreneurs could escape its consequences by various forms of horizontal integration, such as merger by asset acquisition, that were simply not available to competing laborers. As will be discussed in Chapter 20, many defendants in antitrust price-fixing cases merged with one another rather than compete. The nature of the American business corporation was to permit several business investors to act together as a single person. Joint decisions by the owners, directors, or managers of a single corporation were not a "conspiracy" but merely the acts of agents acting for the same "person." A joint decision of the laborers working for a single corporation, however, was conspiratorial.

Throughout American history most labor unions have been unincorporated associations, treated more like large partnerships than corporations for most legal purposes. Because labor unions were not incorporated the real parties in interest in union-management disputes were generally perceived by courts to be the workers themselves rather than the union. The treatise writers paid no attention to this distinction between capital and labor. In all the venom that Arthur Eddy spat at the law's favorable treatment of labor combinations as against combinations of capital, he never even found it relevant that the combinations of labor about which he spoke were combinations of individuals. However, capital interests became a "combination" only when two or more distinct firms were involved. Once two firms had become one by merger, the post-merger firm's price setting was no longer a combination in restraint of trade, because there was no multiplicity of actors. "Combination by consolidation of competing companies, by the formation of a new corporation . . . is legal," even if the purpose of the merger is to "diminish competition" between the merging firms. A few years later in his popular book, *The New Competition,* Eddy vented his wrath at labor combinations even as he praised the business consolidation movement for achieving great economies of scale, and proposed the trade association movement as a mechanism for making industry operate more efficiently.[29]

But the distinction between individuals and corporations did not escape the notice of Progressive critics of American labor policy. In 1924 John R. Commons, the Progressive Era's greatest scholar of American labor, complained bitterly that the law could treat a business corporation worth millions of dollars and representing hundreds of investors as a single "person," while it treated each individual laborer as a person. As a result, any number of capitalists united into one corporation could bargain with labor. But the instant the laborers joined forces to strengthen their bargaining position they were involved in a "conspiracy," and received the law's closest scrutiny.[30] Even liberty of contract, that most individualistic of Gilded Age legal rights, belonged to laborers as individuals, but to incorporated businesses as entities.[31] As a result, collective bargaining agreements were never given the kind of preferred constitutional treatment accorded to other corporate contracts.[32] Although the bare right to strike was eventually accorded constitutional protection,[33] it was a right that had to be exercised within the strictest noncoercive limits.

The unions were caught between a rock and a hard place, however, and their decision not to incorporate was generally their own. Union leaders and lawyers were inclined to believe that the disadvantages of incorporation outweighed the advantages. Incorporation of unions would make them more easily suable and responsible in damages for their acts. Even a liberal, pro-labor lawyer like Louis Brandeis argued in 1902 that the principal consequence of union failure to incorporate was irresponsible behavior. No single entity could be held responsible for the individual acts of union members. The labor leader Eugene

Wambaugh immediately replied that union incorporation would place labor even more firmly under the control of capital.[34]

Historically, Brandeis and Wambaugh were certainly correct that union incorporation would come at a cost. As unincorporated associations, unions were generally not suable in common law damage actions.[35] But the importance of such actions was minimal at best, since most unions had few funds. Furthermore, by the 1890's the Supreme Court had upheld labor injunctions directed against unnamed laborers who had not been personally served with process. The injunction approved in *Debs* purported to apply to "all persons combining and conspiring with them [the named defendants] and all other persons whomsoever." In 1912 this kind of injunction was approved in a federal equity rule of procedure on the theory that the unnamed defendants stood in the same position as those named; therefore their rights were being protected. Many states also passed statutes permitting such injunctions.[36] The labor injunction as thus approved reached as far as the ordinary injunction against an incorporated firm. An injunction against a corporation generally bound only its agents, while the labor injunction bound everyone, whether or not they were acting with the union's authority or even had been served with process. In short, Wambaugh's argument against union incorporation had already lost its force by the time he wrote. Finally in 1922 the Supreme Court held that under federal law unincorporated trade unions were suable because they operated as single entities and wielded great economic power. As Chief Justice Taft noted, the larger the union the more power it had, but the more difficult it was to sue. In the case of the 400,000-member United Mine Workers, the common law effectively left plaintiffs without a remedy.[37]

Union incorporation would have spelled increased judicial control of the internal management of the labor union. Corporate charters would have to be issued by the state, and unions could be disciplined for ultra vires acts, whether or not they were independently illegal. The "danger of submitting a union to the intervention of the courts in its every-day affairs" was sufficient to convince the United Mine Workers president, John Mitchell, that union incorporation was a bad idea.[38]

The Labor Injunction and the Clayton Act

Although the labor injunction arose in the 1880's, its earliest uses were relatively narrow. Courts enjoined violence or other explicitly coercive activities, not mere picketing or striking. Only in the 1910's did federal courts begin enjoining nonviolent secondary boycotts designed to produce closed shops or hot cargo agreements.[39] During the 1920's secondary boycotts were commonly enjoined, and the courts even began enjoining picketing and sometimes nonviolent, purely voluntary strikes.[40]

The elite bar generally approved. James Bradley Thayer chided Richard T. Ely for accusing judges of using their equity powers to take over the government. Such "crude observations" underestimated the neutrality of American judges. Arthur Eddy ridiculed the notion that the *ex parte* injunction directed at unnamed and unserved parties amounted to a "government by injunction," contrary to democratic principles. The injunctions simply commanded people to do that which had been independently determined to be illegal, Eddy argued. "No complaints" about judicial usurpation "have come from the orderly and well-disposed," but only from "those who are the greatest offenders against the peace and order of the community."[41]

The law of labor injunctions was dynamic, becoming more hostile toward labor activities as time went on. One of the biggest blows to organized labor was the Clayton Act. Ironically, it was designed by a Progressive Congress to exempt labor organizing from the federal antitrust laws. Section 6 provided that "the labor of a human being is not a commodity or article of commerce," and that the antitrust laws should not be construed "to forbid the existence and operation of labor . . . organizations . . . ." Section 20 additionally forbade labor injunctions "unless necessary to prevent irreparable injury to property, or to a property right . . . ." Shortly after the Clayton Act was passed Samuel Gompers, then president of the American Federation of Labor, proclaimed it an "Industrial Magna Carta upon which the working people will rear their structure of industrial freedom."[42]

But never did a statute backfire so badly.[43] Congress intended to do three things in the Clayton Act: expand private plaintiff standing to sue business violators, enlarge the scope of illegal business activities, and give labor some kind of exemption for most nonviolent organizational activities.[44] Sections 4 and 16 of the Clayton Act contained expanded private causes of action, the first for damages and the second for injunctive relief. Given the broad labor exemptions created in sections 6 and 20, it seems clear that Congress intended these two sections to create more effective private remedies against business combinations. It did not intend to create a private right of injunction against labor unions.

Earlier cases under the Sherman Act had held that injunctive relief was not available to private parties in labor disputes.[45] In *Paine Lumber Co. v. Neal* (1917) the Supreme Court held that the Sherman Act did not authorize an injunction at the behest of a private party, but Justice Holmes suggested that the majority would find such authorization in the Clayton Act. The Supreme Court granted such an injunction in *Duplex Printing* (1921).[46]

Even more unexpected was the way the *Duplex Printing* decision undermined the Clayton Act's labor "exemption." The Court held that the Clayton Act "is but declaratory of the law as it stood before"— peaceful, completely voluntary strikes were legal, but any kind of coercion, including secondary boycotts, were still to be condemned. In short, the exemption was no exemption at all, and the only thing labor received from the Clayton Act was increased amenability to injunctions at the initiative of employers, boycotted workers, or other private parties. In 1932 J. Stanley Christ, a University of Chicago economist, concluded that as a result of the Clayton Act at least ten injunctions were issued that would not have been issued. Furthermore, in every case where an injunction would have issued under the Sherman Act, the Clayton Act failed to stop it.[47]

To America's elite lawyers during the Gilded Age and Progressive Era, the labor combination presented a difficult but tractable problem in political economy. By viewing "the labor problem" as an economic one, these lawyers believed that they were applying the rule of law—a rule that was substantively fair because it did not discriminate between capital and labor, but was concerned exclusively with maximizing the welfare of society as a whole. In this view, the judiciary's attack on organized labor was simply part of a larger war against monopoly of every kind. But capitalists found legal ways to combine that were unavailable to laborers. Further, the unique structure of the labor market—easy entry and few economies of scale—meant that a body of law intended to be symmetrical treated the American laborers far more harshly than it treated those that employed them.

PART VI

THE ANTITRUST MOVEMENT AND THE THEORY OF THE FIRM

CHAPTER 20

American Merger Policy and the Failure of Corporate Law

The Great Merger Movement and Antitrust

The causes of the trust movement, the rash of American business mergers that began in the 1880's, were both technological and legal. Thanks to the railroads, American markets had become larger than ever before. Firms manufactured more and sold what they produced over a much greater geographic area, but they also competed with more distant firms for the same business. The transportation revolution both created new marketing opportunities and increased the competitiveness of American industry.[1] Mergers helped firms expand in order to take advantage of these bigger markets, but also helped to insulate them from some of the new competition.

The larger markets that the railroads made possible encouraged firms to grow and to specialize. As Adam Smith had already observed in 1776, "the division of labour is limited by the extent of the market."[2] New technology after the Civil War also encouraged firms to grow, for two reasons. First, industrialists developed many manufacturing processes that could produce higher-quality goods more cheaply than could older processes, but the new processes required production in large volume. Good examples are can-making machinery, which made the hand-soldered can obsolete; and wire nail machinery, which produced thousands of nails per hour from a string of steel wire, replacing older methods of cutting nails from sheet iron.[3] These manufacturing processes became subject to "economies of scale," and bigger firms acquired a cost advantage over small firms. Second, the new technologies required higher fixed costs, and fixed costs could be minimized when output was maximized. One effect of new technology was excess capacity. Firms held, and had to pay for, plants that were much larger than necessary to satisfy the demand. The effects of increased productivity were exacerbated by the great 1890's depression, which even further disturbed the balance between demand and the capacity to supply.[4] Mergers often enabled firms to control total market output. In the wake of a merger firms often closed their least efficient plants, for example, or plants that management deemed were no longer needed.

Firms grew for another reason. Market transactions ceased to be the most efficient way to coordinate many distinct but related production processes. Firms began to find that they could lower their costs by integrating backward to sources of supply, or forward into downstream production processes or even into distribution. Much of the great merger movement actually consisted of vertical integration.[5]

The Sherman Antitrust Act was passed in 1890. Five years later the trust movement accelerated sharply and turned into the greatest merger mania America has ever experienced, lasting almost a decade (1895–1904) and involving thousands of consolidations of American business firms.[6] How can it be that, far from stopping the trusts, the Sherman Act permitted this great flurry of corporate consolidations to occur?

Historians have suggested several answers to this question. One is that the mergers were going to occur anyway. The Sherman Act was simply ineffectual or underenforced, and failed to stop them.[7] Another suggestion is that the Sherman Act actually "caused"—or at least contributed to—the great merger wave. The first successful targets of the Sherman Act were "loose" combinations, or cartels, such as the railroad pools and the pipe cartel. The first use of the Sherman Act against a "tight" combination, or merger, aborted in 1895 when the Supreme Court concluded that "manufacturing is not commerce," and held that congressional power under the commerce clause did not empower Congress to go after a multistate manufacturing trust. This early experience with the Sherman Act sent a clear signal to entrepreneurs: if you want to avoid Sherman Act prosecution, form "tight" combinations rather than cartels. Thus the Sherman Act actually forced firms to merge rather than collude.[8] E. C. Knight convinced many contemporaries that, although the Sherman Act might be effective against interstate cartels, merger policy was to be left to the individual states. In 1908 Herbert Knox Smith reported for the Bureau of Corporations that the blame for the great consolidation movement was not so much the Sherman

Act itself as the rigid way it had been applied to loose combinations. As interpreted by the Supreme Court the statute took "no account of intent, methods, and results of combination . . . . In prohibiting combination agreements it has gone far to drive corporations directly to the most extreme and complete form of consolidation."[9]

This chapter argues that any assessment of merger strategies at the turn of the century must place heavier emphasis on the role of state corporate law. The most conspicuous antitrust policy failure of the era was corporate law's inability to develop a policy regarding anticompetitive mergers. Instead, both the federal government and the states developed a model based on the common law of contracts in restraint of trade. Historically, state corporate law had been quite solicitous about corporate structure and regulated it closely. Although the law of contracts in restraint of trade was hostile toward perceived anticompetitive agreements between different firms, it was quite tolerant of business decisions within a single firm, including a firm's decisions about how to grow larger. The law of contracts in restraint of trade had generally not been used to condemn mergers before 1890,[10] although it had been used against noncompetition clauses contained in merger agreements. This suggested that state merger policy should be derived from existing corporate law.

But writing in 1909, the federal judge Walter Chadwick Noyes observed that state antitrust policy had become completely separated from state corporate law. If a particular corporate practice or merger was challenged as anticompetitive, it was no defense that the practice was legal under the state's corporate law. For example, holding-company acts permitted one corporation to acquire another corporation's shares, but they did not permit such an acquisition if the purpose or effect was to monopolize a market.[11]

Combinations and State Policy

Most, but perhaps not all, structural decisions by business firms are calculated by managers to increase profits. Such decisions are complex, because they require consideration of four quite interdependent variables. First, other things being equal, a firm maximizes its profits by minimizing costs through the attainment of scale economies and economies of distribution. Second, a firm can earn more by acquiring a market position that enables it to charge a higher price, and to obtain such a price for the longest possible time. Third, a firm may select a profit-maximizing size and structure for strategic reasons—for example, to increase the costs of its rivals or make entry by potential rivals more difficult.

Finally, a firm maximizes its profits by discovering the least costly method of organization within its legal environment. The cost of litigating and losing lawsuits, or of giving up assets or going through forced reorganization as a result of court decrees, can be as high as the cost of inefficiencies in technology or organization. A less efficient form of organization might even be preferable, if the more efficient form is illegal or poses significant legal risks.

Scholars have expressed two seemingly inconsistent views about trust busting by the states at the turn of the century. On the one side is the view that by the turn of the century the states had virtually "abandoned the field," leaving the job to the federal government.[12] On the other is the view that the states maintained an aggressive policy against the trusts throughout the heyday of the antitrust movement.[13] Both views represent only part of the entire picture. States abandoned, not the enterprise of going after the trusts, but rather the corporate law model of antitrust policy. In its place they adopted legislative antitrust policies based on the common law of trade restraints. This policy choice had a dramatic effect on business firms' selections of lawful, profit-maximizing strategies. It also had one important long-term effect: the state law model of antitrust enforcement became more or less identical to the federal model and gradually became more and more superfluous as federal commerce clause power was expanded in the 1930's and 1940's. Once separated from the law of corporations, state antitrust policy lost most of its distinctiveness. Eventually the states did "abandon the field," but this occurred during the New Deal and after.

Two Legal Models for Dealing with the Trust Problem

By 1900 the word "trust" had become well established in the lexicons of political economists and lawyers. But "antitrust" law had developed along two quite different paths. The first, which one might call the *structural* model, was well established in state corporation law, and was based on a mixture of statutory and common law rules. The second, or *strategic* model, was equally well established in the common law governing agreements in restraint of trade. Both state and federal law dealt with loose combinations such as cartels under the rules applying to restraints on trade. Corporate law was largely irrelevant in cartel cases like *Trans-Missouri* or *Addyston Pipe,* because they involved simple agreements among otherwise competing corporations to fix price or output. But the "tight" combination, or merger, raised an entirely different problem: what is the proper relationship between the right of natural persons—recognized in every state—to form a business firm, and the competing public policy against monopolies? The union of two or more persons into a corporation legal under state law was not automatically an unlawful combination or conspiracy in restraint of trade.

The relationship between state corporate law and federal antitrust policy was complicated. First, under the supremacy clause federal antitrust policy never had to yield in any formal sense to state corporate law, and it never did. In 1912 the Supreme Court made it clear that legality under state corporate law was no defense to a federal antitrust prosecution.[14] But the supremacy clause notwithstanding, federal antitrust policy was equally clearly not designed to preempt all of state corporate law. Whether something was a mere agreement fixing price and output among competing firms or a union of firms into a single entity recognized by state law was quite relevant in Sherman Act cases. As the Supreme Court held in its first Sherman Act decision in 1895, Congress made no attempt "to limit and restrict the rights of corporations created by the States or the citizens of the States in the acquisition, control, or disposition of property; . . . or to make criminal the acts of persons in the acquisition and control of property which the States of their residence or creation sanctioned or permitted." Justice Peckham said the same thing in the *Joint Traffic* railroad cartel case (1898). "[T]he formation of corporations for business or manufacturing purposes has never, to our knowledge, been regarded in the nature of a contract in restraint of trade or commerce."[15]

Progressives were inclined to believe that the evil of the trust combination was caused by some deficiency in state corporate law. At least since Chief Justice Taney's decision in *Bank of Augusta v. Earle* (1839) that a business corporation "exists only in contemplation of law" and "can not migrate to another sovereignty" without permission, it was clear that the business corporation had only those powers that the state gave to it. Thus, if a trust could monopolize a multistate market there must be something awry with the state corporate law system. State antitrusters looked first to corporate law for a solution. Only when it failed did they seek legislation based on the common law of trade restraints. Some of these state statutes were inspired by the Sherman Act; some actually preceded it. Some of the earliest state statutes recognized antitrust fundamentally as a corporate problem. For example, the substantive sections of the Iowa and Illinois statutes, passed in 1890 and 1891, applied only to corporations.[16]

The contemporary literature ambiguously mixed the corporate law and trade restraint approaches to the trust problem. Some writers wrote as if the trust problem were entirely one of corporate structure, to be dealt with under corporation law. For many of these, a federal corporation statute for multistate firms was the best solution. Others wrote as if the trusts must be controlled, if at all, by the law of restraints on trade. Still others, such as Theodore Dwight, dean of the Columbia Law School, mixed the two.[17]

In his dissent in the *Northern Securities* case (1904), Justice Holmes read the Sherman Act as if it adopted the "contract in restraint of trade" approach exclusively. As a result, he concluded, the Sherman Act should not be read to condemn a merger that eliminated all competition between two railroads, because a merger was not a contract in restraint of trade but merely the formation of a new firm. "It would seem to me impossible," Holmes concluded, that the language of the Sherman Act "would send the members of a partnership between, or a consolidation of, two trading corporations to prison —still more impossible to say that it forbade one man or corporation to purchase as much stock as he liked in both." The logical effect of the majority's opinion condemning the merger would "disintegrate society so far as it could into individual atoms."[18]

Both the language and the legislative history of the Sherman Act suggested that Holmes was correct. Congress rejected the attempts to create a federal incorporation law, but instead condemned every "contract, combination . . . and conspiracy in restraint of trade." Why Congress chose the model it did is not entirely clear. In fact, the general intent of Congress in passing the Sherman Act is a matter of dispute. Some have argued that Congress wished to reduce the social cost of monopoly in the American economy. Others have argued that protection of consumers from monopoly wealth transfers was its principal motive.[19] But there is equally good evidence that Congress's rhetoric does not fully account for its true motives, which were to protect various special interest groups representing small business. For example, Senator John Sherman himself may have been the cat's-paw of the independent oil producers and refiners, who wanted protection from both Standard Oil Company and the railroads. Among the most aggressive lobbying organizations were several associations of salesmen and independent distributors, whose positions in the American economy were threatened by larger, vertically integrated firms. The only consumers lobbying Congress were the farmers, but their relationship to big business was complex and ambiguous. The farmers' principal objection appears to have been urbanization and the perceived consolidation of economic power in a few hands. Various labor organizations lobbied Congress as well, but their concerns were that new technology used by the trusts would reduce the number of jobs and that the big firms would then cut wages, not that laborers as consumers would have to pay higher prices.[20]

In any event, many lawyers believed that the approach Congress chose, based on the common law of restraints on trade, was the weaker of the two models for dealing with the trusts and reflected a certain lack of enthusiasm for the entire problem. A federal incorporation statute for firms seeking to do business in more than one state could have placed the multistate firm's structural decisions immediately under federal control. The government could have stipulated in corporate charters when firms could acquire other firms or their assets, come to agreements with them, build or purchase plants in other states, or integrate vertically. The government could have brought quo warranto actions against those who violated their charters. For this reason, Progressive lawyers and politicians continued to clamor for federal incorporation for at least twenty years after the Sherman Act was passed. But the Hepburn Bill of 1908, the most prominent of federal incorporation proposals, was attacked by practically every interest group— some because it was too strong, others because it was seen as exempting registered corporations from antitrust violations. The bill failed to pass.[21]

An important weakness in the corporate law model was its inability to make the distinctions necessary to permit firms to grow to a more efficient size, while prohibiting monopoly. The corporate law approach was too heavy handed. For example, the developing rule discussed below that stock transfer trusts involved corporations in ultra vires partnerships condemned all mergers by stock transfer trust, not only those that were monopolistic. Likewise, the corporate law rule forbidding one corporation from owning the shares of another corporation forbade all holding companies, not merely the anticompetitive ones. But the evolving law of combinations in restraint of trade was based on an economic theory that purported to distinguish competitive from anticompetitive combinations.

By the same token, however, the trade restraints model was believed to be weaker than the corporate law model because of the "rule of reason" inherent in its application. The model of combinations in restraint of trade was drawn from classical political economy, and was filled with economists' ideas about when such contracts were socially harmful and when they should be approved.

The corporate law model was preferred by many courts for precisely this reason: it gave unambiguous answers. In the sugar trust case, which applied New York state corporate law to condemn a common law trust agreement, the lower court had fashioned a restraint-on-trade rule that a stock-transfer trust was contrary to public policy because it tended to create a monopoly. The New York Court of Appeals affirmed the result, but based its rule entirely on corporate law. It was "needless to advance into the wider discussion over monopolies and competition and restraint of trade and the problems of political economy." The court thus condemned the merger without regard to anticompetitive consequences. Under the corporate law model the legality of mergers was determined, not by looking at political economy and the doctrine of monopoly, but by considering basic corporate power vis-à-vis the chartering state. The economic model should be reserved for loose combinations, such as cartels of independent firms, where corporate law did not apply.[22]

Congress itself had good reasons for not selecting the corporations-structural model for the Sherman Act. When the act was passed in 1890, state law still seemed adequate to control corporate structure. The corporation law of most states strictly limited the activities in which a corporation could engage to those enumerated in its charter. Most states forbade corporations from owning the stock of other corporations or from transferring their franchises, or special authorizations from the state, to other corporations. Furthermore, the business corporation was strictly a creature of the law. It had only those powers given to it by the state, and in the 1890's one state was not required to permit another state's corporations to do business within its borders. These limitations seemed to place the state-chartered corporation well under state control.

Combinations in restraint of trade between independent firms were a different matter, particularly if they involved interstate commerce. Throughout the 1890's the Sherman Act was used much more successfully as an anticartel device than as a "trust-busting," or antimerger, device. Its success against cartels was enhanced by Justice Peckham's rejection of the rule of reason in the *Trans-Missouri* case. Read together, *E. C. Knight* and *Trans-Missouri* suggested that the Sherman Act was the most effective tool against multistate cartels, while state corporate law would be more effective against mergers.

But the usefulness of state corporate law to combat mergers was already being undermined. Many American markets had become national, or at least regional. Business firms often competed with firms in other states. The trusts, which were designed in part to eliminate some of this competition, were multistate creatures.

At first, the new multistate firms were formed under common law trust arrangements that actually proved quite vulnerable to state corporate law. But the rise of the asset acquisition merger in the 1880's and of the holding company in the 1890's substantially undermined state power over the multistate business combination. Ironically, given the nomenclature the "antitrust" movement has given us, the business "trust" was never much of a legal problem. Once firms had abandoned the trust form of organization, they were increasingly able to evade state corporate law. The last successful corporate law quo warranto proceedings directed at monopoly occurred during the first decade of the twentieth century, and the basis for these was the state's power to exclude foreign (that is, out of state) corporations. But the states lost even that power during the same decade, when the Supreme Court overruled its earlier decisions and gave the corporation what amounted to a constitutional right to do lawful business in every state.[23]

Three Legal Models of the Business Trust

Standard Oil's S. C. T. Dodd and the other legal geniuses who invented the trusts were most concerned about running afoul of state corporate law. Each of the models they created was cleverly designed to evade the special limitations that states had imposed on corporate power. Perhaps these men lacked the foresight to sense their vulnerability to the law of combinations in restraint of trade; more likely, they sensed their vulnerability but decided that nothing could be done about it. In any event, the legal structure of the trust was directed at establishing the legality of mergers under state corporate law, not under the law governing combinations in restraint of trade.

Although trust arrangements were individually negotiated and each was different, every late nineteenth-century acquisition was organized around one of three legal models: (1) the stock-transfer trust model; (2) the asset-transfer combination; (3) the holding company. Each presented its own problems to state enforcers.

The Stock-Transfer Trust

The classic trust model, which characterized some of the earlier trusts (such as Standard of Ohio before a state court decision forced it to reorganize as a holding company),[24] was the stock-transfer trust. This legal model gave the "antitrust" movement its name. It was also the model that was most vulnerable to state corporate control.

In a stock-transfer trust the holders of stock in different corporations entered common law trust agreements transferring their shares to a common group of trustees in exchange for "trust certificates," reflecting the ownership interest of each individual shareholder. The trustees were obligated by the trust agreement to vote the shares according to the wishes of the trust certificate owners. The trustees then made management decisions for all the participating corporations together, and the boards of directors of each corporation were obligated to vote according to the trustees' orders. The amount of integration could vary from little more than price-fixing arrangements to the effective merger of many corporations into a single firm. The arrangements were designed to be legal under the corporation law of any particular state, and required no changes in the legal structure of a participating corporation. Yet they were agreements between distinct firms, and thus were vulnerable under the common law of trade restraints. At the time the first trusts were formed, however, combinations in restraint of trade were merely unenforceable among the parties. They were not affirmatively illegal in the sense that they could be challenged by the state. This appeared to make the trusts immune from external attack.

Commentators were initially convinced that the stock-transfer trust would successfully permit multistate corporations to evade the strictures of state corporate law. Writing in 1889, the Brown University economist Elisha Andrews was pessimistic, concluding that stockholders in participating companies would not be motivated to challenge trust agreements, since they stood to gain so much from the resulting monopoly profits. As a result, the law of trade restraints would be ineffectual. Further, the state had no legal basis for challenging them under state corporate law, since the corporations did not appear to be doing anything that could be condemned in a quo warranto proceeding. At the time Andrews wrote one state, Louisiana, had already brought a successful action against the cotton seed oil trust. But prevailing opinion was that the Louisiana case, which found that the trustees had presumed to act as a corporation without obtaining a corporate charter, was wrongly decided. Andrews believed that the defendants would win the pending quo warranto proceeding in New York against the sugar trust.[25]

But Andrews underestimated the creativity of state judges intent on destroying monopoly. The New York Court of Appeals did not follow the reasoning of the cotton seed oil decision, but it reached the same result. New York corporate law did not permit its corporations to enter partnerships with other corporations, and the trust was an illegal partnership. In addition, New York corporate law forbade individual shareholders from contracting away their voting power. Further, the law required a corporation to be controlled by its board of directors, but the trust agreements effectively transferred this control to the trustees, leaving the directors with no discretion. Each individual corporation in the trust "has a board of directors nominally and formally in office, but qualified by shares which they do not own, and owing their official life to the board [of trustees] which can end their power at any movement of disobedience."[26] In general, the stock-transfer trust met a bad fate under state corporation law, and by the turn of the century was considered to be an obsolete trust form. Most states found a way to condemn them under corporate law.[27] As Chapter 6 noted, they quickly modified the emergent notion that a state-brought quo warranto proceeding was available only for activities independently shown to violate the public interest. If monopoly was threatened, public injury was presumed.[28]

The result was a per se rule against the common law trusts. The economic questions suggested by the law of contracts in restraint of trade—whether the extent of the restraint as to time or space was unreasonable, or whether it tended to create a monopoly—were simply irrelevant. This was all the more important because at the time the sugar trust case was decided, as will be discussed in Chapter 21, the New York courts as well as those in other states were liberalizing the tests for the reasonableness of contracts in restraint of trade. They had already permitted restraints that covered virtually the entire United States.

In 1898 William W. Cook concluded in his influential treatise on corporations that the *Standard Oil* and *Sugar* decisions "convinced the trusts that their original mode of organization was illegal and must be abandoned." As Ernst von Halle put it in 1900, "It was considered wise to yield in the matter of form. The trusts . . . for the most part reorganized and reappeared in the form of gigantic corporations."[29] These giant corporations were the asset-transfer combination and the holding company. Few common law trusts were organized after 1890.

The Asset-Transfer Combination

The asset-transfer combination evaded the particular legal problems of the stock-transfer trust. Corporations generally were permitted to buy and sell property. In the asset-transfer model a central corporation was formed that then purchased or leased all the productive assets—plants, equipment, patent rights, and so forth—of the individual corporations. Asset-transfer mergers generally reflected a higher degree of integration than did the stock-transfer trusts, for a single corporation and set of stockholders became the owners of all the productive assets.

The asset-transfer merger proved more elusive than the stock-transfer trust. By the end of the century it was widely recognized as superior to the stock-transfer model, since corporate asset transfers were not automatically ultra vires under state corporate law. In his influential treatise on mergers, Judge Walter Chadwick Noyes also noted the "elementary principle" that a corporation "has inherent power to acquire and hold any property, real or personal . . . ." In 1891 Louis Boisot concluded that the asset acquisition was the merger form "least open to legal objection . . . ."[30]

The law of asset acquisitions and the classical corporation. To be sure, the asset-transfer model had its limits. Historically, although a corporation was entitled to buy and sell property, a company that sold all of its plant and equipment and stopped producing could have its charter forfeited for nonuser. In most cases this remedy was a paper tiger, however, for no one was particularly interested in preserving the empty shell of the old corporation. In the second half of the century courts adopted the classical view that the ordinary manufacturing corporation is simply another business firm, and that the public has no interest in whether it continues in business. The same Louisiana court that had struck down the cotton seed stock-transfer trust in 1888 held in 1889 that a monopoly, formed when three steamboat corporations sold all their property to a fourth corporation, was valid. Noyes noted the emergent rule that an ordinary manufacturing corporation was generally free to sell all of its productive assets, leaving only the empty shell.[31]

In the process of condemning the sugar trust, the New York Court of Appeals suggested that a consolidation accomplished by total asset-transfer would have been a legal alternative under New York law. However, the trusts "chose to disregard" the legal route. If there had been a legal consolidation of corporate assets, the individual companies "would have disappeared utterly, and not, as under the trust, remained in apparent existence to threaten and menace the other organizations." More important, under the consolidation statute "the resultant combination would itself be a corporation deriving its existence from the state, owing duties and obligations to the state, and subject to the control and supervision of the state; and not, as here, an unincorporated board, a colossal and gigantic partnership, having no corporate functions, and owing no corporate allegiance."[32] New York policy clearly preferred merger by asset acquisition.

The law of many states required the unanimous consent of shareholders for a sale of all the corporation's productive assets, but as late as the 1880's most manufacturing corporations were either closely held or family owned. In the 1890's, a large number of states began passing statutes that permitted a simple majority of shareholders to divest all the corporation's productive assets.[33] Ultimately a simple majority of shareholders was able to sell all a corporation's productive assets if the corporation was going to be dissolved anyway, as was generally the case in asset acquisition mergers. In *Pringle v. Eltringham Construction Co.* (1897), the Louisiana court noted the "fundamental principle that, in a corporation organized for the exclusive benefit of the corporators or shareholders [that is, not a public utility], the majority of its members may, in their discretion, wind up its business whenever they deem this step to be in the interests of the whole association." As a result, Walter Chadwick Noyes observed, "the power to sell the entire corporate assets follows . . . as an incident to the power to wind up the affairs of the corporation." Noyes noted some dissenting opinion that this rule should apply only to failing concerns. But such a rule would deny the directors the opportunity to act most advantageously for the corporation. Winding up might be more profitable when the corporation had accumulated a surplus and its assets had a high market value. Such "questions of expediency in corporate management" were not proper for court review.[34]

The exception to these rules was that "quasi-public" corporations, such as public utilities or railroads, could not go out of business without the consent of the sovereign that incorporated them. For this reason the Supreme Court had condemned a number of railroad mergers that had occurred when one railroad leased all the track of another railroad, with leases whose duration was often ninety-nine years or more—a longer period than the productive life of the track itself. But most corporations were not "quasi-public," and their purchases of one another's assets were legal, provided that operation of the acquired assets was within the acquiring firm's business purpose clause. In 1891 the Supreme Court made clear that its condemnation of lease consolidations applied only to quasi-public corporations.[35]

The law of assets acquisitions and the theory of competition. Judge Noyes's treatise on corporate mergers noted an important limitation on the asset-transfer merger: the acquisition of property had to be "useful or convenient" for the corporation's operation of the business "for which it was organized."[36] As a result, horizontal acquisitions—for example, a refiner's purchase of the refining plant of a competitor—were generally lawful. However, a vertical acquisition—such as a refiner's acquisition of a railroad or a set of retail outlets—would not be legal unless the acquiring firm also had authority in its charter to operate such facilities.

Noyes's observation was probably made with little thought of political economy or competition. But it revealed a major inconsistency between the corporate law of mergers and the emerging antitrust law that evaluated mergers under the law of contracts in restraint of trade. British and American economists had only recently begun to formulate models illustrating the price and output consequences of the elimination of competition. Under these models mergers of direct competitors were the most anticompetitive. As Chapter 21 will argue, the law of combinations in restraint of trade followed quickly behind and developed a much greater hostility toward agreements among competitors than it had exhibited in the past.

But horizontal mergers were most likely to be legal under the state corporate law of asset acquisitions, for they did not run afoul of business purpose clauses. If a corporation chartered to refine oil should acquire a competitor's oil refinery, the corporation was still doing nothing more than refining oil. Vertical integration was much more likely to violate the business purpose clause, although under the "collateral transactions" rule developed in the second half of the nineteenth century, corporations were frequently allowed to integrate vertically if they could show that the vertically related assets were convenient or advantageous for the conduct of authorized business. For example, a coal-mining company might be permitted to purchase a fleet of steamboats to carry its coal, or a railroad might be permitted to acquire a hotel for its passengers. "Conglomerate" mergers—or the acquisition of assets completely unrelated to the acquiring firm's authorized business—posed the smallest threat to competition, but were the most likely to be challenged under state corporate law. For example, a petroleum refining corporation that acquired a shoe factory would have a difficult time showing that operation of the shoe factory somehow enabled it to carry on its legal purpose more easily. The eminent corporate law treatise writer Victor Morawetz cited the "well-settled" proposition that "a corporation cannot engage in a business wholly distinct from its main enterprise, merely in order to raise funds for the purpose of carrying on the latter . . . ." To the extent that the concern of late nineteenth-century merger policy was the maintenance of "competition," economically defined, state corporate law did an extraordinarily poor job of meeting it. In fact, the law of corporations and the law of contracts in restraint of trade operated at cross-purposes.[37]

The legal status of asset acquisitions. Mergers by asset acquisition were generally legal under state corporate law, unless they were part of a scheme to defraud creditors. However, two variations on the basic asset purchase raised potential legal problems. The first was the problem of covenants not to compete, which often accompanied asset sales. The second problem was the legality of using corporate stock as payment.

When firms intent on becoming dominant acquired the assets of their competitors, they often required them to sign covenants not to reenter the same business. Often these covenants covered a large geographic area and were specified to run for a long time. Although the asset transfers themselves were legal, the noncompetition agreements were sometimes condemned as contracts in restraint of trade.[38] But the law of noncompetition covenants was itself in the process of a liberalizing revolution, and by the turn of the century most noncompetition clauses attending the sale of business assets were legal. For example, in *Diamond Match Co. v. Roeber* the New York Court of Appeals upheld an asset-transfer merger, even though it would condemn the stock-transfer trust in the sugar case three years later. The purchaser, a Connecticut corporation, purchased all the real estate, stock and materials, "trade, trademarks, and good will" of a New York manufacturer of matches. The purchase was part of a scheme to create a match monopoly, and the purchase agreement contained a covenant not to compete that spanned nearly the entire United States. The court could find nothing wrong with the purchase itself, and it approved the covenant not to compete under the emerging New York rule giving broad latitude to such covenants.[39]

The widespread use of covenants not to compete in cases involving asset acquisitions suggests that many of the great mergers of the turn of the century were anticompetitive. Alfred Chandler has argued that the attainment of scale economies and production economies resulting from vertical integration explain virtually the entire trust movement. But many of the great mergers cannot be written off this easily. If the mergers resulted only in reduced costs for the post-merger firms, it is hard to explain the persistent use of legally risky, nationwide, long-term covenants not to compete. Trust managers were obviously frightened by the prospect that those who sold their companies might return someday to compete with the trust. But small-scale entry is generally not a problem for a large corporation in an industry in which scale economies are substantial; the new entrant will always operate at a substantial cost disadvantage. More likely, even though the trusts attained economies of scale, management intended to raise prices so high that even entry on a small scale would be attractive. This happened in at least two Sherman Act cases involving asset acquisitions and non-competition covenants, *American Can* and the first *Corn Products* case, both in 1916.[40]

The second legal problem attending the asset acquisition was the method of payment for purchased assets. In most cases the acquiring firm paid for the assets it acquired, not with cash, but rather with its own stock. By 1890 courts were virtually unanimous in approving such payments. Much more problematic was the ability of selling corporations to receive the shares in exchange for their assets. Corporate law almost uniformly held that one corporation could not acquire shares in another corporation, absent explicit authorization. As the Illinois Supreme Court concluded in 1889, the fact that a gas company was authorized to produce gas and could lawfully acquire other gas-producing plants did not suggest "that the power to purchase stock in other gas companies should also exist. There is no necessary connection between manufacturing gas and buying stocks."[41]

If the corporation whose assets were being acquired had no authority to own stock, then the asset acquisition would have to be paid for with cash or other property. Thus in *Merz Capsule* a federal court applying Michigan law decided that although a New Jersey company could lawfully acquire the assets of a Michigan corporation as far as New Jersey law was concerned, it could not pay for the assets with its own shares. The Michigan corporation had no authority to own the New Jersey shares. The court found it unnecessary to express any opinion on counsel's "learned discussion concerning monopolies, competition, restraint of trade, and like problems of political economy," since the illegality of the transaction under Michigan corporate law was plain enough.[42]

Interestingly, when the Michigan Supreme Court was faced with an almost identical transaction four years earlier it had applied the law of contracts in restraint of trade, not of corporations. In *Richardson v. Buhl* (1889), the Diamond Match Company, a Connecticut corporation, had purchased all the assets of a Michigan corporation in exchange for stock. The Michigan corporation executed a covenant that it would not make matches anywhere for twenty years. The Michigan court relied on the law of contracts in restraint of trade to declare the noncompetition agreement invalid. Then the court launched into a long discussion of the evils of monopoly. Arthur J. Eddy roundly criticized the opinion for relying on vague issues of public policy and political economy, when it had an easy route to the same result via corporate law.[43] The rise of the holding company substantially solved the problem of stocks as payment for assets, for the states that passed such statutes.

The asset acquisition and the emerging vulnerability of corporate law. The rise of the asset-transfer combination brought one point home to state antitrusters: corporate law could not always be relied on to control the trusts. Writing in 1891, Louis Boisot concluded that states wishing to combat asset-acquisition monopolies should forget about corporate law and concentrate instead on the common law of combinations and conspiracies in restraint of trade. Such an approach would require new legislation, however. At common law, contracts in restraint of trade were unenforceable, but they were generally not challengeable by nonparties or the state. The success of the asset-acquisition trust led states to rely less on corporate law as an antimonopoly device and more on state antitrust statutes modeled after the common law of trade restraints, but giving enforcement power to the state itself.[44]

But state corporate law had one legal device remaining: the power of every state to exclude foreign corporations. The *Bank of Augusta* decision (1839) first suggested that, since corporations are creatures of state law, they are not automatically entitled to recognition by other states. The implication was that one state could forbid another state's corporations from owning property or productive assets within its borders. The Supreme Court so held thirty years later in *Paul v. Virginia.*[45] Thus if a New York corporation wished to purchase the plant of a competing corporation in Illinois, the state of Illinois could stop the purchase under its power to prevent the New York corporation from operating in Illinois. Holding-company acts were designed to help multistate corporations evade this state power; they proved remarkably successful.

The Holding Company

The third model of the business trust was the holding company, which came into prominence after 1889, when the "Traitor State," New Jersey, amended its general incorporation act to permit corporations to purchase and hold the shares of other corporations. Previous American decisions consistently held that without express authorization one corporation could not hold the stock of another. Only Maryland followed the English rule that permitted one corporation to own another's stock.[46]

New Jersey had a long history of attentiveness to the desires of the business corporation. In 1865 it had amended its corporation act to permit New Jersey corporations to own productive assets and carry on business in other states. Up to that time states had attempted to limit corporate activities in a variety of ways, one of which was to confine their operations to the incorporating state. In the 1870's and 1880's New Jersey discovered the wealth of tax revenue that could be earned from selling corporate charters to multistate businesses. This prompted the first holding-company act, passed in 1888. The original act was ineffectual because it did not permit New Jersey corporations to use their own shares as payment for the shares of other corporations. That defect was cured by legislation passed in 1889 and 1891. With subsequent amendments in 1893, a New Jersey corporation was effectively able to turn itself into a multistate holding company. Under the 1891 and 1893 amendments, a New Jersey corporation could be formed with only nominal capital paid in, agree to acquire a controlling interest in the shares of another corporation, and then issue shares with a stated value sufficient to pay for the transaction. The shares of the acquired firms were the paid-in capital necessary to support issuance of the holding company's shares.[47]

In 1892 New York also amended its statute to permit holding companies, and over the next decade several states followed suit. But New Jersey had been the first, and it acquired a clear advantage. By 1899 the states had chartered 121 corporations with a capitalization of $10 million or more each. Of these, 61 were chartered in New Jersey. By 1899 every combination that had been dissolved in state quo warranto proceedings during the 1890's had reorganized as a New Jersey corporation.[48]

Holding-company acts like New Jersey's were designed to avoid the legal problems that the trusts had encountered with the states, plus two additional ones. First, although states had the power to exclude foreign corporations, they did not always have the power to control the identity or nature of foreign shareholders. Second, at the time the holding-company acts were passed it was not apparent that a holding company would be deemed a "combination" or "conspiracy" under the Sherman Act.

The holding company and state power to exclude foreign corporations. Those who have seen state corporate law as a powerful antitrust device until the end of the nineteenth century have generally cited the ultimate power that each state had to exclude "foreign" corporations—that is, corporations chartered in a different state—from owning productive assets within their borders.[49] Although states could generally not discriminate against out-of-state sales agents or prevent the flow of goods from other states, nothing in the Constitution required them to permit foreign corporations to build plants or purchase real estate in their territory. Given that the states had this power to exclude foreign corporations, why was it not used more frequently, and why was there a widespread belief by the late 1890's that state corporate law was ineffectual for dealing with multistate firms? The Supreme Court did not overrule the decisions permitting states to exclude out-of-state companies until 1910. If all the states, or even a large number of them, had formulated policies persistently excluding foreign corporations, the interstate trusts would never have survived.

The problem of state incentives. It is easy to make too much of state power to exclude out-of-state corporations. First is the problem of incentives. Control of the trusts was only a small part of the economic policy of each individual state. Gilded Age states were as interested as states today in strengthening and enlarging their own economies. Aggressive attacks on foreign corporations were perceived as likely to discourage new business rather than promote local economies. States benefited even from monopoly production, particularly if much of the product was shipped elsewhere. Manufacturers located in other states had more or less the same right to sell their goods as local manufacturers had.[50] The principal victims of monopoly—consumers—were more widely scattered. As Charles Bostwick noted in 1899, each state wanted to avoid the consequences of monopoly pricing. But at the same time, each wished to "draw to its jurisdiction as much of these vast fortunes and monopolies as possible to provide itself food upon which the State could continue to live and draw its daily sustenance."[51] Thus we see the odd phenomenon of states such as New York being among the first to pass a holding-company act (1892) to permit its own corporations to own the shares of others, but also having an actively enforced state antitrust statute.[52] On the one hand, states did not wish to exclude foreign investment; on the other, they wished to retain the power to avoid the weight of monopoly, particularly when it fell upon them. Holding-company acts facilitated out-of-state investment in local assets as a general matter. State antitrust laws permitted the states to attack the mergers that they deemed harmful to the local economy. Significantly, when "traitor" states such as New Jersey were the *victims* of trusts, they prosecuted just as vigorously as anyone else.[53]

In 1914 the Progressive lawyer Raymond Zilmer applied a reverse Social Darwinism argument to account for state free-riding in the matter of trust policy. The state that pursues the trusts too aggressively, just as the state that is too enthusiastic about controlling child labor,[54] succeeds only in driving its capital elsewhere. As a result, socially "unfit" laws tend to survive. Zilmer concluded that only national legislation could control the giant corporation.

An important effect of aggressive application of state corporate law against the trusts was to drive them elsewhere—and driving them elsewhere was by no means an unmixed blessing. As the New York Court of Appeals wrote in an 1894 decision holding that a foreign corporation could lawfully purchase and sell real property in New York, a state would be foolish to exclude developmental capital merely because it was offered by a foreign corporation: "If our citizens are attracted to other jurisdictions for purposes of incorporation, because of more favorable corporation or taxation laws, I cannot see in that fact, however, and in whatever sense, to be deplored, any reason that they should be prevented from employing here the corporate capital in the various channels of trade or manufacture. That, as it seems to me, would be a rather hurtful policy and one not to be attributed to the State."[55]

The difference between foreign corporations and foreign shareholders. The rise of the holding company undermined the state's power to exclude foreign capital even when it wished to. Although the power to exclude foreign corporations proved to be a substantial impediment to the formation of asset-acquisition mergers, holding companies differed in one critical respect. In the holding company the shareholders, rather than the corporation, were foreign. Suppose that an Illinois corporation owning a single plant in Illinois should sell its plant to a New Jersey corporation. By this asset-transfer merger the Illinois corporation would become an empty shell and the plant, now owned by the New Jersey corporation, would become subject to Illinois's power to exclude out-of-state corporations. Under the holding company form of organization, however, majority shareholders in the Illinois corporation would transfer their *shares* to the New Jersey holding corporation. The plant would continue to be held by a domestic corporation, and the full panoply of constitutional protections for domestic corporations would remain in force.

Whether the state of Illinois could prevent such a transfer depended on its ability (1) to control the transfer of an Illinois corporation's shares to someone who was not a resident of Illinois; and (2) to prevent corporate ownership of the shares of an Illinois corporation. Prevailing opinion was that a state had the power to place these restrictions in the charters of new corporations. However, states could not limit share ownership retroactively. Similarly, a state might have the power to limit future transfers of stock to foreign corporations. However, if it attempted to void past transfers that were legal when they were made, it would have to pay compensation to the owners. In short, at the time the holding-company acts were passed, they appeared to facilitate legal mergers, provided that these occurred before state legislatures had a chance to close the door.

Much of our confusion over the development of the holding company and of state antitrust policy lies in the failure to distinguish between the power of domestic firms to own shares in other corporations and the power of foreign corporations to own shares in domestic corporations. At the turn of the century most states forbade their own corporations from owning the shares of other corporations, whether domestic or foreign. However, as Walter Chadwick Noyes wrote in 1909, courts uniformly held that shares in domestic corporations could be owned by foreign corporations, unless the state explicitly forbade such holdings. In 1898 then Circuit Judge Horace H. Lurton concluded that a foreign corporation had the power to purchase shares in a domestic corporation. "Comity requires that this charter power [in the foreign corporation] shall be recognized as valid if not opposed to some law or policy of the State creating the corporation in which stock has been acquired."[56] Most states had no such policy, because they had confronted the problem so rarely.

Noyes noted that, once a foreign corporation had acquired the shares of a domestic corporation, the state's legislature could not retroactively apply a policy against foreign corporate ownership, because such a policy would violate the contract clause of the Constitution.[57] Nevertheless, the creation of a monopoly could be enjoined as against the domestic policy of a state.[58] As a result, if the law of the state permitted, a state could enjoin the purchase of a domestic corporation's shares by a foreign corporation. In short, the holding-company acts forced the courts to look to the law of monopoly in order to separate the sheep from the goats.

Charles McCurdy has argued that in 1895 the relief requested by the United States government in the *E. C. Knight* antitrust case "was readily available in Pennsylvania courts" as a "simple problem in corporation law."[59] *Knight* did not create a "gap" that left interstate trusts free of regulation altogether. The decision merely left to each state the problem of controlling its own corporations that attempted to expand their productive capacity into other states or, conversely, of excluding foreign corporations that attempted to expand their productive capacity into another state's territory. Pennsylvania law did not authorize its corporations to purchase the stock of foreign corporations. If they did so, Pennsylvania courts could apply the remedy.

But the merger being challenged in *E. C. Knight* was more elusive than McCurdy suggests. The American Sugar Refining Company, a holding company incorporated under New Jersey law, purchased the shares of four different Pennsylvania corporations, each of which owned and operated sugar refineries. The purchase price was shares of stock in the New Jersey holding company.[60] Thus the issue was not whether a Pennsylvania corporation could purchase the stock of a New Jersey corporation, but whether a *shareholder* in a Pennsylvania corporation could sell his stock to someone else—a nonresident corporation—and whether that same shareholder could purchase stock from an out-of-state corporation. These questions raised issues quite different from the question of the state's power to exclude foreign corporations. First, federal or state law probably prevented Pennsylvania prosecutors from imposing such restraints on alienation as a general matter. Several courts had held that shareholders had a right, whether constitutional or at common law, to sell or give away their shares.[61] Second, as noted above, even if Pennsylvania had the general power to create such restraints, its power to impose them on a previously existing corporation posed substantial questions under the contract clause. Finally, the states' power to exclude foreign corporations was irrelevant. The four refineries continued to be held by domestic corporations. Only the shareholders were foreign.

The notion that the *E. C. Knight* decision created a "no man's land"[62]— a haven for trust formation that was out of reach of both the federal government and the states—has been exaggerated. If Pennsylvania wanted to, it could prevent the assembly of a sugar-refining monopoly within its borders. But given the limitations of state corporate law, the problem had to be dealt with under the law of trade restraints, not of corporations.

However, the trade restraints law in most states was far more ambiguous, affected by notions of political economy, and inclined to be tolerant of even monopolies, provided that they were not created by means of an array of restrictive covenants limiting future competition. Perhaps most important, the common law of trade restraints had no alternative to the corporate law's quo warranto proceeding by which the state itself could challenge unlawful acts. The common law of trade restraints was generally enforced by private parties. The result was increased reliance by the states on antitrust statutes that looked very much like the Sherman Act. Walter Chadwick Noyes made it clear that the purpose of state antitrust legislation was to cut through all the formalities of state corporate law. Under the antitrust statutes "the test whether a combination is in violation . . . lies in its object or tendencies and not in its form." Even holding companies that were lawful under state corporate law could constitute unlawful combinations under state antitrust law.[63]

Combination and corporation: The legal theory of the firm. By the end of the century state corporate law seemed to be a failure—or, to view it another way, to have succeeded so well that it had unleashed a power it could no longer control. Writing in 1900, Christopher G. Tiec'eman blamed the entire trust problem on state corporate law. The onl. way to prevent the continuing growth of the giant business corporation, he argued, was to repeal the general corporation acts and make incorporation a special prerogative of the state, just as it had been a century earlier.[64]

The problem of monopoly fell to the antitrust laws, but the regime established by state corporate law continued to exist. The Sherman Act's interpreters faced the difficult question: when is a group of entrepreneurs structured as a single legal entity nevertheless an unlawful "combination" under the Sherman Act? State corporation law generally determined when a group of persons acting together were a single "firm," whose individual members were legally incapable of "combining" or "conspiring," in the parlance of the Sherman Act. But by 1900 it was clear that if entrepreneurs could fall outside the "combination" category simply by organizing themselves into a single entity under state law, they could undermine the Sherman Act.

At the time the Sherman Act was passed, the holding company had just made its first appearance. Congress did not take it very seriously. Nothing in the act's legislative history suggests that Congress gave much thought to the problem of what constitutes a single entity rather than a "combination." Most antitrust scholars in the 1890's believed that the holding company was not covered by the Sherman Act because it was a legal structure for a single business firm, created by the sale of one corporation's property to another corporation. Such a sale was not a cartel of separate entities that would have been characterized as a "combination in restraint of trade" under the common law. In 1901 Arthur J. Eddy argued that the corporate merger was the obvious legal alternative to the common law trust or pool, because the former was not a "combination" within the meaning of the Sherman Act, but merely a purchase and sale of property. "Congress has no power or authority to limit and restrict the right of corporations, created by states or citizens of states, to acquire, control and dispose of property . . . ."[65]

Judge Howell E. Jackson, who joined the Supreme Court in 1893, took this approach in one of the first Sherman Act decisions. In holding that the whiskey trust had not violated the statute, he concluded that Congress lacked the power "to limit and restrict the right of corporations created by the States, or the citizens of the States, in the acquisition, control and disposition of property."[66] The Court agreed in the sugar trust case three years later. The formation of the sugar trust was a sale of property from one set of business owners to another. However, "the act of Congress only authorized the Circuit Courts to proceed by way of preventing and restraining violations of the Act in respect of contracts, combinations, or conspiracies in restraint of interstate . . . commerce."[67]

By a slow process the Court came to reject this presumption that state corporate law determines what is a "combination" and what is a single business firm. The first combinations condemned under the Sherman Act, the railroad pools in the *Trans-Missouri* (1897) and *Joint Traffic* (1898) cases, were simple agreements among different corporations and did not raise the issue. Only in the *Northern Securities* case (1904) did the Supreme Court decide that the Sherman Act could condemn a holding company, and even then four Justices dissented.[68] Justice Brewer felt obliged to write a long concurring opinion explaining that, because a corporation was merely a fictional person and not a natural one, a corporation's acquisition of property could constitute a "combination," while a natural person's acquisition could not.

The *Northern Securities* decision provoked a famous dissent by Justice Holmes. Holmes concluded that the Sherman Act did not apply to the formation of a firm. Its words "hit two classes of cases, and only two, — contracts in restraint of trade and combinations or conspiracies in restraint of trade." The act merely stated the common law, whose objection to contracts in restraint of trade "did not apply to partnerships or other forms, if there were any, of substituting a community of interest where there had been competition."[69]

In commenting on the case, Victor Morawetz conceded that every corporation is a "combination" of its shareholders. However, the mere formation of such a combination should never be considered illegal. Such a rule would strike at the heart of the state's power to define the business firm. Rather, a combination becomes unlawful when it is formed for an illegal purpose. Morawetz concluded that the *E. C. Knight* case was correctly decided, while the *Northern Securities* case was wrong. The lawyer Herbert Pope agreed that some, but not all, corporate mergers were illegal under the *Northern Securities* decision. But the relevant question, he argued with some foresight, was not whether the parties to the merger intended to commit an illegal act. Rather, it was whether the merger gave them effective control of the market.[70]

Even after *Northern Securities,* lawyers continued to argue that corporate asset acquisitions and holding companies legal under state law could not be considered "combinations" under the Sherman Act. Identifying what constituted the business "firm" was a prerogative that belonged to the states. Columbia University's George F. Canfield conceded that a corporation "may in one sense be regarded as a combination of the persons composing it," but only in the sense that "a man, although usually regarded as a unit, may be considered as a combination of his limbs and the other parts of his anatomy."[71]

The notion that the Sherman Act was not intended to interfere with state prerogatives to determine what constitutes a business firm was deeply embedded in the legal mind. Sir Frederick Pollock could explain the *Northern Securities* decision breaking up the holding company only on the theory that the stock transfers at issue were somehow fraudulent. The Northern Securities holding company must have been not a firm at all but merely a cartel, and the transfer of shares a subterfuge. The Supreme Court itself sensed the concern. In a subsequent decision it made clear that it had interpreted the Northern Securities holding company to be the result of real stock transfers creating a new firm. Nevertheless, the union was illegal under the Sherman Act. Judge Noyes read the two decisions broadly. "The States have no power to charter corporations to break such a law" as the Sherman Act.[72]

Nonetheless, even *Northern Securities* did not preempt state corporate law quite as aggressively as Noyes suggested. In fact, the Northern Securities holding company probably violated the law of at least one of the states in which a substantial amount of its railroad business was performed.[73] Not until the Union Pacific Railroad merger case in 1912 did the Supreme Court expressly hold that a merger that was legal under state corporate law could be condemned under the Sherman Act. "That the purchase was legal in the state where made, and within corporate powers conferred by state authority, constitutes no defense, if it contravenes the provision of the anti-trust act."[74]

The Failure of Corporate Law and the Invention of Antitrust

As the federal antitrust movement got under way, many states were passing their own antitrust laws, generally modeled after the common law of restraints on trade, but often closely tied to state corporate law. Some of the statutes made participation in trusts ultra vires, or provided for forfeiture of a corporate charter as a penalty for violation.[75] Others provided that foreign corporations that violated the statute should be denied permission to do business within the state.[76] Others gave minority shareholders the right to object to the creation of asset-transfer trusts.[77]

But the very same states also seemed to be racing with each other to liberalize their corporate laws just as New Jersey had done—to invite the trusts to take advantage of their particular incorporation act. In 1900 Ernst von Halle noted the "strange spectacle of the enactment of the most severe laws against trusts and combinations on the one hand, and on the other of a transformation of the corporation law which facilitated a remodelling of the trusts, and the continued transaction of business in the state."[78] Von Halle concluded that the two policies were incoherent. He noted, for example, that Illinois both had modernized its corporate law to be more like New Jersey's and was also one of the most aggressive enforcers of its antitrust act. He predicted that few giant firms would select Illinois as a situs because the antitrust prosecutions would make them feel unsafe.

But there is an alternative explanation for the phenomenon that von Halle was witnessing. The states were adopting a policy of encouraging efficient or economically beneficial mergers, while condemning those that were anticompetitive. Corporate law was badly designed for this task. The law of combinations in restraint of trade, by contrast, could be used to condemn anticompetitive mergers while permitting the others. As the corporate law treatise writer William W. Cook observed in 1891, the fact that corporate law forced the common law trusts to reorganize as asset acquisitions or holding companies was a great victory in the eyes of the public, even though it had little impact on the size or power of the affected firms. The greatest impact was on the rules of disclosure. The trustee agreements were completely unregulated and almost always secret; the holding companies were required to report assets, earnings, and expenses. Of course, even these reporting requirements were niggardly compared with those that would be required by federal law passed during the Great Depression—but they were better than nothing. Corporate disclosure became one of the principal concerns of the Bureau of Corporations, the 1903 creation of Theodore Roosevelt's Progressive administration.[79]

With remarkable speed the states abandoned corporate law as an antitrust device and turned to antitrust statutes based on the common law of trade restraints. Thomas Carl Spelling's 1893 treatise on trusts and monopolies dwelt almost entirely on corporate law; it included the following as its entire discussion of state antitrust legislation:

> Statutes directed against restraints of trade generally have recently been passed in a few States. Such statutes are of little avail, except as declarations of the common law, and few, if any, decisions of courts have turned upon their substantive provisions.[80]

By 1898, Charles Fisk Beach's influential treatise on monopolies and industrial combinations revealed rapidly expanding application of the new state antitrust laws. The second editions of Noyes's treatise and Frederick Cooke's treatise on combinations and monopolies both contained sections on state antitrust law that were far longer than the corresponding sections on federal antitrust law. The number of state prosecutions in the 1890's and 1900's rivaled or exceeded those of the federal government. State antitrust became the principal device for challenging monopolistic combinations.[81]

But the triumph of state antitrust proved to be short-lived. State antitrust based on the law of corporations was distinctive. Each state was the prime interpreter of its own corporation statute, and remedies such as quo warranto against state corporations were simply not available to the federal government. But once the states turned to statutes that looked like "little Sherman Acts," state antitrust policy increasingly became a carbon copy of federal policy. Given the fact that the large business firm was a multistate creature, much more easily reached by the federal courts, state policy was bound to yield to federal.

CHAPTER 21

The Classical Theory of Competition

Ever since 1890 scholars have debated the relationship between the Sherman Act and the common law of trade restraints. Did the framers intend merely to enact the common law, or did they hope to do something more? Was there an identifiable "common law," or was it merely an "artificial construct"?[1] The great difficulty we have had in understanding the relationship between the Sherman Act and the common law lies in the fact that in 1890 the common law of competition was undergoing the same revolution that political economy experienced as classicism became neoclassicism. This chapter returns to the same economic ideas developed in Chapter 18 with respect to labor combinations. Here, however, the concern is with competition among business firms.

One of the great myths about American antitrust policy is that courts began to adopt an "economic approach" to antitrust problems only in the 1970's. At most, this "revolution" in antitrust policy represented a change in economic models. Antitrust policy has been forged by economic ideology since its inception. But even the common law experienced economic revolutions. The notion that antitrust can be freed from economic policy making if we can only rediscover its common law roots is based on the misconception that the common law itself was somehow exempt from economic policy making.[2] It never was in any branch, and certainly not in the law of monopolies and restraints on trade. The common law responded dramatically to the death of mercantilism and the rise of classicism in the late eighteenth century.[3] It responded equally as classicism collapsed a century later.

Courts had already realized this at the time the Sherman Act was passed, as they wrestled with the problem of how much economic analysis was appropriate in judge-made antitrust policy. As we saw in Chapter 20, judges preferred the relatively traditional approach of state corporate law to what they perceived as the excessively "economic" approach of the common law of trade restraints. But by the 1890's it was clear that the trusts could be reached effectively only under the relatively economic law of combinations in restraint of trade. At the same time, Anglo-American economic theory was nearing the end of a great revolution that we identify today with the rise of neoclassicism. Classical political economy had become neoclassical economics, and by 1890 neoclassicism was already affecting judicial thinking. The important question for courts interpreting the Sherman Act was not whether they would take an "economic approach." That question was settled decisively in Congress's selection of an antitrust model based on the law of restraint of trade rather than corporate law. The only important question was whether courts deciding antitrust cases would draw their economic wisdom by looking back at one hundred years of classicism, or forward to emerging neoclassicism.

Competition and Politics

Political economy and public law became technical and professionalized in the second half of the nineteenth century. Before this they had been far more humanistic. Classical political economists were men of affairs. Political economists and lawyers were concerned with the same policy problems, they tended to view things the same way, and they read and wrote in the same journals. The great legal values of nineteenth-century American lawyers—individualism, liberty of contract, abhorrence of forced wealth transfers—were also the values of classical political economy. To be sure, judges did not often cite works of political economy in legal opinions. But the etiquette of legal citation was a function of lawyers' technique, not of understanding or perception.

During the nineteenth century both law and economics began to develop theories of competition and ideological defenses of competition as a social good. Lawyers and economists each had exaggerated notions about the ability of the other discipline to determine the appropriate limits of competition policy. Political economists typically thought that law would provide all the answers to policy questions about how much competition is enough. Lawyers typically thought that such questions presented a problem in political economy. But each group had a growing faith that something called "competition" was a great good, and that the state should encourage more of it.

Although classicists were concerned to preserve "competition," they did not understand that term as we understand it today. Competition was not a theory about cost-price relationships, as it came to be in neoclassical economics. Nor was it a theory about the "struggle for survival," as it was for some Gilded Age intellectuals and entrepreneurs who adopted models based on the Darwinian law of natural selection. Rather, competition was a belief about the role of individual self-determination in directing the allocation of resources, and about the limits of state power to give privileges to one person or class at the expense of others. The law of competition was classicism's mechanism for keeping special interest politics out of state decision making about the allocation of resource—particularly the allocation of entrepreneurial opportunities. Classicism purported to give the same opportunity to all. It abhorred special privileges. In this sense, classicism was the preeminent device for separating politics and state policy.

With the rise of neoclassicism in the 1870's, political economy became less credible as a device for keeping law and politics distinct. The great British neoclassicist Alfred Marshall and his wife Mary Paley Marshall made perhaps the most valiant attempt to preserve the separation when they argued that the classical name "political economy" should be replaced by "economics":

> The nation used to be called "the Body Politic." So long as this phrase was in common use, men thought of the interests of the whole nation when they used the word "Political"; and then "Political Economy" served well enough as a name for the science. But now "political interests" generally mean the interests of only some part or parts of the nation; so that it seems best to drop the name "Political Economy," and to speak simply of Economic Science, or more shortly, Economics.[4]

For the Marshalls, "economics" had to be separated from "politics." The first dealt with the welfare of society as a whole; the second with the welfare of interest groups.

But the inevitable result of the Marshallian revolution—signaled by the publication of his great *Principles* in 1890, the same year that the Sherman Act was passed[5]—was that the science of economics became more technical and less approachable by the nonspecialist. Neoclassicism became preoccupied first with marginal utility theory, then with cost-price relationships, the geometry of the marginal cost and marginal revenue curves, and the relationship between consumers' surplus and monopoly. Subjectively, economics become increasingly concerned with technique, preoccupied with theory, and less concerned about issues of state policy. The material welfare school of the early twentieth century tried to reestablish the role of economics in policy making[6]—but that effort was effectively torpedoed by the vehement, religious argument of 1930's positivists that changes in marginal utility cannot be compared among different persons. Although a particular individual might prefer a dollar to a doughnut, the positivists argued, no one can compare the amount of pleasure that one person experiences by having a dollar with the amount another experiences by having a doughnut. As a result, economics had little to contribute to our understanding of how a particular policy of dividing entitlements among conflicting interest groups would make society as a whole better or worse off.[7]

Just as the political economist was becoming an expert,[8] American lawyers were developing the rhetoric of legal formalism, which instructed lawyers searching for the law not to look outside their case reports. Many of America's elite lawyers came to believe that the law was a closed system, just as mathematics was. Law had its own techniques, and these were different than the techniques of economics or philosophy. These attitudes created the illusion that law and political economy really never had very much to do with each other.

Nonetheless, even during the heyday of legal formalism people doing economics and people doing law were engaged in the same enterprise. Political economists applied their increasingly sophisticated tools to the understanding of markets. Lawyers and judges surely tried to understand them too, if only to regulate them. Not coincidentally, political economists and lawyers continued to describe markets in the same way. Only when the modern theory of "perfect competition" began to emerge in the 1920's and 1930's, attended by technical notation and the mathematics of marginalism, did economics and law begin speaking about competition in completely different languages. The Babel that resulted was in many ways the worse for both economics and law.

"Public Policy," Economics, and the Common Law

Classical political economists were expressly concerned with public policy, much more than their neoclassical followers. But many nineteenth-century lawyers purported to believe that the common law was purely "private," unconcerned about the sovereign's economic policy. This distinction between classical political economy's expressly "public" and the common law's "private" character was an important part of classical political theory. The public purpose of classical political economy was to show that the state ought to stay out of most legal disputes, except in its role as mediator. The law purported to follow the rules that classical political economy discovered.

Forceful arguments have been made that American common law in the nineteenth century was heavily concerned with economic development.[9] That is undoubtedly true. Nonetheless, most common law rhetoric was distinctly private, expressly eschewing "public policy" concerns unless these had been articulated in a statute. Policy making was for the legislature, not the courts.[10] Americans generally accepted the famous dictum of Justice Borrough that public policy "is a very unruly horse, and when once you get astride it you can never know where it will carry you."[11] As William W. Story put it in the second edition of his treatise on contracts (1847), "Public policy is in its nature so uncertain and fluctuating, varying with the habits and fashions of the day, with the growth of commerce and the usages of trade, that it is difficult to determine its limits with any degree of exactness."[12] Nevertheless, Story was willing to concede that a contract would be void on public policy grounds whenever it "conflicts with the morals of the time and contravenes any established interest of society." In the *License Tax Cases* (1866)[13] Chief Justice Salmon P. Chase opined that a court, unlike a legislature, can "know nothing of public policy . . . ." It "cannot amend or modify any legislative acts. It cannot examine questions as expedient or inexpedient, as politic or impolitic; considerations of that sort must, in general, be addressed to the legislature. Questions of policy determined there are concluded here."

One exception to the bias against importing public policy considerations into legal decisions was the common law of contracts in restraint of trade—that is, contracts in which a person promised not to engage in a particular business, usually for the benefit of some competitor. When Charles Fisk Beach identified why such contracts were void he cited, not a statute, but rather the "general principle" of free labor: that the law must "secure to every citizen the right to pursue his ordinary avocation and dispose of his labor, or of the product thereof, without restraint, and to protect the public from the evil consequences of an agreement under which it would be deprived of the benefits of competition in skilled labor."[14] Or, as Elisha Greenhood stated it, the "capacity of an individual to produce constitutes his value to the public . . . . The actual product belongs immediately to him who employs him, but mediately to the State, and goes to swell the aggregate of public wealth." As a result, the state was rightfully concerned about agreements that restrained people's ability to produce. The law of contracts and combinations in restraint of trade was one of the few areas where the courts expressly accommodated the nineteenth-century state's economic policy.

The explicit articulation of public policy in the law of contracts in restraint of trade was an open door for economic doctrine. When economic theory changed, the legal rules followed quickly. A pressing item on the Gilded Age policy maker's agenda was the formation of a new legal model for the regulation of competition. The eighteenth-century common law of contracts in restraint of trade seemed quite irrelevant to the perceived evils of big business. The classical law of monopolies, which viewed them as exclusive grants from the sovereign, had little to do with the modern, emerging *de facto* monopoly. How the state could regulate enterprise while yet preserving the distinction between public and private law, and the essentially private nature of business transactions in a market economy, became a vexing problem.

Classical and Neoclassical Competition

Within the modern neoclassical model "perfect competition" describes a state of affairs in which price is driven to marginal cost and firms are forced to minimize their costs through innovation and growth to the optimal size. But classicism knew nothing of marginal cost and, in fact, very little of the difference between fixed and variable costs. American classicists wrote little about competition, and wrote about monopoly chiefly to attack exclusive privileges given by the government.[15]

The first generation of economists who might be called neoclassical talked about competition, but even for many of them "competition" referred to a theory about liberty and free choice, not to a description of price-cost relationships. As we have seen, as late as 1888 the M.I.T. economist Francis Walker defined competition as "the operation of individual self-interest, among the buyers and the sellers of any article in any market. It implies that each man is acting for himself solely, by himself solely, in exchange, to get the most he can from others, and to give the least he must himself."[16] Anticompetitive conduct was a restraint on individual freedom, not mere interference with a relationship between prices and costs.

Within a decade, however, "competition" had acquired a much more technical meaning. In the Yale economist Arthur Twining Hadley's *Economics* (1896), which had the benefit of Alfred Marshall's *Principles,* competition was something that existed only among the buyers within a single market, or only among the sellers. Hadley relied on a theory of marginal utility that he borrowed from the English political economist William Stanley Jevons and the influential Austrian School of political economists to explain why demand curves slope downward and to illustrate that under competition output would increase to the point that the demand curve intersected the cost curve.[17] In 1899, John Bates Clark's *Distribution of Wealth,* also relying heavily on the work of the Austrians, developed an even more sophisticated model of "perfect competition," illustrating that social welfare was maximized when "marginal social gain" and "marginal social sacrifice" were equated.[18]

The law actually kept close step with these changes in the conception of "competition," gradually lessening its concern about the restraints on individual freedom that contracts in restraint of trade entailed, and becoming increasingly concerned about arrangements that were anticompetitive in the neoclassical sense, such as price fixing.

The historical concern of the common law of contracts in restraint of trade was coercion, or the elimination of noncontracting parties' freedom to act. Although completely voluntary agreements to eliminate competition, such as by price fixing, were not generally enforceable in court, neither were they indictable offenses or even challengeable by third parties in civil actions.[19] The law stepped in only when entrepreneurs combined to force the recalcitrant to cooperate or adhere to their terms. Thus concerted refusals to deal, or boycotts, were generally condemned. As the lawyer Albert Stickney put it in 1897, "no individual is deprived of a legal right by the act of the owner of merchandise in selling on his own terms, or in refusing to sell on any terms, whether his act is the result of his own separate volition of the moment, or his volition of a former moment in making a contract with others."[20]

This concern with contract and freedom from coercion rather than with cost-price relationships explains why the classical model made little distinction between "horizontal" and "vertical" arrangements in restraint of trade. As Chapter 18 noted, when Francis Walker and Oliver Wendell Holmes, Jr., spoke of "competition," they referred to the rivalry that existed between buyers and sellers as well as that which existed among buyers. Sellers were free to charge whatever price they pleased. They were free to do so unilaterally, and generally they were free to act in concert, provided that their agreements were purely voluntary—that is, that no one was coerced to join the cartel. "[N]o other man suffers a legal wrong, when I simply put a bond on my own freedom," said Albert Stickney in concluding that cartels ought to be legal. Cartels did not jolt the classical lawyer's economic conscience because no one's freedom was being denied. Sellers were free to set their price, and buyers were equally free to say no. Neoclassicism greatly broadened this concept of "coercion" to include what might be called "market coercion," or the deprivation of opportunities that the competitive market itself could be expected to provide.

The regard for liberty in the classical conception of competition helps to explain the common law's concern with consideration in cases challenging agreements in restraint of trade. Early on, courts stressed that promises not to compete would be enforced only if supported by adequate consideration. The court had to satisfy itself that the person who had promised not to compete would not become a charge on the community. The court did this by determining that the promisor had received the market value of his promise.[21] Dicta in *Mitchel v. Reynolds* (1711), which originally adopted a reasonableness rule for covenants in restraint of trade, suggested that the court must determine the adequacy of the consideration. But in *Hitchcock v. Coker* (1837) the court reverted to the usual contract rule that it would determine only if the consideration was legal, but would not inquire into its adequacy. American courts sometimes noted the earlier English rule inquiring into adequacy of consideration in cases involving contracts in restraint of trade. But as early as 1811 they held that nominal consideration could support a contract in restraint. The courts would not inquire into the adequacy of the consideration; however, they would ensure that consideration had been given.[22]

The rationale of the consideration requirement was certainly not that the amount of competition interfered with depended on the presence of consideration. The point was that the doctrine of competition was part of the doctrine of liberty of contract. One could be forced to give up his freedom to make free market choices only if he had been adequately bound by contract, and contracts required consideration. Consideration tended to establish that a refusal to engage in business was voluntary and not coerced.

Contracts and Combinations in Restraint of Trade

Until the rise of the trusts in the 1870's and 1880's, American competition policy was located principally in two bodies of law. First was the law of corporate charters, and the questions about when they implied monopoly rights or when explicit monopoly rights would be recognized. Second was the law of contracts in restraint of trade. In *Navigation Co. v. Winsor* (1873), Justice Joseph P. Bradley gave what became the classic American position on the law of contracts in restraint:

> There are two principal grounds on which the doctrine is founded that a contract in restraint of trade is void as against public policy. One is the injury to the public by being deprived of the restricted party's industry; the other is the injury to the party himself by being precluded from pursuing his occupation, and thus being prevented from supporting himself and his family. It is evident that both these evils occur when the contract is general, not to pursue one's trade at all, or not to pursue it in the entire realm or country. The country suffers the loss in both cases; and the party is deprived of his occupation, or is obliged to expatriate himself in order to follow it. A contract that is open to such grave objection is clearly against public policy. But if neither of these evils ensue, and if the contract is founded on a valid consideration and a reasonable ground of benefit to the other party, it is free from objection and may be enforced.[23]

Bradley's statement expressed both a "public" and a "private" interest in the law of contracts in restraint of trade. As Charles Fisk Beach noted, "the law has regard, on the one hand, to the interests of the person restrained . . . and, on the other hand, it takes account of the interest of the community in providing that it shall not be deprived of the benefit of his business, or exposed to the burden of his support, as a result of his lack of employment."[24] The post–Civil War doctrine of contracts in restraint of trade was heavily imbued with the ideology of "free labor," that each person had a right to pursue a lawful calling. Justice Bradley was second only to Justice Field in bringing free labor ideology to the Supreme Court, and the law of contracts in restraint of trade was its private expression.

During most of the nineteenth century the law of cartels and mergers was not part of the law of contracts in restraint of trade. Few American decisions before 1870 dealt with price fixing[25] and even fewer dealt directly with the competitive consequences of mergers. In 1891 the Minnesota Supreme Court chided a lawyer who had "confounded" his argument by indiscriminately mixing cases involving contracts in restraint of trade with cases involving "combinations between producers or dealers to limit the production or supply of an article so as to acquire a monopoly of it and then unreasonably enhance prices."[26] The law of contracts in restraint of trade and boycotts expressed the classical meaning of "competition," with its emphasis on liberty and freedom from coercion. A voluntary price-fixing agreement was not "anticompetitive" in the sense that anyone's freedom to act was artificially restrained. At common law they might be unenforceable, but they were almost never actionable by nonparticipants. But beginning in the 1890's the law of cartels and mergers became the quintessential expression of neoclassical price theory, particularly of its emerging theory of competition.

This common law distinction between contracts in restraint of trade and price-fixing agreements accounts for some of the confusion concerning the meaning to be given to section 1 of the Sherman Act, which condemned "every contract, combination in the form of trust or otherwise, or conspiracy in restraint of trade." Section 1 was only rarely applied to covenants not to compete in the classical sense. It quickly became, for all practical purposes, a price-fixing and antimerger statute.

One might argue that section 1 of the Sherman Act condemned both "contracts" and "combinations," and that while the first covered covenants not to compete the second covered combinations such as cartels and mergers to monopoly. But the most careful scholars of the common law, such as Justice Holmes, knew that the common law itself made no such distinction. Concern with the voluntary elimination of competition between producers simply had not played much of a part in common law adjudication. Justice Holmes's large lexicon of dissenting antitrust opinions includes this rather startling proposition:

> The court below argues as if maintaining competition were the expressed object of the [Sherman] act. The act says nothing about competition.

The *Northern Securities* case (1904), where Holmes's dissent appeared, condemned a merger between parallel railroad lines that effectively created a monopoly of east-west railroad traffic over a large section of the United States between the Mississippi River and Puget Sound. The merger was accomplished by means of a New Jersey holding company and was completely voluntary. No effort was made to coerce unwilling outsiders to participate, or to keep anyone from practicing his trade.

Holmes explained at some length why contracts or combinations "in restraint of trade" in section 1 of the Sherman Act really had nothing to do with competition. "Contracts in restraint of trade" were defined by the common law as "contracts with a stranger to the contractor's business . . . , which wholly or partially restrict the freedom of the contractor in carrying on that business as otherwise he would." The "trade restrained was the contractor's own."

"Combinations or conspiracies in restraint of trade," Holmes continued, "were combinations to keep strangers to the agreement out of the business." The objection to them was not "to their effect upon the parties making the contract" but rather "to their intended effect upon strangers to the firm and their supposed consequent effect upon the public at large." As such, they "were regarded as contrary to public policy because they monopolized, or attempted to monopolize, some portion of the trade or commerce of the realm."

Holmes argued that the Sherman Act's words "in the form of trust or otherwise" referred not to price-fixing agreements but rather to "exclusionary practices" directed by the large combination against its competitors. Congress's concern "was not the union of former competitors, but the sinister power exercised or supposed to be exercised by the combination in keeping rivals out of the business and ruining those who already were in."

Holmes's *Northern Securities* dissent adopted the classical position that the Sherman Act, like the common law, must be concerned with artificial restrictions placed on the individual's freedom to act. It should not care about purely voluntary arrangements, such as cartels or mergers, that simply had the effect of raising price. The mere voluntary elimination of competition among firms by mutual agreement was not covered by the statute. "[I]t is lawful to abolish competition by any form of union," provided that the union was indeed voluntary.[27]

Holmes never had much regard for American antitrust policy. He was inclined to believe it ineffectual, and once described it to his friend Sir Frederick Pollock as "a humbug based on economic ignorance and incompetence."[28] But Holmes was not the sort of judge who would distort a statute's intended meaning simply because he thought it a bad idea. He believed that Congress had chosen a particular instrument for dealing with the trusts, and that the statute should be interpreted as written. Holmes assumed that the framers of the Sherman Act intended neither more nor less than to enact and thus federalize the common law. As a result, the offenses identified and condemned in the act ought to have their common law meaning.

Holmes was correct about the historical meaning of the common law.

The classical doctrine of contracts in restraint of trade had little or nothing to do with the emerging neoclassical doctrine of competition. Arthur J. Eddy observed in his treatise on combinations (1901) that "the law governing contracts in restraint of trade has no direct connection with the law governing combinations." Nevertheless, "nearly every decision against a combination assigns as one of the reasons for its illegality that it is 'in restraint of trade.'" This "involves a misapprehension and misapplication of the law governing contracts in restraint of trade." A cartel agreement, for example, "is in no sense a contract in restraint of trade, unless it directly seeks to prohibit some one from again embarking in business."[29]

Frederick H. Cooke, whose appreciation of the neoclassical revolution was far greater than either Holmes's or Eddy's, made the same observations in his important treatise on combinations, monopolies, and labor unions (1898), emphasizing even more forcefully the common law's lack of concern about "competition." The law of contracts in restraint of trade would be irrational, he argued, if it were viewed as being concerned about competition. For example, the law condemned a covenant not to compete unlimited as to space covering "one out of a thousand trade competitors in a given city," even though "the continuance of the other nine hundred and ninety-nine would have effectually prevented the danger of monopoly." But the law, "at least until very recently," permitted "the withdrawal of nine hundred and ninety-nine such competitors from carrying on their trade within a given city . . . ," provided that their agreement was limited as to time and space.

Cooke criticized several decisions upholding contracts in restraint of trade because their coverage was limited as to time or space. The "confusion of thought" produced by traditional restraint law had prevented them from seeing the more important issue of "restrictions upon competition."[30] By and large, common law decisions treated contracts in restraint of trade that involved horizontal competitors exactly as they treated those that did not. For example, *Skrainka v. Scharringhausen* (1880) upheld a six-month price-fixing contract among twenty-four stone quarries in a portion of St. Louis. The agreement was not an illegal contract in restraint of trade because it was "amongst the quarrymen of one district of one city, and it does not appear that it embraces all of them . . . . It is limited both as to time and place; and we know of no case in recent times in which a contract such as the one before us has been declared illegal."[31]

That the restraints doctrine was not designed to preserve competition is obvious from the way courts employed the doctrine. Under English law a restraint was "general" if it applied to all of England, or "partial" if it applied to anything less. Similarly, under the American common law, restraints were ordinarily characterized as general if they applied to the entire state, or partial if they applied only to a smaller part. As the Illinois Supreme Court explained this rule in 1901, it had nothing to do with competition, but rather with the fact that each state regulates its own internal affairs, "supports those who become public charges, and is interested in the industries of its citizens." A "general" restraint forbade someone from pursuing his occupation anywhere in the realm, and thus could force him to become dependent on charity or state aid. A "partial" restraint, by contrast, always left him someplace to pursue his calling. It did not matter that markets might encompass either much more or much less than a single state. Writing in 1917, the Harvard antitrust professor Albert M. Kales found the relationship between the restricted area and the sovereign territory of the jurisdiction to be quite irrational. "The rational test is the extent of the business sold and not the boundaries of some political subdivision of the country," he argued, thus suggesting the eventual interpretation of the Sherman Act that evaluated the tendency of an agreement to control trade in some relevant market.[32]

Some of the earliest Sherman Act decisions read the classical common law approach into the act. They followed Holmes, and refused to condemn cartels or mergers unless the defendants had also made contracts that were in restraint of trade at common law. In *Corning* (1892) the judge refused to condemn a merger by asset acquisition because the sellers had not been required to enter noncompetition agreements. In *Terrell* (1892) the court found price fixing among liquor dealers legal under the Sherman Act, because there were no contract terms requiring buyers to deal exclusively with the cartel. Likewise in the whiskey trust case (1892) Judge Jackson interpreted the term "monopolize" to mean either, following the historical meaning of monopoly, an *exclusive* control of some market; or, following the historical doctrine of contracts in restraint of trade, contractual obligations to exclude others from the market. Since the whiskey trust controlled only three-quarters of the liquor sold, it did not do the former, and Judge Jackson could find no efforts by the trust to curtail the production of others. In the cash register trust case (1893), however, the court had no difficulty condemning the defendants for employing coercive methods against others. They had used spies, threats, and intimidation, and had even beaten and bribed employees. The mere attempt to control all of the cash register business did not violate the statute, Judge Putnam concluded, but the coercive methods employed did.[33]

The inevitable direction of both common law and Sherman Act jurisprudence was toward more sanguinity about the public threat of contracts in restraint of trade, and more concern about purely voluntary agreements among competitors who collectively dominated some market. The law gradually accommodated a new, more neoclassical concept of "competition," within which few contracts in restraint of trade were perceived as anticompetitive. Most of them were nothing more than covenants not to compete attending the sale of businesses in competitively structured industries. These simply did not create the opportunity to monopolize a market.

The New York Court of Appeals is the best example of the trend toward increased toleration of traditional contracts in restraint of trade, and increased hostility toward cartels. In *Diamond Match Co. v. Roeber*[34] (1887) the court noted the important difference between contracts in restraint of trade and restraints on competition. In a contract in restraint of trade, such as a covenant not to compete, the contract deprives the participant from carrying on his trade and the "community of any benefit it might derive from his entering into competition." However, "the business is open to all others, and there is little danger that the public will suffer harm from lack of persons to engage in a profitable industry."

A year later in *Leslie v. Lorillard* (1888) the same court approved an arrangement under which the Old Dominion Steamship Company purchased a promise not to compete from a rival, the Lorillard Steamship Company. Dominion apparently purchased no ships or other assets from Lorillard, but only the noncompetition covenant. In upholding the agreement, the New York Court of Appeals concluded that "no contracts are void, as being in general restraint of trade, where they operate simply to prevent a party from engaging or competing in the same business." The court was much more explicit a decade later in *Wood* (1901), when it approved an express agreement, unaccompanied by any transfer of property, under which the defendant promised he would not sell molding-sand in competition with the plaintiff. In fact, when the agreement was struck the defendant was not even in the molding sand business, and had no assets to sell. "[C]ontracts between parties, which have for their object the removal of a rival and competitor in a business, are not to be regarded as contracts in restraint of trade," the court concluded. "They do not close the field of competition, except to the particular party to be affected."[35]

Under this developing model even general restraints, or contracts unlimited as to time or place, could be reasonable. The rule of reason announced in the English case of *Mitchel v. Reynolds* (1711) considered time and space restrictions an important attribute of reasonableness, and many later decisions held that unlimited restraints were inherently unreasonable.[36] In *Nordenfelt* (1894), however, the House of Lords held that limitations as to time and space were only elements to be considered in determining reasonableness. If the restraint covered only a small part of the market, "competition," neoclassically defined, was not injured. In *Oakdale Manufacturing* (1894) the Rhode Island Supreme Court indicated that a covenant not to compete should be legal "even if the restriction [is] unlimited as to both time and territory."[37]

The traditionalist Arthur J. Eddy and the neoclassicist Frederick Cooke expressed dramatically different views of the importance of space and time restrictions in determining the validity of contracts in restraint of trade. Eddy presented the time and space rules as if he had gotten them from the top of a mountain. They were rigid and virtually without exception. Cooke trivialized them, finding the rules themselves irrational—because they usually had nothing to do with competition. Theodore Dwight also criticized the old rules as "based on erroneous views of political economy," and noted that they "have practically disappeared in great trade centres, for example, in England and New York."[38]

Coupled with classicism's traditional harshness toward contracts in restraint of trade was a surprising casualness about cartels. Within the classical model, the simple voluntary price-fixing conspiracy, with no exclusionary practices directed at nonparticipants, was not particularly offensive. Nevertheless, to say that the classical law of cartels was not concerned with competition is not quite accurate. Classicism's emphasis on liberty, together with the absence of any notion of barriers to entry, yielded a complete theory of competition. Within the classical paradigm, monopoly prices could never be earned in any industry unless people were artificially restrained from entering. Such restraints could take two forms. First, they might be a grant of exclusive privileges from the sovereign, which classicism abhorred and classicist jurists repeatedly condemned. Second, the restraint could take the form of a privately created restriction on entry, either by a contract including the restricted person as a willing participant or else by a combination directed at other people as targets. A mere agreement among sellers to fix prices was of little concern, provided that neither the price fixers nor the state forbade others from entering the field. If the cartel members sought to charge monopoly prices, new competition would immediately frustrate their attempt. Classical cases that did condemn cartel agreements generally emphasized the defendants' efforts to exclude or coerce nonparticipants.[39] The mere fact that customers were required to pay a higher price was not a kind of "coercion" that classicism recognized, because the customers were free to walk away and purchase elsewhere. As late as 1892 a court dismissed a Sherman Act indictment that charged lumber dealers with price fixing, because the indictment alleged nothing more than a voluntary attempt by competitors to agree to raise prices. "[C]ompetition is not stifled by such an agreement, and other dealers would soon force the parties to the agreement to sell at the market price, or a reasonable price, at least."[40]

One consequence of the neoclassical revolution in economic theory was a change in the legal definition of "coercion" to encompass the loss of market opportunities that competition would have afforded. When the neoclassical revolution was complete, even the customer forced to pay a high price because of cartelization or monopolization was legally "coerced." The Sherman Act itself reflected this emergent neoclassicism. Not only did the new statute federalize the perceived common law, but it also changed the status of contracts, combinations, and conspiracies in restraint of trade from merely unenforceable to affirmatively illegal. The government or even private parties forced to pay higher prices for monopolized goods had an action under the Sherman Act. Holmes himself noted as much in his *Northern Securities* dissent. Section 7 of the Sherman Act gave a cause of action to any private person "injured in his business or property" by a violation. "This cannot refer to the parties to the agreement, and plainly means that outsiders who are injured in their attempt to compete with a trust or other similar combination may recover for it."[41]

Holmes's opinion was based strictly on the language of the statute, for the common law did not permit damage actions by purchasers from cartels or competitors who were not the targets of boycotts.[42] The importance of this change is underestimated by those who suggest that the Sherman Act adopted the common law, with the relatively minor distinction that arrangements unenforceable at common law became actionable by third parties or the state.[43] This change itself was revolutionary. There was no effective law against price-fixing in the United States before the antitrust movement. The common law made price-fixing agreements unenforceable—but this merely told price fixers that their cartels had to be enforced by means other than judicial action. We have no way of knowing how many cartels existed in nineteenth-century America. Undoubtedly, however, they often survived or thrived free from the legal challenges of customers or other nonparticipants. In small, isolated markets containing only a few sellers—and nineteenth-century America was full of these—cartels were likely widespread and profitable. Recalcitrant members or newcomers could be dealt with through exclusive dealing contracts or other, more subtle, forms of discipline. For all practical purposes, the perceived judicial hostility toward price-fixing agreements was not enough to become even a minimal state "policy." The policy, to the extent it can be articulated, was simply that colluders were on their own. If collusion was mutually beneficial to all participants, it likely went unchallenged.

The development of the modern neoclassical model of perfect competition and of the law's new concern with agreements between competitors were nearly simultaneous events. For example, at the same time that the Court of Appeals of New York became much more tolerant of contracts in restraint of trade in the *Roeber* (1887), *Leslie* (1888), and *Wood* (1901) cases noted previously, it became much more hostile toward price fixing. In *People v. Sheldon* (1893) it held that a voluntary price-fixing agreement among coal dealers was not merely unenforceable but was an indictable criminal conspiracy. To be sure, the New York court limited its criminal holding to cartels governing "an article of prime necessity," but the case represented a distinct departure from the traditional common law rule that, although cartels were unenforceable by members, they could not be challenged by outsiders or by the government unless the cartel's members exercised coercion or intimidation against others. In *De Witt Wire-Cloth* (1891) the New York court concluded that "people have a right to the necessaries and conveniences of life at a price determined by the relation of supply and demand, and the law forbids any agreement or combination whereby that price is removed beyond the salutary influence of legitimate competition."[44]

In the 1890's some American state courts began holding for the first time that price fixing was illegal without regard to the reasonableness of the prices fixed or the market position of the defendants.[45] The framers of the Sherman Act could not have had these cases in mind, for none had yet been decided in 1890. In his famous *Addyston Pipe* decision, of which more will be said later, Judge Taft cited them for the proposition that American courts had always condemned "naked" restraints without inquiry into their reasonableness, and that this per se rule had been enacted into the Sherman Act. In fact, in 1890 American courts had done no such thing.

By the turn of the century, then, the common law's theory of competition had changed completely. The rhetoric had changed relatively less, however, and some courts continued to use the language of contracts in restraint of trade in condemning price fixing and even mergers. The result was a great confusion about what the common law of trade restraints had been, and what the Sherman Act was designed to do.

From the start, the Supreme Court gave the new statute a distinctly neoclassical interpretation. Although Justice Peckham and the Court said in 1897 that the statute reached "every" contract in restraint of trade, the Court was much harsher on cartels than on traditional contracts in restraint of trade. During the period from 1897, when the Supreme Court declared price fixing illegal per se in the *Trans-Missouri* case, until 1911, when the Supreme Court adopted a rule of reason for certain restraints, it continued to hold that common law contracts in restraint of trade—that is, covenants not to compete—were illegal only if unreasonable. In the *Cincinnati Packet* case (1906) the Supreme Court approved a five-year noncompetition agreement attending the sale of two steamboats, noting that the agreement was reasonable and valid at common law. In *Shawnee Compress* (1908) the Court condemned a covenant not to compete contained in a lease agreement, but only because the covenant's coverage was far broader than necessary to protect the lessor's business. The lessor had given away all its business assets and the purpose of the transfer was to create a monopoly. Lower federal courts likewise held that covenants not to compete were legal under the Sherman Act if they adhered to the traditional reasonableness rules. In his *Addyston Pipe* opinion (1898) Judge Taft equated covenants not to compete with "ancillary" restraints that could be legal under the Sherman Act, provided they were reasonably limited.[46]

Judge Taft's Addyston Pipe Opinion

Antitrust scholars have often praised Judge Taft's opinion in *United States v. Addyston Pipe & Steel Co.* (1899) for its expression of the relationship between the Sherman Act and the common law. The great brilliance of the *Addyston Pipe* opinion, argue its admirers, is that Taft showed that the common law had always adopted a distinction between "naked" and "ancillary" restraints, condemning the former automatically, but subjecting the latter to further analysis for reasonableness.

But *Addyston Pipe* contains nothing like the broad distinction between "naked" and "ancillary" restraints that some claim to have found.[47] Taft reserved the rule of reason only for ancillary restraints of a particular type—those found in noncompetition covenants. General production-enhancing joint ventures, or ventures reducing market transaction costs but requiring the sellers to set a uniform price, were not included in Judge Taft's list. The ancillary restraints that courts generally upheld as valid, Taft said, were:

> (1) by the seller of property or business not to compete with the buyer in such a way as to derogate from the value of the property or business sold; (2) by a retiring partner not to compete with the firm; (3) by a partner pending the partnership not to do anything to interfere, by competition or otherwise, with the business of the firm; (4) by the buyer of property not to use the same in competition with the business retained by the seller; and (5) by an assistant, servant, or agent not to compete with his master or employer after the expiration of his time of service.[48]

All five of Taft's examples were of classical covenants not to compete, which had always been analyzed under the rule of reason at common law. He selected these examples because they were the only ones in the law of trade restraints up to that time. His distinction between "naked" and "ancillary" restraints was merely an acknowledgment that the Sherman Act would continue to apply the rule of reason to noncompetition covenants attending the transfer of a business or business asset, or an employment agreement.

Even so, Taft painted an impressionistic, noninterpretivist picture of the law of cartels and contracts in restraint of trade. His *Addyston Pipe* opinion was as important for its disingenuousness as for its brilliance. Most important, he suggested that the common law treated "naked" restraints such as price fixing with more hostility than it treated ancillary restraints such as covenants not to compete. As noted earlier, during most of the nineteenth century, common law judges did precisely the opposite. Further, Taft took a series of opinions holding that "coercive" restraints were illegal but noncoercive ones were not, and read them to say that the common law condemned "naked" restraints but not necessarily those that were ancillary to some other purpose.[49] In the process he totally ignored or misconstrued common law and even Sherman Act decisions approving naked price fixing, pure and simple.[50] Half the opinions he cited only to explain why they were wrong.[51] Finally, Taft relied on several recent decisions that reflected the emerging neoclassical view that price fixing itself was bad, whether or not third parties were coerced, the defendants had market power, or the prices fixed were unreasonable.[52] He cited at least one opinion as condemning a naked restraint which in fact condemned an ancillary restraint for failure of consideration.[53] Several cases that he cited for the common law position on contracts in restraint of trade in fact involved statutes that departed from the common law.[54] Some of the opinions he cited as condemning "naked" restraints actually condemned joint ventures with great efficiency-creating potential. For example, *People v. Sheldon* involved a joint venture that established a uniform grading system for coal and common sales agency, but also facilitated the fixing of prices. The *Morris Run Coal* case, decided by a Pennsylvania court applying a New York statute, rejected the defense that the coal grading and selling joint venture was designed in part "to lessen expenses," because the resulting restraint was "too general" for such an end. In other words, the court applied the classical rule that the restraint could not be broader than necessary to protect the parties' business. In addition, Taft failed to acknowledge that the restraint at issue in the *Trans-Missouri* case, decided by the Supreme Court the previous year, was ancillary—an efficiency-creating cargo-transfer, scheduling, and freight rate agreement among unregulated railroads.

Disingenuous or not, all of this was immensely valuable to emerging federal antitrust policy. First, Taft's analysis ran roughshod over Peckham's approach in *Trans-Missouri* and effectively read the rule of reason back into the Sherman Act. Restraints defined as ancillary were reasonable; they were illegal only if they tended to monopolize. Second, *Addyston Pipe* fused the neoclassical model of competition with the legal doctrine of combinations in restraint of trade. In the process Judge Taft created the illusion that the law of combinations in restraint of trade had always been concerned with "competition," neoclassically defined. The result was a thoroughly neoclassical Sherman Act. Taft's analysis so overwhelmed future antitrust case law that Holmes's dissenting position in *Northern Securities* six years later—although historically more correct—was all but forgotten.

Competition, Liberty, and Coercion

Both the classical law of restraints on trade and the neoclassical law of competition expressed concern about "coercion" of unwilling parties.

The classical American doctrine of contracts in restraint of trade recognized and permitted two kinds of "coercion" as consistent with the
individual's liberty of contract. First, individuals could bind themselves
contractually. Second, individuals agreeing with each other could coerce
third parties, provided that the coercion was expressed in the market
and nowhere else. Today we have little difficulty regarding cartelization
as a form of coercion directed at customers—but in the classical model
the customers were seen as free to walk away, just as sellers were free
to set their prices. As Holmes suggested in his *Dr. Miles* dissent, no one
has a complaint when the seller of a good merely charges all the market
will bear. Those who wish to have the product will purchase it, and
those who find the price too high will not.[55]

But neoclassicists viewed the problem of free choice and restraint in
a more subtle way. Coercion was something that could exist in degrees,
and the market itself could coerce. The new perspective is illustrated in
the theory of consumers' surplus developed in Alfred Marshall's *Principles of Economics*.[56] In Marshall's model every person has a "reservation
price"—or a price more than which he will not pay. Both those who
purchase and those who refuse to purchase from the monopolist or
cartel are "coerced"—either into paying more than the competitive price
or else into not purchasing at all. Both are deprived of what an unrestrained market would offer.

From 1890 until around 1920 courts engaged in considerable debate
over the distinction between "competition" and "coercion" in trade
restraints.[57] Almost everyone agreed that certain kinds of agreements
were "coercive" and ought to be condemned, but determining where
the line should be drawn between competitive and coercive activities
proved to be very difficult. The debate was complicated by the fact that
it became a focal point of an even larger debate over the role of subjective intent in common law adjudication. In 1894 Holmes made his
famous argument that purported questions about intent really reduce
to nothing more than questions of state policy. Actual subjective intent
is almost always irrelevant. Holmes gave his famous illustration about
the sweet shop. If the plaintiff operates the only sweet shop in town, it
is not tortious for the defendant to open a second shop in competition
with the plaintiff, even if the defendant's only motive is to spite the
plaintiff. The state's policy of encouraging competition trumps any
contrary suggestions drawn from the defendant's subjective intent.
Holmes's Harvard colleague James Barr Ames responded that tortious
activity, including injury to competition, should be identified by reference to the actor's intent.[58]

For the time being, the debate over objectivism appeared to leave the problem of identifying anticompetitive restraints untouched. Courts deciding antitrust cases would continue to use subjective criteria for a long time. But one important consequence of the debate was increased attention to objective criteria in determining the plausibility of anticompetitive consequences. For example, in the 1890's and after courts looked increasingly to the economic power or size of the defendants in relation to some "market" in order to determine whether their restraint might be anticompetitive. A good illustrative pair of opposing cases is the Minnesota Supreme Court's *Bohn* opinion of 1893 and the Supreme Court decision in *Eastern States Lumber,* twenty-one years later. The first is a clear illustration of the classical concept of coercion, the second of emergent neoclassicism. Both cases involved the same basic facts. A trade association of lumber dealers agreed with each other that no member would purchase lumber from a wholesaler who also retailed directly to customers. In short, the retailers were trying to prevent the lumber wholesalers from integrating vertically into retailing, probably for one of two reasons. First, the retailers may have been fixing prices, and the wholesalers may have wished to enter retailing themselves in order to evade the cartel. Such integration would have cost the cartel market share and perhaps threatened its existence. Second, the vertically integrated firms may have had lower costs than independent firms and thus threatened the independents' livelihood.

Whatever the motive, the Minnesota court approved the boycott, finding no "coercion" and observing that the plaintiff had the option of either complying with the defendant association's terms or else not dealing with the association. That the defendants had acted in concert was "wholly immaterial." Any single dealer was free to refuse to deal for any reason, and "[w]hat one man may lawfully do singly, two or more may lawfully agree to do jointly. The number who united to do the act cannot change its character from lawful to unlawful."

The United States Supreme Court took a starkly different position two decades later, finding that the publishing of information identifying wholesalers engaged in retailing "tends to directly restrain the freedom of commerce by preventing the listed dealers from entering into competition with retailers." The Court then concluded that "[a]n act harmless when done by one may become a public wrong when done by many acting in concert . . . if the result be hurtful to the public or to the individual against whom the concerned action is directed."[59]

Political economy took nearly a century to develop a model of competition in which certain kinds of business conduct were "coercive" simply because they altered the structure and character of the market. During the last quarter of the nineteenth century judges and political economists simultaneously developed the theory that when a firm or a group of firms acting together comes to dominate a particular market, then their price increases or refusals to deal may be inherently coercive—because the buyers in the market do not have adequate alternatives. Gradually the "rule of reason" used to determine whether to uphold contracts in restraint of trade came to focus on the defendants' position in the market.[60] In 1909 Frederick H. Cooke concluded that the common law test for legality in price-fixing cases had become whether "the agreement [was] among dealers in substantial control of the supply to produce such result."[61] Legality rested on "the circumstance of their having such control, and not by the circumstance of the agreement; in other words . . . the presence or absence of the agreement furnishes no test of legality." Nearly all the cases that Cooke cited were from the years 1890 to 1910. For example, *Slaughter v. Thacker Coal & Coke Co.* (1904) upheld a joint-selling agency and price-fixing agreement among coal dealers that was almost identical to ones previously condemned without market analysis.[62] The court emphasized that the market for coal was competitive; the defendants were only "three small companies out of the vast number of coal producing companies in the State," producing an "utterly insignificant portion" of the entire market.

Cooke also argued that the reasonableness test for covenants in restraint of trade should include an inquiry into the effect of the restriction upon competition. Under this "test of extent" such contracts would be condemned if, "roughly speaking," they resulted in control of "90 or, at any rate, 95 percent. of the supply within a given area." Arthur J. Eddy objected strenuously to all such tests. He found the objective questions whether the defendants had the capacity to injure competition, or whether their agreement had the "tendency" to reduce output, to be irrelevant and harmful. The only basis for liability, he argued, was whether the parties to the agreement had the purpose to commit an illegal act.[63]

As noted earlier, the Sherman Act represented an important structural departure from the common law in that it permitted state or third-party challenges to agreements. This change was radical because most combinations would never have been challenged at all when they could be attacked only by participants. The most important such cases were voluntary mergers by asset acquisition or holding company. Under the common law, illegality meant that a contract could not be enforced; but once an acquisition was completed there was nothing left to enforce.[64] For this reason the common law of trade restraints had never developed rules about the legality of mergers.[65] The federal courts interpreting the Sherman Act were necessarily writing on a clean slate, and with the *Northern Securities* decision they were already beginning to look at market dominance, or the effective elimination of competition. The new legal test, Herbert Pope suggested, was that "[t]o be illegal, the combination must rest upon an understanding or agreement between actual competitors who, by removing competition between their established independent enterprises, are able at the time to control the market or industry in which they are engaged."

The Classical Exception: Articles of Prime Necessity

Classicism recognized one important exception to its position that combinations and cartels did not coerce customers. Customers were not free to walk away if the restraint covered the market for an article of "prime necessity"—something that no one could do without, such as "short rations in a shipwreck," as Holmes put it.[66] Restraints involving the necessities of life were treated more harshly than those involving goods about which buyers had discretion. Customers had the freedom to walk away from shade rollers, insurance, glue, or washing machines.[67] But in condemning the sugar combination (1889) the New York courts placed heavy emphasis on the fact that sugar was a necessity of life.[68] In *Richardson v. Buhl* (1889), the court condemned the Diamond Match Company's attempt to buy out its competition and secure covenants not to compete, citing the fact that matches had become an article of prime necessity.[69] A few of the earlier Sherman Act cases in the lower courts also created distinctions for articles of prime necessity. In its opinion in *United States v. Trans-Missouri Freight Association* (1893), subsequently reversed by the Supreme Court, the Eighth Circuit Court of Appeals suggested that cartels among goods of prime necessity ought to be illegal per se, while cartels involving other goods should be evaluated under a rule of reason. The Second Circuit followed this rule in *Dueber Watch* (1895), holding that when an agreement did not involve an article of prime necessity "it is not the existence of the restriction of competition, but the reasonableness of that restriction" that determines legality: "The goods in question are not articles of prime necessity, as were the flour, coal, and other staple commodities referred to in many of the cases cited upon the argument . . . . Each one of the defendants had an undoubted right to determine for himself the price at which he would sell the goods he made, and he certainly does not lose that right by deciding to sell them at the same price at which a dozen or so of his competitors sell the goods which they make."[70]

By 1890 neoclassicism had begun to develop a model of competition in which the concept of "prime necessity" was all but irrelevant. Marshall's *Principles of Economics* generalized about the difference between the amount that a customer was willing to pay and the price that a competitive market should yield. There was almost always a difference, although it might be larger for articles of prime necessity. But even a cartel covering the most frivolous luxury might raise its price above the competitive level. More important, questions about the "necessity" of an article were far less important in the new competition model than questions about how easily it could be produced and how quickly new producers could enter the field. Agricultural products were certainly articles of "prime necessity," in the common law sense, but they were also relatively easy to produce and the nation was overrun with farmers. Thus the threat of a potato monopoly was probably far less serious than the threat of a gasoline monopoly, even though few people were yet using gasoline. Under the emerging model the fact that gasoline was not an article of prime necessity was far less important than the fact that the technology for refining gasoline was expensive and took a long time to build. As Albert Kales noted in 1917, the courts appeared to be making a distinction between restraints on trade that took specialized assets off the market, and those that removed easily transferable assets. "Where the business is carried on principally with a plant and property which cannot readily be converted to any other use, and will in all probability lie entirely idle during a period provided by the covenant, the restriction is regularly held to be illegal."[71] However, in a case such as *Leslie v. Lorillard* the covenant was justifiably sustained because the subject of the covenant, a steamboat, could easily be transferred to another run.

As we have seen, the judiciary responded to the emergence of neoclassical price theory with an increased hostility toward price fixing. Initially, the hostility was directed at cartels of articles of prime necessity. In 1889 even the Supreme Court took the position that price fixing with respect to an article of "public necessity," in this case illuminating gas, should be illegal, although price fixing in ordinary items might be protected by liberty of contract.[72]

The hostility toward price fixing and other anticompetitive agreements quickly became much more generalized, and the focus on articles of prime necessity began to fall away. In 1884 an Ohio court held that price fixing by tobacco warehousemen was illegal whether or not they provided one of the necessaries of life. "Although courts may be inclined to apply this rule more strictly in cases involving the necessaries of life or services of a *quasi-public* nature, there is no authority for excepting from its operations any legitimate trade or business." Between 1885 and 1910 many courts repudiated the distinction.[73] As mentioned earlier, in *Sheldon* (1893) and *Cummings* (1901) the New York Court of Appeals began taking a harder line against price fixing. At the same time, it gave reduced significance to the distinction between general articles and those of prime necessity. A state might have to show that a price-fixed product was an article of prime necessity in a criminal conspiracy action, but not in a civil action.[74]

In the principal Sherman Act price-fixing cases, *Trans-Missouri* (1897), *Joint Traffic* (1898), and *Addyston Pipe* (1898), the Supreme Court and Judge Taft found it absolutely irrelevant that the price-fixed products were not articles of prime necessity. In *Trans-Missouri* Justice Peckham interpreted the Sherman Act to forbid cartels in products and services of all kinds. In *Addyston Pipe* Taft expressly repudiated any exception for goods not of prime necessity.[75] From that point on the collusion rule became generalized to all goods and services. Frederick H. Cooke concluded that the distinction "seems never to have been very firmly established in our jurisprudence, and the present tendency seems to be in favor of repudiating it as inapplicable . . . ."[76]

The Sherman Act and Liberty of Contract

The doctrine of liberty of contract, drawn largely from classical political economy, held that people had a right to contract for what they pleased. State and federal courts constitutionalized that economic doctrine during the Gilded Age. As a result, the public policy concerns articulated by the law of contracts and combinations in restraint of trade danced dangerously near the edge of the Constitution. Did people have a liberty of contract that entitled them to eliminate competition among themselves? The Supreme Court eventually held that states had the general power to prohibit contracts in restraint of trade, liberty of contract notwithstanding.[77] Arthur J. Eddy argued strenuously that, whatever constraints a state might lawfully place on public utilities, individuals and private corporations had a constitutional right to enter into combinations.[78] But the courts by and large ignored Eddy's argument. A few state antitrust statutes were struck down in opinions containing liberty of contract language. But these statutes impermissibly attempted to govern out-of-state transactions or exempt certain industries from their coverage.[79] State restraint-on-trade legislation or common law rules were struck down on liberty of contract grounds only rarely.

Few people believed the Sherman Act should be declared unconstitutional for interfering with constitutional liberty of contract. Much more important was the issue of how broadly the words "contract, combination . . . or conspiracy in restraint of trade" should be defined, given liberty of contract. Should simple, noncoercive price fixing—often found legal by common law courts—be condemned under the Sherman Act, or only those explicitly coercive agreements, such as concerted refusals to deal, that even common law courts sometimes condemned?

In his dissent in *Trans-Missouri* (1897) Justice (later Chief Justice) Edward D. White argued that the Sherman Act would violate constitutional liberty of contract if it deviated from the common law rule of reason and condemned certain restraints as illegal per se. "If the rule of reason no longer determines the right of the individual to contract, or secures the validity of contracts upon which trade depends and results, what becomes of the liberty of the citizen or of the freedom of trade?"[80] The defendants in the *Joint Traffic, Addyston Pipe,* and *Northern Securities* cases all argued that price-fixing agreements or mergers among voluntary participants were protected by liberty of contract because they were not unreasonable restraints of trade at common law. In *Joint Traffic* the defendants argued that the Sherman Act was unconstitutional if it was interpreted to interfere with the individual's "right to make contracts regarding his own affairs . . . ." But Justice Peckham, though one of the Court's great champions of liberty of contract, adopted the narrow position that railroads were "public franchises" operating with corporate charters granting the state's permission. One could not presume that the franchises entitled them to behave anticompetitively.[81]

This argument suggested implicitly that unincorporated businesses might have the constitutional right to fix prices. But in its *Addyston Pipe* affirmance a year later, the Supreme Court clarified itself, Justice Peckham once again writing the opinion. Although liberty of contract was protected by the Constitution, the power of Congress to regulate interstate commerce was also constitutionally recognized. In a remarkable departure from the traditional principles of federalism, Peckham then held that the commerce clause was not only a division of regulatory power between the federal government and the states. It also divided regulatory power between the federal government and private parties. The doctrine of liberty of contract "has never been . . . held" to include "the right of an individual to enter into private contracts [which] would, if performed, result in the regulation of interstate commerce and in the violation of an act of Congress upon that subject."[82] In short, the Constitution's commerce clause itself defined the limits of liberty of contract.

This turned out to be a brilliant solution to the problem. The Supreme Court decision in *Addyston Pipe,* often ignored, is as important as Judge Taft's much more widely heralded decision for the Sixth Circuit. It completely disassociated the classical concern with liberty of contract from the Sherman Act's concern about elimination of competition. If a restraint was within the power of Congress to regulate interstate commerce, and thus within the jurisdiction of the Sherman Act, then liberty of contract did not apply. This rationalization effectively paved the way for a much more neoclassical federal antitrust policy.

CHAPTER 22

The Rise of
Industrial Organization

The modern science of industrial organization grew out of a great dialogue between lawyers and economists in the waning years of the nineteenth century. The occasion of this debate was the rise of the "trust," or giant business firm, which presented Americans with both an economic opportunity and a threat. The subject of the dialogue was how the law should respond to the trusts, or if it should respond at all.

Both classical and neoclassical economics assume that business firms organize themselves with one goal in mind: maximizing profits. The classical tradition, but neoclassicism more than classicism, also assumes that firms are more or less amoral in selecting a profit-maximizing business structure. Management surely wants to know what can be done legally, because legal penalties reduce profits. But when the firm chooses among lawful strategies it generally selects the most profitable one, with little concern about its effect on other participants in the market.

A firm might wish to increase profits by growing larger—by producing more of a product or by entering a new line of business—for two quite different reasons. First, the firm might reduce its costs. In the case of "horizontal" growth, or increased production of a product the firm already makes, these cost reductions might come from economies of scale, the lower costs that attend higher output. In the case of "vertical" growth, or entry into a new but related line of business, the cost reductions might come from economies in the production process or from the elimination of market transactions. Use of the market is expensive, and a firm might find that producing a needed input is cheaper or more reliable than purchasing it on the market. Some historians have argued that the quest for these cost reductions explains most of the history of business firm growth in the late nineteenth and early twentieth centuries.[1]

But a firm may also employ growth strategies to obtain power or position so that it can charge higher prices. A merger of all or most of the firms that manufacture a product might permit the new firm to charge a monopoly price. A firm might integrate vertically in order to deny an important resource to a competitor, or to make entry by new competitors more difficult. Often it is difficult to determine why a firm has selected a particular growth strategy, or what its competitive consequences might be. Further, a particular growth strategy can simultaneously reduce a firm's costs and enable it to behave anticompetitively. In such cases we cannot know whether the firm's growth is socially beneficial unless we can balance the social gains resulting from lower costs against the social losses resulting from the anticompetitive behavior. Some historians have argued that opportunities for anticompetitive behavior—or to reap the benefits of a noncompetitive market structure—explain Gilded Age business growth strategies as much as do the opportunities to reduce costs.[2]

If American antitrust policy had been dedicated exclusively to maximizing the efficiency of American production, antitrust enforcers would still have been faced with the difficult problem of sorting out these two explanations for firm growth, one generally competitive and the other often anticompetitive. Problematically, the goal of American antitrust policy was more ambiguous. Since antitrust's early history, its enforcers have been as concerned with protecting small businesses from larger competitors or with protecting consumers from wealth transfers deemed unfair as with maximizing efficiency. A policy of protecting small business might condemn both efficient and inefficient growth by larger firms, without distinguishing between them. A policy of protecting consumers from unfair wealth transfers might prevent efficient growth that results in market dominance and higher prices.

The parsing out of the competitive and anticompetitive determinants of firm structure belongs to the science of industrial organization, not yet formally born when the Sherman Act was passed. But political economists were beginning to write about the problem.[3] The development of marginalism, particularly the concepts of marginal cost and marginal revenue, were necessary to create modern industrial organization theory. Modern industrial organization also needed a theory of perfect competition, which in turn depended on a concept of marginal cost. Most of the early American writers on the trust problem knew little of marginalism. For example, the third edition of Francis Walker's *Political Economy* (1888) said nothing about marginal cost or the economic determinants of firm size.[4] Walker also said little about the relationship between bigness, or market dominance, and the ability to charge a monopoly price.

The rise of the American business trust first generated the problems of law and economic policy that spawned modern industrial organization theory. A large group of economists began writing about what determines firm size and structure, when bigness is good, and when it is bad. Like the first classical political economists, the early writers on industrial organization were concerned largely with policy problems. But as the field of industrial organization matured, it became more technical, more theoretical, and less concerned with policy as such.

Empiricism or Positivism? The First Revolt against Neoclassicism

The economics of industrial organization was born during a great war among Anglo-American and European economists over the proper domain of theory and description in economic analysis. The issue was whether Americans would adopt the British-Austrian or the German approaches to industrial theory. The paradigmatic example of the British approach was that of Alfred and Mary Paley Marshall in their *Economics of Industry* (1881). In chapters entitled "Organization of Industry" and "Division of Labour" the Marshalls managed to discuss the phenomena of economies of scale and scope, plant distribution, multiplant economies, and plant specialization with scant mention of a single particular industry. Alfred Marshall's *Principles of Economics*, published in 1890, took an even more theoretical approach to industrial organization. Marshall developed generalized theories of price and output under competition and monopoly, wages, and costs, but said little about individual industries, markets, or firms. His goal was to make universal statements that could be applied to all business firms alike.

But German economics of the same period was dominated by the Historical School, which had survived a bitter methodological debate between German and Austrian schools of political economy. The Austrians had urged a theoretical model similar to English neoclassical price theory, while the Germans advocated a more historical "case study" approach to economic analysis.

American economists were exposed to the historical method in the 1870's, when works by German political economists such as Wilhelm Roscher were popularized in the United States.[5] The historical method received a great boost in 1876, when the railroad regulator Charles Francis Adams, Jr., endorsed it while criticizing British political economy for its naiveté about business firm behavior.[6] The neoclassical model fell apart when applied to the railroads, which did not behave as the model predicted. "In the complex development of modern life, functions are more and more developed which, in their operation, are not subject to the laws of competition or the principles of free trade, and which indeed are reduced to utter confusion within and without if abandoned to the working of those laws." Adams argued that the German method was more appropriate to study the railroads, because it was less inclined to look for universal laws and more willing to treat phenomena in all their uniqueness and complexity.

As if to slap theory in the face, in the 1870's and 1880's many American students who were to become the prominent economists of the next generation selected German rather than English universities for their graduate education.[7] These included Frank W. Taussig, Frank Fetter, John Bates Clark, Richard T. Ely, Simon Patten, and Edwin R. A. Seligman.[8] Although the founders of the American Economic Association, formed in 1885, were careful to qualify their enthusiasm for the German historical methodology, part of the AEA's agenda was to bring more case study analysis to American economics. Its constitution provided that the association should promote "economic research, especially the historical and statistical study of the actual conditions of industrial life." The association's publications over the first three decades are filled with case studies of particular markets or firms.[9]

By the mid-1880's questions about methodology had begun to divide American economists into two groups, the more traditional, English or American trained neoclassicists, and the "new school," taught in the German historical approach. In 1886 Edwin R. A. Seligman, one of the new school, touched off a year-long debate in *Science* magazine with an essay on "Change in the Tenets of Political Economy with Time," proclaiming the "relativity of economic doctrines." Seligman expressed contempt for neoclassicism's search for universality. However, "[t]he new movement in political economy . . . maintains that the explanations of phenomena are inextricably interwoven with the institutions of the period, and that the practical conclusions must not be disassociated from the shifting necessities of the age."[10]

Henry Carter Adams, another member of the new school, followed Seligman with one of the earliest American "law and economics" pieces. In "Economics and Jurisprudence"[11] he argued that a merger of economics and law would result from the recognition that economics is not merely a mathematical system but an ethical and historical system as well. "Having formulated a theory of society in harmony with the teachings of the science of history, the adherents of this [German Historical] school endeavor to bring their economic doctrines into accord with their social theory." He called for a new dialogue between economics and the social sciences.

The Yale traditionalist Arthur Twining Hadley responded to Seligman and Adams, and set the tone for American neoclassicism's critique of historicism. Adams had confused the materials which form the data of science with the science itself, Hadley argued. For example, the science of mechanics consists not of wood or iron, but of a few simple laws. Identification of these laws is essential to science. The historical method "[d]efeats the usefulness of verification as a measure of discovery," Twining urged. "It is only when you assume a rigid law that your verification leads to new discoveries . . . ."

Hadley's point was part of a much broader view of the nature of science. The difficulty with the German method of gross historical observation was that it made the formulation of theories very difficult, and prediction impossible. The point of economic science, as of all science, is to strip away complexity and identify those things that phenomena have in common and that will predict their behavior. Hadley concluded that even the members of the German School made theoretical advances only "by an abandonment of the so-called historical method, and by a rigid application of deductive reasoning combined with careful verification."[12]

From the 1880's on, American industrial organization theory and eventually American antitrust policy were divided into two camps. The neoclassical camp was becoming positivistic in its methodology, highly theoretical, ideologically conservative, suspicious of empirical research, and inclined to view the work of the other side as merely "anecdotal"— one of the worst of scientific pejoratives. The historical camp was committed to a more traditional empiricism, suspicious of theory (which it believed could easily be manipulated for political ends), hostile toward simplification, opposed to universalism, highly committed to the use of statistical evidence, and much more tolerant of ad hoc government intervention in the market. Within American economic departments the historical school suffered for its lack of sympathy with the dominant marginalist approach to price theory and welfare economics, as well as its close identification with the "institutionalist" economics of such renegades as Thorstein Veblen, Wesley Mitchel, and John R. Commons. Some economists trained in the historical school, such as John Maurice Clark, Frank W. Taussig, and Frank Fetter, abandoned it in favor of a more orthodox neoclassicism.[13]

But for several decades the historical approach dominated industrial organization theory.[14] Harvard's economics department, one of the finest in the country during the first two decades of the twentieth century, was heavily committed to the historical, case-study method. Its series of Harvard Economic Studies were mostly case studies of particular industries.[15] During the early twentieth century the historical approach was adopted by the government agencies charged with making American industrial policy. The United States Bureau of Corporations used the historical model to analyze business firms such as American Tobacco and United States Steel. When the Federal Trade Commission succeeded the Bureau of Corporations in 1914, it produced its own series of historical case studies.[16]

Some pragmatic Americans tried to choose the most useful from both the analytic and historical methods. For example, Simon N. Patten urged the simultaneous use of both approaches. William Watts Folwell argued in 1882 that although the British tradition was valuable as an analytic device, the historical method was much more useful for determining "practical" questions of state policy.[17] This quickly became a popular position on the German Historical School, and was argued by American mavens of political economy in the eighties and nineties, liberal and conservative alike. Francis Walker included a section on the "two schools" in his *Political Economy*.[18] The British School insists "that the proper premises of pure Political Economy consist of a few certain facts of human nature, of human society, and of the physical constitution of the earth." These theorems, "not more than five or six in number, constitute all the premises proper to the inquiry." By contrast, the German School believed the duty of political economy was to "explain the phenomena of wealth"; "the economist must inquire how men do, in fact, behave in regard to wealth, constituted as they are, and under the conditions and circumstances in which they are placed." As a result "nothing that importantly influences the production and distribution of wealth can be neglected," and "all human history" becomes the economist's domain. The economist who uses such a method may not dismiss as irrelevant "any cause, structural or dynamic, physical or moral, which affects the production, exchange, distribution or consumption of wealth." He may only plead "the lack of information, the limitations of the human faculties, or the need, for popular instruction, of very brief and very general statements of principle."

Walker placed his finger on one very important difference between the analytic and historical approaches to political economy. The analysts not only reduced the number of relevant postulates to a very small number; they also excluded any postulates that were not "economic," in a narrow sense. Within the neoclassical system, morals, psychology, and sociology had little to contribute to the understanding of the behavior of the economic individual or firm. The historical approach was far more holistic and more inclined to explain every phenomenon, even those for which no rational "economic" explanation was available.

In his 1896 *Economics*, Arthur Twining Hadley softened his earlier hostility toward the historical method. "[E]very good economist now employs both methods by turns," he conceded, "being guided in his choice by the character of the problem he is investigating." Hadley concluded that "most of the every-day work of economists involves the deductive method rather than the historical." For example, "[i]f we ask why the price of wheat is falling . . . we take human nature as we find it, and consider how commercial motives operate in affecting demand and supply in various lines of industry." But "in more difficult questions involving moral judgment, the historical method must be combined with the deductive." Thus, "if we ask whether trades-unions are a good thing or a bad thing, it is not enough to consider their momentary effect on wages, prices, and demand for labor . . . ."[19]

The object of the early economic writing on industrial organization was to consider whether the giant trusts were good or bad. The writers were engaged in policy or, in Hadley's terms, "moral" inquiries. They considered not merely why the prices of commodities rose or fell, but whether the fundamental change that the trusts wrought in the structure and character of American economic life was good or evil. The earliest economic studies of the trust problem were dominated by broad, historically based inquiries that examined all aspects of the development of a particular firm.

In 1888 and 1889 Jeremiah W. Jenks, perennial defender of the trusts, made historical studies of the Michigan Salt Association and the whiskey trust. Jenks believed that the salt cartel had been of value in preventing ruinous competition, ensuring product quality, and saving transportation costs through coordination of deliveries. He found little risk of higher prices, since the Michigan producers were in competition with New York producers. Jenks came to similar conclusions about the Distillers and Cattle-Feeders Trust: although its principal purpose was to curtail production, reduced production was necessary to prevent ruinous competition.[20]

Most historical studies of the trusts were more critical than those of Jenks. Charles Edgerton's study of the Wire-Nail Association argued that the cartel was formed because new technology had created enormous excess capacity in the nail industry. Without cartelization, competition would have forced some firms out of business. But no sooner had the cartel raised the price of nails than even more firms began to enter the market—so many that the cartel had to pay nail machinery manufacturers to stop making additional equipment.[21]

Some of the earliest writers of books on the trust problem argued that the trusts were good and that any attempt to regulate them would be harmful. Others, most notably John Bates Clark, called for modest state intervention. Still others, such as Richard T. Ely, argued for much more substantial control.[22] In spite of their German educations and stated commitment to the historical method, both Clark and Ely took generally analytic approaches to the trust problem. They spoke in generalized terms of the wastes of competition, economies of scale, and market dominance.

In the 1920's a second generation of studies appeared. The economists in this second group were less confident that the large firms would produce lower prices, and much more concerned about the threat of monopoly. They relied heavily on historical case studies of the individual firm or market. A 1921 book by the Stanford economist Eliot Jones included intensive historical studies of a half-dozen combinations, in addition to a general discussion of the effects of dominant firms on productive efficiency and prices. The individual industry studies in one part of the book were designed to confirm the more analytic conclusions in the other part. The University of Missouri economist Myron W. Watkins took the same approach in his *Industrial Combinations and Public Policy* (1927). The first part of the study, entitled "The Economics of the Organization of Industrial Control," generalized about what prompted firms to combine with others, possible economies or threats to competition, and the relationship between large-scale production and public welfare. The second part, entitled "Experience with Industrial Combination in Certain Industries in the United States," contained case studies of the United States Steel Company, International Harvester Company, and the glass, paper, and corn products industries.

The case study approach to industrial organization has had a firm place in the discipline ever since. It has come under attack for its antitheoretical bias and for its presumed proclivity to provide anticompetitive explanations to ambiguous behavior. But many case studies from early on, such as those of Jenks, were quite favorable to the trusts. And if the case studies were inclined to exaggerate the competitive dangers of business firm decision making, the theoretical models of firm behavior were inclined to understate them. For example, Ronald Coase's path-breaking article "The Nature of the Firm" (1937), discussed below, attempted to develop a general theory about firm growth and size with almost no reference to anticompetitive behavior. In the 1920's Frank A. Fetter concluded that neoclassical price theory was too sterile to provide the policy maker with reliable descriptions or predictions of firm behavior. He insisted that economics take more seriously the "human factor in the economic relationship" and become "emancipated from the bonds of a mere price conception."[23]

Historicism and the Rule of Reason

Litigators and courts were particularly enthusiastic users of the historical method. It provided the raw material and the framework for the arguments in early Sherman Act antitrust cases, such as *Addyston Pipe* (1898) and the first *United States Steel* case (1915). The judicial decisions developing the rule of reason in antitrust cases required the courts to consider the historical development of a firm and its market in determining whether it should be condemned.[24] This was in stark contrast to the per se rule developed in the *Trans-Missouri* (1897) and *Joint Traffic* (1898) cases, where Justice Peckham refused to consider any economic peculiarities of the railroad industry that might make cartelization reasonable. The historical method came to dominate rule of reason analysis, and the rule-of-reason came to dominate antitrust policy making in the areas where the trusts were a principal concern: monopolization and mergers.

One might argue that the historical, or case study, approach is inherent in the law, particularly the common law, which has a strong historical, antitheoretical bias. But the common law's historicism in a particular case had generally been limited to a few simple determinations about motive or intent. For example, the "rule of reason" in common law restraints cases had come to mean only that contracts in restraint of trade were reasonable if they were limited as to time and place and gave no more protection than necessary for the maker's business. The common law rule of reason never required a broad inquiry into the history of the firm or of the market in which it operated. That the rule of reason in antitrust cases would go much further became clear in the Supreme Court's opinion in *Chicago Board of Trade* (1918), in which Justice Brandeis wrote what has become the classic statement of the antitrust rule of reason. "The true test of legality is whether the restraint imposed is such as merely regulates and perhaps thereby promotes competition or whether it is such as may suppress or even destroy competition," wrote Brandeis. In order to apply this test a court "must ordinarily consider the facts peculiar to the business to which the restraint is applied; its condition before and after the restraint was imposed; the nature of the restraint and its effect, actual or probable. The history of the restraint, the evil believed to exist, the reason for adopting the particular remedy, the purpose or end sought to be attained, are all relevant facts."[25] Antitrust policy makers had committed themselves to the historical approach to industrial analysis.

Historicism Attacked: The Neoclassical Theory of the Firm

In the 1920's and 1930's the historical method encountered sharp criticism from a rising group of positivist economists, particularly at the University of Chicago, who tried to add rigor to their discipline by identifying economic science with the ability to predict.[26] As Frank Knight argued in his essay "The Limitations of Scientific Method in Economics,"[27] the detailed historical inquiries add little to our ability to predict. "Merely historic facts are of no direct practical use, and it would conduce to clear thinking to separate sharply scientific from historical truth in the terminology." In general, "a scientific proposition must hold good for a class of objects or situations . . . . [T]ruth cannot be considered scientific unless it is demonstrable, which means that it must be alike for all observers and accurately communicable." The ad hoc, firm-specific historical inquiries into the development of individual business firms failed to measure up to this test. "The primal question in regard to a science of history," as with any science, is whether its observed elements are "classifiable and verifiable."

The most famous expression of the new classicism in industrial organization was Ronald Coase's essay "The Nature of the Firm" (1937).[28] Coase developed a powerful global model for explaining why firms grow: a firm does something for itself whenever doing so is cheaper than buying the same thing on the market. The market itself is a costly device, Coase observed. In order to use it efficiently one must have good information about prices and the quality and usability of the products and services offered by others. One must also have confidence that the sellers will be able to produce the right amount of a good when it is needed, and that they will sell at a competitive price. Gathering information and then negotiating the right transaction can be expensive. Often a firm's managers will decide that the firm could produce a particular good or service more cheaply for itself. When this happens the firm "integrates" into a new area: it provides its own raw materials, transportation, legal, accounting, or distribution services. In the process, of course, the firm becomes bigger and the amount of some market left to others becomes relatively smaller.

"The Nature of the Firm" contained little room for strategic decisions to integrate that might not be motivated by the firm's simple desire to reduce its own costs. Coase's essay never cited any of the numerous historical studies of the development of individual firms. Further, it assumed away a large literature on the separation of ownership and control in the large corporation. That literature argued that since the large firm is not managed by its principal owners, other goals than cost reduction or profit maximization might influence its actions. Coase's article never mentioned the influential work by Adolf Berle, Jr., and Gardiner Means, *The Modern Corporation and Private Property*, which had appeared five years earlier.[29] Berle and Means's book came to be identified with the theory that separation of ownership and control in the business firm distorted its motives. However, their work did little more than summarize a set of observations that dated back at least to the work of Alfred Marshall in the 1890's.[30]

Coase's article established the continuing legitimacy of two rival approaches to industrial organization and antitrust analysis in the United States. The neoclassical models that followed after Coase were "long-run" or "equilibrium" models. They generally assumed that entry by competitors was easy, and they expressed little concern about the time it might take entry to occur. The long-run models minimized the effects of imperfections in markets, such as scarcity of raw materials. They generally played down the advantages that might accrue to the "first mover"—the first firm to enter an industry—particularly when the capital and time requirements for entry were very large, much of the investment would be lost if the firm had to exit early, and economies of production and distribution were substantial. In the long run, when time counts for nothing, monopoly almost never occurs. Like most policy problems, it exists only for those of us for whom time matters.

CHAPTER 23

The Fixed-Cost Controversy

One picture of the relationship between economics and antitrust law is that economists supply the economic theory, while antitrust lawyers and courts consume it and decide how it should be used. According to this theory, antitrust policy makers certainly accept some ideas that do not come from economists, but these ideas are "noneconomic"—that is, they are concerned with some value other than the optimal allocation of scarce resources.

An alternative view is that, over time, law and economics have contributed to a common perspective on human behavior. Industrial organization theory surely influenced the law, but the law shaped economic thinking about problems of industrial organization as well. Even when they came to speak different languages, economists and lawyers drew their ideas from each other. The notion that economists teach lawyers but do not learn very much from them is built on a rather formal view of the science of economics. The alternative notion, that law and economics are engaged in dialogue, is built on a broader view of economics as a behavioral science. Industrial organization in particular is first a behavioral science, and only secondly a formal one.

The British neoclassical theory of the firm described in the preceding chapter eventually triumphed in the United States in the 1950's. The neoclassical theory suggested that industrial organization is a formal, exclusively economic science. But throughout the nineteenth century lawyers and economists subscribed to a common "theory of the firm." They even developed a common vocabulary to describe what they saw.

They began to part company only in the 1930's, when economics became far more technical, and lawyers began to become more preoccupied with distributive, or noneconomic, concerns, which they identified as the "public" content of legal policy.

The roots of modern industrial organization theory—both the neoclassical and the American historical methods—lay heavily in the law itself, or in the law's frequent, generally unattributed, borrowings from classical political economy. Even the most neoclassical tenets, expressed today with a high degree of formality, such as the theory of ruinous competition and the potential competition doctrine, have a long history in a field as informal and antitheoretical as the law.

When the first American antitrust law was enacted in 1890 many economists argued that the statute would do more harm than good. The business combinations that had sprung up in the previous generation, they believed, were creatures of economic necessity.[1] The new antitrust law would either fail or else it would lay waste to these engines of efficiency at great cost to society. Henry Carter Adams had already anticipated the problem in 1887 when, writing in the first journal of the newly formed American Economic Association, he argued that many American businesses had achieved economies of scale—they could operate more cheaply only if they were very large. The natural gravitation of business in such industries was toward monopoly, and "no law can make them compete."[2]

Part of the economists' fear was that by breaking the giant trusts into smaller firms the Sherman Act would deprive modern business of these economies of scale. Antitrust would then produce higher rather than lower prices. But higher costs alone would not ruin a firm, provided that its competitors had higher costs as well. A more serious concern was that in many American industries the trusts were necessary because competition had simply become unworkable. If forced to compete, firms in these industries would naturally be driven to ruin. The principal cause of this "ruinous competition" was the presence of high fixed costs.

Within classical political economy general "overproduction"—a permanent or long-term imbalance of supply and demand—was impossible. New investment in an industry would continue to occur as long as supplies were low and monopoly profits were being earned, but it would stop once supply and demand reached equilibrium and prices were competitive. Both conservatives and radicals within the classical tradition accepted these propositions. For example, the conservative political economist Francis Wayland argued in his *Elements of Political Economy*

(1837) that increased productivity could yield nothing but good for the community. Everyone's standard of living would be raised because more could be produced at a profitable rate. The radical Jeffersonian Thomas Cooper made virtually the same argument in his *Lectures on the Elements of Political Economy* (1830), noting that increases in supply or in demand could cause nothing more than temporary imbalances in the market, which would always tend to right itself. As late as 1888 Francis A. Walker spoke of the "absurdity" of any notion of general overproduction, because it supposed "that men will labor to produce that which they have not the desire to consume." There might be brief periods of surplus or shortage, but these were simply distortions caused by motion in the market. Markets always tended toward an equilibrium in which supply and demand were perfectly matched at a competitive price.[3]

But Walker's posture was more defensive than Wayland's or Cooper's. Classicism's optimistic notion that supply and demand would always seek a balance was being attacked as it had never been before. The issue rose at the fringes of academic economics, in a policy debate over the tariff and the eight-hour day. In 1881 George Basil Dixwell argued that classical political economy's position that tariffs were economically harmful had become obsolete, given America's proclivity to over-produce. If the flood of imported goods were not stopped, overproduction and periodic panic would be recurring problems.[4] In 1889 David A. Wells, the former federal revenue commissioner and a prominent economist, published *Recent Economic Changes*,[5] which attacked orthodox political economy and argued that, left unrestricted or unregulated, American industry would overproduce. That same year, the businessman and magazine editor George Gunton argued that American productivity had increased so enormously that overproduction was sure to result unless American workers were given less time to work and more time to consume.[6] Others argued that overproduction was a real problem, but that it could not be solved by anything as simple as reducing the hours of labor or raising the tariff. For example, in 1889 Andrew Carnegie argued that the entire trust movement was nothing more than an attempt to combat overinvestment in American industry and the resulting ruinous competition. John Bates Clark argued in 1887 that certain industries were so prone to overproduction that the firms in them must either collude or face "widespread ruin." In 1897 Carroll D. Wright, head of the federal Bureau of Labor, argued that overproduction was becoming a chronic problem in American industry, and that it could be solved only if industry itself were organized under more cooperative lines. The reason for the tendency to overproduction, Carnegie, Clark, and Wright all noted, was the rising proportion of fixed costs in American industry.[7]

By 1890, when the Sherman Act was passed, economists were becoming involved in a great "fixed-cost controversy," which waged in the economics literature for more than a quarter century. For at least a generation among academic economists the development of the modern model of costs appeared to undermine the classical argument that general overproduction or misallocation of resources is impossible. A corollary was that collusion, or at least coordination of output, among the firms in such industries would be a good thing.

The classicists and even the early neoclassicist economists had paid surprisingly little attention to the problem of cost. They wrote little about what costs are, what kinds of costs there are and how they should be classified, or what the relationship is between cost and price or between cost and profit. Francis A. Walker's textbook on political economy contained no discussion of marginal cost, and little about the difference between fixed and variable costs. Arthur Twining Hadley's *Economics* (1896) contained rather full discussions of fixed costs and marginal utility, but little of variable cost or marginal cost.[8]

But Hadley set out one of the economists' principal economic arguments against the Sherman Act: that combination was virtually inevitable in industries with high fixed costs. The argument was an extension of a model explaining railroad rates that Frank Taussig[9] had developed a few years earlier. The basic argument was that in markets with relatively high fixed costs competition would continually drive prices to variable costs, without enough remaining to cover payment for the capital investment.

Hadley's theory of ruinous competition was simple. If new cost-reducing and output expanding technology lowers the cost of producing to substantially less than the market price, investors will rush to enter the new market. Many capitalists will invest in the new technology, each without knowing precisely what the others are doing. The result is excess capacity: "more goods are produced than the community can pay for at prices which cover the expense to the producers." In any industry with large capital investments in expensive, durable, specialized manufacturing equipment, such overproduction is a threat. "The larger the fixed capital involved in an industry, the greater is the danger of such over-production."

Once the investment has been made and the equipment is in place, "the owners have invested their capital in a form which they cannot readily change." They must produce as long as the price is sufficient to cover their variable, or operating, costs. Hadley had identified an anomaly that resulted from neoclassical political economy's development of the fixed and variable cost curves. In industries with high fixed costs, the price needed to attract new investment into an industry was much higher than the price that would force existing firms to withdraw. Firms would come into a market only if the price were high enough to cover anticipated total costs—that is, the sum of fixed and variable costs. Once in the market, however, they would continue to produce as long as prices covered variable costs. Classicism had always assumed that in any market there was a single "profitable" price. If prices were higher than that level, new firms would come in; if they were lower, existing firms would withdraw. Equilibrium depended on the proposition that profitable prices invited entry while unprofitable prices caused immediate exit. But the presence of high fixed costs suggested that firms already in the market would stay in as long as prices covered their operating costs and contributed something to the amortization of fixed costs. The result was that capital-intensive industries thrust into competition would charge ruinous prices that would eventually drive them to bankruptcy. For Hadley, combination was the only viable solution.

By the 1890's the theory of "ruinous competition" was as fully developed in American law as it was in political economy. The legal theory of ruinous competition was that in some markets competition would simply not work, at least under certain conditions. Firms constrained to compete would be driven into bankruptcy, and eventually consumers would be left facing only a monopoly firm, free to charge whatever price it pleased. In 1900 the New York bankruptcy lawyer William Miller Collier argued that the purchase and closing of plants by the trusts was socially beneficial because it reduced excess capacity in the industry and thus ameliorated the effects of ruinous competition.[10] In the 1880's and 1890's a number of courts had already begun to suggest that railroad "pools" or cartels should be legal, because they were necessary to protect the railroads from ruinous competition.[11] Justice Peckham's Supreme Court opinion in the *Trans-Missouri* case, which condemned a railroad cartel under the Sherman Act, summarized the economic literature on high fixed costs, ruinous competition, and cartelization quite well:

> When a railroad is once built, it is said, it must be kept in operation; it must transport property, when necessary in order to keep its business, at

the smallest price and for the narrowest profit, or even for no profit, provided running expenses can be paid, rather than not to do the work; that railroad property cannot be altered for use for any other purpose, at least without such loss as may fairly be called destructive; that competition while, perhaps, right and proper in other business, simply leads in railroad business to financial ruin and insolvency, and to the operation of the road by receivers in the interest of its creditors . . . ; that a receiver is only bound to pay operating expenses, so he can compete with the solvent company and oblige it to come down to prices incompatible with any profit for the work done . . . .[12]

It is little appreciated how deeply the notion that competition can sometimes be "ruinous," or contrary to the interests of both business firms and society, is embedded in American law. The first discussion of ruinous competition in a United States Supreme Court opinion appeared in 1837, in the *Charles River Bridge* case. The basic theory presented there was no different from the theory developed by Taussig and Hadley more than a half century later, although the economic terminology was less technical. Toll bridges were firms that had an extraordinarily high percentage of fixed costs. If forced to compete with each other, competition would drive tolls down to a level barely sufficient to cover the costs of operating the bridge, without enough left over to service the debt. Daniel Webster traced the phrase "ruinous competition" to Chancellor Kent, whose *Commentaries* were published in the late 1820's. The company's grant of the right to build a bridge implied a monopoly at common law, Webster argued, because the bridge would be profitable only if it had protection from competition. "[I]n order to make this protection available, it must, of necessity, have [an exclusive right over] some local extent, sufficient, at least, to keep down ruinous competition; or, in other words, that it must be exclusive between Charlestown and Boston." Justice Story's dissent from the Supreme Court's opinion denying the monopoly right concluded that the authorization of a second bridge in competition with the first was "wholly repugnant to the avowed objects of the [Charles River Bridge Company's] grant, which are to confer a benefit, and not to impose an oppressive burden, or create a ruinous competition."[13]

In the 1870's the theory of ruinous competition began to appear regularly in American judicial decisions. Many of these involved public utilities, although some involved ordinary manufacturing as well. Defendants accused of forming illegal cartels or combinations in restraint of trade typically raised "ruinous competition" as a defense: they would surely have been driven out of business but for the challenged agreement. For example, in 1876 former Supreme Court Justice John A. Campbell successfully defended a price-fixing agreement between two railroads by arguing that the agreement was necessary to prevent ruinous competition. In *Nutter v. Wheeler* (1874) a federal court in Massachusetts concluded that "ruinous competition" both explained and justified resale price maintenance: "the prohibition against selling below the trade price is a very common one between a manufacturer and those who buy of him to sell again, and is intended to prevent a ruinous competition between sellers of the same article." Several state courts held that price-fixing or market division schemes were enforceable if the cartel members had a bona-fide fear of ruinous competition. Some courts cited the fear of ruinous competition in permitting apparent mergers to monopoly. For example, in approving a merger in 1895, the New York Court of Appeals observed that "not all combinations are condemned, and self preservation may justify prevention of undue and ruinous competition . . . ." And in approving price fixing and resale price maintenance in the proprietary drug industry in 1903, the New York Court of Appeals noted that "competition may be carried to such an extent as to accomplish the financial ruin of those engaged therein, and thus result in a derangement of the business, an inconvenience to consumers, and in public harm." Other courts were presented with ruinous competition defenses but rejected them.[14]

Many courts used "ruinous competition" language in approving public utility mergers or in determining whether local governments should be permitted to erect utilities in competition with existing privately owned utilities. Such cases involved firms with very high fixed costs, and the argument was the same as that being developed in the economic literature. For example, in *Walla Walla v. Walla Walla Water Co.* (1898), the Supreme Court held that a city could not build a public waterworks in competition with a privately owned waterworks when the grant to the latter was exclusive by its terms, and the public waterworks would engage in ruinous competition with the private one. Several varieties of this case appeared during the 1890's and 1900's, most of them relying on the ruinous competition doctrine. In 1896 the Supreme Court of Pennsylvania held that even if a municipal grant to a waterworks were nonexclusive, the city would not be permitted to erect its own waterworks in competition. "If anything be manifest, it is that if two water mains be laid side by side on the same street, equally accessible to the householder on each side, conveying double the quantity needed, with double sets of hydrants, pumping stations, offices, salaries and expenses, one or the other must be abandoned." In approving a merger of two San Diego waterworks in 1895, the California Supreme Court noted that the market was a natural monopoly most cheaply served by a single firm. In such a situation, competition was inherently ruinous.[15]

Some of the earliest Sherman Act cases also relied on the ruinous competition doctrine. In *Dueber Watch* (1893), one of the earliest Sherman Act suits by a private plaintiff, the court dismissed the complaint of a concerted boycott that was apparently motivated by the plaintiff's price cutting, which frustrated the defendants' cartel. The judge found it totally irrational to interpret the Sherman Act to "extend to every agreement where A. and B. agree that they will not sell goods to those who buy of C." Such an interpretation "would strike at all agreements by which honest enterprise attempts to protect itself against ruinous and dishonest competition." In the Eighth Circuit's opinion in the *Trans-Missouri* railroad cartel case (1893), Judge Sanborn accepted a "ruinous competition" defense, concluding that the "plain object" of the cartel was "to prevent competitors from resorting to secret, unfair, and ruinous methods of warfare, to make competition fair and open . . . ."[16]

But the Supreme Court reversed the Eighth Circuit's *Trans-Missouri* decision in 1897 and expressly rejected ruinous competition as a defense to a Sherman Act price-fixing case. Justice Peckham made the observations about high fixed costs and ruinous competition noted previously. But then he concluded that (1) the ruinous competition argument was not unanimously accepted, but was quite controversial; and (2) a "ruinous competition defense would force the court to decide what a reasonable rate of profit in a particular industry should be," and courts were not up to that task. In the *Joint Traffic* case two years later, the prominent legal scholar James Coolidge Carter devoted 100 pages of his brief for the railroad association to arguing that railroad cartels or pooling agreements were essential to the railroads' economic survival. Any statute forbidding such agreements was therefore an unconstitutional deprivation of the railroads' property without due process of law.[17] The Solicitor General argued in response that high capital cost had become a fact of life in many American industries, and the difference between them and the railroads was merely one of degree, not of kind. So "[w]hy should the railroads be singled out from all the great interests of this country, and alone be authorized to combine and prevent competition and keep up prices?" With a colorful mixture of Social Darwinism and utilitarianism he then suggested that the railroads' "ruinous competition" argument was nothing more than a cover for an agreement to retard innovation. "Competition drives the weak to the wall, the fittest survive, but the greatest good to the greatest number results." Only competition could guarantee "the most improved plant, the best trained labor, the most economical management, the wisest business sagacity and foresight." In accepting the argument of the Solicitor General, Justice Peckham concluded that there was no federally protected "property" right to be free of the rigors of competition, whatever the consequences. If competition in the railroad industry was ruinous, that fact was a function of the market itself, and not of state policy.

In the famous *Addyston Pipe* case, the trial court (1897) had upheld the cartel arrangement, accepting the defense that "ruinous competition" would drive the steel pipe manufacturers into bankruptcy if they could not fix prices. Judge Taft wrote the appellate opinion reversing the trial court and holding that "ruinous competition" was not a defense to price fixing. Thereafter Sherman Act decisions rejected "ruinous competition" defenses in cartel and resale price maintenance cases.[18]

"Ruinous competition" had a brief revival after the rule of reason was developed in the 1911 *Standard Oil* and *American Tobacco* decisions. Litigants argued that the concept of "reasonable" restraints included cartels designed to protect the participants from ruinous competition. In the *Standard Sanitary Manufacturing* (1911) case the lower court rejected a ruinous competition defense because it would require a court to determine in each case if the prices fixed were reasonable, given the condition of the market. "After all was done and said, the margin of doubt would usually remain large." In the Supreme Court Herbert Noble then argued for the cartel members that the Sherman Act "does not condemn a fair and reasonable attempt to avoid loss by means of trade agreements which are intended to prevent nothing but the cutting of rates below the reasonable expense of production and reasonable profit thereon; . . . ." But the Court rejected the argument with almost no comment.[19]

In the tugboat cartel case in 1913 the defendants argued ruinous competition strenuously, perhaps with some merit. The United States sought dissolution of a merger to monopoly of the tugboat operators in several Great Lakes harbors, accomplished by a New Jersey holding company. The tugboat market was probably not unlike the railroad market in the earlier railroad cartel cases or the municipal utilities markets. Fixed costs were high, and price competition among tugboat operators might have driven prices to operating costs. Nevertheless, the court concluded that "ruinous competition" could not be a defense to a Sherman Act prosecution. However, the court later held that the condition of the market before the merger should be considered in determining the remedy. In this case it made no sense to break up the firm into its constituents, because that would only restore the ruinous competition. Rather, the holding company was permitted to continue, but "exclusive" contracts between customers and individual participants in the holding company were forbidden.[20]

In the 1916 *Corn Products* decision the court accepted the ruinous competition defense in principle. The corn products industry, which had large fixed costs, appeared to be suffering from substantial excess capacity. However, "the immediate result of the combination was such a rise in price as attracted new capital into an industry whose producing capacity, on paper, was already more than the market would take." The court found no public benefit in fixing the "price at a point where, with ample capacity, new capital came in . . . ."[21]

Finally, ruinous competition played an important role in the 1920 *United States Steel* case.[22] The lower court noted that the practice initiated by the Carnegie Steel Company of "running full"—that is, of producing at capacity in spite of high inventory and low orders in order to minimize fixed costs—had led to ruinous competition which the steel merger had been designed to cure. In approving the merger, the Supreme Court emphasized the defendants' lack of market control. It paid little attention to the ruinous competition defense, except to note that at least one of the challenged acquisitions had been submitted to President Theodore Roosevelt, and that he had approved it because of the distressed conditions in the industry. The "ruinous competition" defense was laid to rest a second time in *Trenton Potteries* (1927), when the Supreme Court clarified that the rule of reason announced in the *Standard Oil* decision did not apply to naked price-fixing agreements, regardless of the reasonableness of the prices fixed.[23]

By the turn of the century the fixed-cost controversy divided liberal and conservative economists, with the liberals in this case resting firmly on the traditional classical view that competition would not be ruinous in the long run in any industries except a few natural monopolies. The Progressive economists Richard T. Ely, Edwin R. A. Seligman, H. R. Seager, and Charles Bullock all denied that there was any "such thing as general over-production."[24] As a result, courts should enforce the antitrust laws aggressively and ignore "ruinous competition" as a defense.

The economic debate over the "ruinous competition" hypothesis climaxed in the economics literature in the 1910's and 1920's. In 1915 Princeton University's Oswald Knauth argued that competition was almost certain to be ruinous and wasteful in industries in which the required capital investment was high and assets specialized, so that failing firms could not easily switch into other markets.[25] Knauth even argued that innovation in competitively structured, capital-intensive industries was ruinous. It forced firms to adopt new technologies before existing machinery, in which heavy investment had been made, had outlived its usefulness. For these reasons, the 1911 *Standard Oil* decision was wrong as a matter of economics, while the *American Tobacco* decision of the same year was probably correct. The difference was the large amount of specialized capital investment that was required to refine and distribute petroleum products. "The destruction of capital through competition in the tobacco industry is negligible; in the oil business the risk is tremendous and must be insured against by means of higher prices . . . ." Knauth urged the government to consider more carefully the result of any breakup that might occur in the *International Harvester* and *United States Steel* antitrust cases, which were currently being litigated. In each, he suggested, the wastes brought about by excessive competition would likely outweigh any benefits that might result from competitive prices.

In 1918 the University of Texas economist Spurgeon Bell argued that the great merger movement of the preceding decade had been caused by two factors. First was the firms' desire to reduce costs. But "the character of the price competition which prevailed also had much to do with the consolidations." However, Taussig argued that the overproduction, or ruinous competition, argument proved too much, and that it was most commonly used as "an excuse for trying to build up a monopoly which will restrict production, and secure (or try to secure) regularity at the expense of extra levies on the public."[26] Taussig's view came to dominate until the early thirties. An economists' consensus emerged that high capital costs, standing alone, did not make competition impossible. Competition would be ruinous, if anywhere, only in a few natural monopoly markets, such as public utilities and perhaps the railroads.

For example, Eliot Jones argued that, although the ruinous competition hypothesis probably applied to railroads, ordinary manufacturing was different. Jones noted that even capital-intensive manufacturing industries had ratios of fixed to variable costs far lower than those that prevailed in the railroad industry. The higher the percentage of fixed costs, the greater the likelihood of ruinous competition. In addition, for the railroads even some operating expenses were "fixed," in the sense that they did not vary over the short run with the amount of freight. Labor and fuel were ordinarily regarded as variable costs. However, a scheduled train could generally accommodate additional freight at very little increase in the amount of labor or fuel. "This would seldom be true of manufacturing industries, whose costs in much larger degree are comprised of costs of raw materials, which necessarily vary almost directly as the scale of operations." Myron Watkins wrote similarly in 1927 that, except in a few natural monopoly industries, high fixed costs would yield overproduction only if producers lacked the foresight to keep the construction of plant capacity in check. Both Watkins and Jones attempted to show that "ruinous competition did not explain the formation of many of the trusts." Many of the individual firms had been profitable at the time the trusts were formed; many trusts had actually increased their productive capacity after they were formed.[27]

The fixed-cost controversy drove economists toward more complex models of markets. In defending the ruinous competition hypothesis, Spurgeon Bell made a suggestion that was to play an important role in the competition theory of the next decade: that firms can avoid ruinous competition by product differentiation. Bell assumed that a tendency toward ruinous competition existed in most capital-intensive industries. Profits in such industries were destined to be very low unless the sellers could find ways to avoid competing with one another. However, when a manufacturer successfully differentiated its product from that of its competitors its profits rose, because it could price to that part of the buying public that preferred its own unique offering. As soon as its brand or style became "standardized," however, profit margins would fall once again. The result would be continual attempts to develop new product variants that would distinguish the seller's product from those of others. "If fixed costs are large there must be a style or brand competition on the one hand or, on the other hand, consolidation of producers similar to that which took place in the steel industry, in the railroads, and in various large plant industries producing goods of a comparatively staple character." In short, for some capital-intensive firms product differentiation was an alternative to consolidation. Bell believed this explained why so many trusts were formed in markets for staple commodities that could not easily be differentiated, such as salt or sugar.[28]

Eliot Jones disagreed with Bell about the tendency toward ruinous competition, except where fixed costs were extraordinarily high. But he agreed that product fungibility exacerbated any tendency toward ruinous competition that might already exist. "Competition is hardly likely to be ruinous except where a comparatively slight difference in price will cause purchasers to patronize one concern rather than another," he concluded. The railroads were continually bedeviled by their inability to distinguish their services. Customers were generally indifferent as to which railroad carried their freight, and therefore they shopped for the lowest bidder. "[W]herever there has been a marked development of brands and trade marks, or wherever competition is upon a quality or style basis," Jones observed, "prices may be maintained by favored concerns, even above a normal competitive level."[29]

The fixed-cost controversy came to an end when economists began to emphasize the difference between short-run and long-run perspectives. In 1914 John Maurice Clark noted that in the short run excess capacity might exist in many markets, and firms might suffer substantial losses. However, no new investment would be made in such a market and when plants wore out they would not be replaced. Eventually, competitive equilibrium would be restored. The reconstructed competition model of the 1920's emphasized the long run. Frank H. Knight argued that whether the concept of "cost of production" included capital costs depended entirely on the period of time that one was studying. Over the long run capital assets would have to be replaced and must be paid for. The firm varying its sales from day to day might neglect to take these into account. Prices would be ruinous only for those who ignored the long run. And Taussig argued in 1922 that "overproduction" was merely a short-run problem. "Sooner or later—perhaps after a considerable interval, if the operations involve large plants—some of the producers will withdraw, supply will lessen, price will rise, and overproduction will cease."

John Maurice Clark's consensus-forming book on overhead costs in 1923 ended the debate, at least for a time. Clark acknowledged that the "ruinous competition" theorists such as Hadley spoke the truth; in the short run firms might tend to overproduce. However, Clark concluded, by using cost-accounting techniques and by being aware of the amount of capacity on the market at any given time, firms should be able to avoid long-run problems of ruinous competition. "In the actual development of business, as of other things, the long-run consequences often come not so much as the result of far-sighted planning as from the cumulative effect of a series of things done from short-run motives,"

Clark acknowledged in 1926. Such short-sightedness could be a costly error. But for Clark the solution was neither collusion nor state regulation, but rather careful business planning. Firms in concentrated, heavy industries needed to be more aware of factors such as total industry capacity, the construction plans of competitors, and changes in anticipated demand. Each firm acting individually could avoid being thrust into ruinous competition if it kept one eye on the long-run horizon.[30]

Of course, the "answer" that the overproduction problem existed only for the short run was no answer at all if the short run was thirty years and an industry was in distress the entire time. Likewise, the fact that long-run equilibrium was theoretically possible did not mean that it was likely to occur. For this reason the overproduction argument has surfaced repeatedly in various guises, even in the 1980's.[31] The theory of ruinous competition has been surprisingly robust.

The work of Jones, Bell, and J. M. Clark suggested new difficulties with the neoclassical competition model, just as the theory of perfect competition was being formed. Under the emerging model, firms in industries with high fixed costs producing fungible, or staple, commodities were always at risk. Such industries would likely experience periods, or "cycles," during which they would be able to sell at a price barely higher than variable costs—that is, they would lose money. These firms could reduce their vulnerability to periods of low demand in one of two ways. First, they could consolidate, creating in the process a more concentrated industry structure less prone to competition. Second, they could differentiate their products from those of their competitors. In most cases, capital-intensive industries would do both. The result was product-differentiated oligopoly in which each firm behaved as much like a monopolist as a perfect competitor. Edward Chamberlin developed this "theory of monopolistic competition" in his work by that title published in 1933.[32]

Even before Taussig and Clark argued that firms could prevent ruinous competition through better knowledge of competitors' production plans, legal writers were moving in that direction. Arthur Eddy argued in 1914 that competing firms should seek to avoid ruinous competition by forming trade associations for mutual protection. By exchanging "knowledge regarding bids and prices," they could keep "prices at reasonably stable and normal levels." Competition in the modern era requires competitors "competing under conditions that enable each to know and fairly judge what the others are doing." In

1922 Milton Nelson concluded that "a knowledge of all conditions that might have a bearing on the supply of, and the demand for, a given commodity" could result "in similar exchanges taking place on similar terms," which would be good for most markets. The work of Eddy and Nelson contributed to the great trade association movement of the 1910's and 1920's.[33]

Eddy and Nelson were careful to tell firms that the simple exchange of price information was not the same thing as price fixing. The Federal Trade Commission protested that often trade associations were nothing more than fronts for cartels,[34] but firms managed to convinced the Supreme Court that specific agreements to charge a certain price, not merely the exchange of price and output information, were necessary to condemn association activities.[35] In praising the trade association movement, Franklin D. Jones of the Justice Department emphasized how wasteful competition could be—particularly the carrying of large amounts of excess capacity—in a regime in which firms had very poor information about what their competitors were doing.[36] The trade association movement achieved its greatest success when Herbert Hoover, then Commerce Secretary, began to preach it in the 1920's,[37] and it became an important part of Hoover's associationalist platform. When the movement had run its course, ruinous competition moved on, and next appeared in the Codes of Fair Competition as part of the first New Deal.[38]

CHAPTER 24

Potential Competition

In the 1890's most political economists and many elite lawyers believed that the public had no great interest in voluntary agreements that eliminated competition among the parties involved. This belief was guided by two tenets of classical political economy that remained prominent in the emerging neoclassical economics of industrial organization. One was an optimistic appreciation of the economies that might result from large-scale manufacturing and distribution. Influential studies of the trusts, such as those of Jeremiah Jenks and Ernst von Halle were filled with praise for the large firm's ability to reduce the costs of production, and expressed little concern for the threat to competition. Neoclassicists such as Arthur Twining Hadley wrote of the trusts as if their potential to achieve economies of scale was infinite, while their threat to competition negligible. Even the Progressive Richard T. Ely was overwhelmed by the trusts' ability to achieve cost reductions through large-scale production and distribution.[1]

The second tenet was that "potential" competition—or the continual entry of newcomers into a market—would discipline any firm or group of firms that attempted to charge monopoly prices. Classical political economists generally analyzed markets from the premise that entry was easy and could be accomplished very quickly. The only limitation on new entry to which they gave much thought was monopoly grants from the government. Within this model private, *de facto* monopoly was seldom a problem. Prominent commercial lawyers like New York's Albert Stickney scoffed at the notion that price-fixing conspiracies could

ever be anticompetitive: "No such combination has ever had any substantial result, other than to make a slight rise in prices, in some local
market, for a very short time." The sociologist Franklin H. Giddings
argued in 1887 that the doctrine of potential competition was an important corollary of the doctrine of conservation of energy in physics.
Competition was a type of energy. Although the total amount could not
be changed, its form might change from actual to potential. When there
was less actual competition, there was necessarily more potential competition. The Illinois economist and clergyman Julian M. Sturtevant
argued that long-term monopoly was impossible, for there "will ever be
those who will be eager to produce a commodity at a price equal to the
cost of production." Even the great oil monopoly would expire, because
the high price would invite inventors to look for new methods of providing lighting and energy. The corporate law treatise writer William
W. Cook argued that one of the greatest pitfalls awaiting the trust was
"the certainty of new competitors . . . . Even after a trust becomes an
absolute monopoly it is never safe. Its vast profits are a tempting prize,
to be contended for by the wealth and enterprise of all men."[2]

As Chapter 21 observed, the common law had been relatively sanguine about cartels but quite hostile toward covenants not to compete.
Both positions were part of a model in which the potential for entry
was regarded as very important. Noncoercive price-fixing agreements
were not a subject of much concern, because monopoly prices would
always be undermined by new entry. It was artificial *restriction* on entry
that concerned classical political economists—whether the restraint came
from the sovereign in the form of a monopoly franchise or from private
parties in the form of covenants not to compete or concerted agreements
not to do business with new entrants.

A robust potential competition doctrine had remarkable implications
for antitrust policy. Most economists at the turn of the century believed
that increasing business concentration and large firm size could yield
two possible results. First, they could lead to substantial efficiencies in
production and distribution. Second, they could produce market dominance, or the ability of one firm or a small group of firms to charge
prices well above costs. A strong theory of potential competition effectively neutralized the second possibility. Even if a firm should end up
with 75 or 80 percent of its market, it would not charge monopoly prices
as long as it faced the immediate expansion of smaller rivals or competitive entry by newcomers. The result for economists who accepted
the classical theory of competition was that the trusts could have only
beneficial consequences, not harmful ones.

For economists who had particularly exaggerated notions about economies of scale the trusts were not merely beneficial but a form of salvation. Jeremiah Jenks and popularizers such as George Gunton and Andrew Carnegie wrote ad nauseam about the "wastes" of actual competition—needless duplication of facilities, overproduction, higher transportation costs, and so on.[3] Gunton concluded that potential competition was more than sufficient to keep prices at the competitive level, without unnecessary waste: "[When] the gates for the admission of new competitive capital are always open, the economic effect is substantially the same as if the new competitor were already there; the fact that he *may come* any day has essentially the same effect as if he *had come*, because to *keep him out* requires the same kind of influence that would be necessary to *drive him out*."[4]

Arthur Twining Hadley believed that competition could be wasteful in industries with high fixed costs: ". . . the competition of different concerns always involves a loss, from the need of maintaining too many selling agencies, the expense of unnecessary advertising, and the lack of proper utilization of fixed capital." However, Hadley reassured his readers, such duplication was unnecessary. The trust that presumed to charge high prices was asking for trouble. New entry by competitors would follow quickly. Even more cautious economists such as John Bates Clark argued in the 1880's and 1890's that potential competition would generally be sufficient to prevent monopoly pricing by the trusts. Speaking at the Chicago Trust Conference in 1899, Clark concluded that "potential competition . . . is the power that holds the trusts in check. The competition that is now latent, but is ready to spring into activity if very high prices are exacted, is even now efficient in preventing high prices."[5]

But by 1901 Clark had became more cautious, suggesting that potential competition would keep the trusts in check only if the trusts were forbidden to engage in predatory pricing or other exclusionary practices calculated to "terrorize" potential competitors into staying out of the market. A substantial minority of economists found the classical potential competition doctrine naive. Brown University's Elisha Andrews raised several objections. First, although monopoly profits might attract new entry, virtually no one outside the monopoly firm knew what its profits were. Second, the capital required to compete against the trusts was so large that almost no one was capable of raising it. Finally, Andrews observed, small competitors of the trust would find it much more profitable to reap the rewards of monopoly rather than trying to fight it. When a monopolist or cartel raises prices, small firms making the same product can increase their prices as well. "Establishments not in the combination, so long as its monopoly endures, are, in spite of themselves, its parasites, lifted up and nourished by its power." They would likely be content with their high current profits, rather than risk the wrath of the dominant firm.[6]

Richard T. Ely argued in 1900 that economies of scale themselves tended to deter entry by competitors. If the biggest companies could do things more cheaply than smaller firms could, a new entrant would immediately find itself at a disadvantage. Ely went so far as to conclude that the undoing of competition was inherent in the notion of economies of scale. Charles J. Bullock of Williams College made the same observation in 1901. If it costs a small firm a dollar to make a product but the dominant firm only eighty cents, the monopolist could "maintain the price at ninety-nine and nine-tenths cents without inviting competition."[7]

One of the most incisive perspectives on the trusts and potential competition came from the lawyer William Miller Collier, of New York, who argued in 1900 that the real anticompetitive evil of the trusts was not their control of large market shares but rather their tendency to carry large amounts of excess capacity. Ordinarily, Collier explained, potential competition can be relied on to discipline monopoly pricing. If the dominant firm carries enormous excess capacity, however, "the potential competitor will hesitate a very long time." He "knows that there is no need of new factories; and that the demand of the public will not sustain both the new factory and the old factory." More problematically, Collier argued, this carrying of excess capacity by dominant firms was strategic:

> This knowledge of the potential competitor that there is really not room for a new establishment in the industry is also knowledge possessed by the trust managers; and knowing that, they realize that even though they raise their prices somewhat above the fair profit mark, yet there is a very powerful restraint upon the establishment of new competition . . . . It is not the aggregation [of capital] that stops the establishment of new competitive enterprises, but the fact that the total capacity is in excess of demand.[8]

Collier believed that the sugar trust, Standard Oil, and Carnegie Steel were among the dominant firms that had used excess capacity as a device for earning current monopoly returns while at the same time discouraging new entry.

Collier's perspective on potential competition was ahead of his time;

he certainly was more sophisticated than the average business lawyer. John Maurice Clark would make the same arguments in the economics literature fourteen years later, when he also argued that potential competition would lose its efficacy in industries with high fixed costs and excess capacity. This model of strategic entry deterrence by scale economies and excess capacity remains prominent today.[9]

Common law courts had known about potential competition for a long time. As early as the 1820's English cases had cited potential competition as a justification for upholding cartel agreements. Inherent in the classical economic theory adopted by the courts was the notion that purely "voluntary" restraints on trade, such as price-fixing agreements, were harmless because any attempt to charge monopoly prices would be promptly disciplined by customer defection or new entry. Some American courts held that price fixing was not a public problem as long as the cartel made no effort to exclude others from doing business as well. For example, in 1886 a New York federal court refused to condemn a washing machine manufacturers' cartel, because the parties "did not contemplate suppressing the manufacture or sale of machines by others," and these would quickly enter the business in response to a monopolistic price increase. Frederick H. Cooke argued in 1909 that potential competition should be given greater consideration in cases involving the apparent elimination of competition.[10]

Some early Sherman Act cases also reflect the classical optimism about potential competition. In *United States v. Nelson* (1892) the court dismissed an indictment alleging naked price fixing among sellers of lumber. "Competition is not stifled by such an agreement, and other dealers would soon force the parties to the agreement to sell at the market price, or a reasonable price, at least." In approving price fixing among watch manufacturers, the Second Circuit concluded in 1895 that the public could not possibly be injured by price fixing. If "the combining defendants fix the price too high, they restrain their own trade only; the public will buy the goods it wants, not from them, but from their competitors."[11]

The classical perspective on entry by competitors suggested that collusion was a much greater problem in markets where entry was restricted by law than in ordinary markets. In 1893 the Texas Supreme Court concluded that "there is a stronger reason for holding illegal combinations to enhance prices among those engaged in occupations which are licensed, and are protected from unlicensed competition, than among those of whom no license is required." Likewise, in an 1895

Sherman Act case the Second Circuit suggested that price fixing among "public or quasi public" businesses, such as "railroads or gaslighting companies," be treated more severely than price fixing among ordinary commodities. As Frederick H. Cooke put it, combinations in restraint of trade should be dealt with more harshly if they occurred in businesses of a "public character." An important difference between such businesses and ordinary businesses, he noted, is that historically one could engage in business of a public character only by obtaining a charter, or franchise, from the state. Collusion in such markets was more threatening, because new competition would have to await the state's decision to permit additional firms to enter.[12]

Around the turn of the century a large treatise literature on utilities and public service companies began to emerge. By and large these writers, whose work was discussed in Chapter 11, noted that restraints on competition were dealt with more severely in such industries. In the railroad industry, in particular, this suggested a major anomaly in the classical model. The railroads were natural monopolies subject to high fixed costs and economies of scale. Competition among railroads would almost always be "ruinous." But one could not enter the railroad market without special permission from the state. As a result, collusion among railroads would not be effectively disciplined by potential competition. Forced to compete, the railroads would be driven into bankruptcy. But if permitted to collude, they would almost certainly charge monopoly prices. Only statutory rate regulation would yield both competitive pricing and normal profits.

One reason for classicism's casual attitude toward private monopoly was its failure to distinguish between "long-run" and "short-run" phenomena. Today we think of most of the concerns of the classicists as long-run issues. The classicists were interested in the general, or final, effects of policies, not in the temporary dislocations that might occur in some markets as a result of one firm's control over an important resource. In the long run, monopolies and cartels tend to correct themselves, of course. Outsiders are attracted by the high profits and look for ways to enter the market. The new entry drives prices back to the competitive level.

But the cost to society of even a "short-run" monopoly can be very high, particularly if the short run is not all that short. The growth of capital-intensive industry in the last half of the nineteenth century brought the realization that, even if entry into some markets was unrestrained, it was nevertheless risky and could take a long time. In his

Economics (1896), Arthur Twining Hadley observed that a trust's potential to earn monopoly profits was in large part a function of the time it
took for new competitors to enter. In some capital-intensive industries
characterized by substantial scale economies and specialized, durable
assets, new entry took a long time or might never occur. The potential
for monopoly profits was comparatively large. For example, railroads
could "charge high rates for a long time without calling a competitor
into being; for business which gives unusual profit to one road may
afford very inadequate remuneration to more than one." In other industries, entry was quick and monopoly profits all but impossible.[13]

The developing antitrust law quickly acquired a healthy skepticism
about potential competition. In his *Addyston Pipe* opinion, Judge Taft
established the premise that short-run, or temporary, monopoly was an
important concern of the Sherman Act. "It may be . . . that local
monopolies cannot endure long, because their very existence tempts
outside capital into competition," Judge Taft conceded. However, "the
public interest may suffer severely while new competition is slowly developing." For this reason Judge Taft rejected the English holding that
cartels were not a matter of public concern as long as they were faced
with potential competition.[14]

After *Addyston Pipe* potential competition was no longer a defense to
price fixing in Sherman Act cases. In *American Can* (1916) the court
noted that the can combination's efforts to raise prices were persistently
doomed to failure. The can trust was largely the product of Edwin
Norton, an entrepreneurial wizard who had managed to acquire control
of the best can-making technology and then launched an elaborate
program of purchasing rivals' plants, shutting them down, and even
dismantling them. The purchase agreements contained covenants forbidding the sellers from making cans for fifteen years within three
thousand miles of Chicago. Norton also either acquired every manufacturer of can-making machinery, purchased from them covenants that
they would not make the machinery for anyone but American Can, or
negotiated contracts requiring the machinery makers to sell their full
output to American Can.[15]

These efforts notwithstanding, American Can's first substantial price
increase flooded the market with the cans of competitors. It became
"apparently profitable for outsiders to start making cans with any antiquated or crude machinery they could find in old lumber rooms . . . .
Any number of people began to make cans, or, at least, began to try to
make them." At first, American Can tried to buy out these new com

petitors one at a time. But the company was almost out of money, and for every plant it purchased outsiders found it "easy enough to start some more." Nevertheless, the court condemned the can company for monopolizing and for entering into numerous combinations in restraint of trade.

Likewise, in the *Corn Products* case (1916) Judge Learned Hand found two propositions equally well proved. First was the government's argument that the defendant corn products trust went to extraordinary lengths, including predatory pricing and purchase and dismantling of competitors' plants, to exclude newcomers from the market. Second was the defendants' argument that "regardless of what their efforts [to acquire a monopoly] may have been, in fact the conditions of the industry were such that they could not do so but have been slipping back proportionately from the very outset." Nonetheless, Hand refused to hold that the Sherman Act required a showing that the combination "was able to exclude" all others. If that were the test, there could be "no restraint of trade without a patent or control of some natural source."[16]

The potential competition doctrine, like the controversy over ruinous competition, threw economists and lawyers into a common debate about theory, firm behavior, and public policy. The debate long antedates the Sherman Act, and its existence should disabuse anyone of the notion that economics in antitrust policy is a recent discovery. Judges and lawyers involved in antitrust cases at the turn of the century did exactly what judges and lawyers do today—they took the best economic theory available to them and tried to apply it to vexing issues of policy.

CHAPTER 25

Vertical Integration and Resale Price Maintenance

A firm is vertically integrated when it produces for itself some good or service that it would otherwise purchase on the market. Under this definition, all firms are vertically integrated to one degree or another. When we consider vertical integration as a policy problem, we generally think of firms that begin to supply for themselves something that they had previously procured from others. Good examples are International Harvester's acquisition of the Wisconsin Steel Company, which gave Harvester the ability to manufacture its own steel for making farm implements, or United States Steel's acquisition of the Bessemer Steamship Company, which permitted it to transport its own raw material and finished products.[1]

A firm can integrate vertically in three different ways. First, it might build its own new plant or facility in a vertically related market. This method of vertical integration has only infrequently been condemned as anticompetitive. Second, a firm might acquire an existing firm operating in a vertically related market. Such vertical mergers have often been challenged under the antitrust laws. Third, a firm might enter into a long-term contract creating a formal, ongoing relationship with another firm. Franchise contracts, exclusive dealing contracts, tying contracts,[2] resale price maintenance agreements, and vertical nonprice agreements specifying dealer location can all be forms of vertical integration by contract.

The Theory of Vertical Integration before the New Deal

American antitrust policy has always felt ambivalent about vertical integration. Since the 1910's the courts had seemed aware of the potential of vertical integration to reduce a firm's costs and make it operate more efficiently.[3] But they were also anxious that vertical integration might somehow increase monopoly power or deny to other entrepreneurs opportunities that were rightfully theirs.[4] That these two public concerns about vertical integration—the first motivated by a desire for business efficiency, the second by a wish to treat small businesses fairly—were fundamentally inconsistent helps explain the erratic nature of American policy toward vertical integration.

The trust movement, particularly the merger wave of 1895–1905, included a great deal of vertical integration. What motivated this integration is a matter of some controversy. Writing during the middle of the wave, the Harvard economist William F. Willoughby had little but praise for the tendency of the large firms to integrate vertically—part of a "wonderful development of an industrial system." In his 1977 study of the development of American business enterprise, Alfred D. Chandler, Jr., argued that most nineteenth-century vertical integration was efficient, designed to achieve "economies of speed" in the production or distribution process. In 1990 Chandler modified that position slightly, conceding that some uses of vertical integration were strategic and exclusionary.[5]

But others cite "abundant evidence" that vertical integration was frequently motivated by the integrating firm's desire to enhance a dominant market position, most generally by denying competitors some source of supply or channel of distribution.[6] United States Steel made repeated efforts to integrate into raw materials in order to deny access to competitors. International Paper did the same thing. American Smelting & Refining and Anaconda Copper attempted to gain monopoly control of ore deposits. National Cordage, the American Tin Plate Company and American Can all attempted to cut off their competitors' access to manufacturing machinery.

Whatever the actual motives, it seems clear that policy makers in the nineteenth and early twentieth centuries had difficulty balancing the values and threats of vertical integration. Both the preclassical and classical legal traditions had their own legacy of ambivalence. In England the preclassical crime of "badgering" or "regrating" was codified in a 1552 statute that actually compelled vertical integration in agricultural products, by forcing farmers to do their own distributing. The statute forbade people from obtaining "any corn . . . or other . . . victual . . . to be sold, and to sell the same again in any fair or market holden or kept in the same place, or in any other fair or market within four miles thereof . . . ." The middleman, in this view, served no useful function in society except to enhance the price of commodities.[7]

With the rise of the classical concept of the market, however, the middleman's functions began to be appreciated. The English law against regrating was repealed in 1772. Statutes condemning regrating never took hold in the United States, although a few states passed laws that were enforced for a short time.[8] In 1853 the American treatise writer William W. Story noted that such statutes attempted to prohibit activities that were "the very life of trade." Without them, "all wholesale trade and jobbing would be at an end." By the time Story wrote the middleman, or "jobber," had become an important part of American commerce. In a series of important decisions in the 1870's and 1880's, the Supreme Court protected the "drummer," or middleman selling products manufactured in other states, from discriminatory state taxation. Thus the interstate distribution network received constitutional sanction.[9]

Neither classical political economy nor classical legal theory regarded vertical integration as threatening. Resale price maintenance and exclusive dealing, probably the most common forms of vertical integration by contract in the eighteenth and nineteenth centuries, were both legal at common law. In the *Pullman* case (1891) Justice John Marshall Harlan explained why an exclusive dealing contract between a railroad and a manufacturer of sleeping cars was not contrary to public policy. His explanation was orthodox classicism:

> Instead of furnishing its own drawing-room and sleeping cars, as it might have done, [the railroad] employed the plaintiff, whose special business was to provide cars of that character, to supply as many as were necessary to meet the requirements of travel. It [the railroad] thus used the instrumentality of another corporation in order that it might properly discharge its duty to the public. So long as the defendant's lines were supplied with the requisite number of drawing-room and sleeping cars, it was a matter of indifference to the public who owned them.[10]

Under this view, vertical integration was nothing more than the consequences of a firm's decision about whether to produce some essential product or service internally, or to purchase it by general or exclusive contract from someone else. Presumably, the firm would do this in the way most advantageous to itself. As Judge Taft described *Pullman* in his famous *Addyston Pipe* opinion six years later: "The railroad company may discharge this duty itself to the public, and allow no one else to do it, or it may hire some one to do it, and, to secure the necessary investment of capital in the discharge of the duty, may secure to the sleeping-car company the same freedom from competition that it would itself in discharging the duty."[11]

The one place nineteenth-century American law was hostile toward vertical integration was the doctrine of ultra vires in American corporate law, which generally forbade business corporations from engaging in unauthorized activities. The principal legal vehicle for regulating corporate vertical integration was the business purpose clause contained in either the incorporation statute or the corporate charter. Although the clauses seldom limited the size to which a firm could grow—i.e, its horizontal growth—they almost always enumerated the types of business in which firms could engage. They applied to vertical integration, both by acquisition and by new entry. If a railroad's charter did not authorize it to operate a trackside hotel, then the railroad could neither purchase a hotel or hotel-operating firm nor build its own hotel. Furthermore, in order to challenge such a venture one did not need to show an injury to competition or a threat of monopoly. Operation in an area not permitted by the charter or the corporation statute was simply illegal.

The historical concern of the corporate law of ultra vires was not competition or protection from trade restraints but rather a general distrust of the corporate form of organization, particularly of its unlimited ability to amass capital. But as the nineteenth century wore on, that fear was generally allayed. One effect of the classical revolution in American corporate law, as we have seen, was to broaden considerably the range of permissible corporate business activities.

Historically, courts in condemning actions as ultra vires made no distinction between vertical integration and the more general range of unauthorized activities. But in the final decades of the nineteenth century courts began to treat actions challenged as ultra vires more leniently if they involved vertical integration. For example, in 1896 the Supreme Court held that a railroad could be permitted to operate a hotel even though such power was not granted in its charter, because the railroad had acquired the hotel in order "to furnish reasonable and necessary accommodations to its passengers and employees . . . ."[12] Presumably if the railroad had decided to operate a business in an unrelated market, the court would have been less tolerant.

The doctrine giving preferred treatment to vertical integration, which came to be called the "collateral transactions" rule, was that a corporation might engage in business not expressly permitted in its charter if the transactions enabled it to perform its authorized business more efficiently. The rule appears to have been developed in cases involving common carriers, particularly the railroads. Common carriers, unlike other firms, were required by law to provide "collateral" services to their customers—such as a guarantee of safe arrival, accommodations in the case of a breakdown, or even transportation to destinations that were not located along the tracks. From these extra obligations the courts fashioned the rule that railroads could engage in business activities necessary to provide these collateral services, even if their charter permitted them only to operate a railroad.

Victor Morawetz's treatise on corporation law contained this economic argument for the collateral transactions rule:

> Business corporations are formed for the pecuniary profit of their shareholders. Economy is, therefore, essential in the proper management of the corporate affairs; and it is implied in the charter of every corporation of this character that it may adopt all such means as will enable it to attain its legitimate purpose in the most profitable manner. A transaction may *prima facie* appear to be wholly foreign to the business for which a corporation was formed; and yet, if it be auxiliary to any legitimate purpose of the company, and adapted to attain the same more advantageously, it is impliedly authorized.

Under this rule, Morawetz suggested, a company chartered to operate a railroad might be justified in purchasing and working a coal mine in order to provide coal for its internal operations; but it could not "buy coal or anything else as a speculation, with the intention of selling it again." Nor could a firm engage in unrelated business merely in order to raise funds for the pursuit of its legitimate business. However, Morawetz clearly preferred the relatively broad rule that had been adopted by English courts that the railroad which had purchased a coal mine for internal operations should also be permitted to sell its surplus coal on the open market, effectively entering the coal business as well. Morawetz relied on several recent American cases that had approved vertical integration challenged as ultra vires.[13]

By the turn of the century corporations could be chartered to engage in any lawful business activity. The collateral transactions rule was unnecessary for corporations with such charters. Further, the doctrine of ultra vires was generally confined to challenges by stockholders themselves, or to quo warranto proceedings in which the corporation was accused of doing something independently unlawful or contrary to the public interest.

Thus at the time the Sherman Act was passed both the common law of trade restraints and classical corporate law were quite tolerant of vertical integration. Judicial interpretations of the Sherman Act adhered to these principles for two decades. But in the *American Tobacco* case (1911) the Supreme Court first suggested that vertical integration might facilitate the creation of a monopoly by "foreclosing" competitors from needed inputs. In its 1911 report on the United States Steel Company, the Federal Bureau of Corporations acknowledged the value of vertical integration in steel manufacturing, but concluded that the constituent firms involved in the merger that created the great company had already been fully integrated. Something other than increased efficiency must have motivated the firms to merge.[14]

The Bureau's 1913 report on the farm implement trust concluded similarly that International Harvester, which manufactured several lines of agricultural machinery, had a policy of entering exclusive dealing arrangements with every available dealer in a community. Each dealer was given the right to sell a particular Harvester line, but forbidden from selling the machinery of competitors. The result, concluded the report, was that Harvester's competitors were denied access to adequate retail outlets for their competing products. In 1918 the government obtained a consent decree limiting International Harvester to dealing with a single dealer in any town. A 1920 report of the Federal Trade Commission argued that part of the blame for the high price of farm implements lay in the fact that International Harvester had integrated back into the production of steel, giving it a monopolistic advantage over its competitors.[15]

Increased congressional hostility toward vertical integration by contract appeared in 1914 in the Clayton Act, which condemned tying arrangements and exclusive dealing that might injure competition, and in the Federal Trade Commission Act, which created the Federal Trade Commission and authorized it to go after "unfair" competition. "Unfair" competition became a term of art for a group of practices that included many types of vertical integration. In 1920 the Supreme Court held that tying contracts were not "unfair competition" under the Federal Trade Commission Act, just as it had held in 1912 that they did not violate the Sherman Act. But in 1917 it condemned the tying of unpatented products to patented ones, and began a series of decisions increasingly hostile toward tying arrangements.[16]

The economic rationalization of these concerns followed very shortly. Economists quickly came to absorb the same fears about vertical integration that the courts expressed in the 1900's and 1910's, and these became an acceptable, if controversial, part of mainstream American economics. In 1919 Frank W. Taussig, whose neoclassical credentials were impeccable, wrote about vertical integration in terms very reminiscent of earlier case law and government reports:

> The iron and steel manufacture offers an unusually tempting field for vertical combination, chiefly, it would seem, because of the concentration of the supplies of raw materials, —coal and iron ore. Those who, at any stage of rising demand, possess the mines of coal and iron, have the whip hand in the situation; hence the manufacturers of the more finished forms of iron and steel have sought to gain control of the mines, by purchase or amalgamation . . . .
> Vertical combination and horizontal combination may go hand in hand. The American Tobacco Company has attempted to combine all the establishments manufacturing tobacco for smoking and chewing; and the extension of its operations into the retail disposal of its products has been the outgrowth of the endeavor to form and strengthen this all-embracing horizontal combination.[17]

Taussig went on to note that vertically integrated firms could also perform more efficiently than unintegrated firms. But the seed was planted. Even in the economics literature vertical integration had become an ambiguous practice, sometimes good but sometimes evil, and worthy of antitrust scrutiny. In 1921 Eliot Jones identified certain instances of vertical integration as anticompetitive—such as Standard Oil Company's acquisitions of pipelines, which denied its competitors access to markets. In 1927 Myron Watkins wrote of vertical integration as one of the "tactical" uses of combination, which could enable the dominant firm "to hinder and obstruct the business operations of rivals." Watkins concluded that exclusive dealing was almost always anticompetitive. Good dealers, he argued, would not agree to deal exclusively in a single manufacturer's line unless the manufacturer were very powerful. Why give up the opportunity to deal in everyone's goods in exchange for the right to deal in those of a single supplier? However, the dealer cannot be "indifferent to the proposals of the manufacturer who produces, say, more than half of the total output of a particular type of goods." In addition, Watkins opined, it would generally be "uneconomical" to develop a distribution network to deal in only one line of goods; so exclusive dealing was not likely to have an efficiency explanation. With respect to tying, Watkins concluded that in most cases the requirements were anticompetitive, because through them firms "extended the scope of a legalized monopoly," usually a patented product, by requiring purchasers to take an unpatented product as well.[18]

These fears about vertical integration became most prominent in the 1930's when many economists came to regard vertical integration as anticompetitive as a general matter, and not merely in the unusual case involving a resource that could not be duplicated by competitors. For example, in his *Theory of Monopolistic Competition* (1933) Edward Chamberlin argued that in oligopoly markets "universal" vertical integration would be "compelled," not because of increased efficiency, but as a defensive mechanism. Each firm in an oligopoly market would integrate vertically into another oligopoly market in order to avoid paying monopoly prices there. Under the theory of monopolistic competition, these firms already engaged in extreme product differentiation and carried abundant excess capacity. The result of the vertical integration was excess capacity at every stage of production and distribution, "much duplication of distributive machinery, and higher margins of profit which attract more people into the field and bring still more waste . . . ." The University of Chicago economist Henry Simons similarly believed that vertical integration was harmful more often than it was competitive.[19]

Arthur R. Burns, in his ponderous but influential *The Decline of Competition* (1936), argued that vertical integration was both a cause and a result of a general decline in competition. Any efficiencies that might result from vertical integration were likely to be dwarfed by its anticompetitive effects.[20] "Integration may result from attempts to secure economies in production and marketing," Burns conceded. "In large measure, however, it is explicable in terms of considerations that would be absent from a purely competitive world." The picture Burns painted was bleak. In a world of oligopolistic industries prices were high. Firms integrated vertically in order to avoid paying monopoly prices to someone else. For example, both International Harvester and Ford Motor Company manufactured their own steel in order to avoid monopolistic steel prices. But the result of this vertical integration, Burns lamented, was that big firms became even bigger, concentrated industries even more concentrated, and prices even higher. Industrial concentration and vertical integration were wrapped together and caught in an upward spiral. Burns concluded that courts should be far more concerned with vertical integration than they had been in the past.

In their 1932 book on the American business corporation, Berle and

Means had argued that vertical integration could actually make the large corporation less efficient because its costs became "indeterminate"—it would have unreliable information about the cost of functions that it performed for itself rather than purchased on the marketplace.[21] Burns agreed. Disputing the traditional neoclassical view, he argued that vertical integration reduced the efficiency of most firms by shielding transactions from the market. "Where little vertical integration occurs the efficiency of producers is checked at a great many points along the chain of operations . . . ; costs of production are separated for each stage and the market facilitates the frequent comparison of costs and utilities." However, if the firms in an industry tend to be vertically integrated, "the market affords opportunity for comparing only the aggregate cost of all stages of production." As a result, inefficiencies would be disguised and firms slower to adopt more efficient procedures. Burns relied on two 1920's Federal Trade Commission studies that had concluded that in the steel and petroleum industries rate of return was actually inversely proportional to the extent of vertical integration.[22]

The classical model suggested that such inefficiencies would be self-correcting. If vertically integrated firms were less efficient, they would be unable to compete with unintegrated rivals. But in the case of American industry the tendency to integrate vertically in order to avoid oligopoly was too strong. The result was the simultaneous perpetuation of both oligopoly and inefficient, vertically integrated firm structures. Frank A. Fetter argued to the same effect in his pessimistic *Masquerade of Monopoly* (1931).[23]

In "The Nature of the Firm" (1937), Ronald Coase argued that the principal characteristic of the firm was "the suppression of the price mechanism." To the extent the firm was vertically integrated, it eliminated market transactions. By 1937 this view was already well developed in the economic literature, but it had come from different sources than those Coase looked to. Both Berle and Means and Arthur Burns had argued that vertical integration suppresses prices. For them, however, this made vertical integration inefficient. Coase assumed that the suppression of the price mechanism by integration was an unmitigated good, simply by assuming away the arguments on the other side. By avoiding the market, firms did no more than avoid its costs. Coase neither cited nor discussed Burns's *Decline of Competition* or Berle and Means's *Modern Corporation*. He assumed that markets are imperfect and that firms have imperfect information about them, but he also assumed that firms have nearly perfect information about their own costs.[24]

By 1940 economists were divided into two camps. Orthodox neoclassicists, holding to the conclusions of Coase's "Nature of the Firm," continued to hold the minority view for some time. These tended to rely on the model of perfect competition, subject to some qualifications, and to emphasize long-run rather than short-run concerns. Over the long run firms are vertically integrated precisely to the extent that integration reduces the costs of production and distribution. Within this model, all firms were presumed to be profit-maximizers.

The majority camp was more distinctly post-classical, heavily influenced by Chamberlin's theory of monopolistic competition and more clearly concerned about imperfections in the market. Even more important, they were more impressed by short-run, strategic considerations than were the neoclassicists. For example, the emerging theory of the "price squeeze" suggested that a vertically integrated monopolist or oligopoly could manipulate the price structure in a market in order to deter unintegrated entry. The government first argued the price squeeze in the *Corn Products* case in the 1910's, where the theory was that the corn products monopoly sold corn solids to syrup mixers at a high price, but sold its own finished corn syrup at a low price, in order to drive the syrup mixers out of business. The theory was refined somewhat in the 1930's and 1940's, and the most famous case in which the courts applied it involved the Aluminum Company of America (Alcoa).[25]

Finally, the post-classicists were dubious about the efficiencies of the business firm's own internal operations. Coase assumed that firms had good knowledge about their own costs. Both Berle and Means and Arthur Burns assumed the contrary. This debate—closely related to the debate about the consequences of the separation of ownership and control in the modern business firm—has never been resolved. Even the question whether firms maximize profits remains controversial and normative.

Resale Price Maintenance and the Drug Cartel

One of the most perplexing of the early Sherman Act antitrust cases is the Supreme Court's *Dr. Miles* decision (1911)[26] condemning resale price maintenance agreements. Resale price maintenance occurs when a manufacturer or wholesaler requires retailers to resell its product at a specified price. Within the neoclassical model such an agreement eliminates no competition between the manufacturer and the retailer, because they are not in "competition" with each other. But resale price maintenance agreements were viewed as eliminating competition *among* the retailers of a particular brand. The Sherman Act's per se rule against resale price maintenance, which survives to this day, grew out of the tension between classical and neoclassical price theory that the Supreme Court perceived in 1911. Classicism, with its emphasis on liberty and freedom from unbargained for coercion, found resale price maintenance legal.[27] Neoclassicism, with its heightened concern about collusion, was more suspicious.

Nineteenth-century manufacturers imposed resale price maintenance on their dealers for a variety of reasons. Undoubtedly they sometimes used it to encourage retailers to make sufficient investment in their stores and provide adequate services at sale. By guaranteeing a minimum markup and eliminating price competition among its retailers, a manufacturer could effectively force the retailers to engage in this kind of nonprice competition, and so maximize sales.[28]

But manufacturers were not always the instigators of resale price maintenance; it was also procured by groups of small retailers intent on protecting themselves from the lower prices charged by larger stores. In the 1930's the small retailers accomplished this by lobbying for "fair trade" laws, which effectively legalized resale price maintenance in many states.[29]

In the late nineteenth century resale price maintenance was legal. The principal political task of the small retailers was to convince the suppliers to impose resale price maintenance on the larger retailers. This was accomplished through a series of agreements that were simultaneously vertical and horizontal. First, the small retailers would agree with each other to obtain resale price maintenance agreements from their suppliers. Then they would take their campaign to the suppliers, perhaps with threats of a boycott of any supplier that refused to comply.[30] The suppliers themselves might also agree with each other to impose resale price maintenance, and to refuse to deal with distributors or retailers that refused to cooperate. In 1903 the New York Court of Appeals summarized allegations concerning collusion and resale price maintenance in the over-the-counter drug industry:

> At one time the sale of these goods was largely made through traveling sales agents, who worked upon commissions . . . . Later on they were sold largely through the druggists, but many of the manufacturers did not maintain a uniform price. They would supply goods to some of the wholesalers upon more favorable terms than to others; thus permitting large dealers to make a profit, while a great number of the smaller druggists

found the handling of proprietary goods unprofitable. This resulted in the organization of the National Wholesale Druggists' Association, an unincorporated body, which in 1882 and 1883 represented 90 per cent. of the wholesale jobbing trade of the United States. At a meeting of this association a plan was devised and adopted for the conduct of the business of the sale of proprietary goods, which was in the form of a petition addressed to the proprietors, asking them to fix a uniform jobbing price for fixed quantities, and also a selling price by the druggists, which they were to agree to maintain . . . .

This cartel was to dominate the proprietary drug industry in the United States for thirty years, and the legality of its resale price maintenance agreements was assessed twice by the United States Supreme Court. The druggists' cartel, which was gradually uncovered through a series of judicial decisions attacking both the horizontal and the vertical agreements, accounts for a great deal of our current law of resale price maintenance.[31]

The plaintiff in the *Dr. Miles* case was Dr. Miles Medical Company, a large manufacturer of patent medicines based in Elkhart, Indiana, which sold its products nationwide to wholesale distributors. The distributors then sold the medicines to retail druggists. The contract by which Dr. Miles sold its drugs to the distributors required the distributors to sell the drugs to the retailers at a specified price, and the retailers in turn to sell the medicines to the public at a specified price.

By 1911 the discount department store was well established in America. These stores sought to buy products in large quantities at discount prices, and then to sell them more cheaply to consumers. They were opposed at every stage by older, smaller retailers who had higher costs and resold products at higher prices.[32] One large distributor of patent medicines, John D. Park & Sons of Cincinnati, persistently resold medicines to discounters at a lower price than its contract with Dr. Miles permitted. In order to obtain enough Dr. Miles medicine to satisfy the discounters' requests, John D. Park often talked other distributors into selling it large quantities at discount prices. Dr. Miles Company finally sued Park to enjoin it from breaking the resale price maintenance contracts. Park raised the common law and the Sherman Act as a defense, arguing that the resale price maintenance contracts were illegal.

John D. Park had been a thorn in the drug industry's side for nearly thirty years. In the early 1880's he had begun violating resale price maintenance agreements with manufacturers of patent medicines. He was sued by Seth A. and Horace S. Fowle, who made Wistar's Balsam of Wild Cherry. In *Fowle v. Park* (1889)[33] the Supreme Court accepted the classical position and rejected Park's argument that resale price maintenance agreements were unenforceable contracts in restraint of trade. The *Dr. Miles* case was identical to the *Fowle* case except that Park now had the benefit of the Sherman Act.

Within the classical model of political economy, resale price maintenance agreements were quite harmless. Manufacturers were free to insist on the terms upon which products would be resold; retailers and their customers were free to walk away from bargains they found objectionable. Resale price maintenance agreements were generally perceived as completely voluntary as between the parties to the agreement.[34] No one was being coerced in any sense that classical political economy recognized, although some distributors and retailers certainly would have preferred to buy without the restraint on resale prices. Most courts found resale price maintenance agreements legal at common law.[35] The few courts that condemned them generally did so on the theory that resale price maintenance was merely a variant on the common law offense of "forestalling"—or buying up a product in order to resell it at an enhanced price.[36]

Given that both classical political economy and the common law were so tolerant of resale price maintenance agreements, why did the Supreme Court interpret the Sherman Act to make them illegal per se? One reason is that by this time the Supreme Court was adopting a more neoclassical conception of coercion, in which consumers were presumed to be entitled to the price that would be offered in a market free of restraint. Although it might be difficult to see how a manufacturer without market power could use resale price maintenance to charge monopoly prices, it was clear that under resale price maintenance customers were not receiving all the benefits of price competition at every market level. The "public is entitled to whatever advantage may be derived from competition in the subsequent traffic," the Supreme Court concluded in *Dr. Miles*.[37]

Equally important was that by 1911 neoclassicism had given the courts a heightened sensitivity to collusion, and judges had begun to realize that resale price maintenance often facilitated price fixing. If retailers wanted to fix the price of a product, nothing could be more effective than to have the manufacturer of that product "impose" the cartel price on the retailers through resale price maintenance agreements. The horizontal price-fixing agreement would likely not be enforceable in court, as an agreement in restraint of trade. And any concerted boycott

344 · THE ANTITRUST MOVEMENT

by conspiring retailers directed at discounting retailers might be condemned. However, at common law the resale price maintenance agreement was legal and enforceable. Combining retailers would try to force manufacturers to impose such agreements on discounting retailers, thereby making the cartel legally enforceable at the apparent behest of the manufacturers. In that way an unenforceable price-fixing agreement became a legally enforceable one.

A manufacturer would ordinarily prefer not to deal with colluding retailers, because the higher markup by retailers reduced the demand for the manufacturer's product. One way to avoid dealing with retailer cartels was through vertical integration. The manufacturer might open its own distribution outlets or retail stores. But if the retailers were well established and powerful and vertical integration into retailing was not a realistic option for the manufacturer, dealing with the cartel may have been the only alternative. For example, the maker of a patent medicine such as the Dr. Miles Company could not easily open its own retail stores in order to avoid the effects of a retail druggists' cartel. Drugs are sold most efficiently through stores that sell hundreds of brands. Dr. Miles, as other drug manufacturers, decided that the best way to deal with the retail drug cartel was to do business with it.

In its *Dr. Miles* decision the Supreme Court relied heavily on Justice Horace Lurton's conclusion in another case involving Park, made when Lurton was still a circuit judge, that when a manufacturer imposes resale prices on all its dealers, prices are fixed horizontally as well as vertically. In such situations, "competition between retailers is destroyed, for each such retailer can obtain his supply only by signing one of the uniform contracts prepared for retailers, whereby he covenants . . . not to sell at less than a standard price named in the agreement. Thus all room for competition between retailers, who supply the public, is made impossible."[38]

In the early twentieth century, when the modern law of resale price maintenance emerged, cartelization and price maintenance contracts seemed to go hand in hand. Two years before *Dr. Miles* the Supreme Court had held that the Sherman Act condemned simultaneous price fixing and resale price maintenance in the wallpaper industry. In that case as in *Dr. Miles*, Judge Lurton had written the opinion for the appellate court condemning the cartel.[39] It was once again clear that price fixing among competitors was being facilitated by resale price maintenance contracts.

The *Dr. Miles* lawsuit was only one of a series of lawsuits exposing the proprietary drug cartel, certainly one of the largest in American history.

The existence of the cartel, alleged but never proved in John D. Park's original lawsuit against the National Wholesale Druggists Association, had finally been established in *Loder v. Jayne* in 1906. The plaintiff in that case was a Boston druggist who also had been sued by Dr. Miles for violating a resale price maintenance agreement. Jayne was able to prove a cartel involving the Proprietary Association of America, which included 90 percent of drug manufacturers; the National Wholesale Druggists' Association, which included 95 percent of wholesale druggists in the United States; and the National Association of Retail Druggists, whose membership included 90 percent of America's retail druggists. The record confirmed John D. Park's earlier allegations that the drug manufacturers and wholesalers were pawns of the substantial power of the retail druggists' association. The retail druggists met periodically to set minimum retail drug prices and to collect the names of "aggressive cutters," or retailers who systematically sold drugs at a lower price. The fact that the retailers set the price is important. A supplier or manufacturer might have good, pro-competitive reasons for wanting to enforce a particular resale price on a retailer, but it is difficult to come up with a competitive explanation why suppliers would want to let a cartel of retailers fix their prices. Under the agreement, the manufacturers and wholesalers refused to deal with anyone labeled an "aggressive cutter" by the National Association of Retail Druggists. Part of the written evidence of this cartel was a series of resale price maintenance agreements between individual manufacturers and wholesalers, and individual wholesalers and retailers. Jayne had been identified by the retail druggists as an aggressive cutter.[40]

Some courts that knew about the horizontal price-fixing conspiracy condemned the resale price maintenance agreements as nothing more than part of the conspiracy. Others, looking only at challenges to the vertical resale price maintenance contracts, upheld them because they were not restraints of trade at common law. For example, in another suit involving aggressive cutter John D. Park & Sons, the court acknowledged that the drug industry appeared to be subject to resale price maintenance agreements that "cover the entire trade in complainant's medicine . . . ." However, the plaintiff had not been able to establish the horizontal agreement, and the court found that the vertical resale price maintenance agreements standing alone were not contracts in restraint of trade. In yet another suit involving aggressive cutter Jacobs' Pharmacy, the court condemned the concerted refusal to deal with price cutters as an unlawful boycott.[41]

Early in the twentieth century some courts began to rule that resale price maintenance agreements were illegal at common law only when they facilitated price fixing among competitors or when the firm imposing resale price maintenance controlled the entire market. For example, in approving a resale price maintenance arrangement covering olive oil, the California Supreme Court noted in 1909 that the agreement did "not relate to any olive oil except that manufactured by plaintiff." There was "no suggestion that this comprises all, or any large proportion, of the olive oil manufactured or sold in the market." The court saw no reason to condemn the contract. The dealer upon whom the agreement was imposed was free to "sell other olive oil at any price and on any conditions satisfactory to him."[42]

In *Park v. Hartman,* the opinion upon which the Supreme Court relied so heavily in the *Dr. Miles* case, Judge Lurton made clear that he was condemning the resale price maintenance agreement *only* because the record showed that resale price maintenance was being used to facilitate collusion. The "covenants restricting sales and resales have as their prime object the suppression of competition between those who buy to sell again." The "main purpose" of the agreement was to benefit the retailers "by breaking down their competition with each other." Likewise in *Park v. National Wholesale Druggists* the New York Court of Appeals applying the common law found it perfectly legal for "manufacturers individually to agree with their customers that those customers shall sell the particular goods manufactured by the vendor for a certain price." However, it was an unlawful restraint of trade "for such manufacturers to become a party to a combination which shall prevent any of his customers from obtaining other goods of other manufacturers because those customers violate the agreement with him in respect to a cutting of prices . . . ."[43]

The Supreme Court went further in *Dr. Miles*. It simply rejected the common law rule approving resale price maintenance agreements. In the process it condemned all such arrangements because some of them might be used anticompetitively. But that is the nature of judicial rule making in revolutionary times, and in 1911 the ruling ideology of trade restraints was still experiencing convulsive change.

The market for economic ideas is no different from the market for products or services. When a demand appears, someone will try to supply it, from whatever source. The demand for a theory of industry organization and performance was generated by the rise of the American business trust. The supply came from economics, history, the developing social sciences, and the law. Economists trying to understand how markets work used ideas that had been generated by lawyers and judges for nearly a century.

But the urge to monopolize appears in intellectual markets as much as in commercial ones. "Formalism" is the principal tool of the intellectual monopolist. Legal formalists argued in the late nineteenth century that the law provided its own source of supply, and that one need not look elsewhere. In economics, the analytic, positivistic theory of the firm attempted to make industrial organization a much more rigorous, formal science than it had been before. This required that economics disregard sources that did not have a particular pedigree. This new, positivistic industrial organization eventually rejected not only the legal tradition but also a well-developed, more eclectic literature in economics itself.

Many of the insights of the formal theory of industrial organization, such as the ruinous competition and potential competition doctrines and the post-classical concern about vertical integration, were really borrowed from the law. This suggests that formalism in economics, just as formalism in law, is not so much a methodology as a rhetoric. During the heyday of legal formalism American lawyers professed that the law was a rigorous, closed system; but all the while they borrowed their ideas wholesale from classical political economy. Economists, it seems, did much the same.

Epilogue: Classical Enterprise in Decline

The Limits of the Classical Market

Neoclassical political economy and classical business enterprise crashed together. The intellectual event signaling the fall of the former was the publication of Joan Robinson's *Economics of Imperfect Competition* and Edward Chamberlin's *Theory of Monopolistic Competition* in 1933. The event signaling the fall of the latter was the publication of a work by Adolph Berle, Jr., and Gardiner Mean, *The Modern Corporation and Private Property,* in 1932. Each of these three books in its own way represented theories of business firm behavior that were inconsistent with the classical models that preceded them. The economics of Robinson and Chamberlin functioned within a neoclassical model in which "markets" were considered to be the fundamental unit of business analysis, but the work of these two economists contributed greatly to the breakdown of that model. Berle and Means's work came out of an institutionalist economic tradition that had become important in America during the Progressive Era, and that placed much more emphasis on the behavior of the individual firm. Although the approaches taken by Robinson and Chamberlin on the one hand and Berle and Means on the other were dramatically different, both were responses to the same phenomena: the awesome growth of the business corporation and the apparent failure of the classical competition model.

Over a century's time classical political economy had developed a model of "perfect competition" within which most economic concepts were analyzed. The perfect competition model, which was not fully drawn until after the turn of the century, was built on three important assumptions: (1) all firms making a particular product make exactly the "same" product, subject only to such size or quality variations as individual purchasers might wish in a particular transaction; (2) individual firms have unrestricted, easy entry into and exit from markets; and (3) all firms have the same costs per unit of output, or "constant returns to scale," no matter what their size. Although a working model of perfect competition had not yet been developed, most of the great works in the classical tradition assumed these market characteristics, even as late as Alfred Marshall's great synthesis of neoclassical economics in 1890. In fact, the explicit articulation of the perfect competition model in the 1920's invited the attack on the model that followed in the 1930's and 1940's. Similarly, just as the perfect competition model was maturing in the economics literature, the structure of the business firm had substantially changed in ways that called into question the three fundamental assumptions of perfect competition. The result was an economic theory that appeared unable to explain everyday price and output phenomena.[1]

Classicism's theory of competition looked a good deal like the model for evolution by natural selection developed in 1859 by Charles Darwin. The popularizers of competition theory used Darwinian analogies liberally. For example, Jeremiah W. Jenks, who taught industrial economics at Cornell, wrote a popular book glorifying monopolies and trusts because of their efficiencies. The "one who shows on the whole the greatest power of self-reliance, self-direction, and skill—the fittest—is the one who, in the competitive struggle, survives." In his famous article "Wealth," Andrew Carnegie explicitly compared the process of economic competition to the struggle of the species for survival. People like Jenks and Carnegie were confident that competition would force firms to produce the best product at the lowest cost or else decline and eventually close down. If a new innovation came along that made products better or cheaper to produce, it would have to be copied by every firm in the market. Those that did not copy it would suffer the consequences. In this way the invisible hand—market competition—would always guarantee consumers the best possible combination of price and quality.[2]

But the one development that this model of competition did not account for was that one firm or a small group of firms might become so "fit" that it drove everyone else from the market. At that point the theory fell apart, and competitive evolution stopped dead. Once competition disappeared the invisible hand could no longer guarantee that the market acting alone would produce the best combination of product quality and price. Ironically, the very success of the business corporation appeared to produce just this situation. The federal antitrust laws were the first broadly supported attempt to solve the monopoly problem, in this case by shoring up the competition model so that the invisible hand could be made to work once again. But by the second and third decades of the twentieth century economists widely perceived that the antitrust laws were not up to the job. More radical, more regulatory approaches seemed necessary in a market that was far less than perfect.

The Revolution in the Theory of Competition

As we have seen, the competition model of classical and much of neoclassical political economy assumed fungible products, small firms, easy entry and exit from business, and constant returns to scale. In such a market every firm charged the competitive price, and a firm that attempted to charge more would quickly lose all its sales.

But the classical model of competition contained a fundamental antinomy: the very nature of political economy was to suggest ways in which firms could "economize," and fundamental to the notion of economizing was the principle that specialization and volume could reduce costs. Adam Smith, the grandfather of classicism, recognized this when he suggested that the "extent of the market" explains the "division of labor," or specialization.[3] As firms specialize they can do things more cheaply, but the number of units of output of a single firm increases. For example, a craftsman who produced an entire carriage might be able to complete only four or five per year. But if he specialized and produced only wheels, he might make enough per year to equip one hundred carriages. He might be able to make the resulting wheels at a much lower cost, but the market would have to be big enough to absorb one hundred carriages. As population density increased and transportation technology made markets larger, so that one manufacturer could supply many more people, further specialization became feasible. Firms thus became larger and more specialized as a natural result of competitive processes.

Inherent in the classical competitive process was each firm's urge to increase the "extent" of its market, and in so doing reduce its relative production costs through economies of scale. Early classicists such as

David Ricardo recognized that the assumption of constant returns to scale in the competitive model did not describe real world behavior very accurately.[4] But Ricardo never spent much time revising the model to account for the problem of decreasing costs.

One important corollary of the theory of decreasing costs was product differentiation, also inconsistent with the classical model. As a general rule a single shop could manufacture four hundred identical carriage wheels per year at a lower cost per unit than two different shops could each manufacture two hundred wheels. This suggested that eventually a market would contain only a single carriage wheel manufacturer, as larger firms with lower costs continually drove smaller ones from the market. But two, five, or even more competing shops continued to exist in many markets, because each made a product somehow distinguishable from the offerings of competitors. Some shops had a reputation for manufacturing wheels of the highest quality that commanded a relatively high price; others a poorer quality wheel that might be cheaper; still others a sturdy wheel that was not particularly elegant. Each of these shops filled a distinct niche in a single market.

Once again, classical political economy recognized the existence of product differentiation and price difference within a market. In the 1840's John Stuart Mill acknowledged that the theory that all firms in the same market sell at exactly the same price did not seem to be supported by fact. Even a single town like London had its "cheap shops" and "dear shops," serving different groups of customers.[5] But once again, the notion of product differentiation did not force any substantial revision of the perfect competition model, even in the neoclassical period. In a footnote in the fourth edition of his *Principles* (1898), Alfred Marshall suggested that product differentiation was a natural result of competition.[6] As a result of product differentiation, Marshall concluded, each individual firm in a market might face a slightly different demand for its product, rather than all the firms being in precisely the same position, as the classical theory assumed. But Marshall let the matter rest with that observation. He appeared not to realize its implication: that the firms in product-differentiated markets do not "compete" as much as firms in markets where products are perfectly fungible. Firms in product-differentiated markets begin to behave more like individual monopolists.

Equally important was the impact of decreasing costs on ease of entry into business. The classical model always assumed that monopoly profits in an unregulated industry were impossible. If any particular industry were earning higher profits than another, new competitors would enter until returns were equalized. As late as the 1880's this argument was applied even in industries where economies of scale were obvious, such as the railroads. For example, Gerritt Lansing argued that rate regulation of railroads was unnecessary because, as long as they were not protected by legal monopolies, new railroads would be built until the rate of return was driven down to the competitive level.[7]

But increasing returns tended to give large incumbent firms advantages over both new rivals and prospective entrants. In 1890 Marshall had already observed that smaller manufacturers in industries subject to such economies did not have as many resources to devote to research or experimentation, nor could they distribute or market as efficiently. Marshall concluded that "the advantages which a single powerful firm has over its smaller rivals in those industries in which the Law of Increasing Return acts strongly " might be enough to give it "a practical monopoly of its own branch of production."[8]

The development of the railroad, more than anything else, prompted the theoretical reformulation of competition doctrine. A specialized branch of political economy, extensive enough to be called "railroad economics," began to develop in the United States in the 1860's and virtually exploded in the 1870's. Initially the writing on railroad economics was specific to the context, emphasizing the uniqueness of railroads, particularly their high fixed costs, extensive economies of scale, and extreme amounts of price discrimination. American economists such as Arthur Twining Hadley and Frank W. Taussig noted an important phenomenon caused by high fixed, or "overhead," costs: under competition prices would be driven to variable costs without enough left over to cover the fixed costs. As a result collusion, consolidation, and price discrimination seemed inherent in the industry.

As the economic literature on the railroads developed in the 1880's and 1890's it became increasingly theoretical and conceptual, and began to view railroads as only a rather extreme example of characteristics that were widespread in modern industry: high capital, or fixed, costs; substantial economies of scale; price discrimination; and the likelihood of "ruinous" competition if too many firms operated in the same market niche.

Many of the mechanical and distributional innovations developed in the nineteenth and early twentieth centuries gave the firms that used them substantial scale economies. This was certainly true of the railroads, mass production, steam and electric power, and oil and gas production and distribution.[9] By the turn of the century it was widely believed that economies of scale both explained and "justified" the growth of the trusts. Jeremiah Jenks concluded that "[o]nly great establishments can get the best equipment for cheap production; only such can secure the ablest men . . .; only such can make the enormous savings in the cost of selling goods which comes from doing away with the competitive bidding of travelling men. . . ."[10] In a book remarkable for its time, Charles Whiting Baker argued that the notions of economies of scale and competition were fundamentally in conflict: firms could take advantage of new methods of production and distribution, both of which required very large investments, only if they grew large enough to saturate entire markets. The Progressive Richard T. Ely acknowledged the pervasiveness and force of economies of scale, but suggested that monopoly pricing was a serious possibility and called for more government control.[11]

Except for the work of Ely and one or two others,[12] this early writing by economists on the "trust problem" contained remarkable optimism about large corporate growth. When the Sherman Act was passed in 1890 economists were generally critical, believing that it threatened to rob firms of the economies of scale that would increase economic growth and improve Americans' standard of living.[13] The literature also reveals how poorly developed the economic model of competition was, even as late as 1900. For most of these early writers on the trusts the fact of economies of scale counted for almost everything, while the decrease in the number of firms operating in the market counted for very little. In the words of George Stigler, the economists of the turn of the century were inclined to treat "the unregulated corporation as a natural phenomenon."[14] Without much apparent concern about the threat of monopoly pricing, writers such as Jenks advocated the broad use of cartels, unrestricted joint ventures, and trusts to achieve scale economies. At the same time Jenks wrote of "competition" as if it would produce nothing but waste from duplicated effort. For example, he referred to the ability of trusts to eliminate "the expense of competitive selling," as a result of which "the product might be sold for half the price."[15] Within this economic view the unregulated classical business corporation reigned supreme.

As is often the case, the classical theory of competition did not change until an overwhelming array of unexplained facts made the existing model unacceptable. By the turn of the century it was clear that different prices in the same market, product differentiation, and economies of large size were not anomalous but a large and apparently permanent part of the industrial economy.[16]

In the second two decades of the twentieth century economists as a group became much more concerned about the more threatening consequence of the trusts: monopoly pricing.[17] To be sure, these economists were just as sensitive to the phenomena of high capital costs and scale economies as their predecessors had been. But the trusts ceased to be a (nearly) unmixed blessing. The new attitude is prominent in Eliot Jones's 1921 book on trusts,[18] which concluded that although the giant trusts had lowered production costs they had also eliminated wholesome competition. In the process they raised prices. Unlike the earlier writers on trusts, Jones explicitly incorporated the economic theory of the monopoly price into his analysis of trust behavior. Jones argued that the great efficiencies proclaimed for the trusts by earlier economists had been seriously exaggerated. Further, what they gained in productive efficiency they lost in other inefficiencies brought about by the lack of competitive incentives. "Whereas competition provides a stimulus to the introduction of improved methods, the tendency of monopoly is toward stagnation."[19]

John Maurice Clark wrote the first book-length study of the law of decreasing costs in 1923. He also tried to face the fundamental problem of the "inevitability" of business concentration brought about by economies of scale. Like his predecessors, Clark recognized a fundamental contradiction between decreasing costs and perfect competition, particularly if decreasing costs were so substantial that there was room for only a few firms in an industry. Once these firms had become established entry would no longer be easy, and larger firms would have a substantial cost advantage over the smaller ones. Clark came to believe that the unregulated market was no longer adequate to control the competitive process. He supported the federal antitrust laws, as well as other regulatory restraints on the large business corporation.[20] He continued to believe that private business was more efficient than government-owned enterprise, but that widespread control of pricing, wages and working conditions, and consumer contracts would be necessary.

The debate over economies of scale and decreasing costs substantially undermined the perfect competition model just as it was being articulated. In a market subject to increasing returns to scale bigger firms tended to have lower costs than smaller firms. If a "minimum efficient scale" firm in a market had to be big enough to control, say, 25 percent of the sales, there would be room in such a market for only four firms. Entry into such markets was not easy, as classicism had always presumed, but very difficult. One could not be confident that unregulated competition would deliver the optimal mixture of price and quality.

Finally, economics literature in the 1920's argued that firms exacerbated the imperfections in the competitive market by artificially differentiating their products in order to minimize head-to-head competition. As a result they would end up behaving more like monopolists than competitors, even though there were many firms in the market. Price would be set more on the basis of customer demand, which was different to the extent the products were differentiated, rather than on individual firm cost. Significantly, however, competition existed on a continuum, with some industries being inherently less competitive than others. "The difference between the Standard Oil Company in its prime and the little corner grocery store is quantitative rather than qualitative," Harold Hotelling wrote in the year the Great Depression began. "Between the perfect competition and monopoly of theory lie the actual cases."[21]

This great upheaval in competition theory culminated in Chamberlin's *Theory of Monopolistic Competition* and Robinson's *Economics of Imperfect Competition*. Both sought to destroy the dichotomy between perfect competition and pure monopoly that characterized earlier price theory by creating a general economic theory of competition in "imperfect" markets—that is, real world markets in which scale economies obtained, entry was difficult, and products were differentiated. Chamberlin in particular described a competitive world with only a modest resemblance to Adam Smith's. Product differentiation was excessive, as firms sought to distinguish their offerings. Prices were relatively high, since each firm had the power to charge more than its economic costs.[22] Output was lower than it would be under perfect competition, since price was higher. Competitive entry by new firms was difficult, because start-up costs were very high, the number of sales needed to attain minimum efficient scale was large, and product differentiation supported by advertising gave established firms large advantages over new entrants in customer preference. The apparent simultaneous failures of the market economy in the Great Depression and of classical economic theory appeared more than coincidental. The time seemed ready for a much more regulatory theory of political economy and of state policy toward business. Thus the death of classical price theory. The death of classical enterprise law was not far behind.

The Business Corporation in the Post-Classical Era

In *The Modern Corporation and Private Property*[23] Adolf A. Berle, Jr., and Gardiner C. Means argued that an inherent attribute of the modern business corporation was the separation of ownership and control. Stockholders representing the greater part of a corporation's shares generally have little or nothing to say about the real management of the corporation's affairs. Such decisions are in the hands of managers, whose ownership interest is generally small. More important, the interest of managers and the interest of stockholders are not always the same. As a result, the corporation may not behave as the theory of competition suggests it should.

"It is of the essence of revolutions of the more silent sort that they are unrecognized until they are far advanced," Berle and Means wrote. Although they argued their controversial thesis in 1932, the phenomenon they described was prominent by the middle of the nineteenth century, particularly in American railroads. Alfred Chandler has shown that the separation of ownership and control was essential to the modern business corporation's ability to command its resources efficiently.[24] Part I of this book argues that separation of ownership and control was inherent in the developing legal structure of the classical business corporation. Corporations in competition are constantly looking for ways to reduce their costs, and the most effective way is often to internalize transactions that formerly have been made in the marketplace. The result of such vertical integration, however, is that more and more corporate transactions are taken out of the market, where price and offering are more or less given, and placed within the corporation itself, where they are subject to considerable discretion. Furthermore, the corporation's internal business affairs quickly become too complex to be handled by a large group of stockholders who, with the rise of the modern securities market, are likely to show at best a part-time interest in the corporation's activities. Such responsibility then falls on the corporation's managers.

Berle and Means were not the first to document the separation of ownership and control. Alfred Marshall had observed in 1890 that although only the shareholders "are the ultimate undertakers of business risks," they "as a rule know but little of what is being done and what ought to be done." As a result large corporations are "hampered by internal frictions and conflicts of interest between shareholders and debenture holders, between ordinary and preferred shareholders, and between all these and the directors." Marshall concluded that the corporations "seldom have the enterprise, the energy, the unity of purpose and the quickness of action" of unincorporated businesses.[25]

Such arguments became common in the institutionalist tradition of Progressive Era economics.[26] Much of that literature explicitly related the separation of ownership and control to the trust movement. For example, in 1925 Robert Brookings included a chapter entitled "The Separation of Ownership and Management" in his *Industrial Ownership: Its Economic and Social Significance*. Brookings concluded that the separation of management from ownership "began to be conspicuous at about the turn of the century and was a by-product of what was then regarded as a much more important change, namely, the formation of industrial trusts." Although the attainment of monopoly was the most widely publicized feature of the trusts, of far greater significance was "the transfer of the ownership of a substantial portion of the capital of industrial corporations to a wide investing and speculative public . . . ." The corporation's owners no longer took an active role in the affairs of the corporation. As a result, Brookings argued, management no longer felt the immediate consequences of the corporation's economic decisions. This justified more intensive government regulation of management's relationship with owners, labor, and the public in general.[27]

The rise of big business and the growth of industrial concentration were important premises of Berle and Means's book. In fact, Book I of *The Modern Corporation and Private Property* was substantially devoted to corporate growth. Because of the widespread phenomenon of interlocking directorates—the same person serving as director of more than one company—about two thousand people served as directors of the two hundred largest corporations. This economic power controlled by a "few persons" is "a tremendous force which can harm or benefit a multitude of individuals, affect whole districts, shift the currents of trade, bring ruin to one community and prosperity to another," they concluded. "The organizations which they control have passed far beyond the realm of private enterprise—they have become more nearly social institutions."[28] Berle and Means then argued that because these directors and corporate managers lacked substantial ownership interests in their firms, they also lacked the proper incentives to make their management efficient and in the public interest.

The explicitly economic nature of this premise notwithstanding, one is struck by the general absence of theoretical economics in *The Modern Corporation and Private Property*. Berle, a lawyer, selected Means as a co-author because Means was an economist. But Means's chief contribution was several chapters of statistics showing how corporations had grown, how concentrated they had become, and how share ownership was widely dispersed.[29] Except for an occasional citation to Adam Smith and one to Thorstein Veblen's *Absentee Ownership,* there was no discussion of economic literature. One brief discussion in chapter 3 of Book IV suggested that the theory of competition as envisioned by Adam Smith, which assumed small business units that had little fixed capital and overhead costs, no longer applied in modern business.[30] But they said nothing about alternative economic mechanisms for analyzing firm behavior. This was a book written for lawyers. Correspondingly, most economists ignored Berle and Means. As noted earlier, for example, in his important article on the nature of the firm five years later,[31] Ronald Coase never cited Berle and Means's work and virtually ignored the "legal" literature on the structure of the business firm. The year 1932 was still part of the great age of specialization, and citation to works in another discipline was considered more a sign of weakness than of strength.

Nevertheless, Berle and Means's study contributed greatly to the breakdown of the classical corporation in legal theory, because it appeared to undermine the most essential premise in classical political theory: that the "invisible hand" would turn each firm's desire to maximize its own profit into a grand, market-based scheme that would maximize the wealth of society. Berle and Means pointed to the rather awesome possibility that corporations were *not* individual profit-maximizers. Shareholders certainly had the motive to maximize profits, but they had "surrendered all disposition . . . to those in control of the enterprise." The "traditional logic of profits" suggested that the profits should go to the managers, because they were the ones who had the power to make the firm run profitably, and profits were the classical incentive to efficiency. But the managers received salaries that were often set without obvious relation to profit.[32]

Berle and Means argued that competition could no longer be trusted to guarantee efficient corporate behavior. They assumed, although without citation, most of the arguments in the new economics literature attacking the classical concept of competition. For example, they argued that in an age of high corporate concentration competition either became "cut-throat and destructive or so inactive as to make monopoly or duopoly conditions prevail." Competition as envisioned by the classicists was no longer possible as an "effective . . . regulator of industry and of profits. . . ." Berle and Means concluded that since the corporation was no longer being run to serve the interests of its shareholders, who were highly diffuse in American society, it should be run to serve the interests of the public at large. Since the claims of shareholders to any control were weak, and directors lacked the motive to run corporations in the public interest, their supervision had to be subjected to "the paramount interests of the community." These concerns legitimately included "fair wages, security to employees, reasonable service to their public, and stabilization of business. . . ." That view was of course anathema to the classical theory of the corporation, which had sought to privatize the ordinary corporation as much as possible, distinguishing only public service corporations for differential treatment.

Influence is hard to measure. The Great Depression undoubtedly did far more than any book to undermine Americans' faith in the classical market system. Nevertheless Berle and Means contributed much to the rhetoric of government policy toward business in the New Deal and after. *Time* magazine called *The Modern Corporation and Private Property* "the economic Bible of the Roosevelt administration."[33] The attitude toward corporate size expressed in Berle and Means showed up in government policy in a number of ways, particularly in the passage of the Securities Act of 1933, the creation of the Securities Exchange Commission in 1934, and the federal government's brief flirtation with organized cartelization in the National Industrial Recovery Act.[34] The same attitude appeared in the developing governmental hostility toward vertical integration by business firms. Although separation of ownership and control is related to large corporate size, it is much more a function of the number of *different* activities in which a corporation engages than of the size of the individual transactions. A very large firm that does nothing but purchase raw materials, manufacture mousetraps by the millions, and sell them to any buyer who comes along may have operations that are not appreciably more complex than those of a much smaller firm that makes them by the dozen. But intracorporate activity becomes more difficult to coordinate when the corporation enters into the distribution, retailing, transportation, advertising, and perhaps production of raw materials. As a result, the degree of vertical integration, rather than absolute size, is the largest contributor to separation of ownership and control. The "visible hand" in Chandler's history of American business[35] is not mere corporate size but rather the substitution of management decisions for market decisions—when firms integrated vertically, they used the market less but internal management more.

To the extent that vertical integration was an inherent attribute of the classical business corporation, state policy eventually made room for it. Legislatively, charters with broader business purpose clauses became common by the 1880's, and eventually states began passing general incorporation acts that authorized corporations to engage in any lawful business. Judicially, the doctrine of ultra vires was gradually relaxed so as to permit corporations to engage in activities only loosely related to those identified in their charters.

But in the wake of monopolistic competition and the study by Berle and Means a new theory of industrial organization emerged that renewed the concern about vertical integration. The worries were two-fold. One was that large firms could entrench or solidify their monopoly power. Arthur R. Burns's massive 1936 study of competition in American industry relied on both Berle and Means and the new literature on competition to conclude that, although vertical integration might produce some cost savings, on the whole it "diminishes the effectiveness of the market as a stimulus to the improvement of methods of production" and can enable a firm to "impose a levy upon the output of its less integrated rivals. . . ."[36]

The other concern was that vertical integration was often pursued by corporate management in spite of the fact that it was inefficient, unprofitable to the individual firm, and harmful to society as a whole. Managers pursued vertical integration because they enhanced their own power by reaching as far as they could in every direction, by maximizing output rather than profits, and perhaps by making the affairs of the corporation so complex that the average stockholder could not appreciate what was going on. Berle and Means argued that the modern vertically integrated corporation's costs had become "indeterminate": it had its fingers in so many pies that it could not segregate and identify the costs of producing a particular product.[37] The corporation needed to be saved from its own managers, who were undermining its ability to maximize its profits. This observation had an analogue in the 1930's and 1940's literature on the theory of the firm, which developed a consensus that the long-run average cost curve of the firm was U-shaped rather than continually downward sloping: in short, firms could become *too* big, and then their costs would rise.[38] But if, as Berle and Means suggested, costs became indeterminate when firms grew very large, corporate managers would not even know when their companies had become inefficient dinosaurs.

The situation seemed to beg for legal regulation of firm size, and explains the great increase in law and policy makers' concern about vertical integration and mergers in the 1930's and 1940's, first in the reports of the Federal Trade Commission and the New Deal's Temporary National Economic Committee, and later in case law.[39] The eventual result was passage of the Celler-Kefauver Act in 1950, which greatly strengthened the merger provision of the Clayton Act and made it explicitly applicable to vertical mergers.[40]

By the end of the New Deal little was left of the classical corporation. Its internal dealings with shareholders and many of its debtor-creditor relations were substantially regulated by the federal securities acts. Its labor relations were regulated by the new federal labor laws. Its relations in the general market, with consumers and suppliers, became increasingly regulated by the antitrust laws and the Federal Trade Commission, which tried to impose on it a duty to engage in only "fair" competition. In 1938 the Federal Trade Commission Act was amended to establish that the Federal Trade Commission had jurisdiction over a firm's "unfair or deceptive act or practice," whether or not the antitrust laws were violated.[41] For the emerging category of utilities and "public service" companies, regulation was even more complete, including restrictions on entry and price controls.

But the post-classical corporation was not much like the preclassical corporation either. The distinctiveness of the corporate form of private enterprise was gone, perhaps forever. Shareholders never regained the control they once had. Limited liability remained the rule, and corporations remained "persons" for the purposes of constitutional law. After the 1920's the corporation, in common with all forms of business organization, entered a new era in which it could experience once again the benefits and burdens of governmental regulation. The invisible hand of the market had been struck aside by the very visible hand of the state.

Notes

Index

Notes

Introduction

1. Daniel A. Raymond, *The Elements of Constitutional Law and of Political Economy* (4th ed. 1840).
2. See Paul K. Conkin, *Prophets of Prosperity: America's First Political Economists*, chs. 1–4 (1980); Forrest McDonald, *Novus Ordo Seclorum: The Intellectual Origins of the Constitution* 106–142 (1985).
3. 1 Theodore Sedgwick, *Public and Private Economy* 30–31 (1836).
4. See Donald N. McCloskey, *The Rhetoric of Economics* (1985).

1. Classical Political Economy and the Business Corporation

1. Opinion of the Justices, 58 Me. 590, 592 (1871).
2. See Carter Goodrich, *Government Promotion of American Canals and Railroads, 1800–1900* (1960); Mark W. Summers, *Railroads, Reconstruction, and the Gospel of Prosperity: Aid under the Radical Republicans, 1865–1877* (1984); Lloyd J. Mercer, *Railroads and Land Grant Policy: A Study in Government Intervention* (1982).
3. See *Mercantilism: System or Expediency?* (Walter Minchinton ed. 1969).
4. For example, Joseph Chitty, Jr., *A Treatise on the Law of the Prerogatives of the Crown* 120–133 (1820).
5. Joseph K. Angell & Samuel Ames, *A Treatise on the Law of Private Corporations Aggregate* 24, 372 (1832).
6. Hess v. Werts, 4 Serge & Rawle 356 (Pa. 1818); Lachomette v. Thomas, 5 Rob. 172 (La. 1843); Pierce v. Bryant, 87 Mass. (5 Allen) 91 (1862).
7. Angell & Ames, note 5 at 24 n.1; 3 James Kent, *Commentaries on American Law* 35 (2d ed. 1832). See Ronald E. Seavoy, *The Origins of the American*

365

Business Corporation, 1784–1855, at 97–98 (1982); Lawrence M. Friedman, *A History of American Law* 200 (2d ed. 1985).

8. Charles River Bridge v. Warren Bridge, 36 U.S. (11 Pet.) 420, 546 (1837).

9. For example, see John Chipman Gray, *Nature and Sources of the Law* 48–55 (1909); Sir Frederick Pollock, "Has the Common Law Received the Fiction Theory of Corporations," 27 *L. Q. Rev.* 219 (1911). For the development in England and continental Europe, see Frederick Hallis, *Corporate Personality: A Study in Jurisprudence* xxxviii–lxiii (1930).

10. 9 U.S. (5 Cranch) 61, 86 (1809).

11. 43 U.S. (2 How.) 497, 557–558 (1844).

12. Marshall v. Baltimore & Ohio R.R. Co., 57 U.S. (16 How.) 314 (1853); *Dodge,* 59 U.S. (18 How.) 331 (1855). See Charles A. Wright, *Law of Federal Courts* 149 (4th ed. 1983).

13. Angell & Ames, note 5 at 209–210, 220.

14. Yarborough v. the Bank of England, 16 East. 6 (1812).

15. Angell & Ames, note 5 at 221. See Berks v. Dauphin Turn. Road v. Alyers, 6 Serg. & Rawle 17 (Pa. 1820) (permitting suit on a debt to the corporation by the "President, Managers and Company of the Berks and Dauphin Turn. Road"); Minot v. Curtis, 7 Mass. 444 (1811) (permitting an incorporated church to be sued in the name of the individuals who comprised it). See also 2 Kent, note 7 at 235.

16. 25 U.S. (12 Wheat.) 64, 92 (1827).

17. See anon., "Corporations," 4 *Am. Jurist* 298, 302–303 (1830). Early decisions include Portsmouth Livery Co. v. Watson, 10 Mass. 91 (1813) (denying defendant's plea in abatement that action brought against corporation should have been brought against the shareholders); Hayden v. Middlesex Turnpike Co., 10 Mass. 39 (1813) (assumpsit can be brought against corporation itself).

18. For example, Ogdensburgh Bank v. Van Rensselaer, 6 Hill 240 (N.Y. 1843); Verplanck v. Mercantile Ins. Co., 2 Paige 438 (N.Y. 1831); Porter v. Nekervis, 25 Va. (5 Rand.) 359 (1826) (bank cashier could not sue in his own name). See Joseph K. Angell, *A Treatise on the Law of Private Corporations Aggregate* 372–403, 568–609 (3d ed. 1846).

19. Smith v. Hurd, 53 Mass. (12 Met.) 371, 386 (1847).

20. See Dodge v. Woolsey, 59 U.S. (18 How.) 331 (1855); William W. Cook, *The Corporation Problem* 7 (1891).

2. Vested Corporate Rights

1. For example, James L. Kainen, "Nineteenth-Century Interpretations of the Federal Contract Clause: The Transformation from Vested to Substantive Rights against the State," 31 *Buff. L. Rev.* 381 (1982).

2. Green v. Biddle, 21 U.S. (8 Wheat.) 1, 75–76 (1823).

3. Ogden v. Saunders, 25 U.S. (12 Wheat.) 213 (1827); Sturges v. Crowninshield, 17 U.S. (4 Wheat.) 122, 200–201, 206–207 (1819); Mason v. Haile, 25 U.S. (12 Wheat.) 370 (1827).

4. For example, Roscoe Pound, "Liberty of Contract," 18 *Yale L. J.* 454 (1909).

5. Charles River Bridge v. Warren Bridge, 36 U.S. (11 Pet.) 420 (1837); Slaughter-House Cases, 83 U.S. (16 Wall.) 36 (1873).

6. *Charles River Bridge* at 639 (Story, J., dissenting); see Morton J. Horwitz, *The Transformation of American Law, 1780–1860* at 118 (1977).

7. On the drafting of the contract clause, see Benjamin F. Wright, *The Contract Clause of the Constitution* 4–33 (1938); Robert L. Hale, "The Supreme Court and the Contract Clause" (pts. 1–3), 57 *Harv. L. Rev.* 512, 621, 852 (1944); Forrest McDonald, *Novus Ordo Seclorum: The Intellectual Origins of the Constitution* 274 (1985). The application of the *ex post facto* clause to regulatory and corporate law issues was undermined by Calder v. Bull, 3 U.S. (3 Dall.) 386 (1798), which held that the clause referred only to criminal statutes. On the contract clause and *ex post facto* laws, see Ogden v. Saunders, 25 U.S. (12 Wheat.) 213, 286 (1827); Francis Wharton, "Retrospective Legislation and Grangerism," 3 *Int'l Rev.* 50 (1876); Justice David Brewer, "Protection to Private Property from Public Attack," 55 *New Englander & Yale Rev.* 97 (1891) (Yale Law School address).

8. Wright, note 7 at 15–17, 127.

9. *Fletcher*, 10 U.S. (6 Cranch) 87 (1810); *Dartmouth College*, 17 U.S. (4 Wheat.) 519 (1819); *Sturges*, 17 U.S. (4 Wheat.) 122 (1819); *Ogden*, 25 U.S. (12 Wheat.) 213 (1827).

10. 29 U.S. (4 Pet.) 514, 558 (1830).

11. For example, Francis Wharton observed that Benjamin Franklin was conspicuous among members of the Convention as a "student of political economy" who believed "that justice and expediency require that freedom of contract should be absolute." Wharton, *Commentaries on American Law* 549 (1884).

12. See Horwitz, note 6 at 160–173.

13. Alexander Hamilton, *Papers on Public Credit, Commerce, and Finance* 3, 5, 40–42 (Samuel McKee ed. 1934).

14. The best general study of mercantilist political economy is Eli F. Heckscher, *Mercantilism* (2 vols. 2d ed. 1962). On mercantilism in colonial America, *see* George L. Beer, *The Old Colonial System, 1660–1754* (2 vols. 1912); McDonald, note 7 at ch. 4.

15. Alexander Hamilton, *Report on Manufactures* 204, 214–217, 237–238 (Dec. 5, 1791), in Hamilton, *Papers on Public Credit, Commerce, and Finance* (Samuel McKee ed. 1934). On Hamilton's mercantilist political economy, see Jacob E. Cooke, *Alexander Hamilton* 100 (1982) (concluding that Hamilton "set forth economic doctrines that Smith's *Wealth of Nations* was designed to topple").

16. Daniel A. Raymond, *Thoughts on Political Economy* (1820); Raymond, *The Elements of Political Economy*, vol. 1, chs. 16 & 17, vol. 2, ch. 8 (1823). Quotations from vol. 2 at 163, 173, 174. See Charles P. Neill, *Daniel Raymond: An Early Chapter in the History of Economic Theory in the United States*, Johns Hopkins Univ. Studies in Historical and Political Science (1897); Michael J. L. O'Connor, *Origins of Academic Economics in the United States* (1944); Paul K. Conkin, *Prophets of Prosperity: America's First Political Economists* 77–107 (1980).

17. See Chapter 3; Harry N. Scheiber, *Ohio Canal Era: A Case Study of Government and the Economy, 1820–1861* (1969).

18. 2 Joseph Story, *Commentaries on the Constitution of the United States* 247–248 (1851). The first edition was published in 1833, before *Charles River Bridge* was decided.

19. 6 James Madison, *Writings of Madison* 100 (G. Hunt ed. 1900–1910).

20. Thomas Jefferson, *Notes on the State of Virginia* 161–165 (W. Peden ed. 1955). See Drew McCoy, *The Elusive Republic: Political Economy in Jeffersonian America* 175 (1980).

21. See Chapter 14. Horwitz, note 6 at 160–210; P. S. Atiyah, *The Rise and Fall of Freedom of Contract* (1979).

22. *Bronson*, 42 U.S. (1 How.) 311 (1843); *Gantley's Lessee*, 44 U.S. (3 How.) 707 (1845). See also Howard v. Bugbee, 65 U.S. (24 How.) 461 (1861).

23. Gelpcke v. Dubuque, 68 U.S. (1 Wall.) 175 (1864).

24. *Gunn*, 82 U.S. (15 Wall.) 610 (1873); *Edwards*, 96 U.S. (6 Otto) 595 (1878); Home Building and Loan Assn. v. Blaisdell, 290 U.S. 398 (1934) (sustaining Depression-era statute placing moratorium on mortgage foreclosures).

25. Charles River Bridge v. Warren Bridge, 36 U.S. (11 Pet.) 420 (1837).

26. 47 U.S. (6 How.) 507 (1848). The case is discussed further in Harry N. Scheiber, "The Road to *Munn:* Eminent Domain and the Concept of Public Purpose in the State Courts" 329, 379, in *Law in American History* (Donald Fleming & Bernard Bailyn eds. 1971).

27. See Chicago, Burlington & Quincy R.R. Co. v. Chicago, 166 U.S. 226 (1897).

28. Boston & Lowell R.R. Co. v. Salem & Lowell R.R. Co., 68 Mass. (2 Gray) 1 (1854). See also East Hartford v. Hartford Bridge Co., 17 Conn. 78 (1845); Piscataqua Bridge v. The New Hampshire Bridge, 1 N.H. 35 (1834).

29. *Fanning*, 41 U.S. (16 How.) 524 (1853); Richmond, Fredericksburg & Potomac R.R. Co. v. Louisa R.R. Co., 54 U.S. (13 How.) 71 (1851); Bridge Proprietors v. Hoboken Co., 68 U.S. (1 Wall.) 116 (1864). The *Hoboken* charter provided "that it should not be lawful for any person or persons whatsoever to erect, or cause to be erected . . . any other bridge or bridges over or across the said river." 1 Wall. at 118.

30. See Horwitz, note 6 at 134–136.

31. Ohio Life Insurance & Trust Co. v. Debolt, 57 U.S. (16 How.) 416, 435–436 (1853).

32. Mass. Laws, May sess., 1806, to Jan. sess., 1809, p. 467. See Wright, note 7 at 59. Dartmouth College v. Woodward, 17 U.S. (4 Wheat.) 518, 712 (1819). See Shields v. Ohio, 95 U.S. 319 (1877); Peik v. Chicago & Northwesten Ry. Co., 94 U.S. 164 (1877); Greenwood v. Freight Co., 105 U.S. 13 (1881); Spring Valley Water Works v. Schottler, 110 U.S. 347 (1884).

33. Delaware Const., art. 1, § 25 (1831). See Louisiana Const., tit. VI, art. 124 (1845), giving the legislature "the power to revoke the charters of all corporations whose charters shall not have expired" by January 1890.

34. 19 Mich. 259, 273–274 (1869). See Alan Jones, "Thomas M. Cooley and the Michigan Supreme Court; 1865–1885," 10 *Am. J. Leg. Hist.* 97 (1966).

35. Thomas M. Cooley, *A Treatise on the Constitutional Limitations Which Rest upon the Legislative Power of the States of the American Union* 335 (2d ed. 1871).

36. Id. at 333–339; the Supreme Court eventually followed. Manigault v. Springs, 199 U.S. 473 (1905).
37. Thorpe v. Rutland & Burlington R.R. Co., 27 Vt. 140, 149 (1854).
38. See Horwitz, note 6 at 134–136. Slaughter-House Cases, 83 U.S. (16 Wall.) 36, 83 (1873).
39. Cooley, note 35 at 342. Cooley was undoubtedly referring to The Case of Monopolies, 11 Coke 84b, 77 Eng. Rep. 1260 (K.B. 1602) (applying common law to deny enforcement of royal grant giving the exclusive right to manufacture and import playing cards).
40. Cooley, note 35 at 343 n.1 (6th ed. 1890). See also Norman, "Legal Restraints on Modern Industrial Combinations and Monopolies in the United States," 33 *Am. L. Rev.* 499 (1899), concluding similarly.
41. On the first, see Butcher's Union Slaughter-House & Live-Stock Landing Co. v. Crescent City Live-Stock Landing & Slaughter-House Co., 111 U.S. 746 (1884). On the second, see St. Tammany Water Works v. New Orleans Water Works, 120 U.S. 64 (1887); Louisville Gas Co. v. Citizens' Gas Co., 115 U.S. 683 (1885).
42. Thomas M. Cooley, "Limits to State Control of Private Business," 1 *Princeton Rev.* (ser. 4) 233, 265 (1878); Cooley, "State Regulation of Corporate Profits," 137 *N. Am. Rev.* 205, 207–212 (1883).
43. Francis Wharton, *Commentaries on Law* § 483 at 554, 556 (1884).
44. See Christopher Tiedeman, *The Unwritten Constitution of the United States* 54–66 (1890).
45. Christopher Tiedeman, *A Treatise on State and Federal Control of Persons and Property in the United States* (1900). Quotations from 2 id. at 952–959. See Clyde Jacobs, *Law Writers and the Courts*, ch. 2 (1954).
46. *Fertilizing Co.*, 97 U.S. 659 (1878); *Ruggles*, 108 U.S. 526, 533 (1883). See A. Russell, "Status and Tendencies of the Dartmouth College Case," 30 *Am. L. Rev.* 321 (1896).
47. Stone v. Farmers' Trust Co., 116 U.S. 307, 325, 330 (1886); Stone v. Illinois Central R.R. Co., 116 U.S. 347 (1886); Stone v. New Orleans & Northeastern R.R. Co., 116 U.S. 352 (1886).

3. Politics and Public Goods

1. Thomas Cooper, *Lectures on the Elements of Political Economy* 246 (2d ed. 1830).
2. For a chronological list of general incorporation acts, see Justice Louis Brandeis's dissenting opinion in *Liggett v. Lee*, 288 U.S. 517, 549 (1933). On the municipal bond cases, see Charles Fairman, *Reconstruction and Reunion, 1864–1888*, pt. 2, at 918–1116 (Holmes Devise History of the Supreme Court, vol. VII, 1971); L. A. Powe, "Rehearsal for Substantive Due Process: The Municipal Bond Cases," 53 *Tex. L. Rev.* 738 (1975).
3. J. Willard Hurst, *The Legitimacy of the Business Corporation in the Law of the United States, 1780–1970*, at 116–120 (1970).
4. See New York Const., art. 1, § 9 (1821); Ronald E. Seavoy, *The Origins of the American Business Corporation, 1784–1855*, at 60–61, 177–180 (1982);

Louis Hartz, *Economic Policy and Democratic Thought* 57 (1948); Robert H. Wiebe, *The Opening of American Society* 245 (1984).

5. New York Const., art. 7, § 9 (1846). In 1906, when James Gray wrote his treatise on the taxing power, virtually every state had a similar provision in its constitution. James Gray, *Limitations of the Taxing Power, Including Limitations upon Public Indebtedness* 140–157 (1906).

6. New York Const., art. 8, § 1 (1846).

7. Opinion of the Judges, 58 Me. 590, 603 (1871).

8. For example, State ex rel. Burlington R.R. Co. v. Wapello County, 13 Iowa 388 (1862); People v. Salem, 20 Mich. 452 (1870). Approving railroad subsidies: Gelpcke v. Dubuque, 68 U.S. (1 Wall.) 175 (1864); Rogers v. Burlington, 70 U.S. (3 Wall.) 654, 665–666 (1865). See *Topeka*, 87 U.S. (20 Wall.) 655, 659–660, 663 (1875). Other cases are discussed in Herbert Hovenkamp, "The Classical Corporation in American Legal Thought," 76 *Geo. L. J.* 1593, 1636–1637 (1988).

9. Thomas M. Cooley, *A Treatise on the Constitutional Limitations Which Rest upon the Legislative Power of the States of the American Union* 487 (1st ed. 1868).

10. John F. Dillon, *Treatise on the Law of Municipal Corporations* (1872).

11. Commercial National Bank v. Iola, 6 F. Cas. no. 3061 at 221, 222–223 (D. Kan. 1873), aff'd, 22 L.Ed. 463 (1875). The affirmance was inadvertently omitted from the U.S. Reports.

12. Weismer v. Village of Douglas, 64 N.Y. 91, 101 (1876).

13. For example, the bonds issued in Railroad Co. v. County of Otoe, 83 U.S. 667, 669 (1872) were conditioned on the railroad's establishing a connection in Nebraska City, Nebraska. See also Green v. Dyersburg, 10 F. Cas. no. 5756 at 1099, 1100 (W.D. Tenn. 1879), where the bond authorization required the railroad to build a depot "within half a mile of the court house."

14. See Sharpless v. Mayor of Philadelphia, 21 Pa. St. 147 (1853); Stewart v. Supervisors of Polk County, 30 Iowa 9 (1870); see also Gray, note 5 at 129–132; Thomas M. Cooley, *A Treatise on the Law of Taxation* 77 n.1 (1876).

15. Joseph A. Joyce, *A Treatise on Franchises, Especially Those of Public Service Corporations* §§ 7, 11 (1909).

4. The Corporate Personality

1. Santa Clara Co. v. Southern Pacific R.R., 118 U.S. 394, 396 (1886); see also 422–423 (Field, J., concurring). For background see John Flynn, "The Jurisprudence of Corporate Personhood: The Misuse of a Legal Concept" 131, in *Corporations and Society: Power and Responsibility* (Warren J. Samuels & Arthur S. Miller eds. 1987); Howard J. Graham, "An Innocent Abroad: The Constitutional Corporate 'Person,'" 2 *UCLA L. Rev.* 155 (1955).

2. Pembina Consolidated Silver Mining & Milling Co. v. Pennsylvania, 125 U.S. 181, 189 (1888). See also Missouri Pacific Ry. Co. v. Nebraska, 164 U.S. 403, 417 (1896) (holding that the takings clause applies to a corporation).

3. Morton J. Horwitz, "Santa Clara Revisited: The Development of Corporate Theory," 88 *W. Va. L. Rev.* 173, 174 (1985).
4. For example, Blackman v. Central R.R. Co., 58 Ga. 189 (1877); Silk Mfg. Co. v. Campbell, 27 N.J.L. 539 (1859); see Chapter 1.
5. Slaughter-House Cases, 83 U.S. (16 Wall.) 36 (1873).
6. Yick Wo v. Hopkins, 118 U.S. 356 (1886); Powell v. Pennsylvania, 127 U.S. 678, 687 (1888) (upholding statute forbidding manufacture and sale of oleomargarine). The first incorporation decision was Chicago, Burlington & Quincy R.R. Co. v. Chicago, 160 U.S. 226 (1897), incorporating the fifth amendment eminent domain clause.
7. *Dodge*, 59 U.S. (18 How.) 331 (1856); *Pollock*, 157 U.S. 429, 553 (1895). See also Hawes v. Oakland, 104 U.S. 450 (1881) (detailing requirements for federal shareholder derivative suits). *Smyth*, 169 U.S. 466, 517–518 (1898).
8. *Corbus*, 187 U.S. 455, 463–465 (1903); Davis & Farnum Mfg. Co. v. Los Angeles, 189 U.S. 207, 220 (1903). See, for example, Ex parte Young, 209 U.S. 123, 143 (1908).
9. John R. Commons, *Legal Foundations of Capitalism* 296–297 (1924).
10. Shaffer & Munn v. Union Mining Co., 55 Md. 74 (1880); Leep v. St. Louis, Iron Mountain Ry., 58 Ark. 407, 427 (1894); State v. Brown & Sharpe Mfg. Co., 18 R.I. 16, 25 A. 246 (1892).
11. 38 U.S. (13 Pet.) 519, 587–589 (1839).
12. *Allgeyer*, 165 U.S. 578 (1897); *Coppage*, 236 U.S. 1 (1915); *McGuire*, 219 U.S. 549, 566–568 (1911).
13. *Bank of Augusta*, 38 U.S. (13 Pet.) at 587–589; Paul v. Virginia, 75 U.S. (8 Wall.) 168, 181 (1868); Ducat v. Chicago, 77 U.S. (10 Wall.) 410 (1870); Philadelphia Fire Assn. v. New York, 119 U.S. 110 (1886).
14. 125 U.S. 181, 187 (1888).
15. Insurance Co. v. Morse, 87 U.S. (20 Wall.) 445, 543 (1874). Unconstitutional conditions cases: Southern Pacific Co. v. Denton, 146 U.S. 202, 207 (1892); Martin v. Baltimore & Ohio R.R., 151 U.S. 673, 684 (1894); Barrow Steamship Co. v. Kane, 170 U.S. 100, 111 (1898); Ludwig v. Western Union Telegraph Co., 216 U.S. 146 (1910). Commerce clause: Welton v. Missouri, 91 U.S. 275 (1875). The corporate exclusion cases are Western Union Telegraph Co. v. Kansas, 216 U.S. 1 (1910); Ludwig v. Western Union Telegraph Co., 216 U.S. 146 (1910). See Gerard C. Henderson, *The Position of Foreign Corporations in American Constitutional Law* 112–131 (1918); Charles R. McCurdy, "American Law and the Marketing Structure of the Large Corporation, 1875–1890," 38 *J. Econ. Hist.* 631 (1978).

5. Limited Liability

1. 6 Geo. IV, ch. 91 (1825). See 1 Joseph S. Davis, *Essays in the Earlier History of American Corporations* 447 (1917), quoting article in *Gazette of the United States,* Oct. 1792, arguing that limited liability explained popularity of incorporation; and see 2 id. at 267–268, describing the 1789 charter of the Baltimore Manufacturing Company, which provided for limited liability only when subscriptions were fully paid; 2 id. at 317. Joseph K. Angell &

Samuel Ames, *A Treatise on the Law of Private Corporations Aggregate* 349, 357 (1832).

2. See Morton J. Horwitz, "Santa Clara Revisited: The Development of Corporate Theory," 88 *W. Va. L. Rev.* 173, 208–209 (1985).

3. E. Merrick Dodd, *American Business Corporations until 1860,* at 387–451 (1954).

4. Thomas Cooper, *Lectures on the Elements of Political Economy* 247, 250 (2d ed. 1830).

5. Davis, note 1; Dodd, note 3; Oscar Handlin & Mary Handlin, *Commonwealth: A Study of the Role of Government in the American Economy—Massachusetts, 1774–1861,* at 144–150 (1941; rev. ed. 1969). Angell and Ames concluded that broad shareholder liability was "peculiar to Massachusetts." Angell & Ames, note 1 at 361. The anonymous author of "Manufacturing Corporations," 2 *Am. Jurist* 92, 101 (1829), agreed.

6. Mass. Laws, Jan. sess., 1809, c. 65, p. 464; Act of Jan. 28, 1822, Mass. Laws 1818–1822, c. 38, p. 619; Commonwealth v. Blue-Hill Turnpike Corp., 5 Mass. 420 (1809); Spear v. Grant, 16 Mass. 9 (1819); Seymour Thompson, *A Treatise on the Liability of Stockholders in Corporations* 54 (1879).

7. See Angell & Ames, note 1 at 362.

8. Anon., "Manufacturing Corporations," 2 *Am. Jurist* 92, 93, 105, 116–117 (1829); see also anon., "Corporations," 4 *Am. Jurist* 298, 307 (1830).

9. Act of Feb. 23, 1830, Mass. Laws 1828–1831, c. 53, p. 325; Act of May 15, 1851, Mass. Acts and Resolves 1849–1851, c. 133, p. 633. See Dodd, note 3 at 385; Handlin & Handlin, note 5 at 144–150.

10. Briggs v. Penniman, 8 Cowen 392, 295 (N.Y. 1826) (stockholders individually liable for a sum equal to stock subscription after corporation's assets were seized). N.Y. Rev. Stat., vol. 1, ch. 18, tit. 3, § 5 at 300 (1828). See Charles Haar, "Legislative Regulation of New York Industrial Corporations, 1800–1850," 22 *New York History* 195, 205–206 (1941).

11. 1848 N.Y. Laws, ch. 40; Ronald E. Seavoy, *The Origins of the American Business Corporation, 1784–1855,* at 192 (1982); Horwitz, note 2 at 208.

12. See 1 William W. Cook, *A Treatise on Stock and Stockholders, Bonds, Mortgages, and General Corporation Law* § 215 at 273 (3d ed. 1894); Wakefield v. Fargo, 90 N.Y. 213, 217 (1882) (only "menial or manual services" covered); Coffin v. Reynolds, 37 N.Y. 640 (1868) (secretary not covered); Aikin v. Wasson, 24 N.Y. 482 (1862) (contractor not covered).

13. See 1 Cook, note 12 at § 212, p. 270; Chase v. Lord, 77 N.Y. 1 (1879) (applying limited liability under the statute); Matter of the Empire City Bank, 18 N.Y. 199, 218 (1858) (same).

14. These included the statutes of Pennsylvania, Indiana, and Michigan, as well as others. See Herbert Hovenkamp, "The Classical Corporation in American Legal Thought," 76 *Geo. L. J.* 1593, 1655 (1988).

15. *Wood,* 3 Mason 308, 30 F. Cas. 435 (1824); Sawyer v. Hoag, 84 U.S. (17 Wall.) 610 (1873).

16. See Alfred D. Chandler, Jr., *The Visible Hand: The Managerial Revolution in American Business* 21–24 (1977).

17. 14 Wend. 58 (N.Y. 1835).

18. See Horwitz, note 2 at 210.
19. 6 Seymour I. Thompson & John Thompson, *Commentaries on the Law of Private Corporations* § 3418 at 29, 33–34 (2d ed. 1909).

6. Corporate Power and Its Abuse

1. Terrett v. Taylor, 13 U.S. (9 Cranch) 43, 51 (1815); see 2 Joseph S. Davis, *Essays in the Earlier History of American Corporations* 227 (1965).
2. Joseph K. Angell & Samuel Ames, *A Treatise on the Law of Private Corporations Aggregate* 510 (1832).
3. Charter of Richmond James River Co., Act of Jan. 23, 1804, Dec. sess., 1803, ch. 103, § 9; see Bruce A. Campbell, *Law and Experience in the Early Republic: The Evolution of the Dartmouth College Doctrine, 1780–1819*, at 252–253 (Ph.D. diss., Michigan State Univ., 1973).
4. Angell & Ames, note 2 at 487, 510.
5. The cases are discussed in Herbert Hovenkamp, "The Classical Corporation in American Legal Thought," 76 *Geo. L. J.* 1593, 1660–1662 (1988).
6. State v. Société Républicaine, 9 Mo. App. 114, 120 (1880).
7. Day v. Ogdensburg R.R., 107 N.Y. 129 (1887); In re Brooklyn R.R., 125 N.Y. 434 (1891); Oliphant Co. v. Borough of Oliphant, 196 Pa. St. 553 (1900).
8. 2 Thomas C. Spelling, *A Treatise on Injunctions and Other Extraordinary Remedies* 1562 (2d ed. 1901).
9. For example, People v. North River Sugar Refining Co., 121 N.Y. 582 (1890) (illegal trust); Manderson v. Commercial Bank, 28 Pa. St. 379 (1857) (ultra vires discount of paper). For other cases, see Hovenkamp, note 5 at 1662.
10. See 2 William W. Cook, *A Treatise on the Law of Corporations Having a Capital Stock*, ch. 38 (7th ed. 1913).
11. Angell & Ames, note 2 at chs. 5–11, esp. 469–474, 479.
12. 1 Victor Morawetz, *A Treatise on the Law of Private Corporations* § 364 at 349 (2d ed. 1886). See Chapter 25. See Thomas v. West Jersey R.R., 101 U.S. 71 (1879) (railroad's lease of its assets held ultra vires); Clyde L. Colson, "The Doctrine of *Ultra Vires* in United States Supreme Court Decisions," 42 *W. Va. L. Q.* 179, 213 (1936), 42 *W. Va. L. Q.* 297 (1936); Jacksonville, Mayport, Pablo Ry. & Navigation Co. v. Hooper, 160 U.S. 514 (1896).
13. 1 William W. Cook, *Treatise on Stock and Stockholders, Bonds, Mortgages, and General Corporation Law* 971–973 (3d ed. 1894); 1 Cook, *Corporations*, note 10 at vii–viii (4th ed. 1898).
14. For example, North Side Ry. Co. v. Worthington, 30 S.W. 1055 (Tex. 1895) (suggesting different standard for ultra vires in the case of corporation chartered under general act).
15. For example, 1 Bruce Wyman, *Public Service Corporations* §§ 703–710 (1911); 2 Cook, *Corporations*, note 10 at §§ 895, 897, 908; Cook, *Stock & Stockholders*, note 13 at 971–973 (3d ed. 1894).
16. Angell & Ames, note 2 at 475–480.
17. For example, Middlesex Turnpike Corp. v. Locke, 8 Mass. 268 (1811);

Indiana & Ebensburgh Turnpike Co. v. Phillips, 2 Pen. & Watts 184 (Pa. 1830); Hartford & New Haven R.R. Co. v. Croswell, 5 Hill 383 (N.Y. 1843).

18. 2 Spelling, note 8 at 1566.

19. State v. Railroad Co., 50 Ohio St. 239, 33 N.E. 1051 (1893); State v. Minn. Thresher Mfg. Co., 40 Minn. 213, 41 N.W. 1020 (1889); State v. Kill Buck Turnpike Co., 38 Ind. 71 (1871); State v. Essex Bank, 8 Vt. 489 (1836).

20. Spelling, note 8 at 1576. For example, State v. Minn. Thresher Mfg. Co., 40 Minn. 213 (1889); State v. Kill Buck Turnpike Co., 38 Ind. 71 (1871).

21. Hodges v. New England Screw Co., 3 R.I. 9, 18 (1853); Godbold v. Branch Bank, 11 Ala. 191 (1847).

22. 1 Morawetz, note 12 at § 243. *Spering's*, 71 Pa. 11, 24 (1872); Hun v. Cary, 82 N.Y. 65, 71 (1880). See, for example, Railroad Co. v. Lockwood, 84 U.S. (17 Wall.) 357, 382–383 (1873).

23. Smith v. Prattville Mfg. Co., 29 Ala. 503 (1857) (". . . mere errors of judgment . . . do not entitle a stockholder to relief . . . ."); Neall v. Hill, 16 Cal. 145 (1860) (requiring gross negligence or willful misconduct). Other cases are discussed in Hovenkamp, note 5 at 1667–1668. *Briggs*, 141 U.S. 132 (1891). See 2 Cook, *Stock & Stockholders*, note 13 at § 703, p. 1031 n.1 (3d ed. 1894); 3 Seymour D. Thompson, *Commentaries on the Law of Private Corporations* § 4101 at 2995 (1st ed. 1895).

24. C. B. Rhoads, "Personal Liability of Directors for Corporate Mismanagement," 65 *U. Pa. L. Rev.* 128, 132 (1917).

25. 2 Spelling, note 8 at 1567, citing Ward v. Farwell, 97 Ill. 593 (1881); Insurance Co. v. Needles, 113 U.S. 574 (1885); plus many others.

7. A Moral Theory of Political Economy

1. See *The Classical Economists and Economic Policy* (Alfred W. Coats ed. 1971); Raymond G. Cowherd, *Political Economists and the English Poor Laws* (1977); Rajani K. Kanth, *Political Economy and Laissez-Faire* 159–160 (1986).

2. But see Drew R. McCoy, *The Elusive Republic: Political Economy in Jeffersonian America* (1980); Andrew W. Foshee, "Jeffersonian Political Economy and the Classical Republican Tradition," 17 *Hist. Pol. Econ.* 523 (1985).

3. P. S. Atiyah, *The Rise and Fall of Freedom of Contract* 537–542 (1979); John T. Ward, *The Factory Movement, 1830–1855* (1962); Mark Blaug, "The Classical Economists and the Factory Acts—A Re-examination," 72 *Q. J. Econ.* 145 (1972).

4. See Bruce Kuklick, *The Rise of American Philosophy: Cambridge, Massachusetts, 1860–1930*, at 10, 18–21 (1977); Herbert W. Schneider, *A History of American Philosophy* 216–220 (2d ed. 1963). On Scottish Realism, see *The Origins and Nature of the Scottish Enlightenment* (Roy H. Campbell & Andrew S. Skinner eds. 1982); *Wealth and Virtue: The Shaping of Political Economy in the Scottish Enlightenment* (Istvan Hont & Michael Ignatieff eds. 1983).

5. Garry Wills, *Inventing America: Jefferson's Declaration of Independence* (1978).

6. Atiyah, note 3 at 298; Jeffrey T. Young, "The Impartial Spectator and Natural Jurisprudence: An Interpretation of Adam Smith's Theory of the Natural Price," 18 *Hist. Pol. Econ.* 365 (1986).

7. Thomas M. Cooley, "Limits to State Control of Private Business," 1 *Princeton Rev.* (ser. 4) 233, 271 (1878).
8. Tyson & Brother–United Theatre Ticket Offices v. Banton, 273 U.S. 418, 429 (1927); Adkins v. Children's Hospital, 261 U.S. 525, 558 (1923).
9. See Thomas J. Lewis, "Adam Smith: The Labor Market as the Basis of Natural Rights," 11 *J. Econ. Issues* 21 (1977).
10. Herbert Hovenkamp, *Science and Religion in America, 1800–1860* (1978).
11. Thomas Malthus, *An Essay on the Principle of Population* (1798) (Edward A. Wrigley & David Souden eds. 1986). Malthus did not establish either proposition empirically or mathematically. Ellen Paul, *Moral Revolution and Economic Science: The Demise of Laissez-Faire in Nineteenth-Century British Political Economy* 80–83 (1979).
12. See Herbert Hovenkamp, "Evolutionary Models in Jurisprudence," 64 *Tex. L. Rev.* 645, 651–671 (1985).
13. Thomas Malthus, "A Summary View of the Principles of Population," in Malthus, *On Population: Three Essays* 33–40 (1798; 1960 rep.). See Samuel Hollander, "On Malthus's Population Principle and Social Reform," 18 *Hist. Pol. Econ.* 187, 215–227 (1986); Cowherd, note 1 at 27–30.
14. Malthus, *An Essay on the Principle of Population* vii (London 1803).
15. See Paul, note 11 at 134–135, 180–181.
16. See Richard Hofstadter, *Social Darwinism in American Thought* 31, 143–147, 156–157 (rev. ed. 1955). On English political economists and Malthus's iron law, see Mark Blaug, "The Empirical Content of Ricardian Economics," 64 *J. Pol. Econ.* 41, 46–48 (1956). See Hovenkamp, "Evolutionary Models," note 12 at 651–671.
17. David Ricardo, *The Principles of Political Economy and Taxation* 54 (1817) (Ronald M. Hartwell ed. 1971).
18. Id. at 105. See Kanth, note 1 at 105–106; Paul, note 11 at 161. Even Alfred Marshall accepted the theory and devoted substantial attention to it. Alfred Marshall, *Principles of Economics,* bk. 4, ch. 3 (1890).
19. Young, note 6; Atiyah, note 3 at 603.
20. See Alfred W. Coats, "Benthamism, Laissez-Faire, and Collectivism," 11 *J. Hist. Ideas* 357 (1950).
21. John Stuart Mill, "On the Definition of Political Economy; and on the Method of Investigation Proper to It," in J. S. Mill, *Essays on Some Unsettled Questions of Political Economy* 120 (1844).
22. See Herbert Hovenkamp, "The First Great Law & Economics Movement," 42 *Stan. L. Rev.* 993 (1990).
23. See Atiyah, note 6 at 603; Paul, note 11 at 232–236.
24. See, for example, Joseph A. Schumpeter, *Capitalism, Socialism, and Democracy* 75 (1942); Schumpeter, *Economic Doctrine and Method* 84–85 (1954).
25. See Gunnar Myrdal, *The Political Element in the Development of Economic Theory* (1965); T. W. Hutchison, *On Revolutions and Progress in Economic Knowledge* (1978).
26. James Mill, "An Essay of the Impolicy of a Bounty on the Exportation of Grain," in J. Mill, *Selected Economic Writings* 57 (R. Winch ed. 1966). See also Joseph A. Schumpeter, *History of Economic Analysis* 515–520 (1954).

376 · Notes to Pages 73–81

27. See Friedrich Engels, *Condition of the Working Class in England* (1844).
28. See Alfred W. Coats, "The Culture and the Economists: Some Reflections on Anglo-American Differences," 12 *Hist. Pol. Econ.* 588 (1980).
29. Francis Wayland, *The Elements of Moral Science* 25 (1835). See Hovenkamp, *Science and Religion*, note 10 at 3–18.
30. Adam Smith, *Theory of Moral Sentiments* (London 1759).
31. Francis Wayland, *The Elements of Political Economy* vi, 166 (1837).
32. Wayland, *Moral Science*, note 29 at 54.
33. 261 U.S. at 558–559.
34. For example, Alexander H. Everett, "Stewart's Moral Philosophy," 31 *N. Am. Rev.* (1830). On the hostility of American Scottish Realists toward Bentham, see Peter J. King, *Utilitarian Jurisprudence in America: The Influence of Bentham and Austin on American Legal Thought in the Nineteenth Century* 139–266 (1986).
35. See 2 Joseph Dorfman, *The Economic Mind in American Civilization, 1606–1865*, at 836 (1946); 1 & 3 Henry Carey, *Principles of Political Economy*, vol. 1 at 213, vol. 3 at 68 (1837).
36. *Lochner*, 198 U.S. 45, 52–53 (1905); *Adkins*, 261 U.S. at 542.

8. The Classical Theory of Federalism

1. See generally Harry N. Scheiber, "State Law and 'Industrial Policy' in American Development, 1790–1987," 75 *Cal. L. Rev.* 415 (1987); Scheiber, "Federalism and the American Economic Order, 1789–1910," 10 *L. & Soc. Rev.* 57 (1975).
2. Felix Frankfurter, *The Commerce Clause under Marshall, Taney, and Waite*, chs. 1 & 2 (1937).
3. See Illinois Central R.R. v. McKendree, 203 U.S. 514, 530 (1906); Addyston Pipe & Steel Co. v. United States, 175 U.S. 211, 247 (1899); Robert P. Reeder, *The Validity of Rate Regulation, State and Federal* 16 (1914).
4. See U.S. Senate, Select Committee on Interstate Commerce, Report no. 46, 49th Cong., 1st sess., Jan. 18, 1886, at 28–38. See also the statement of John Reagan, U.S. House of Rep., Committee on Commerce, *Arguments and Statements*, H. Misc. Doc. no. 55, 47th Cong., 1st sess., 1882. See Chapter 12.
5. United States v. E. C. Knight Co., 156 U.S. 1 (1895). See Chapter 20.
6. Alan Jones, "Thomas M. Cooley and 'Laissez-Faire Constitutionalism': A Reconsideration," 53 *J. Am. Hist.* 751 (1966); William E. Nelson, *The Roots of American Bureaucracy, 1830–1900*, at 148–155 (1982); Marvin Meyers, *The Jacksonian Persuasion: Politics and Belief* 141–156 (1957); Michael Les Benedict, "Laissez-Faire and Liberty: A Re-Evaluation of the Meaning and Origins of Laissez-Faire Constitutionalism," 3 *L. & Hist. Rev.* 293 (1985).
7. Hammer v. Dagenhart, 247 U.S. 251 (1918). Raymond Zilmer, "State Laws: Survival of the Unfit," 62 *U. Pa. L. Rev.* 509 (1914); National Child Labor Committee, *Objectives of the Committee* (1904); E. Brandeis, "Labor Legislation," in 3 *History of Labor in the United States, 1896–1932*, at 399–420 (John

R. Commons ed. 1935). See generally Stephen B. Wood, *Constitutional Politics in the Progressive Era: Child Labor and the Law* (1968).

8. 41 U.S. (16 Pet.) 1 (1842); 95 U.S. 714, 720 (1877); Wabash, St. Louis & Pacific Ry. Co. v. Illinois, 118 U.S. 557 (1886); 165 U.S. 578 (1897).

9. For example, New York Life Ins. Co. v. Dodge, 246 U.S. 357 (1918) (state could not apply its substantive law to a contract that had been executed in a different state); Western Union Telegraph Co. v. Chiles, 214 U.S. 274 (1909) (due process clause forbade one state from applying its tort law to a tort that had been committed in a different state); Western Union Telegraph Co. v. Brown, 234 U.S. 542 (1914) (commerce clause forbade a state from applying its tort law to a tort committed in a different state).

10. Frederick H. Cooke, *The Commerce Clause of the Federal Constitution* § 57 at 116–117 (1908).

11. Western Union Telegraph Co. v. Call Publishing Co., 181 U.S. 92 (1901).

12. *Call Publishing,* 181 U.S. at 99, 101–102, quoting 1 James Kent, *Commentaries* 471 (4th ed. 1840).

13. John F. Dillon, *Removal of Causes from State Courts to Federal Courts* 2–3 (3d ed. 1881).

14. 41 U.S. (16 Pet.) 1 (1842).

15. Scott v. Sanford, 60 U.S. (19 How.) 393 (1857).

16. Joseph Story, *Commentaries on the Law of Bills of Exchange, Foreign and Inland* 4 (5th ed. 1857) (1st ed. 1843). See also Isaac Edwards, *Bills of Exchange and Promissory Notes* 1 (1857).

17. For a more comprehensive history, see 8 William Holdsworth, *A History of English Law* 126–170 (1926). For the American development, which lagged behind English development, see Morton J. Horwitz, *The Transformation of American Law, 1780–1860,* at 213–215 (1977); Tony Freyer, *Forums of Order: The Federal Courts and Business in American History* (1979).

18. 2 William Blackstone, *Commentaries on the Laws of England* 466 (1765–1769); Story, *Bills of Exchange,* note 16 at 621–622.

19. Story, *Bills of Exchange,* note 16 at 29–30; Story, *Commentaries on the Conflict of Laws, Foreign and Domestic* 314–320, 360–361 (5th ed. 1857).

20. Act of Sept. 24, 1789, 1 Stat. 78–79 (1845). For some history of the section, see Charles Warren, "New Light on the History of the Federal Judiciary Act of 1789," 37 *Harv. L. Rev.* 49, 80 (1923).

21. Buckner v. Finley & Vanlear, 27 U.S. (2 Pet.) 586, 590–593 (1829).

22. Story, *Conflict of Laws,* note 19 at 10.

23. Van Reimsdyk v. Kane, 28 F. Cas. 1062, 1064–1065 (D.R.I. 1812) (no. 16,871), aff'd in part, remanded on other grounds sub nom. Clarke v. van Reimsdyk, 13 U.S. (9 Cranch) 153 (1815).

24. That is, the law of the legal situs, or location, of the thing in dispute. Justice Story applied this rule two years later on the issue whether tenants ejected from land were entitled to compensation for improvements they had made to the land. Rights affecting real property, Justice Story concluded, were "regulated and governed by the law of the place where the land is situated." Society for the Propagation of the Gospel v. Wheeler, 22 F. Cas. 756 (C.C.N.H. 1814).

25. Williams v. Suffolk Ins. Co., 29 F. Cas. 1402, 1405 (C.C. Mass. 1838).
26. See Story, *Bills of Exchange,* note 16 at 218.
27. Swift v. Tyson, 41 U.S. (16 Pet.) 1, 20 (1842).
28. Bank of Sandusky v. Scoville, Barton & Mooney, 24 Wend. 115 (N.Y. Sup. Ct. 1840); Bank of Salina v. Babcock, 21 Wend. 499 (N.Y. Sup. Ct. 1839); see also cases cited in Tony Freyer, *Harmony and Dissonance: The* Swift and Erie *Cases in American Federalism* 166–167 & n.18 (1981).
29. 59 U.S. (18 How.) 517, 519–520 (1855).
30. See Bernard Schwartz, *From Confederation to Nation: The American Constitution, 1835–1877* (1973); Edward S. Corwin, "National Power and State Interposition, 1787–1861," 10 *Mich. L. Rev.* 535 (1912).
31. *Gelpcke,* 68 U.S. (1 Wall.) 175 (1864). For detailed history see Charles Fairman, *Reconstruction and Reunion, 1864–1888,* pt. 2 at 918–1116 (Holmes Devise History of the Supreme Court, vol. VII, 1971). See State ex rel. Dox v. Board of Equalization, 10 Iowa 157 (1859); Ring v. County of Johnson, 6 Iowa 265 (1858); State ex rel. Burlington & Mississippi River R.R. v. County of Wapello, 13 Iowa 388, 390 (1862).
32. Freyer, *Harmony and Dissonance,* note 28 at 45–100.
33. Id.; see also Horwitz, note 17 at 253–268.
34. Horwitz, note 17 at 97–101.
35. 149 U.S. 368, 373 (1893).
36. See Georg Cohn, "The Beginnings of the International Assimilation of Commercial Law," in Alejandro Alvarez, *The Progress of Continental Law in the Nineteenth Century* 351 (1918). In 1818, Daniel Webster attacked the British courts for interfering with the uniformity of the commercial law by enacting insular and confusing statutes that were inconsistent with international merchant practice. See [Daniel Webster], "Wheaton's Reports, Vol. III," 8 *N. Am. Rev.* 63 (1818); Charles M. Cook, *The American Codification Movement: A Study of Antebellum Legal Reform* 104 (1981).
37. 3 Joseph Story, *Commentaries on the Constitution* 564 (1833).

9. An Economic Interpretation of the Constitution

1. Good recent histories of the fourteenth amendment are William E. Nelson, *The Fourteenth Amendment: From Political Principle to Judicial Doctrine* (1988); Michael K. Curtis, *No State Shall Abridge: the fourteenth amendment and the Bill of Rights* (1986); Judith A. Baer, *Equality under the Constitution: Reclaiming the Fourteenth Amendment* (1983); Chester J. Antieau, *The Original Understanding of the Fourteenth Amendment* (1981).
2. Civil Rights Act of 1866, ch. 31, § 1, 14 Stat. 27.
3. Charles Fairman, *Reconstruction and Reunion, 1864–1888,* pt. 1, at 1285–1288 (Holmes Devise History of the Supreme Court, vol. VII, 1971); Earl M. Maltz, "Reconstruction without Revolution: Republican Civil Rights Theory in the Era of the Fourteenth Amendment," 24 *Hous. L. Rev.* 221, 277 (1987).
4. *Plessy,* 163 U.S. 537 (1896); *Lochner,* 198 U.S. 45 (1905). See, for example, Sidney Fine, *Laissez-Faire and the General Welfare State* (1956); Richard

Kluger, *Simple Justice* (1976); Robert G. McCloskey, *American Conservatism in the Age of Enterprise* (1951); McCloskey, *The American Supreme Court* 102–105 (1960); William F. Swindler, *Court and Constitution in the Twentieth Century: The Old Legality, 1889–1932* (1969); Aviam Soifer, "The Paradox of Paternalism and Laissez-Faire Constitutionalism: United States Supreme Court, 1888–1921," 5 *L. & Hist. Rev.* 249 (1987). See also Edward S. Corwin, "The Doctrine of Due Process of Law before the Civil War," 24 *Harv. L. Rev.* 366, 460 (1911).

5. See Eric Foner, *Reconstruction: America's Unfinished Revolution, 1863–1877* (1988), esp. chs. 3 & 8; Herman Belz, *Emancipation and Equal Rights: Politics and Constitutionalism in the Civil War Era* 109–110 (1978); Herbert Hovenkamp, "Social Science and Segregation before Brown," 1985 *Duke L. J.* 624, 648–651. The concept of civil rights also included the right to vote, which the fifteenth amendment ensured.

6. Civil Rights Cases, 109 U.S. 3 (1883); Hovenkamp, note 5 at 648–651.

7. On the historical distinction between civil rights, political rights, and social rights, see Alexander Bickel & Benno Schmidt, *The Judiciary and Responsible Government, 1910–1921,* at 753 (Holmes Devise History of the Supreme Court, vol. IX, 1984); Hovenkamp, note 5 at 642–651.

8. See Maltz, note 3 at 267, 273–274. For the historical arguments for incorporation, see Horace E. Flack, *The Adoption of the Fourteenth Amendment* (1908).

9. Francis Wharton, *Commentaries on Law, Embracing Chapters on the Nature, the Source, and the History of Law; on International Law, Public and Private; and on Constitutional and Statutory Law* (1884), esp. chs. 14–17 at 681–731.

10. Thomas M. Cooley, *A Treatise on the Constitutional Limitations Which Rest upon the Legislative Power of the States of the American Union* (1868); John Norton Pomeroy, *An Introduction to the Constitutional Law of the United States* § 256 (1886); Christopher Tiedeman, *A Treatise on State and Federal Control of Persons and Property in the United States* (2d ed. 1900); Tiedeman, *A Treatise on the Limitations of Police Power in the United States* (1886); John Dillon, *The Law of Municipal Corporations* (2d ed. 1873); [Isaac Parker], "Constitutional Law," 94 *N. Am. Rev.* 435–463 (1862). The work of others is summarized in Herbert Hovenkamp, "The Political Economy of Substantive Due Process," 40 *Stan. L. Rev.* 379, 397–398 (1988).

11. The *American Economic Review* was preceded by the American Economic Association's *Publications,* sometimes called the *Quarterly,* which was first published in 1887.

12. For example, in 1890–1894 the *North American Review* published twenty major articles on legal subjects, and eleven major articles on political economy. In 1880–1884 the *Princeton Review,* which ceased publication in 1888, published eleven major articles on legal subjects, and thirteen on political economy.

13. A. N. Holcombe, "The Legal Minimum Wage in the United States," 2 *Am. Econ. Rev.* 21, 25, 26 (1912).

14. See Peter H. Lindert, "Unequal English Wealth since 1670," 94 *J. Pol. Econ.* 1127, 1152 (1986) (distribution of wealth in England in 1860 was far more

unequal than in the United States); Jeffrey G. Williamson, "Earnings Inequality in Nineteenth-Century Britain," 40 *J. Econ. Hist.* 457 (1980).

15. See Muller v. Oregon, 208 U.S. 412, 419 (1908); Adkins v. Children's Hospital, 261 U.S. 525, 559–560 (1923). In Buchanan v. Warley, 245 U.S. 60 (1917), the Court received a 200-page social science brief on race discrimination, but did not refer to it in its opinion. See Hovenkamp, "Social Science," note 5 at 657–663.

16. For example, Adams v. Tanner, 244 U.S. 590, 605 n.6 (1917).

17. See Benjamin G. Rader & Barbara K. Rader, "The Ely-Holmes Friendship, 1901–1914," 10 *Am. J. Leg. Hist.* 128, 138–140 (1966). The decision was National Cotton Oil Co. v. Texas, 197 U.S. 115 (1904). The definition of monopoly came from Richard T. Ely, *Monopolies and Trusts* 14, 38, 96 (1900). Justice McKenna, who wrote the *National Cotton Oil* opinion, later told Holmes that the definition was probably Ely's.

18. Lochner v. New York, 198 U.S. 45, 75 (1905) (Holmes, J., dissenting).

19. Richard Hofstadter, *Social Darwinism in American Thought* (rev. ed. 1955). See Henry S. Commager, *The American Mind* 82–90, 373 (1950); Herbert Hovenkamp, "Evolutionary Models in Jurisprudence," 64 *Tex. L. Rev.* 645 (1985).

20. See, for example, Robert C. Bannister, *Social Darwinism: Science and Myth in Anglo-American Social Thought* (1979); Donald C. Bellomy, "'Social Darwinism' Revisited," 1 *Persp. Am. Hist.* (n.s.) 1 (1984). These argue that evolutionary models guided sciences and culture less than we have thought, that most uses of Darwinian or Spencerian metaphors outside the biological sciences were purely rhetorical, and that Spencer was not cited all that much in American scientific and literary writing. See also H. I. Sharlin, J. Wall, & D. Hollinger, "Spencer, Scientism, and American Constitutional Law," 33 *Annals of Science* 457 (1976).

21. For an attempt to place Holmes's "Darwinism" into perspective, see Hovenkamp, "Evolutionary Models," note 19 at 656–664. In 1902, Holmes described Spencer's *Social Statics* to Ely as "absurd." Rader & Rader, note 17 at 132.

22. For example, William J. Ghent, *Our Benevolent Feudalism* (1902).

23. Robert M. Crunden, *Ministers of Reform* 70 (1982).

24. See Henry F. May, *Protestant Churches and Industrial America* 39–87 (1967).

25. For example, Paul Murphy, *The Constitution in Crisis Times, 1918–1969* (1972).

10. Market Failure and Constitutional Classicism

1. See Thomas K. McCraw, *Prophets of Regulation* (1984).

2. See Mary O. Furner, *Advocacy and Objectivity: A Crisis in the Professionalization of American Social Science, 1865–1905* (1975).

3. See Charles Reich, "The New Property," 73 *Yale L. J.* 733 (1964); Kenneth J. Vandevelde, "The New Property of the Nineteenth Century: The Development of the Modern Concept of Property," 29 *Buffalo L. Rev.* 325 (1980).

4. See Oliver W. Holmes, Jr., *The Common Law* 246 (1881).

5. Gibbons v. Ogden, 22 U.S. (9 Wheat.) 1 (1824) (commerce clause); Charles River Bridge v. Warren Bridge, 36 U.S. (11 Pet.) 420 (1837) (contract clause); Corfield v. Coryell, 6 F. Cas. 546 (C.C.E.D. Pa. 1823) (article IV privileges and immunities clause); Slaughter-House Cases, 83 U.S. (16 Wall.) 36, 69, 74–81 (1873) (thirteenth amendment; fourteenth amendment due process, equal protection, and privileges and immunities clauses); Livingston v. Van Ingen, 9 Johns. 507, 560–561 (N.Y. 1812) (patents clause); Norwich Gas Light v. Norwich City Gas Co., 25 Conn. 18, 37–38 (1856) (police power); The Binghamton Bridge, 70 U.S. (3 Wall.) 51, 82 (1865) (J. Grier, dissenting) (legislature cannot bind successors). See Herbert Hovenkamp, "Technology, Politics, and Regulated Monopoly: An American Historical Perspective," 62 *Tex. L. Rev.* 1263, 1280–1286 (1984).
6. 36 U.S. (11 Pet.) 420 (1837). See Stanley Kutler, *Privilege and Creative Destruction: The Charles River Bridge Case* 25–26 (1971).
7. See Joseph Chitty, Jr., *A Treatise on the Law of the Prerogatives of the Crown* 120–133 (1820); see also Chapter 11.
8. 3 William Blackstone, *Commentaries on the Laws of England* 218–219 (1765–1769); Morton J. Horwitz, *The Transformation of American Law, 1780–1860,* at 110 (1977).
9. See Jora R. Minasian, "Indivisibility, Decreasing Cost, and Excess Capacity: The Bridge," 22 *J. L. & Econ.* 385 (1979).
10. 36 U.S. (11 Pet.) at 616 (Story, J., dissenting).
11. See Charles River Bridge v. Warren Bridge, 24 Mass. (7 Pick.) 344, 504 (1829) (Putnam, J., dissenting).
12. See Kutler, note 6 at 32–45.
13. *Charles River Bridge,* 36 U.S. (11 Pet.) at 546; Horwitz, note 8 at 135. See 1 Bruce Wyman, *Public Service Corporations* §§ 90–117 (1911), and cases cited therein. In 1865 the Supreme Court reaffirmed both sides of the *Charles River Bridge* rule. In Turnpike Co. v. State, 70 U.S. (3 Wall.) 210 (1865), the Supreme Court refused to imply a monopoly provision in a turnpike charter that contained no explicit provision. In The Binghamton Bridge, 70 U.S. (3 Wall.) 51, 54 (1865), the Court enforced a monopoly provision in a bridge charter.
14. 83 U.S. (16 Wall.) 36–83 (1873); 94 U.S. 113, 136 (1877).
15. 36 U.S. (11 Pet.) at 606–607, 638–639; 21 Jac., ch. 3 (1623).
16. Justice Marcus Morton of the Supreme Judicial Court of Massachusetts agreed with Justice Story, but added that the amount of money that the monopoly franchise could charge must be regulated by the state, generally by stipulation in the charter. Charles River Bridge v. Warren Bridge, 24 Mass. (7 Pick.) 344, 447 (1829). Most Massachusetts charters, including the Charles River Bridge's 1785 charter, set the rates that the grantees could charge: "Each foot passenger (or one person passing), two-thirds of a penny; one person and horse, two pence two-thirds of a penny; single horse cart or sled, or sley, four pence; wheelbarrows, hand-carts, and other vehicles capable of carrying like weight, one penny, one-third of a penny; single horse and chaise, or sulkey, eight pence; coaches, chariots, phaetons and curricles, one shilling each; all other wheel carriages or sleds drawn by more

than one beast, six pence; meat cattle and horses passing the said bridge, exclusive of those rode or in carriages or teams, one penny, one-third of a penny; swine and sheep, four pence for each dozen, and at the same rate for a greater or less number; and in all cases the same toll shall be paid for all carriages and vehicles passing the said bridge, whether the same be loaded or not loaded; and to each team one man and no more shall be allowed as a driver to pass free from payment of toll, and in all cases double toll shall be paid on the Lord's day; and at all times when the toll gatherer shall not attend his duty the gate or gates shall be left open." Quoted in Kutler, note 6 at 10.

17. 36 U.S. (11 Pet.) at 639.
18. See Howard J. Graham, "Justice Field and the Fourteenth Amendment," 52 *Yale L. J.* 851 (1943); Charles R. McCurdy, "Justice Field and the Jurisprudence of Government-Business Relations: Some Parameters of Laissez-Faire Constitutionalism, 1863–1897," 61 *J. Am. Hist.* 970 (1975).
19. 94 U.S. 113, 148 (1876).
20. See George T. Brown, *The Gas Light Company of Baltimore: A Study of Natural Monopoly* (1936), esp. 63–70; 6 Irston R. Barnes, *The Economics of Public Utility Regulation* 26–27 (1942).
21. John Stuart Mill, *The Principles of Political Economy* 143 (1848; 1926 rep.).
22. Norwich Gas Light Co. v. Norwich City Gas Co., 25 Conn. 18, 32–33, 37–39 (1856) (quoting Conn. Const., art. 1, § 1).
23. 6 Wis. 526, 535 (1858).
24. 1 Wyman, note 13 at § 51, p. 43.
25. Slaughter-House Cases, 83 U.S. (16 Wall.) 36 (1873).
26. Charles Fairman, *Reconstruction and Reunion, 1864–1888*, pt. 1, at 1321–1327 (Holmes Devise History of the Supreme Court, vol. VI, 1971); Laurence Tribe, *American Constitutional Law* § 7–2 (2d ed. 1988); Jordan, "Last of the Jacksonians," in Yearbook 1980, Supreme Court Historical Society 85–86 (1980). A thorough compilation of the best evidence supporting the consensus position is found in two articles by the legal realist Mitchell Franklin. Franklin, "The Foundations and Meaning of the Slaughterhouse Cases" (pts. 1 & 2), 18 *Tul. L. Rev.* 1, 218 (1943).
27. William A. Dunning, *Reconstruction, Political and Economic, 1865–1877* (1907). See also Walter L. Fleming, *The Sequel of Appomattox* (1919); Claude G. Bowers, *The Tragic Era* (1929); E. Merton Coulter, *The South during Reconstruction, 1865–1877* (1947). The most thorough critique of the Dunning School is Eric Foner, *Reconstruction: America's Unfinished Revolution, 1863–1877* (1988). Also critical is Bruce Loewenberg, *American History in American Thought* 433 (1972). A corrective on the carpetbaggers is Richard N. Current, *Those Terrible Carpetbaggers* (1988).
28. Ella Lonn, *Reconstruction in Louisiana after 1868*, at 42–43 (1918).
29. 3 Charles Warren, *The Supreme Court in United States History* 258 (1922).
30. See Alfred D. Chandler, Jr., The Visible Hand: The Managerial Revolution in American Business 300–301 (1977).
31. Franklin, note 26 at 1–3, 5, 11, 14; Sigfried Giedion, *Mechanization Takes Command* 220–222 (1948); Joe G. Taylor, *Louisiana Reconstructed* 314–363 (1974).

32. Howard N. Rabinowitz, *Race Relations in the Urban South, 1865–1890* (1978).
33. Transcript of Record No. 476 at 1, Slaughter-House Cases, 83 U.S. (16 Wall.) 36 (1873) (petition).
34. The Crescent City slaughterhouse operated this way: "A short distance from the scale is an immense hall, set apart from the slaughtering of the beeves. Here every modern improvement which ingenuity could suggest, in the opinion of your committee, has been provided, and a constantly flowing stream of water sweeping over the spacious floor removes all blood or other refuse as fast as they accumulate. Notwithstanding the fact that numbers of carcasses were in the apartment at the moment of your committee's visit, none of the revolting spectacles nor the frightful stench which in other localities have made the word slaughter-house a synonym for horror were to be observed." Supplemental Brief of Defendants in Error at 4, Slaughter-House Cases, 83 U.S. (16 Wall.) 36 (1873) (quoting the report of the special committee appointed to investigate the Crescent City Live-Stock Landing and Slaughter-House Company, Journal of the House of Representatives, State of Louisiana, Feb. 28, 1872). A New Orleans grand jury issued a similar report. See id. at 5–7.
35. Louisiana ex rel. Belden v. Fagan, 22 La. Ann. 545, 551 (1870). See G. Dargo, Jefferson's Louisiana 3 (1975); Walter M. Lowrey, "The Engineers and the Mississippi," 5 *La. Hist.* 233 (1964).
36. John Duffy, "Pestilence in New Orleans," in *The Past as Prelude: New Orleans, 1718–1968,* at 88, 110, 221–222 (1968).
37. Franklin, note 26 at 221–223 (citing Landry, "History of Yellow Fever in New Orleans," 96 *New Orleans Med. & Surgical J.* 6, 7–8 (1943)).
38. The cause of the epidemics eventually was tied to a mosquito, *Aedes Aegypti,* which lived in the river and fed on decomposing animal tissue. See Dennis East, "Health and Wealth: Goals of the New Orleans Public Health Movement, 1879–1884," 9 *La. Hist.* 245 n.1 (1968).
39. The report of the grand jury stated: "In consideration of the prevalence of cholera and other diseases in our midst, the grand jury makes a special report upon the impurity of the water taken from the river, and supplied by pipes to the city, caused by throwing offal, refuse from slaughterhouses, etc., into the river . . . . The superintendent of the water works states that the suction pipes of the river occasionally become clogged by such matter being drawn into them, requiring constant attention to keep their orifices clear . . . . How many slaughterhouses exist above the works, I can not say, but their entire removal to the lower part of the city would be a public benefit. A petition signed by more than five hundred of our most prominent citizens for such removal of slaughterhouses was addressed to the Council last spring . . . . Every diligence is exercised now to keep the suction pipes clear from all effete substances, and after the water is pumped into the reservoir, a laborer is engaged throughout the day in skimming the scum which forms upon the surface. Many persons of this city (especially the poorer classes, amongst whom most of the deaths of cholera have lately taken place), use the hydrant water for drinking and other purposes. We recommend that the city . . . petition to the Legislature to pass an act that there should not be allowed to exist any slaughterhouses, or similar places,

above the city within a specified number of miles. We consider such an act of legislation necessary, because should the city authorities cause the removal of such establishments from the upper portion of the city, they would be re-established barely above the city limits, and would be as great nuisances then as now." Louisiana ex rel. Belden v. Fagan, 22 La. Ann. 545, 552–553 (1870).

40. *Belden*, 22 La. Ann. at 553 (quoting *Journal*).
41. The Public Health Act, 1875, 38 & 39 Vict., ch. 55, created public abattoirs in England. The first public abattoirs in France were built by Napoleon I early in the nineteenth century, when Napoleon tried to solve a drinking-water problem similar to the one that faced New Orleans. Under an arrangement similar to that followed by the Crescent City slaughterhouse, private butchers in France took their animals to the public slaughterhouses, where they were slaughtered for a relatively small fee. See Alexander J. G. Devron, "Abattoirs," 6 *Transactions*, Am. Pub. Health Assn. 1 (1881); Giedion, note 31 at 209–211.
42. Slaughter-House Cases, 83 U.S. (16 Wall.) at 40–43.
43. John A. Campbell, former Justice of the United States Supreme Court, made the allegation in arguing the case for the plaintiffs: "The common rights of men have been taken away [by this statute], and have become the *sole and exclusive privilege* of a single corporation." Plaintiff's Brief at 12, Slaughter-House Cases, 83 U.S. (16 Wall.) 36 (1873).
44. See Slaughter-House Cases, 83 U.S. (16 Wall.) 36, 42 (1873) (quoting 1869 Charter, § 7); Brief of Defendants in Error at 10, Slaughter-House Cases (Brief of Charles Allen); and 83 U.S. at 62: ". . . the Slaughter-House Company is required, under a heavy penalty, to permit any person who wishes to do so, to slaughter in their houses; and they are bound to make ample provision for the convenience of all the slaughtering for the entire city. The butcher then is still permitted to slaughter, to prepare and to sell his own meats; but he is required to slaughter at a specified place and to pay a reasonable compensation for the use of the accommodations furnished him at that place." See Franklin, note 26 at 225. The price drops were caused by technological innovations, including automatic slaughtering; skinning, cutting, and packing machines; and refrigerated cars. Giedion, note 31 at 213–246.
45. See Cooper v. Schultz, 32 How. Pr. 107, 132 (N.Y. Comm. Pl. 1866) (upholding a municipal statute excluding slaughterhouses from the city and tracing the history of New York City regulation of slaughtering). In 1868 the New York Court of Appeals upheld the same statute. Metropolitan Bd. of Health v. Heister, 37 N.Y. 661 (1868). See City of Milwaukee v. Gross, 21 Wis. 243, 247 (1866).
46. Lonn, note 28 at 42–43.
47. See Kutler, note 6 at 11–12.
48. Transcript of Record No. 479 at 24–25, Slaughter-House Cases, 83 U.S. (16 Wall.) 36 (1873) (judgment signed by Judge Leaumont).
49. Brief of Defendants in Error at 10, Slaughter-House Cases, 83 U.S. (16 Wall.) 36 (1873).

50. Charles F. Beach, Sr., *A Treatise on the Law of Monopolies and Industrial Trusts* 54–55 (1898).
51. 57 U.S. (16 How.) 314, 335 (1853).
52. Frost v. Belmont, 6 Allen 152, 159 (1863). See also Trist v. Child (1874), 88 U.S. (21 Wall.) 441, 450 (1874) (refusing to enforce agreement for lobbying as "contrary to the plainest principles of public policy").
53. Durbridge v. Slaughterhouse Co., 27 La. Ann. 676 (1875).
54. La. Const. of 1879, arts. 248, 258.
55. Butchers' Union Slaughter-House & Live-Stock Landing Co. v. Crescent City Live-Stock Landing & Slaughter-House Co., 111 U.S. 746 (1884).
56. Darcantel v. People's Slaughterhouse & Refrigerating Co., 44 La. Ann. 632, 635–638, 647–648 (1892); Barthet v. City of New Orleans, 24 F. 563 (E.D. La. 1885).

11. Regulation and Incorporation

1. On price regulation in seventeenth-century America, see J. R. T. Hughes, *Social Control in the Colonial Economy* 132–135 (1976); Forrest McDonald, *Novus Ordo Seclorum: The Intellectual Origins of the Constitution* 14–15 (1985).
2. Jeffrey T. Young, "The Impartial Spectator and Natural Jurisprudence: An Interpretation of Adam Smith's Theory of the Natural Price," 18 *Hist. Pol. Econ.* 365 (1986).
3. Lord Hale, "De Portibus Maris," in *A Treatise in Three Parts* (ca. 1670), reprinted in 1 *A Collection of Tracts Relative to the Law of England* 45, 78 (Francis Hargrave ed. 1787).
4. 1 William Blackstone, *Commentaries on the Laws of England* 263–264, 273 (1765–1769). The most elaborate development of the common law doctrine is Joseph Chitty, Jr., *A Treatise on the Law of the Prerogatives of the Crown* (1820). On the early American experience, see 2 Joseph S. Davis, *Essays in the Earlier History of American Corporations* 228–230 (1917).
5. Munn v. Illinois, 94 U.S. 113, 146–149 (1877). The other Granger cases were Chicago, Burlington & Quincy R.R. Co. v. Cutts, 94 U.S. 183 (1877); Peik v. Chicago & Northwestern Ry. Co., 94 U.S. 164 (1877); Chicago, Milwaukee & St. Paul R.R. Co. v. Ackley, 94 U.S. 179 (1877); Winona & St. Peter R.R. Co. v. Blake, 94 U.S. 180 (1877); Stone v. Wisconsin, 94 U.S. 181 (1877). For economic background, see Stuart Bruchey, *Enterprise: The Dynamic Economy of a Free People,* ch. 10 (1990).
6. Wabash, St. Louis & Pacific Ry. v. Illinois, 118 U.S. 557, 569 (1886).
7. *Peik,* 94 U.S. at 176.
8. Chicago, Burlington & Quincy R.R. Co. v. Iowa, 94 U.S. 155, 162 (1877).
9. Stone v. Farmers' Trust Co., 116 U.S. 307 (1886); Stone v. Illinois Central R.R. Co., 116 U.S. 347 (1886); Stone v. New Orleans & Northeastern R.R. Co., 116 U.S. 352 (1886). Justice Field noted in a concurring opinion in *Ruggles,* 108 U.S. 536 (1883) that the *Munn* decision did "not relate to corporations."
10. 2 Christopher Tiedeman, *A Treatise on State and Federal Control of Persons and Property in the United States* 975–977 (1900).

11. 2 William W. Cook, *A Treatise on Stock and Stockholders, Bonds, Mortgages, and General Corporation Law*, pt. VI, at 1486 (3d ed. 1894); Isaac F. Redfield, *A Practical Treatise on the Law of Railroads* (1858). The regulated industry treatises are Joseph A. Joyce, *Joyce on Franchises* (1909); Bruce Wyman, *Public Service Corporations* (2 vols. 1911); Oscar L. Pond, *Law of Public Utilities* (1913); Nedham C. Collier, *Collier on Public Service Companies* (1918).

12. 110 U.S. 347, 354 (1884); 169 U.S. 466 (1898).

12. The Railroads and the Development of Regulatory Policy

1. Among the first to make this observation was John Stuart Mill. See *The Principles of Political Economy* 143 (1848; 1926 rep.). See also the Progressive Era economist Richard T. Ely's discussion of market failure and natural monopoly in Ely, "The Nature and Significance of the Corporation," 75 *Harper's Mag.* 71 (1887); and Henry Carter Adams, "Relation of the State to Industrial Action," *Publications*, Am. Econ. Assn. 55 (Jan. 1887). For the contemporary understanding of natural monopoly in the railroad industry by one of its most notable regulators, see Charles Francis Adams, Jr., "The Railroad System" 360–366, in Charles F. Adams, Jr., & Henry Adams, *Chapters of Erie and Other Essays* (1871).

2. Harold U. Faulkner, *Politics, Reform, Expansion, 1890–1900*, at 75 (1959); Alfred D. Chandler, Jr., *The Railroads: The Nation's First Big Business* (1965).

3. See Thomas K. McCraw, *Prophets of Regulation* 1–79 (1984). Works in the public interest genre include 1 Isaiah L. Sharfman, *The Interstate Commerce Commission: A Study in Administrative Law and Procedure* (1931); Charles Beard & Mary Beard, *The Rise of American Civilization* 329 (1927); E. Johnson & T. Van Metre, *Principles of Railroad Transportation* 499–508 (1916). For the Progressive view of this period, see Edward Chase Kirkland, *A History of American Economic Life* 285 (1969); Harold U. Faulkner, *The Decline of Laissez Faire, 1897–1917*, at 187–191 (1951). On the theory that congressional intent respecting the Interstate Commerce Act was undermined by the Supreme Court, see Gabriel Kolko, *Railroads and Regulation, 1877–1916*, at 80–82 (1965). Other sources are discussed in Herbert Hovenkamp, "Regulatory Conflict in the Gilded Age: Federalism and the Railroad Problem," 97 *Yale L. J.* 1017, 1020 (1988).

4. Albert S. Bolles, "Difficulties and Dangers of Government Rate-Making," 181 *N. Am. Rev.* 873 (1905) (capture by railroads); H. T. Newcomb, "The Diminished Dollar and Railway Rates," 189 *N. Am. Rev.* 561 (1909) (capture by shippers); Logan G. McPherson, "The Farmer, the Manufacturer, and the Railroad," 186 *N. Am. Rev.* 405 (1907) (same); Hugo R. Meyer, "Railway Rates as Protective Tariffs," 14 *J. Pol. Econ.* 1 (1906) (capture by large cities at the expense of more rural areas); M. O. Lorenz, "Railway Rates as Protective Tariffs—Another View," 14 *J. Pol. Econ.* 170 (1906) (responding to Meyer). Others are noted in Hovenkamp, "Regulatory Conflict," note 3 at 1021.

5. George H. Miller, *Railroads and the Granger Laws* (1971); Lee Benson, *Mer-*

chants, Farmers, and Railroads: Railroad Regulation and New York Politics, 1850–1887 (1955).

6. Kolko, note 3.
7. See Lance Davis & Douglass C. North, *Institutional Change and American Economic Growth* 157–166 (1971); Robert H. Wiebe, *The Search for Order, 1877–1920,* at 133–363 (1967); Paul MacAvoy, *The Economic Effects of Regulation: The Trunk-Line Railroad Cartels and the Interstate Commerce Commission before 1900* (1965). See also Edward C. Kirkland, *Dream and Thought in the Business Community, 1860–1900,* at 1–28 (1956); James Weinstein, *The Corporate Ideal in the Liberal State, 1900–1918* (1968). But see Edward Purcell, "Ideas and Interests: Businessmen and the Interstate Commerce Act," 54 *J. Am. Hist.* 561 (1967). Purcell notes that "business" interests were far less unified than either Kolko or other revisionist historians such as Lee Benson suggested. The most comprehensive counterargument to Kolko is Albro Martin, *Enterprise Denied: Origins of the Decline of American Railroads, 1897–1917* (1971). For good summaries of the dialogue between the Progressive critique and the revisionists, see Stephen Skowronek, *Building a New American State: The Expansion of National Administrative Capacities, 1877–1920,* at 125–150 (1982); Thomas K. McCraw, "Regulation in America: A Review Article," 49 *Bus. Hist. Rev.* 159 (1975).
8. For example, Richard A. Posner, "Theories of Economic Regulation," 5 *Bell J. Econ. & Mgmt. Sci.* 335 (1974); George Stigler, "The Theory of Economic Regulation," 2 *Bell J. Econ. & Mgmt. Sci.* 3 (1971).
9. See Richard A. Posner, *Economic Analysis of Law,* chs. 9, 12, 13, 19 (3d ed. 1986).
10. Federal regulation exclusively: Robert L. Rabin, "Federal Regulation in Historical Perspective," 38 *Stan. L. Rev.* 1189 (1986) (federal regulation); Martin, *Enterprise Denied,* note 7; Kolko, note 3. State regulation: Miller, note 5; Benson, note 5. Although Benson's book discusses federal legislation as well, it does so entirely from the perspective of New York lobbyists and political concerns.
11. Thomas M. Cooley, "State Regulation of Corporate Profits," 137 *N. Am. Rev.* 205, 215 (1883). See also Robert Garrett, "The Railway Problem," 129 *N. Am. Rev.* 361 (1879); Isaac L. Rice, "A Remedy for Railway Abuses," 134 *N. Am. Rev.* 134 (1882).
12. *Smyth,* 169 U.S. 466 (1898); Minnesota Rate Cases, 230 U.S. 350 (1913).
13. On the Interstate Commerce Act, see Kolko, note 3 at 35–70; Rabin, note 10 at 1209–1213; Martin, *Enterprise Denied,* note 7; Albro Martin, "The Troubled Subject of Railroad Regulation in the Gilded Age—A Reappraisal," 61 *J. Am. Hist.* 339 (1974). On the Sherman Act, see Chapters 20 & 21.
14. For example, Miller, note 5; Benson, note 5.
15. Illinois had a more complex constituency, since Chicago was a major shipping point. See Miller, note 5 at 59–96.
16. See Raymond De Roover, "Monopoly Theory Prior to Adam Smith: A Revision," 65 *Q. J. Econ.* 492 (1951); William Letwin, "The English Common Law Concerning Monopolies," 21 *U. Chi. L. Rev.* 355 (1954).

17. See Charles Nott, "Monopolies," 1 *Int'l Rev.* 370 (1874).
18. Gerrit Lansing, "The Railway and the State," 138 *N. Am. Rev.* 461, 462–463 (1884).
19. Indeed, by the time Lansing wrote, many European countries had begun to socialize their railroad systems. See Arthur T. Hadley, *Railroad Transportation: Its History and Its Laws* 236–237 (1885).
20. There is some controversial evidence to the contrary. See Robert Fogel, *The Railroads and American Economic Growth: Essays in Econometric History* (1964). Fogel's thesis—that the railroads made only a modest contribution to American economic growth—is criticized in Peter D. McClelland, "Railroads, American Growth, and the New Economic History: A Critique," 28 *J. Econ. Hist.* 102 (1968). See also Donald N. McCloskey, *The Rhetoric of Economics* 114–119 (1985).
21. Hadley, note 19 at 66. See also C. F. Adams, Jr., "Railroad System," note 1 at 356.
22. See Kolko, note 3 at 18–25; see generally Benson, note 5.
23. For example, Lloyd Bryce, "The Railway Problem: I. The Legislative Solution," 164 *N. Am. Rev.* 327 (1897); James J. Waite, "The Railway Problem: II. A Mercantile View," 164 *N. Am. Rev.* 338 (1897); Albert B. Stickney, *The Railway Problem* (1891); Christopher S. Patterson, "The Railway Problem," 13 *Princeton Rev.* (ser. 4) 36 (1884); Albert Fink, *The Railroad Problem and Its Solution* (1880); Garrett, note 11. See also Ray Morris, "The Railway Crisis: A Way Out," 4 *Yale Rev.* (n.s.) 520 (1915); E. James, "The Railway Question," 2 *Publications*, Am. Econ. Assn. 236 (July 1887).
24. In fact, frequently they did not have to pay for it, and this accounts for a great deal of the overdevelopment. See Chapter 3; Carter Goodrich, *Government Promotion of American Canals and Railroads, 1800–1900* (1960); Lloyd J. Mercer, *Railroads and Land Grant Policy: A Study in Government Intervention* (1982).
25. The ratio of fixed to variable costs given here is consistent with the ratios found to obtain in 1873 on the Louisville & Nashville and Great Southern Railroad by Albert Fink, "Cost of Railroad Transportation," 1 *J. Railroad Transp.* 46, 53 (1874); and Albert Fink, *Cost of Railroad Transportation, Railroad Accounts, and Governmental Regulation of Railroads* (1875).
26. See anon., "The New Jersey Monopolies," 104 *N. Am. Rev.* 428 (1867); John K. Towles, "Early Railroad Monopoly and Discrimination in Rhode Island, 1835–55," 18 *Yale Rev.* 299 (1909); Thomas M. Cooley, "Limits to State Control of Private Business," 1 *Princeton Rev.* (Ser. 4) 233, 261 (1878). In addition, a few early decisions held that railroad charters implied monopoly rights. For example, Boston & Lowell R.R. v. Salem & Lowell R.R., 68 Mass. (2 Gray) 1, 32–34 (1854).
27. U.S. Senate, Select Committee on Interstate Commerce, Report no. 46, 49th Cong., 1st sess., Jan. 18, 1886, at 48–51.
28. For reluctance of railroads to build competing lines in the absence of state subsidy, see Goodrich, note 24 at 238. See also G. S. Callender, "The Early Transportation and Banking Enterprises of the States in Relation to the Growth of Corporations," 17 *Q. J. Econ.* 111 (1902), arguing that the sub-

sidies were necessary for the railroads to develop in many markets. See also William W. Cook, *The Corporation Problem* 12–15 (1891), arguing that many railroads would not have been built but for the subsidies.

29. See Chapter 3. Quincy v. Jackson, 113 U.S. 332 (1885); City of Jonesboro v. Cairo & St. Louis R.R. Co., 110 U.S. 192 (1884) (decided under state law). T. Payson, "Taxation for Railroads by New England Towns," 16 *Am. L. Rev.* 893 (1882) (arguing against public subsidies and taxation for railroads); W. B. J., "County Subscriptions to Railroad Corporations," 11 *Am. L. Reg.* (n.s.) 737 (1872) (arguing against subsidies); C. A. Kent, "Municipal Subscriptions and Taxation in Aid of Railroads," 9 *Am. L. Reg.* (n.s.) 649 (1870) (favoring subsidies).

30. For example, Rice, note 11 at 134.

31. On the development of the American pooling system, see Alfred D. Chandler, Jr., *The Visible Hand: The Managerial Revolution in American Business* 122–144 (1977). Supporting pooling were E. R. A. Seligman, "Railway Tariffs and the Interstate Commerce Law" (pt. 2), 2 *Pol. Sci. Q.* 369, 389 (1887); Hadley, *Railroad Transportation*, note 19, at 74–79; Hadley, "The Prohibition of Railway Pools," 4 *Q. J. Econ.* 158 (1890); William Z. Ripley, *Railroads: Finance and Organization* 575–608 (1915); Thomas M. Cooley, "Popular and Legal Views of Traffic Pooling," 27 *Railway Rev.* 15 (1887); Waite, note 23 (same). Others are discussed in Hovenkamp, note 3 at 1039–1041.

32. Ch. 309, 36 Stat. 539, 547–552 (1910). See ICC, *Annual Report* 16–20 (1898); *Annual Report* 13 (1900). United States v. Trans-Missouri Freight Assn., 166 U.S. 290 (1897); United States v. Joint Traffic Assn., 171 U.S. 505 (1898).

33. Robert H. Bork, *The Antitrust Paradox: A Policy at War with Itself* 22–26 (1978).

34. ICC, *Annual Report* 25 (1889). United States v. Trans-Missouri Freight Assn., 58 F. 58, 67, 76, 79–80 (8th Cir. 1893). James Coolidge Carter made this argument before the Supreme Court to no avail. *Brief for the Trans-Missouri Association, Appellees*, 16–17 (1897). On standardization of operations in the railroad industry, see Alfred D. Chandler, Jr., *Scale and Scope: The Dynamics of Industrial Capitalism* 54–56 (1990).

35. Ch. 3591, 34 Stat. 584 (1906); see William Z. Ripley, *Railroads: Rates and Regulation* 190, 209 (1912).

36. See Ripley, *Railroads: Rates and Regulation*, note 35 at ch. 12; Julius Grodinsky, *The Iowa Pool: A Study in Railroad Competition, 1870–1884*, at 53–67 (1950). For an economic analysis of why the railroad trunk-line cartels were so unsuccessful, see MacAvoy, note 7.

37. See Ripley, *Railroads: Finance and Organization*, note 31. See also Charles F. Adams, Jr., "The Government and Railroad Corporations," 112 *N. Am. Rev.* 31 (1871). Making essentially the same arguments are Leonard Bacon, "Railways and the State," 30 *New Englander & Yale Rev.* 713 (1871); Frank H. Dixon, "Railroads in Their Corporate Relations," 23 *Q. J. Econ.* 34 (1908). Others are discussed in Hovenkamp, note 3 at 1043.

38. For example, Naomi R. Lamoreaux, *The Great Merger Movement in American Business, 1895–1904*, at 159–186 (1985); Chandler, note 34 at 315–339;

Hans B. Thorelli, *The Federal Antitrust Policy: Origination of an American Tradition* 294–303 (1955); Weinstein, note 7 at 67–69; 1 Sharfman, note 3 at 33. But see George Bittlingmayer, "Did Antitrust Policy Cause the Great Merger Wave?" 28 *J. L. & Econ.* 77 (1985).

39. See *Brief of Appellees Freemont, Elkhorn and Missouri Valley Railroad Co.* 52, United States v. Trans-Missouri Freight Assn.; John F. Crowell, "Railway Receiverships in the United States: Their Origin and Development," 7 *Yale Rev.* 319 (1898), noting that in 1895 $1.00 of every $4.00 worth of railway securities was controlled by receivers.

40. For example, Hadley, *Railroad Transportation,* note 19 at 63–74; C. F. Adams, Jr., "The Railroad System," note 1 at 360–366; F. W. Taussig, "A Contribution to the Theory of Railway Rates," 5 *Q. J. Econ.* 438 (1891); Seligman, note 31 at 222, 222–227 (1887); Cooley, note 31.

41. Smyth v. Ames, 169 U.S. 466, 493–494 (1898). Bryan lost the case; the Supreme Court found the Nebraska rate confiscatory. See Chapter 13.

13. Federalism and Rate Discrimination

1. See Jackson v. Rogers, 2 Show. 327 (1683).
2. Western Union Telegraph Co. v. Call Publishing Co., 181 U.S. 92, 101–102 (1901), quoting 1 James Kent, *Commentaries* 471 (4th ed. 1840).
3. On the common law position, see Cook v. Chicago, Rock Island & Pacific Ry. Co., 81 Ia. 551, 46 N.W. 749 (1890); Messenger v. Pennsylvania R.R. Co., 7 Vroom (36 N.J.) 407 (1872); Fitchburg R.R. v. Gage, 12 Gray (Mass.) 393 (1859); Commonwealth v. Louisville & Nashville R.R. Co., 112 Ky. 783, 68 S.W. 1103 (1902); 4 Byron K. Elliott & William F. Elliott, *A Treatise on the Law of Railroads* § 1467, at 154–156 (2d ed. 1907); Joseph Beale & Bruce Wyman, *The Law of Railroad Rate Regulation, with Special Reference to American Legislation* § 851 (1907).
4. 1 Ida M. Tarbell, *The History of The Standard Oil Company* 44–49 (1904); Frank Norris, *The Octopus* 56 (1901; 1964 rep.); Beale & Wyman, note 3 at §§ 749, 750. See also J. Walter Lord, "A Brief Review of the Subject of Federal Railroad Regulation," 181 *N. Am. Rev.* 754 (1905).
5. Henry Demarest Lloyd, "Story of a Great Monopoly," 47 *Atlantic Monthly* 317, 322 (1881); Arthur T. Hadley, *Railroad Transportation: Its History and Its Laws* 119–121 (1885).
6. See Schofield v. Lake Shore & Michigan Southern Ry. Co., 43 Ohio St. 571, 3 N.E. 907 (1885) (condemning agreements under which Standard Oil Company obtained rates lower than its competitors).
7. Ch. 3591, 34 Stat. 584 (1906). See William Hill, "Recent Utterances of Mr. Hill and Mr. Harriman upon Railway Problems," 14 *J. Pol. Econ.* 627 (1906), noting that the statute was interpreted to prevent railroads from owning the stock of any industry along the road, for such an industry would likely want to ship on the closest available line; Frank H. Dixon, "The Interstate Commerce Act as Amended," 21 *Q. J. Econ.* 22 (1906).
8. Schofield v. Lake Shore & Michigan Southern Ry. Co., 43 Ohio St. 571, 3 N.E. 907 (1885); Cook v. Chicago, Rock Island & Pacific Ry. Co., 81 Ia.

551, 46 N.W. 749 (1890) (condemning secret rebates); Louisville, Evansville & St. Louis Consolidated R.R. v. Wilson, 132 Ind. 517, 32 N.E. 311 (1892). For the economics of such cheating, see Herbert Hovenkamp, *Economics and Federal Antitrust Law* § 4.1 (1985).

9. Hadley, note 5 at 112–113; F. W. Taussig, "A Contribution to the Theory of Railway Rates," 5 *Q. J. Econ.* 438 (1891); John Bates Clark, "Some Neglected Phases of Rate Regulation," 4 *Am. Econ. Rev.* 565 (1914). See the Cullom Committee Report, U.S. Senate, Select Committee on Interstate Commerce, Report no. 46, 49th Cong., 1st sess., Jan. 18, 1886, at 184–194.

10. Norris, note 4 at 56.

11. 2 & 3 D. Moore, *Moore on Carriers,* chs. 14 & 32 (1914); 2 Bruce Wyman, *Public Service Corporations* §§ 1310–1338 (1911); Isaac F. Redfield, "Regulation of Interstate Traffic on Railways by Congress," 22 *Am. L. Reg.* (o.s.) 1, 13 (1874). Many others are discussed in Herbert Hovenkamp, "Regulatory Conflict in the Gilded Age: Federalism and the Railroad Problem," 97 *Yale L. J.* 1017, 1050 (1988).

12. For example, Carl N. Degler, *The Age of the Economic Revolution, 1876–1900,* at 24 (1977).

13. Joseph Potts, "The Science of Transportation," 1 *J. Soc. Sci.* 115, 124 (1870).

14. See Gerrit Lansing, "The Railway and the State," 138 *N. Am. Rev.* 461, 466 (1884): "Markets that are common to various points of production or supply control the rates from all these points by the competition which may exist with any one of them. The lowest rate to the market by any route controls the rates by all the other routes."

15. Charles F. Adams, Jr., "Railway Problems in 1869," 110 *N. Am. Rev.* 116, 133 (1870).

16. For example, William Z. Ripley, *Railroads: Rates and Regulation* 217–222 (1912); Hugo Meyer, "Government Regulation of Railway Rates," 7 *Publications,* Am. Econ. Assn. 61 (1906).

17. Hadley, note 5 at 117.

18. For example, Hadley, note 5 at 265; Hadley, "Private Monopolies and Public Rights," 1 *Q. J. Econ.* 28 (1886); Marshall M. Kirkman, *Railroad Revenue: A Treatise on the Organization of Railroads and the Collection of Railroad Receipts* (1879).

19. Taussig, note 9 at 438, 442, 454, 458. Disagreeing, is M. B. Hammond, "Railway Rate Theories of the Interstate Commerce Commission," 25 *Q. J. Econ.* 1, 279, 471 (1910 & 1911).

20. For example, Robert Garrett, "The Railway Problem," 129 *N. Am. Rev.* 361 (1879).

21. William P. Shinn, "The Relations of Railways to the State," 26 *Railway Rev.* 121, 122 (1886) (emphasis added).

22. United States v. E. C. Knight Co., 156 U.S. 1 (1895). For identification of an intrastate bill of lading as determining jurisdiction, see Cincinnati, New Orleans & Texas Pacific Ry. Co. v. I.C.C., 162 U.S. 184, 193 (1896).

23. Gabriel Kolko, *Railroads and Regulation, 1877–1916* (1965).

24. Wabash, St. Louis & Pacific Ry. Co. v. Illinois, 118 U.S. 557 (1886).

25. George H. Miller, *Railroads and the Granger Laws* 3-41, 172-173 (1971); Lee

Benson, *Merchants, Farmers, and Railroads: Railroad Regulation and New York Politics, 1850–1887*, at 29–54 (1955).

26. 25 Stat. 124 (1886); Cong. Rec., 1888-1889, at 2322. See 2 Lewis H. Haney, *A Congressional History of Railways in the United States* 195 (1910).

27. Wabash, St. Louis & Pacific Ry. Co. v. Illinois, 118 U.S. 557 (1886).

28. Munn v. Illinois, 94 U.S. 113 (1877), plus companion cases; Spring Valley Water Works v. Schottler, 110 U.S. 347, 354 (1884) (Waite, C.J., also the author of the Court's opinion in *Munn*); Chicago, Milwaukee & St. Paul Ry. v. Minnesota, 134 U.S. 418 (1890); *Smyth,* 169 U.S. 466 (1898).

29. Principally in Chicago, Milwaukee & St. Paul Ry. Co. v. Minnesota, 134 U.S. 418 (1890), which struck down a state statute that authorized a commission to set rates and made its findings unreviewable. For a summary of the criticisms see Stephen A. Siegel, "Understanding the Lochner Era: Lessons from the Controversy over Railroad and Utility Rate Regulation," 70 *Va. L. Rev.* 187, 212–259 (1984).

30. See Chapter 11. A list of several state charters regulating railroad rates is given in Minnesota Rate Cases, 230 U.S. 352, 412 (1913).

31. Thomas M. Cooley, "State Regulation of Corporate Profits," 137 *N. Am. Rev.* 205, 210–211 (1883); Cooley, "Limits to State Control of Private Business," 1 *Princeton Rev.* (ser. 4) 233, 254–255 (1878); 1 Isaac F. Redfield, *The Law of Railways* 448–450 (3d ed. 1867).

32. Francis Wharton, "Retrospective Legislation and Grangerism," 3 *Int'l Rev.* 50, 61 (1876). See also David Brewer, "Protection to Private Property from Public Attack," 55 *New Englander & Yale Rev.* 97 (1891) (Yale Law School commencement address); Lyman H. Atwater, "The Regulation of Railroads," 7 *Princeton Rev.* (ser. 4) 406 (1881). Justice Field made a similar argument in his dissent in Stone v. Wisconsin, 94 U.S. 181, 183 (1877).

33. Beale & Wyman, note 3 at §§ 101, 102.

34. For example, in Smyth v. Ames, 169 U.S. 466, 528–539 (1898), the Court found that 7.5 percent of the railroad revenues generated in Nebraska came from intrastate traffic. See also id. at 543, concluding that the Chicago, Burlington & Quincy's intrastate earnings accounted for only 5 percent of its total earnings; Ames v. Union Pacific Ry., 64 F. 165, 186 (C.C.D. Neb. 1894). And see the chart in Minnesota Rate Cases, 230 U.S. 352, 438 (1913), showing about 12 percent of Minnesota's traffic at that time to be local.

35. See the argument of the Attorney General of Nebraska, 169 U.S. at 486; White, "Government Control of Transportation Charges" (pts. 1–4), 37 *Am. L. Reg.* (n.s.) 721 (1898); 38 *Am. L. Reg.* (n.s.) 151, 288, 355 (1898-1899).

36. Munn v. Illinois, 94 U.S. 113 (1877); Chicago, Burlington & Quincy R.R. Co. v. Iowa, 94 U.S. 155 (1877); Peik v. Chicago & Northwestern R.R. Co., 94 U.S. 164 (1877); Winona & St. Paul R.R. Co. v. Blake, 94 U.S. 180 (1877).

37. *Wabash,* 118 U.S. at 576–580.

38. For example, Henry Clews, "Legislative Injustice to Railways," 148 *N. Am. Rev.* 319 (1889).

39. Ames v. Union Pacific R.R. Co., 64 F. 165, 171 (C.C.D. Neb. 1894), aff'd *sub nom.* Smyth v. Ames, 169 U.S. 466 (1898). The statute was struck down, however, as denying the railroad a fair rate of return on its investment.

40. Louisville & Nashville R.R. Co. v. Kentucky, 183 U.S. 503, 518–519 (1902).
41. Maurice H. Robinson, "State Regulation of Railways," 166 *N. Am. Rev.* 398, 398 (1898).
42. Robert Mather, "How the States Make Interstate Rates," 32 *Annals,* Am. Acad. Pol. & Soc. Sci. 102, 104 (1908).
43. See Minnesota Rate Cases, 230 U.S. 350, 435, 438 (1913). The problem is discussed more fully in an earlier article upon which the litigants may have relied. Maurice H. Robinson, "The Legal, Economic, and Accounting Principles Involved in the Judicial Determination of Railway Passenger Rates," 16 *Yale Rev.* 355 (1908).
44. Woodrow Wilson, "The States and the Federal Government," 187 *N. Am. Rev.* 684 (1908); Henry Wade Rogers, "The Constitution and the New Federalism," 188 *N. Am. Rev.* 321 (1908).
45. Ch. 708, 32 Stat. 847 (1903). The Elkins Act permitted the railroads to draft and propose rates jointly, and then prevented any particular railroad from deviating from those rates. Hepburn Act, ch. 3591, 34 Stat. 584 (1906); Mann-Elkins Act, ch. 309, 36 Stat. 539 (1910).
46. ICC, *Annual Report* 73–75 (1889); Interstate Commerce Act, § 1, ch. 104, 24 Stat. 379 (1887); Hepburn Act, ch. 3591, 34 Stat. 584 (1906). See Minnesota Rate Cases, 230 U.S. at 417–418.
47. 230 U.S. at 417, 432–433.
48. Houston, East & West Texas Ry. Co. v. United States, 234 U.S. 342, 347, 351–355 (1914). See William C. Coleman, "The Commerce Clause and Intrastate Rates," 12 *Col. L. Rev.* 321 (1912); Note, "The Evolution of Federal Regulation of Intrastate Rates: The Shreveport Rate Cases," 28 *Harv. L. Rev.* 34 (1914).
49. See William Z. Ripley, *Railroads: Rates and Regulation* 394 (1912). On the Texas Railroad Commission at this time, see Lewis H. Haney, "Railway Regulation in Texas," 19 *J. Pol. Econ.* 437 (1911).
50. Act of Feb. 28, 1920, ch. 91, 41 Stat. 456; Act of May 8, 1920, ch. 172, 41 Stat. 590; 1 Isaiah L. Sharfman, *The Interstate Commerce Commission: A Study in Administrative Law and Procedure* 177–244 (1931). See, for example, Rates, Fares, and Charges of the New York Central R.R. Co., 59 I.C.C. 290 (1920); Intrastate Rates within Illinois, 59 I.C.C. 391 (1920); Wisconsin Passenger Fares, 59 I.C.C. 391 (1920), enforced *sub nom.* Wisconsin R.R. Comm'n v. Chicago, Burlington & Quincy R.R. Co., 257 U.S. 563, 585–586 (1922).

14. Historical Explanation and Substantive Due Process

1. In re Jacobs, 98 N.Y. 98 (1885) (striking down statute forbidding cigar manufacturing in tenement houses).
2. See *Adkins,* 261 U.S. 525, 545 (federal minimum wage law); Morehead v. New York ex rel. Tipaldo, 298 U.S. 587 (1936) (state minimum wage law); Lochner v. New York, 198 U.S. 45 (1905) (state maximum hours law); Weaver v. Palmer Bros., 270 U.S. 402 (1926) (statute regulating quality of bedding materials); Jay Burns Baking Co. v. Bryan, 264 U.S. 504 (1924) (statute requiring standardized weights for bread); Louis K. Liggett Co. v. Baldridge, 278 U.S. 105 (1928) (state licensing of pharmacists); New State

Ice Co. v. Liebmann, 285 U.S. 262 (1932) (statute conditioning entry into ice business on demonstration of "necessity" and inadequacy of existing facilities); Ribnik v. McBride, 277 U.S. 350, 357 (1928) ("[T]he fixing of prices for food or clothing, of house rental or of wages to be paid, whether minimum or maximum, is beyond the legislative power").

3. Labor supported wage and hour laws. James L. Bates, *The United States, 1898–1928,* at 141–143 (1976); John D. Buenker, *Urban Liberalism and Progressive Reform* 42–79 (1973). Many industrialists supported rate regulation. See Chapters 12 and 13. Established business firms also supported many of the licensing and entry restrictions. See Lawrence M. Friedman, "Freedom of Contract and Occupational Licensing, 1890–1910: A Legal and Social Study," 53 *Calif. L. Rev.* 487, 497 (1965).
4. For example, Roscoe Pound, "Liberty of Contract," 18 *Yale L. J.* 454 (1909).
5. See Edward A. Purcell, *The Crisis of Democratic Theory: Scientific Naturalism and the Problem of Value* (1973); Herbert Hovenkamp, "Evolutionary Models in Jurisprudence," 64 *Tex. L. Rev.* 645, 677–683 (1985).
6. See generally Robert M. Crunden, *Ministers of Reform* (1982); Richard Hofstadter, *The Age of Reform* (1955).
7. See William E. Nelson, "The Impact of the Antislavery Movement upon Styles of Judicial Reasoning in Nineteenth-Century America," 87 *Harv. L. Rev.* 513 (1974); Harry N. Scheiber, "Instrumentalism and Property Rights: A Reconsideration of American 'Styles of Judicial Reasoning' in the Nineteenth Century," 1975 *Wis. L. Rev.* 1.
8. See, for example, Pound, note 4; Roscoe Pound, "Mechanical Jurisprudence," 8 *Col. L. Rev.* 605 (1908); Hovenkamp, note 5 at 677–683. Progressive histories include Henry S. Commager, *The American Mind* 359–373 (1950); Morton G. White, *Social Thought in America: The Revolt against Formalism* 59–75 (1957).
9. 198 U.S. 45, 75 (1905).
10. For example, Pound, "Mechanical Jurisprudence," note 8.
11. 158 U.S. 564, 581–582 (1895).
12. 209 U.S. 123, 160 (1908).
13. Christopher Tiedeman, *The Unwritten Constitution of the United States: A Philosophical Inquiry into the Fundamentals of American Constitutional Law* 80 (1890).
14. Christopher C. Langdell, *A Selection of Cases on the Law of Contracts* (1871).
15. See Morton J. Horwitz, *The Transformation of American Law, 1780–1860,* at 253–266 (1977). On the obsession of Gilded Age social scientists, particularly economists, with being scientific, see Mary O. Furner, *Advocacy and Objectivity: A Crisis in the Professionalization of American Social Science, 1865–1905* (1975).
16. See, for example, Joseph Beale & Bruce Wyman, *The Law of Railroad Rate Regulation* 24–40 (1906).
17. On the absence of distributive concerns in classical political economy, see P. S. Atiyah, *The Rise and Fall of Freedom of Contract* 335–338 (1979).
18. Charles Beard, *An Economic Interpretation of the Constitution of the United States* (1913).
19. See, for example, Lawrence M. Friedman, *A History of American Law* (2d ed.

1985); Horwitz, note 15; J. Willard Hurst, *Law and Economic Growth: The Legal History of the Lumber Industry in Wisconsin, 1836–1915* (1964); William E. Nelson, *Americanization of the Common Law: The Impact of Legal Change on Massachusetts Society, 1760–1830,* at 145–165 (1975); Mark Tushnet, *American Law of Slavery* (1981).

20. See William G. Sumner, "Rights," in 1 *Essays of William Graham Sumner* 358 (1934); Sumner, "Some Natural Rights," in id. at 363; see also Hovenkamp, "Evolutionary Models," note 5 at 669–670.
21. However, some judges have done so since very early in the nineteenth century. See Horwitz, note 15; Herbert Hovenkamp, "The Economics of Legal History," 67 *Minn. L. Rev.* 645 (1983).
22. Theodore Sedgwick, *Public and Private Economy* 31 (1836). See Introduction.
23. For example, Charles F. Adams, Jr., "The Granger Movement," 120 *N. Am. Rev.* 394, 399–400 (1875); Richard T. Ely, *Property and Contract in Their Relations to the Distribution of Wealth* (1914); E. R. A. Seligman, "Is the Income Tax Constitutional and Just?" *Forum,* March 1895, at 56; John R. Commons, *Legal Foundations of Capitalism* (1924).
24. Oliver W. Holmes, "The Path of the Law," 10 *Harv. L. Rev.* 457, 467–468 (1897). In 1906 Holmes suggested to Sir Frederick Pollock that the Justices incorporated the "prejudices of [their] class" in constitutional opinions. Letter of June 23, 1906, 1 *Holmes-Pollock Letters: The Correspondence of Mr. Justice Holmes and Sir Frederick Pollock, 1874–1932,* at 127 (M. D. Howe ed. 1961). See also Arnold M. Paul, *Conservative Crisis and the Rule of Law: Attitudes of Bar and Bench, 1887–1895,* at 232–237 (1960); Benjamin Twiss, *Lawyers and the Constitution: How Laissez-Faire Came to the Supreme Court* 13–17 (1942).
25. For example, Village of Euclid v. Ambler Realty Co., 272 U.S. 365 (1926).
26. 83 U.S. (16 Wall.) 36, 83 (1873) (Field, J., dissenting). See Chapter 10.
27. 165 U.S. 578 (1897). See William E. Nelson, *The Roots of American Bureaucracy, 1830–1900,* at 152–153 (1982).
28. See, for example, Chicago, Burlington & Quincy R.R. v. McGuire, 219 U.S. 549 (1911) (approving Iowa statute that voided limitation of liability for injury clauses in railroad employment contracts); New State Ice Co. v. Liebmann, 285 U.S. 262 (1932); Frost v. Corporate Comm'n, 278 U.S. 515 (1929); Louis K. Liggett Co. v. Baldridge, 278 U.S. 105 (1928); Frost & Frost Trucking Co. v. Railroad Comm'n, 271 U.S. 583 (1926).
29. See Bessette v. People, 193 Ill. 334, 62 N.E. 215 (1901) (blacksmiths); People v. Beattie, 96 A.D. 383, 89 N.Y.S. 193 (1904) (same); Wyeth v. Thomas, 200 Mass. 474, 86 N.E. 925 (1909) (undertakers); People v. Ringe, 197 N.Y. 143, 90 N.E. 451 (1910) (same); People ex rel. Tyroler v. Warden, 157 N.Y. 116, 51 N.E. 1006 (1898) (ticket agents); Noel v. People, 187 Ill. 587, 58 N.E. 616 (1900) (druggists); Schnaier v. Navarre Hotel & Importation Co., 182 N.Y. 83, 74 N.E. 561 (1905) (plumbers); State ex rel. Richey v. Smith, 42 Wash. 237, 248, 84 P. 851, 854 (1906) (plumbers). Thomas M. Cooley, "Limits to State Control of Private Business," 1 *Princeton Rev.* (ser. 4) 233, 263–266 (1878). For one contemporary scholar's analysis see Frank J. Goodnow, *Social Reform and the Constitution* 292–328 (1911).
30. See Chapters 12 and 13.

31. See Horwitz, note 15 at 253–268.
32. See Henry J. Abraham, *Justices and Presidents: A Political History of Appointments to the Supreme Court* 24–48 (2d ed. 1985).
33. See Nelson, *Bureaucracy*, note 27; Michael Les Benedict, "Laissez-Faire and Liberty: A Re-Evaluation of the Meaning and Origins of Laissez-Faire Constitutionalism," 3 *L. & Hist. Rev.* 293 (1985); Charles R. McCurdy, "Justice Field and the Jurisprudence of Government-Business Relations: Some Parameters of Laissez-Faire Constitutionalism, 1863–1897," 61 *J. Am. Hist.* 970 (1975).
34. Legal Tender Cases, 79 U.S. (12 Wall.) 457, 580 (1871) (Chase, C.J., dissenting).
35. Oscar Handlin & Mary Handlin, *Commonwealth: A Study of the Role of Government in the American Economy—Massachusetts, 1774–1861* (1941; rev. ed. 1969); Harry N. Scheiber, *Ohio Canal Era: A Case Study of Government and the Economy, 1820–1861*, at 88–94 (1969); Gordon Wood, *The Creation of the American Republic, 1776–1787*, at 53–65 (1969).
36. Lochner v. New York, 198 U.S. 45, 64 (1905).
37. For example, State v. Santee, 111 Iowa 1, 82 N.W. 445 (1900) (striking down statute generally prohibiting use of certain lamp fuels but creating exception for the "Welsbach hydrocarbon incandescent lamp"); see also People v. Gillson, 109 N.Y. 389, 17 N.E. 343 (1888); Wynehamer v. People, 13 N.Y. 378 (1856).

15. The American School of Political Economy

1. See Chapter 7.
2. E. K. Hunt, *History of Economic Thought* 123 (1979); Phyllis Deane, "Contemporary Estimates of National Income in the First Half of the Nineteenth Century," 8 *Econ. Hist. Rev.* (2d ser.) 339 (1956); Rajani K. Kanth, *Political Economy and Laissez-Faire* (1986).
3. Willard Phillips, *A Manual of Political Economy, with Particular Reference to the Institutions, Resources, and Condition of the United States* 117, 134–149 (1828).
4. See Lewis H. Haney, *History of Economic Thought* 315–329 (3d ed. 1936); Abraham D. H. Kaplan, *Henry Charles Carey: A Study in American Economic Thought* (1931); Paul Conkin, *Prophets of Prosperity: America's First Political Economists* 261–296 (1980).
5. "We cannot close our eyes to the notorious fact that earnings everywhere, in all occupations, have greatly increased—not alone in States where the minimum wage law obtains but in the country generally." Adkins v. Children's Hosp., 261 U.S. 525, 560 (1923).
6. Jacob N. Cardozo, *Notes on Political Economy* iii (1826).
7. Gulian C. Verplanck, *An Essay on the Doctrine of Contracts: Being an Inquiry How Contracts Are Affected in Law and Morals, by Concealment, Error, or Inadequate Price* 107–131 (1825). Verplanck did argue for more intervention by courts, but on moral rather than economic grounds. Alexander H. Everett, "Verplanck's Essay on Contracts," 22 *N. Am. Rev.* 253 (1826).
8. See Henry Vethake, *The Principles of Political Economy* 101–102, 110–115

(2d ed. 1844); 3 Henry Carey, *Principles of Political Economy* 55–57 (1837); Alexander H. Everett, "M'Culloch's Political Economy," 25 *N. Am. Rev.* 112, 118 (1827).

9. See Richard Hofstadter, *Social Darwinism in American Thought* 55–56 (rev. ed. 1955).

10. James McVikar, *Outlines of Political Economy* 120–122 (1825). Daniel A. Raymond, an earlier Federalist, had written a treatise on political economy that said almost nothing about Malthus. Raymond, *The Elements of Political Economy* (1823). See also Samuel P. Newman, *Elements of Political Economy* 254 (1835).

11. Thomas Cooper, *Lectures on the Elements of Political Economy* (1826). See also George Tucker, "On Density of Population," in Tucker, *Essays on Various Subjects of Taste, Morals, and National Policy* (1822) (agreeing with Cooper). Francis Wayland made similar arguments, although he did not cite Malthus. Wayland, *The Elements of Political Economy* 125–127 (1837).

12. Or else they suggested that Malthus was so preoccupied with Britain's own agricultural problems that he generalized from Britain to the rest of the world. See Van Buren Denslow, "American Economics," 139 *N. Am. Rev.* 12 (1884).

13. Cardozo, note 6 at 44; Vethake, note 8 at 109–110, 120–124; Everett, "M'Culloch's Political Economy," note 8 at 141; Alexander H. Everett, *New Ideas in Population* (1823); Everett, "Political Economy," 28 *N. Am. Rev.* 368 (1829). See Joseph J. Spengler, "Alexander Hill Everett: Early American Opponent of Malthus," 9 *New Eng. Q.* 97 (1936). On Jefferson, see Drew McCoy, *The Elusive Republic: Political Economy in Jeffersonian America* 194–195 (1980).

14. Elisha Andrews, "Are There Too Many of Us?" 155 *N. Am. Rev.* 596, 606–607 (1892); Denslow, note 12 at 12–14, who appears to have taken the observation from Carey. Carey performed a "simple calculation" showing that even a conservative geometric progression would have the population doubling every generation. Had this happened since the time of Adam and Eve, people would "not now find standing-room upon the earth." 3 Carey, note 8 at 54.

15. 3 Carey, note 8 at 54–56. Francis Wayland agreed; Wayland, note 11 at 339–340.

16. See, for example, Andrews, note 14; Denslow, note 12.

17. Henry George, *Progress and Poverty: An Inquiry into the Cause of Industrial Depressions and of the Increase of Want with Increase of Wealth—The Remedy* (1879).

18. Phillips, note 3 at 109; Wayland, note 11 at 382–384; Newman, note 10 at 274. See Joseph Dorfman, "Economic Thought," in *The Growth of the Seaport Cities, 1790–1825,* at 151 (D. Gilchrist ed. 1967); James H. Thompson, "Willard Phillips: A Neglected American Economist," 16 *Hist. Pol. Econ.* 405 (1984).

19. Cardozo argued that land will not produce unjust rents in a competitive market, but that rents might easily exist when a "monopoly of land is established": "[W]hen the soil has been purchased as an instrument of

political influence, or as a source of dignity and power, its price will not be subject to the rules which govern its market-value as a commodity, in those countries where it is sought purely for the profit that can be made from it. Something must be paid for the additional value acquired by land in consequence of these circumstances." Cardozo, note 6 at 26–27; see also Phillips, note 3 at 122.

20. Carey, note 8. On Carey's critique of Ricardo, see Kaplan, note 4 at 35–41, 48–51. See also Cardozo, note 6 at 31–32; Wayland, note 11 at 386–390.
21. See Carey, note 8 at 27–35; Vethake, note 8 at 95.
22. "Carey on the Population and Political Condition of Mankind," 7 *N.Y. Rev.* 306 (1840); "Carey's Principles of Political Economy," 3 *N.Y. Rev.* 1 (1838).
23. See Jacob Oser & William C. Blanchfield, *The Evolution of Economic Thought* 348 (3d ed. 1975).
24. John Bates Clark, "Capital and Its Earnings," 3 *Publications,* Am. Econ. Assn. 88 (1889).
25. See Chapters 20–23.
26. 1 Richard T. Ely, *Property and Contract in Their Relations to the Distribution of Wealth* 79–91 (1914).
27. For example, Charles F. Adams, Jr., "The Granger Movement," 120 *N. Am. Rev.* 394 (1875); Frank Norris, *The Octopus* (1901).
28. See Alfred Marshall, *Principles of Economics,* bk. 7, ch. 10 (1890). On the lack of attention to monopoly in neoclassical British economic theory, see P. S. Atiyah, *The Rise and Fall of Freedom of Contract* 616–617 (1979).
29. Arthur C. Pigou, *The Economics of Welfare* 746–747 (1920; 4th ed. 1932). See T. W. Hutchison, *On Revolutions and Progress in Economic Knowledge* 94–120, 175–199 (1978); Hovenkamp, "The First Great Law & Economics Movement," 42 *Stan. L. Rev.* 993 (1990).
30. See Chapter 18; John F. Henry, "John Bates Clark and the Marginal Product: An Historical Inquiry into the Origins of Value-Free Economic Theory," 15 *Hist. Pol. Econ.* 375 (1983); Joel Jalladeau, "The Methodological Conversion of John Bates Clark," 7 *Hist. Pol. Econ.* 209 (1975).

16. The Wages Fund

1. William G. Sumner, "Protective Taxes and Wages," 136 *N. Am. Rev.* 270, 271 (1883). See generally Scott Gordon, "The Wage-Fund Controversy: The Second Round," 5 *Hist. Pol. Econ.* 14 (1973); Doris G. Phillips, "The Wages Fund in Historical Context," 1 *J. Econ. Issues* 321 (1967).
2. Francis Wayland, *The Elements of Political Economy* 339 (1837). For similar views, see Henry Carey, *Essay on the Rate of Wages* 30–32 (1835); Samuel P. Newman, *Elements of Political Economy* 246 (1835).
3. William G. Sumner, "Wages," in Sumner, *Collected Essays in Political and Social Science* 36, 50 (1885).
4. A. L. Perry, *Elements of Political Economy* 122 (1866). Perry's book succeeded Wayland's text after the Civil War as the most popular American economics textbook. See Gordon, note 1 at 20.
5. The doctrine was championed by J. R. M'Culloch in the 1820's and by

Nassau Senior in the 1830's. See J. R. M'Culloch, *The Principles of Political Economy* 292–332 (1825); Nassau Senior, *An Outline of the Science of Political Economy* 2–3, 49 (1836); Senior, *Three Lectures on the Rate of Wages* 36 (1830).

6. John Stuart Mill, "Book Review," in 5 *Collected Works* 680 (J. Robson ed. 1967). See Robert B. Ekelund, "A Short-Run Classical Model of Capital and Wages: Mill's Recantation of the Wages Fund," 28 *Oxford Econ. Papers* 66 (1976); Walter Stanley Jevons, *The Theory of Political Economy* 257–258 (1871); Alfred Marshall, "The Theory of Business Profits," 1 *Q. J. Econ.* 477 (1887); Marshall, "Wages and Profits," 2 *Q. J. Econ.* 218 (1888); Marshall, *Principles of Economics* 567 (1890).

7. The earliest statement of the wage-fund doctrine in America that I have found is in Alexander H. Everett, "M'Culloch's Political Economy," 25 *N. Am. Rev.* 112 (1827). American writers before Everett discussed wages almost entirely as a function of the monopoly price of land. For example, 1 Daniel A. Raymond, *The Elements of Political Economy* 191–203 (1823). See also Perry, note 4 at 122; Jacob N. Cardozo, *Notes on Political Economy* 40–41 (1826); Newman, note 2 at 243; Willard Phillips, *A Manual of Political Economy, with Particular Reference to the Institutions, Resources, and Condition of the United States* 117 (1828); Henry Vethake, *The Principles of Political Economy* 100 (2d ed. 1844); Carey, *Essay*, note 2; Silas MacVane, *The Working Principles of Political Economy* (1890); F. W. Taussig, *Wages and Capital: An Examination of the Wages Fund Doctrine* 96–107 (1896); Henry T. Terry, "The Services Capital Renders to Labor," 45 *New Englander & Yale Rev.* 498 (1886).

8. See Carey, *Essay*, note 2; 1 Henry Carey, *Principles of Political Economy* 15–19 (1837).

9. Francis Walker, "The Wage-Fund Theory," 120 *N. Am. Rev.* 84, 102 (1875); see also Walker, *The Wages Question* 142–144, 405–406 (1876).

10. Francis Walker, "The Source of Business Profits," 1 *Q. J. Econ.* 265 (1887). See James P. Munroe, *A Life of Francis Amasa Walker* (1923).

11. Silas MacVane, "The Theory of Business Profits," 2 *Q. J. Econ.* 1 (1887); Simon Patten, "President Walker's Theory of Distribution," 4 *Q. J. Econ.* 34 (1889); F. W. Taussig, "The Employer's Place in Distribution," 10 *Q. J. Econ.* 67 (1895); John Bates Clark, "Distribution as Determined by a Law of Rent," 5 *Q. J. Econ.* 289 (1891); Franklin H. Giddings, "The Theory of Profit-Sharing," 1 *Q. J. Econ.* 367, 369–372 (1887). Many others are discussed in Herbert Hovenkamp, "The Political Economy of Substantive Due Process," 40 *Stan. L. Rev.* 379, 435 (1988).

12. Stuart Wood, "A New View of the Theory of Wages," 3 *Q. J. Econ.* 462 (1889); 1 Richard T. Ely, *Property and Contract in Their Relations to the Distribution of Wealth* 2–4 (1914).

13. John Bates Clark, "The Possibility of a Scientific Law of Wages," 4 *Publications*, Am. Econ. Assn. 39, 49 (1889).

14. Henry George, *The Science of Political Economy* 445 (1898; rep. 1981); George, *Progress and Poverty: An Inquiry into the Cause of Industrial Depressions and of the Increase of Want with Increase of Wealth—The Remedy* 50–79, 206–207, 212–213, 215, 310–311 (1879).

15. Adkins v. Children's Hosp., 261 U.S. 525, 557 (1923).

17. Market Failure and the Constitution

1. See David P. Currie, "The Constitution in the Supreme Court: The Protection of Economic Interests, 1889–1910," 52 *U. Chi. L. Rev.* 324, 381 & n.341 (1985).
2. For example, Paul Murphy, *The Constitution in Crisis Times, 1918–1969*, at 68–72 (1972); Laurence H. Tribe, *American Constitutional Law* 570–574 (2d ed. 1988). Contemporary scholars made the same criticism. For example, Robert E. Cushman, "The Social and Economic Interpretation of the Fourteenth Amendment," 20 *Mich. L. Rev.* 737, 749 (1922); W. F. Dodd, "The Growth of Judicial Power," 24 *Pol. Sci. Q.* 193, 194 (1909).
3. Lochner v. New York, 198 U.S. 45, 56–57 (1905).
4. Munn v. Illinois, 94 U.S. 113, 127 (1876). See Chapters 12 and 13.
5. Tyson & Brother–United Theatre Ticket Offices v. Banton, 273 U.S. 418, 431 (1927); Felix Frankfurter, *The Commerce Clause under Marshall, Taney, and Waite* 87 (1937); *Banton*, 273 U.S. at 446 (Holmes, J., dissenting).
6. Thomas M. Cooley, *A Treatise on the Constitutional Limitations Which Rest upon the Legislative Power of the States of the American Union* 736–739 (1868). See Walton Hamilton, "Affectation with Public Interest," 39 *Yale L. J.* 1089 (1930); Breck P. McAllister, "Lord Hale and Business Affected with a Public Interest," 43 *Harv. L. Rev.* 759 (1930). A few cases suggest that monopolization of a market would justify legislative intervention. For example, Williams v. Standard Oil Co., 278 U.S. 235, 240 (1929). The Court was divided on the question whether *de facto* monopoly status was sufficient to warrant price regulation. See Budd v. New York, 143 U.S. 517 (1892) (6–3 decision involving grain elevator, as in *Munn*).
7. See Chapter 10; Ellen Paul, *Moral Revolution and Economic Science: The Demise of Laissez-Faire in Nineteenth-Century British Political Economy* 195–196 (1979). The one classicist with a well-developed doctrine of externalities was Edwin Chadwick, a utilitarian who did most of his writing in the 1830's and 1840's. See P. S. Atiyah, *The Rise and Fall of Freedom of Contract* 332–334 (1979).
8. Arthur C. Pigou, *Wealth and Welfare* (1912); Pigou, *The Economics of Welfare* (1920). Quotations from the fourth edition, 1932 at 183, 192–196. See Frank Knight, "Some Fallacies in the Interpretation of Social Cost," 38 *Q. J. Econ.* 582 (1924). Pigou's most notable critic was Ronald Coase; Coase, "The Problem of Social Cost," 3 *J. L. & Econ.* 1 (1960).
9. Tyson & Brother–United Theatre Ticket Offices v. Banton, 273 U.S. 418, 451 (1927) (Stone, J., dissenting).
10. Lochner v. New York, 198 U.S. 45, 57, 62 (1905). Justice Peckham continued: "In our judgment it is not possible in fact to discover the connection between the number of hours a baker may work in the bakery and the healthful quality of the bread made by the workman." Some dissenters, such as Justices Stone and Holmes, believed unequal bargaining power and the resulting unreasonableness in contract terms should justify regulation. Ribnik v. McBride, 277 U.S. 350, 361–362 (1928) (Stone dissent); *Banton*, 273 U.S. at 448–450 (Stone dissent); Coppage v. Kansas, 236 U.S. 1, 26–27 (1915) (Holmes).

11. Louis D. Brandeis, Brief for Defendant in Error, Muller v. Oregon, 208 U.S. 412 (1908) (No. 107) reprinted in 16 *Landmark Briefs and Arguments of the Supreme Court of the United States: Constitutional Law* 63 (P. Kurland & G. Casper eds. 1975). Much of the brief consisted of statements by workers that they liked factory legislation. Said one worker: "I decidedly prefer to work the hours fixed by the Factory Acts . . . . I have never had any illness since the Factory Act came into operation." Said another: "I have been six years employed in the sewing department. I am very well satisfied with the Factory Acts as they are, and I think all the sewers are of opinion that it is a good law . . . ." Id. at 100–101. On the quality of the brief's information, see David P. Bryden, "Brandeis's Facts," 1 *Const. Comm.* 281 (1984); on its sexism, see Mary E. Becker, "From *Muller v. Oregon* to Fetal Vulnerability Policies," 53 *U. Chi. L. Rev.* 1219, 1221–1225 (1986).
12. Brandeis Brief, note 11 at 50–51 (quoting *Report of the Massachusetts Bureau of Labor Statistics* 504 (1871); S. F. Breckinridge, "Legislative Control of Women's Work," 14 *J. Pol. Econ.* 107, 108–109 (1906)).
13. *Muller*, 208 U.S. at 421–422.
14. *Welch*, 214 U.S. 91, 107–108 (1909); *Euclid*, 272 U.S. 365, 391–394 (1926).
15. See Eric G. Behrens, "The Triangle Shirtwaist Company Fire of 1911: A Lesson in Legislative Manipulation," 62 *Tex. L. Rev.* 361 (1983).
16. Pigou, *Economics of Welfare*, note 8 at 183, 192.

18. Classical Theory and the Labor Cartel

1. For example, In re Debs, 158 U.S. 564 (1895).
2. Oliver W. Holmes, Jr., "The Path of the Law," 10 *Harv. L. Rev.* 457, 467–468 (1897).
3. Leo Pasvolsky, "'Yellow' and 'Red' Trade Unions," 215 *N. Am. Rev.* 621 (1922); Richard J. Hinton, "American Labor Organizations," 140 *N. Am. Rev.* 48, 59 (1885); Samuel P. Orth, *The Armies of Labor* 82 (1919); Jane Addams, "The Present Crisis in Trade Union Morals," 179 *N. Am. Rev.* 178 (1904); Allan Pinkerton, *Strikers, Communists, Tramps, and Detectives* (1878); Francis Dewees, *The Molly Maguires: The Origin, Growth, and Character of the Organization* (1877); Edward W. Martin, *The History of the Great Riots* (1877). See also David Grimstead, "Antebellum Labor: Violence, Strike, and Communal Arbitration," 19 *J. Soc. Hist.* 5 (1985); Linda Schneider, "The Citizen Striker: Workers' Ideology in the Homestead Strike of 1892," 23 *Labor Hist.* 47 (1982); William M. Dick, *Labor and Socialism in America: The Gompers Era* 11–12 (1972); Robert H. Wiebe, *The Search for Order, 1877–1920* (1967); Samuel P. Hays, *The Response to Industrialism* (1957).
4. For example, Arnold M. Paul, *Conservative Crisis and the Rule of Law: Attitudes of Bar and Bench, 1887–1895* (1960); Christopher L. Tomlins, *The State and the Unions: Labor Relations, Law, and the Organized Labor Movement in America, 1880–1960* (1985); Mark Kelman, "American Labor Law and Legal Formalism: How 'Legal Logic' Shaped and Vitiated the Rights of American Workers," 58 *St. John's L. Rev.* 1 (1983). But see Chapter 14.
5. Henry Pelling, *A History of British Trade Unionism* 16, 52–185 (2d ed. 1972);

John V. Orth, "English Combination Acts of the Eighteenth Century," 5 *L. & Hist. Rev.* 175, 177–179, 181–183, 196 (1987); C. R. Dobson, *Masters and Journeymen: A Prehistory of Industrial Relations, 1717–1800,* at 122 (1980).

6. Commonwealth v. Pullis (1819). No official report was published, but large parts of the record and opinion appear in 3 John R. Commons et al., *A Documentary History of American Industrial Society* 59–236 (1910). See B. W. Poulson, "Criminal Conspiracy, Injunctions, and Damage Suits in Labor Law," 7 *J. Leg. Hist.* 212, 215 (1986). For further discussion of cases, see Herbert Hovenkamp, "Labor Conspiracies in American Law, 1880–1930," 66 *Tex. L. Rev.* 919, 922–924 (1988).

7. *Hunt,* 45 Mass. (4 Met.) 111 (1842); Bowen v. Matheson, 96 Mass. (14 Allen) 499, 502 (1867).

8. See United States v. Frisbie, 28 F. 808 (C.C.E.D. La. 1886); United States v. Donau, 11 Blatchf. 168 (2d Cir. 1873); Robert S. Wright, *The Law of Criminal Conspiracies and Agreements* 130–134 (1887); Hampton L. Carson, *The Law of Criminal Conspiracies and Agreements as Found in the American Cases* 110–111 (1887); W. A. Martin, *A Treatise on the Law of Labor Unions* 9–13 (1910); Charles F. Beach, Sr., *A Treatise on the Law of Monopolies and Industrial Trusts* § 78 (1898).

9. Gregory v. Duke of Brunswick, 134 Eng. Rep. 866, 1178 (1843–1844).

10. Frederick H. Cooke, *The Law of Combinations, Monopolies, and Labor Unions* 33 (2d ed. 1909). See Toledo, Ann Arbor Ry. Co. v. Pennsylvania Co., 54 F. 730 (C.C. Ohio 1893); Pickett v. Walsh, 192 Mass. 582, 586 (1906).

11. Cooke, note 10 at 104; Arthur Eddy, *The Law of Combinations, Embracing Monopolies, Trusts, and Combinations of Labor and Capital; Conspiracy, and Contracts in Restraint of Trade* (1901).

12. Hopkins v. Oxley Stave Co., 83 F. 912, 919 (8th Cir. 1897).

13. For example, Tomlins, note 4; David M. Gordon, Richard Edwards, & Michael Reich, *Segmented Work, Divided Workers: The Historical Transformation of Labor in the United States* (1982); Philip S. Foner, *History of the Labor Movement in the United States* (4 vols. 1955); Eugene V. Debs, *Writings and Speeches of Eugene Debs* (1948); Upton Sinclair, *The Jungle* (1906); Jacob Riis, *How the Other Half Lives* (1890).

14. 2 Eddy, note 11 at 876–998, 1330–1331. See Allyn A. Young, "The Sherman Act and the New Anti-Trust Legislation," 23 *J. Pol. Econ.* 417, 420 (1915); James A. Emery, "Labor Organizations and the Sherman Law," 20 *J. Pol. Econ.* 599, 612 (1912).

15. Louis D. Brandeis, Brief for Defendant in Error, Muller v. Oregon, 208 U.S. 412 (1908); *Seventh Annual Report of the Bureau of Labor Statistics of the Senate of New York* (1899); David Ziskind, "The Use of Economic Data in Labor Cases," 6 *Chi. L. Rev.* 607 (1930); Edward A. Ross, *Sin and Society: An Analysis of Latter-Day Iniquity* (1907); Washington R. Gladden, *Jesus Christ and the Social Question* (1900); Lincoln Steffans, *The Shame of the Cities* (1902).

16. For example, Roscoe Pound, "Liberty of Contract," 18 *Yale L. J.* 454 (1909). Even Arthur Eddy acknowledged that it was "impossible for isolated factories, or the factories in particular cities . . . to yield to the demand for a ten-hour . . . day at the same wages; or to the demand for increased wages

. . . unless practically all the factories engaged in the same industry are successfully subjected to the same demand. Nearly all industries are conducted upon so close a margin between cost and price that even a very small increase in the cost of turning out the product must be accompanied by a corresponding increase in price." 1 Eddy, note 11 at § 382, p. 249.

17. Anon., "The Organization of Labor," 135 *N. Am. Rev.* 118, 119 (1882); John Mitchell, *Organized Labor* 184 (1903); Frank U. Quillin, *The Color Line in Ohio: A History of Race Prejudice in a Typical Northern State* 6–7, 125–166 (1913). See also Robert D. Parmet, *Labor and Immigration in Industrial America* (1981); Herbert Hovenkamp, "Social Science and Segregation before *Brown*," 1985 *Duke L. J.* 624, 662–663. For the problem at its worst, see Alexander P. Saxton, *The Indispensable Enemy: Labor and the Anti-Chinese Movement in California* (1971).

18. See Alexander Keyssar, "Unemployment and the Labor Movement in Massachusetts, 1870–1916," at 233, in *The New England Working Class and the New Labor History* (Herbert G. Gutman & Donald H. Bell eds. 1987); Alfred D. Chandler, Jr., *The Visible Hand: The Managerial Revolution in American Business* 256–260 (1977).

19. See Chapter 16. For the contemporary perception, see Edward Atkinson, "The Hours of Labor," 142 *N. Am. Rev.* 507, 507–508 (1886); Edith Abbott, "The Wages of Unskilled Labor in the United States, 1850–1900," 13 *J. Pol. Econ.* 321 (1905), and the many reports and earlier articles that she discusses; Davis R. Dewey, *Employees and Wages* (1903). On comparison of British and American working conditions, see Edward Brooks, "English Aristocracy and English Labor," 111 *N. Am. Rev.* 352 (1870).

20. 1 Theodore Sedgwick, *Public and Private Economy* 224–225 (1836). See also James A. Emery, "Labor Organizations and the Sherman Law," 20 *J. Pol. Econ.* 599, 599–601 (1912).

21. See Shelton Stromquist, *A Generation of Boomers: The Pattern of Railroad Labor Conflict in Nineteenth-Century America* 30–32, 100–127 (1987).

22. For example, Brown v. Jacobs Pharmacy Co., 115 Ga. 429, 434, 41 S.E. 553, 555 (1902) (output restriction agreement not enforceable); Culp v. Love, 127 N.C. 457, 37 S.E. 476 (1900) (agreement between two sellers that one would not sell meat and the other would not sell flour unenforceable). Other cases are discussed in Hovenkamp, "Labor Conspiracies," note 6 at 932–933.

23. Frank J. Goodnow, "Trade Combinations at Common Law," 12 *Pol. Sci. Rev.* 212 (1897). See also Donald Dewey, "The Common-Law Background of Antitrust Policy," 41 *Va. L. Rev.* 759 (1955).

24. 1 Eddy, note 11 at § 565, p. 486. United States v. Addyston Pipe & Steel Co., 85 F. 271, 279 (6th Cir. 1898), aff'd, 175 U.S. 211 (1899).

25. For example, Martell v. White, 200 Mass. 255, 263–264, 69 N.E. 1085, 1088–1089 (1904) (condemning manufacturers' association that levied fines against nonparticipants in association); Boutwell v. Marr, 71 Vt. 1, 42 A. 607 (1899) (same). 1 Eddy, note 11 at §§ 560, 563, pp. 474–475, 483. See Bruce Wyman, "Competition and the Law," 15 *Harv. L. Rev.* 427, 436–445 (1902), identifying "fraud, disparagement and coercion" as three unac-

ceptable kinds of competition, and describing each; Oliver W. Holmes, Jr., "Privilege, Malice, and Intent," 8 *Harv. L. Rev.* 1 (1894); William D. Lewis, "Should the Motive of the Defendant Affect the Question of His Liability," 5 *Colum. L. Rev.* 107, 123 (1905); James B. Ames, "How Far an Act May Be a Tort Because of the Wrongful Motive of the Actor," 18 *Harv. L. Rev.* 411 (1905).

26. Bohn Mfg. Co. v. Hollis, 54 Minn. 223, 234, 55 N.W. 1119 (1893); see 1 Eddy, note 11 at § 560, pp. 475–476 & n.1. Eastern States Retail Lumber Dealers' Assn. v. United States, 234 U.S. 600 (1914).

27. 14 Wend. 9–10, 19 (N.Y. 1835). For example, Alpheus T. Mason, *Organized Labor and the Law* 64–65 (1925); Francis B. Sayre, "Labor and the Courts," 39 *Yale L. J.* 682, 685–687 (1929); Harry P. Robinson, "Organized Labor and Organized Capital," 7 *J. Pol. Econ.* 327 (1898). The New York court adhered to this distinction in Master Stevedores' Assn. v. Walsh, 2 Daly 1 (N.Y. 1867).

28. See George Stigler, "Perfect Competition, Historically Contemplated," 65 *J. Pol. Econ.* 1, 10–11 (1957).

29. Francis A. Walker, *Political Economy* 263 (3d ed. 1888).

30. Cooke, *Combinations*, note 10 at 98, quoting L. D. Willcut & Sons Co. v. Driscoll, 200 Mass. 100, 125, 85 N.E. 897, 904 (1908).

31. Vegelahn v. Guntner, 167 Mass. 92, 107, 44 N.E. 1077, 1081 (1896).

32. Dr. Miles Medical Co. v. John D. Park & Sons Co., 220 U.S. 373, 412–413 (1911).

33. The notion appears in Alfred Marshall, *Principles of Economics*, bk. 3, ch. 4 at 175–183 (1890).

34. Albert Stickney, *State Control of Trade and Commerce by National or State Authority* 188–189 (1897).

35. George Gunton, *Trusts and the Public* 78–79, 188–190 (1899) (from editorials in *Gunton's Magazine*, 1897, 1899); see also Gunton, *Principles of Social Economics* 409–413 (1891).

36. See Henry R. Hatfield, "The Chicago Trust Conference," 8 *J. Pol. Econ.* 1 (1899); Jeremiah W. Jenks, "How Trusts Affect Prices," 172 *N. Am. Rev.* 906 (1901); Arthur T. Hadley, "Private Monopolies and Public Rights," 1 *Q. J. Econ.* 28 (1886); Irving R. Fisher, *Elementary Principles of Economics* 304–305 (1911); Frank Fetter, *The Principles of Economics* 312–322 (1904); 1 F. W. Taussig, *Principles of Economics* 49–66 (2d ed. 1919).

37. Jeremiah W. Jenks, "Economic Aspects of the Recent Decisions of the United States Supreme Court on Trusts," 20 *J. Pol. Econ.* 346, 349 (1912).

38. Albert S. Bolles, "The Rights and Methods of Labor Organizations," 176 *N. Am. Rev.* 563 (1903).

39. John R. Commons, "Labor's Attitude toward Industrial Efficiency," 1 *Am. Econ. Rev.* 463 (1911); note, "Industrial Efficiency and the Interests of Labor," 2 *Am. Econ. Rev. Supp.* 117 (1912).

40. Arthur T. Hadley, *Economics: An Account of the Relations between Private Property and Public Welfare* 158, 159, 368 (1896); C. Bertrand Thompson, "Relations of Scientific Management to Labor," 30 *Q. J. Econ.* 311, 332–323 (1915); 2 Taussig, note 36 at 306–309, 317 (3d ed. 1922). See also C. Reinold

Noyes, "The Economics of Trade Unionism," 213 *N. Am. Rev.* 16 (1921);
W. Bourke Cockran, "Effect Produced by Combinations, Whether of Capital
or Labor, upon the General Prosperity of the Community" 462, in *Chicago
Conference on Trusts* (1900); J. L. Laughlin, "The Unions v. Higher Wages,"
14 *J. Pol. Econ.* 129 (1906).

41. Arthur J. Eddy, *The New Competition* 51 (1914).

42. See Frederick W. Taylor, *Shop Management* (1911); Taylor, *The Principles of
Scientific Management* (1911); Henry L. Gantt, *Work, Wages, and Profits* (2d
ed. 1919); George Gunton, *Wealth and Progress: A Critical Examination of the
Labor Problem* (1887). See also Stephen H. Haber, *Efficiency and Uplift:
Scientific Management in the Progressive Era, 1890–1920* (1964); David
Montgomery, *The Fall of the House of Labor: The Workplace, the State, and
American Labor Activism, 1865–1925,* at 216–256 (1987); Albro Martin, *Enter-
prise Denied: Origins of the Decline of the American Railroads, 1897–1917,* at
220–222 (1971); Thomas K. McCraw, *Prophets of Regulation* 92–93
(1984).

43. Josephine Goldmark, *Fatigue and Efficiency* (1912); see also R. F. Hoxie,
"Why Organized Labor Opposes Scientific Management," 31 *Q. J. Econ.* 62
(1916); C. Bertrand Thompson, "The Literature of Scientific Management,"
28 *Q. J. Econ.* 506, 549–553 (1914).

44. John Bates Clark, "The Law of Wages and Interest," 1 *Annals,* Am. Acad.
Pol. & Soc. Sci. 43, 44 (1890); Clark, "The Possibility of a Scientific Law of
Wages," 4 *Publications,* Am. Econ. Assn. 37 (1889); Clark, "Capital and Its
Earnings," 3 *Publications,* Am. Econ. Assn. 92 (1888). Clark's mature position
appears in *The Distribution of Wealth* (1899).

45. Eric Foner, *Free Soil, Free Labor, Free Men: The Ideology of the Republican Party
before the Civil War* 261–300 (1970); Foner, *Reconstruction: America's Unfinished Revolution, 1863–1877,* at 156–157 (1988).

46. Slaughter-House Cases, 83 U.S. (16 Wall.) 36, 83–130 (1873), quoting A.
Smith, *Wealth of Nations,* bk. 1, ch. 10, pt. 2 (1776). See William E. Forbath,
"The Ambiguities of Free Labor: Labor and the Law in the Gilded Age,"
1985 *Wis. L. Rev.* 767, 773 (1985); Charles Fairman, *Reconstruction and
Reunion, 1864–1888,* pt. 2, at 1117–1300 (Holmes Devise History of the
Supreme Court, vol. VII, 1971); Charles R. McCurdy, "The Roots of Liberty
of Contract Reconsidered: Major Premises in the Law of Employment,
1867–1937," *Yearbook of the Supreme Court Historical Society* 20 (1984).

47. For example, In re Jacobs, 98 N.Y. 98 (1885); Godcharles v. Wigeman, 113
Pa. 431, 6 A. 354 (1886).

48. See Eric Foner, *Politics and Ideology in the Age of the Civil War* 62 (1982);
David Montgomery, *Beyond Equality: Labor and the Radical Republicans, 1862–
1872,* at 230–295 (1967).

49. Gunton, *Principles,* note 35 at 179.

50. J. M. Hollander, "Political Economy and the Labor Question," 176 *N. Am.
Rev.* 563, 565–566 (1903); Francis Walker, "The Wage-Fund Theory," 120
N. Am. Rev. 84 (1875); Walker, *The Wages Question* (1876); Walker, "The
Doctrine of Rent and the Residual-Claimant Theory of Wages," 5 *Q. J.
Econ.* 417, 421 (1891).

51. See John Bates Clark, "Distribution as Determined by a Law of Rent," 5 *Q. J. Econ.* 289 (1891); Walker, "The Doctrine of Rent," note 50 at 417, 421; Silas MacVane, "The Theory of Business Profits," 2 *Q. J. Econ.* 1 (1887).
52. Francis Walker, "The Source of Business Profits," 1 *Q. J. Econ.* 265, 283 (1887).
53. John Bates Clark, *The Distribution of Wealth* 83, 100, 102–103 (1899); Clark, *Essentials of Economic Theory* 145, 127 (1907); Simon Patten, *The Theory of Prosperity* 45–46 (1902).
54. Clark, *Distribution*, note 53 at 63.

19. Coercion and Its Meaning

1. J. L. Laughlin, "The Unions v. Higher Wages," 14 *J. Pol. Econ.* 126 (1906).
2. *Pullis* was not officially reported, but appears in 3 John R. Commons et al., *A Documentary History of American Industrial Society* 59–236 (1910); *Hunt,* 45 Mass. (4 Met.) 111 (1842).
3. Union Pacific Ry. v. Ruef, 120 F. 102, 128 (C.C.D. Neb. 1902); In re Debs, 158 U.S. 564, 599 (1895). See Charles Schwab, "What May Be Expected in the Steel and Iron Industry," 172 *N. Am. Rev.* 655 (1901); Rufus Hatch, "The Labor Crisis," 142 *N. Am. Rev.* 602, 606 (1886).
4. Henry Clews, "The Labor Crisis," 142 *N. Am. Rev.* 598, 603 (1886).
5. United States v. Trans-Missouri Freight Assn., 166 U.S. 290 (1897); Eastern States Retail Lumber Dealers' Assn. v. United States, 234 U.S. 600 (1914); Montague v. Lowry, 193 U.S. 38 (1904); United States v. Union Pacific R.R. Co., 226 U.S. 61 (1912).
6. See Shelton Stromquist, *A Generation of Boomers: The Pattern of Railroad Labor Conflict in Nineteenth-Century America* 79–99 (1987).
7. United States v. Jellico Mountain Coal Co., 46 F. 432 (C.C.M.D. Tenn. 1891).
8. The principal ones, in chronological order, are United States v. Amalgamated Council, 54 F. 994 (E.D. La. 1893); Waterhouse v. Comer, 55 F. 149 (N.D. Ga. 1893); United States v. Elliott, 62 F. 801 (E.D. Mo. 1894); Thomas v. Cincinnati, 62 F. 803 (S.D. Ohio 1894); United States v. Agler, 62 F. 824 (D. Ind. 1894); In re Grand Jury, 62 F. 828 (N.D. Ill. 1894); In re Grand Jury, 62 F. 834 (S.D. Cal. 1894); In re Grand Jury 62 F. 840 (N.D. Cal. 1894); United States v. Debs, 64 F. 724 (N.D. Ill. 1894); United States v. Cassidy, 67 F. 698 (N.D. Cal. 1895).
9. For example, Samuel Gompers, "The Sherman Law, Amend It or End It," 17 *Am. Federationist* 197, 202 (March 1910); M. Garland, "An Iron and Steelworker's View of Combination" 349, 352 in *Chicago Conference on Trusts* (1900) (Garland was a past president of the Amalgamated Association of Iron and Steel Workers).
10. 21 Cong. Rec. 2611–2612, 2728–2731 (1890). Alpheus T. Mason, *Organized Labor and the Law* 122–127 (1925); Joseph A. Joyce, *A Treatise on Monopolies and Unlawful Combinations or Restraints* 175 (1911); James A. Emery, "Labor

Organizations and the Sherman Law," 20 *J. Pol. Econ.* 599, 604–606 (1912). For the contrary view, see Edward Berman, *Labor and the Sherman Act* 11–51 (1930).

11. Loewe v. Lawlor, 208 U.S. 274, 301 (1908).
12. William H. Taft, *The Anti-Trust Act and the Supreme Court* 97 (1914).
13. See generally *The Pullman Strike* (Leon Stein ed. 1969); *The Pullman Boycott of 1894* (C. Warne ed. 1955); Almont Lindsey, *The Pullman Strike* (1942); C. J. Primm, "Labor Unions and the Anti-Trust Law: A Review of Decisions," 18 *J. Pol. Econ.* 129, 137 (1910).
14. See Joseph H. Beale & Bruce Wyman, *The Law of Railroad Rate Regulation, with Special Reference to American Legislation,* chs. 7 & 8 (1907); Joseph J. Feely, "The Right to Strike: Its Limitations," 191 *N. Am. Rev.* 644, 646 (1910).
15. Richard T. Ely, "Natural Monopolies and the Workingman," 158 *N. Am. Rev.* 294 (1894).
16. 44 Stat. 577 (1926). See generally Robert H. Zieger, *Republicans and Labor, 1919–1929* (1969).
17. See generally Gerald G. Eggert, *Railroad Labor Disputes: The Beginnings of Federal Strike Policy* (1967).
18. Toledo Ann Arbor & North Michigan Ry. Co. v. Pennsylvania Co., 54 F. 730, 54 F. 746 (N.D. Ohio 1893); In re Debs, 158 U.S. 564, 586 (1895). See Felix Frankfurter & Nathan Greene, *The Labor Injunction* 6 (1930); Donald L. McMurry, "The Legal Ancestry of the Pullman Strike Injunctions," 14 *Indus. & Lab. Rel. Rev.* 235 (1961).
19. United States v. Trans-Missouri Freight Assn., 166 U.S. 290, 312 (1897).
20. Oliver W. Holmes, Jr., "Privilege, Malice, and Intent," 8 *Harv. L. Rev.* 1, 8 (1894).
21. W. W. Montague & Co. v. Lowry, 193 U.S. 38 (1904). See James A. Emery, "Labor Organizations and the Sherman Law," 20 *J. Pol. Econ.* 599 (1912); Primm, note 13; Albert Kales, "Coercive and Competitive Methods in Trade and Labor Disputes," 8 *Cornell L. Q.* 128, 145 (1923).
22. John Mitchell, *Organized Labor* 283 (1903).
23. H. E. Hoagland, "Closed Shop versus Open Shop," 8 *Am. Econ. Rev.* 752 (1918); Howard T. Lewis, "The Economic Basis of the Fight for the Closed Shop," 20 *J. Pol. Econ.* (1912); 2 F. W. Taussig, *Principles of Economics* 304–305 (3d ed. 1922). See also Walter G. Merritt, "The Closed Shop," 195 *N. Am. Rev.* 66, 71–72 (1912), arguing that closed shops would yield "monopolistic prices."
24. Retail Lumber Dealers v. State, 49 So. 1021 (Miss. 1909) (state law); Jackson v. Stanfield, 137 Ind. 592 (1893) (state law); Eastern States Lumber Dealers v. United States, 234 U.S. 600 (1914) (federal antitrust law). Kales, note 21 at 128.
25. Folsom v. Lewis, 208 Mass. 336 (1911); Martineau v. Foley, 225 Mass. 107 (1916); Sarros v. Nouris, 15 Del. Ch. 391, 138 A. 607 (1927); Erdman v. Mitchell, 207 Pa. 79 (1903); Duplex Printing Press Co. v. Deering, 254 U.S. 443 (1921); Bedford Cut Stone Co. v. Journeymen Stone Cutters' Assn. of N. Am., 274 U.S. 37 (1927); Lohse Door Co. v. Fuelle, 215 Mo. 421 (1908)

(hot cargo strike); Booth v. Burgess, 72 N.J. Eq. 181 (1906) (same). See W. W. Montague & Co. v. Lowry, 193 U.S. 38 (1904) (condemning tile sellers' association's concerted refusal to deal with nonmembers).

26. For example, Loewe v. Lawlor, 208 U.S. 274 (1908) (enjoining threats and intimidation); O'Brien v. United States, 290 F. 185 (6th Cir. 1923) (enjoining threats and intimidation of nonemployees); Dail-Overland v. Willys-Overland, 263 F. 171 (N.D. Ohio 1919) (violence, intimidation); United States v. Cassidy, 67 F. 698 (N.D. Cal. 1895) (enjoining violence, intimidation, plus union members' seizure of employer's property); Williams v. United States, 295 U.S. 302 (1923) (putting quicksilver in locomotive boilers); Vandell v. United States, 6 F.2d 188 (2d Cir. 1925) (dynamiting of railroad tracks); United States v. Debs, 64 F. 724 (N.D. Ill. 1894) (violence, vandalism, intimidation of nonemployees).

27. United States v. Debs, 64 F. 724, 763 (N.D. Ill. 1894). On the extension of the Sherman Act beyond the common law, see John R. Commons & John B. Andrews, *Principles of Labor Legislation* 112–122 (3d ed. 1927); and see Bedford Cut Stone Co. v. Journeymen Stone Cutters' Assn. of N. Am., 274 U.S. 37, 58 (1927), Brandeis arguing in dissent that the Sherman Act must be interpreted by "principles of the common law."

28. Lowe v. Lawlor, 208 U.S. 274, 297 (1908) (Danbury hatters); Gompers v. Bucks, 221 U.S. 418, 439 (1911); Duplex Printing Press Co. v. Deering, 254 U.S. 443, 467–468, 478 (1921); Coronado Coal Co. v. United Mine Workers of Am., 268 U.S. 295, 310 (1925).

29. 1 Arthur Eddy, *The Law of Combinations, Embracing Monopolies, Trusts, and Combinations of Labor and Capital; Conspiracy, and Contracts in Restraint of Trade* 200 (1901), citing Oakdale Mfg. Co. v. Garst, 18 R.I. 484, 28 A. 973 (1894); Trenton Potteries Co. v. Olyphant, 43 A. 723 (1899). Arthur Eddy, *The New Competition* 50–54 (1914).

30. John R. Commons, *Legal Foundations of Capitalism* 296–298 (1924).

31. See Chapter 4; Santa Clara v. Southern Pacific R.R. Co., 118 U.S. 394 (1886) (holding that a corporation is a "person" under the fourteenth amendment).

32. See William E. Forbath, "The Ambiguities of Free Labor: Labor and the Law in the Gilded Age," 1985 *Wis. L. Rev.* 767 (1985).

33. Wolff Packing v. Court of Industrial Relations, 262 U.S. 522 (1923).

34. See Frederick H. Cooke, *The Law of Combinations, Monopolies, and Labor Unions* 105 n.13 (2d ed. 1909), noting the availability of incorporation for labor unions in many states; Louis D. Brandeis, "The Incorporation of Trade Unions," 15 *Green Bag* 11 (1903); Eugene Wambaugh, "Should Trade Unions be Incorporated?" 15 *Green Bag* 260 (1903).

35. See Pickett v. Walsh, 192 Mass. 572, 582–583, 78 N.E. 753, 760–761 (1906) (unincorporated trade union could not be sued, except in names of all individual members); Karges Furniture Co. v. Woodworkers' Local 131, 165 Ind. 421, 422–423, 75 N.E. 877, 878 (1905) (same). Some states passed statutes permitting unincorporated labor unions to be sued. See United States Heater Co. v. Iron Molders' Union, 129 Mich. 354, 88 N.W. 889

(1902) (applying statute permitting suit against unincorporated associations of five or more members).

36. In re Debs, 158 U.S. 564, 570 (1895). See Joseph Story, *Equity Pleadings* §§ 94, 97 (8th ed. 1870); Frankfurter & Greene, note 18 at 83–88 (including list of state statutes); Federal Equity Rule 38, promulgated Nov. 4, 1912, 226 U.S. 659 (1912).

37. United Mine Workers v. Coronado Co., 259 U.S. 344, 388–389 (1922). See Stanley I. Kutler, "Chief Justice Taft, Judicial Unanimity, and Labor: The Coronado Case," 24 *The Historian* 68 (1961); Kutler, "Chief Justice Taft and the Delusion of Judicial Exactness—A Study in Jurisprudence," 48 *Va. L. Rev.* 1407, 1410–1414 (1962).

38. Mitchell, note 22 at 230.

39. For example, Irving v. Neal, 209 F. 471 (S.D.N.Y. 1913). See Leo Wolman, *The Boycott in American Trade Unions* 50 (1916); Daniel Ernst, "The Woodtrim War: A Case Study in the History of Labor Activism, Antitrust Litigation, and Legal Culture, 1910–1917" (Institute for Legal Studies, Working Paper, 1988).

40. In addition to the decisions noted earlier, see the detailed discussion in William E. Forbath, "The Shaping of the American Labor Movement," 102 *Harv. L. Rev.* 1109, 1148–1158 (1989); and Herbert Hovenkamp, "Labor Conspiracies in American Law, 1880–1930," 66 *Tex. L. Rev.* 919 (1988).

41. James B. Thayer, "American Judges and the Interests of Labor," 5 *Q. J. Econ.* 503, 504 (1891); 2 Eddy, note 29 at 1155–1157. See also Francis M. Burdick, "Injunctions in Labor Disputes," 188 *N. Am. Rev.* 273 (1908); Howard T. Lewis, "The Peril of Anti-Injunction Legislation," 188 *N. Am. Rev.* 577 (1908).

42. 38 Stat. 780, §§ 6, 20 (1914); Samuel Gompers, "Editorial," 21 *Am. Federationist* 971 (1914); see also the Harvard labor economist Philip G. Wright, "The Contest in Congress between Organized Labor and Organized Business," 29 *Q. J. Econ.* 235, 235 (1914); Daniel Davenport, "An Analysis of the Labor Sections of the Clayton Anti-Trust Bill," 80 *Central L. J.* 46 (1915).

43. See Dallas L. Jones, "The Enigma of the Clayton Act," 10 *Industrial and Labor Relations Rev.* 201 (1957); Stanley I. Kutler, "Labor, the Clayton Act, and the Supreme Court," 3 *Labor History* 19 (1962).

44. On the ambiguous nature of the intended exemption, see Daniel Ernst, "The Labor Exemption, 1908–1914," 74 *Iowa L. Rev.* 1151 (1989).

45. Blindell v. Hagan, 54 F. 40, aff'd, 56 F. 696 (5th Cir. 1893); National Fireproofing Co. v. Mason Builders' Assn., 169 F. 259 (2d Cir. 1909).

46. *Paine*, 244 U.S. 459 (1917); Duplex Printing Press Co. v. Deering, 254 U.S. 443, 463–464, 470–472 (1921). See Berman, note 10 at 104–110; Alpheus Mason, "The Labor Clauses and the Clayton Act," 18 *Am. Pol. Sci. Rev.* 489, 512 (1924).

47. J. Stanley Christ, "The Federal Courts and Organized Labor," 5 *J. Bus.* 103, 283 (1932) at 104. See also Edwin E. Witte, *The Government in Labor Disputes* 84 (1932), which concluded that courts granted nearly every injunction requested.

20. American Merger Policy and the Failure of Corporate Law

1. See Ralph L. Nelson, *Merger Movements in American Industry, 1895–1956*, at 78–89 (1959); Stuart Bruchey, *Enterprise: The Dynamic Economy of a Free People*, ch. 11 (1990).
2. Adam Smith, *The Wealth of Nations*, bk. 1, ch. 1, pt. 3 (1776).
3. See United States v. American Can Co., 230 F. 859, 879 (D. Md. 1916), appeal dism'd, 256 U.S. 706 (1921); Charles E. Edgerton, "The Wire-Nail Association of 1895–1896 and Other Iron and Steel Pools," 12 *Pol. Sci. Q.* 246 (1897).
4. See Charles Hoffman, *The Depression of the Nineties: An Economic History* 9–42 (1970).
5. See Harold C. Livesay & Patrick G. Porter, "Vertical Integration in American Manufacturing, 1899–1948," 29 *J. Econ. Hist.* 494 (1969).
6. See Nelson, note 1 at 37 (counting 3,238 mergers during the period 1895–1905); Naomi R. Lamoreaux, *The Great Merger Movement in American Business, 1895–1904* (1985); Conant, "Industrial Consolidations in the United States," 7 *Q. Pub. Am. Statistical Assn.* (n.s.) 1 (1901).
7. For example, Martin J. Sklar, *The Corporate Reconstruction of American Capitalism, 1890–1916*, at 159–163 (1988); Gabriel Kolko, *The Triumph of Conservatism: A Reinterpretation of American History, 1900–1916* (1967); Thomas K. McCraw, "Rethinking the Trust Question" 1, in *Regulation in Perspective: Historical Essays* (T. K. McCraw ed. 1981); Nelson, note 1 at 89–100, 106–126.
8. United States v. E. C. Knight Co., 156 U.S. 1 (1895). George Bittlingmayer, "Did Antitrust Policy Cause the Great Merger Wave?" 28 *J. L. & Econ.* 77 (1985); John J. Binder, "The Sherman Antitrust Act and the Railroad Cartels," 31 *J. L. & Econ.* 443 (1988). Contemporary arguments for this position include George F. Canfield, "Is a Large Corporation an Illegal Combination or Monopoly under the Sherman Anti-Trust Act?" 9 *Col. L. Rev.* 95, 113 n.27 (1909) (Sherman Act "fosters the very thing it was designed to check"; if the act were amended to condemn only "unreasonable" agreements among competitors, firms such as the Northern Securities Company and United States Steel would not have to merge as an alternative); Francis Walker, "The Law concerning Monopolistic Combinations in Continental Europe," 20 *Pol. Sci. Q.* 13, 39 (1905). But see Nelson, note 1 at 89–100, 106–126 (noting that *Addyston Pipe*, which can best be credited with encouraging firms to merge rather than to collude, occurred in the middle of the great merger wave).
9. Bureau of Corporations, *Annual Report* 5 (1980). See Robert L. Raymond, "The Federal Antitrust Act," 23 *Harv. L. Rev.* 353, 376–377 (1910); J. D. Forrest, "Anti-Monopoly Legislation in the United States," 1 *Am. J. Soc.* 411, 424 (1896); Edward B. Whitney, "Constitutional Questions under the Federal Anti-Trust Law," 7 *Yale L. J.* 285 (1898); Bureau of Corporations, James Weinstein, *The Corporate Ideal in the Liberal State, 1900–1918*, at 63–68 (1968).

10. See Herbert Pope, "The Legal Aspect of Monopoly," 20 *Harv. L. Rev.* 167, 181 (1907).

11. Walter C. Noyes, *A Treatise on the Law of Intercorporate Relations* 812–813 (2d ed. 1909).

12. See Charles R. McCurdy, "The Knight Sugar Decision of 1895 and the Modernization of American Corporation Law, 1869–1903," 53 *Bus. Hist. Rev.* 304, 322 (1979); Hans B. Thorelli, *The Federal Antitrust Policy: Origination of an American Tradition* 265, 595 (1955).

13. See James May, "Antitrust Practice and Procedure in the Formative Era: The Constitutional and Conceptual Reach of State Antitrust Law, 1880–1918," 135 *Pa. L. Rev.* 495, 501–504 (1987); Steven L. Piott, *The Anti-Monopoly Persuasion: Popular Resistance to the Rise of Big Business in the Midwest* 4 (1985).

14. United States v. Union Pacific R.R. Co., 226 U.S. 61 (1912).

15. United States v. E. C. Knight Co., 156 U.S. 1, 16 (1895); United States v. Joint-Traffic Assn., 171 U.S. 505, 567 (1898).

16. See Lincoln Steffans, "New Jersey: A Traitor State," 25 *McClure's Magazine* 41 (1905); S. McReynolds, "The Home of the Trusts," 4 *The World's Work* 2526 (1902); *Bank of Augusta*, 38 U.S. (13 Pet.) 519, 588 (1839). See Iowa Code § 5060 (1897); Illinois Laws 1891, § 1 at 206 (Starr & Curtis ed., 1896).

17. See Seymour D. Thompson, *Abuses of Corporate Privilege, Reports of the Ninth Annual Meeting of the Bar Assn. of the State of Kansas* 43 (1892); Thompson, "Notes of Recent Decisions," 29 *Am. L. Rev.* 293 (1895); Theodore Dwight, "The Legality of 'Trusts,'" 3 *Pol. Sci. Q.* 592 (1888).

18. Northern Securities Co. v. United States, 193 U.S. 197, 406, 411 (1904).

19. Robert H. Bork, *The Antitrust Paradox: A Policy at War with Itself*, chs. 1 & 2 (1978); Bork, "Legislative Intent and the Policy of the Sherman Act," 9 *J. L. & Econ.* (1966); Robert S. Lande, "Wealth Transfers as the Original and Primary Concern of Antitrust: the Efficiency Interpretation Challenged," 34 *Hastings L. J.* 65 (1982); Hovenkamp, "Antitrust's Protected Classes," 88 *Mich. L. Rev.* 1 (1989).

20. See Jack Blicksilver, *Defenders and Defense of Big Business in the United States, 1880–1900*, at 122–128 (1985).

21. See Melvin I. Urofsky, "Proposed Federal Incorporation in the Progressive Era," 26 *Am. J. Leg. Hist.* 160 (1982); Sklar, note 7 at 228–285.

22. People v. North River Sugar Refining Co., 3 N.Y. Supp. 401, 409–413 (Cir. Ct., New York County, 1889); 121 N.Y. 582, 626, 24 N.E. 834 (1889). The approach was criticized by Edward A. Harriman, "Voting Trusts and Holding Companies," 13 *Yale L. J.* 109 (1904), who argued that stock trusts should be legal in themselves but subject to the law of combinations in restraint of trade.

23. For example, Attorney General ex rel. Wolverine Fish Co. v. A. Booth & Co., 143 Mich. 89, 102, 106 N.W. 868, 872 (1906); State ex rel. Hadley v. Standard Oil Co., 218 Mo. 1, 378–379, 116 S.W. 902, 1018–1019 (1908), aff'd, 224 U.S. 270 (1912). See Western Union Telegraph Co. v. Kansas, 216 U.S. 1 (1910).

24. State v. Standard Oil Co., 49 Ohio St. 137, 184 (1892). On the Ohio decree, and the subsequent reconstruction of Standard as a New Jersey holding company, see Bruce Bringhurst, *Antitrust and the Oil Monopoly: The Standard Oil Cases, 1890–1911*, at 10–39 (1979); 2 Allan Nevins, *Study in Power: John D. Rockefeller, Industrialist and Philanthropist* 223–230 (1953); Peter Collier & David Horowitz, *The Rockefellers: An American Dynasty* 29–33 (1976).

25. Elisha Andrews, "Trusts According to Official Investigations," 3 *Q. J. Econ.* 117, 131–136 (1889). Reported decisions relating to the cottonseed oil litigation include: State v. American Cotton-Seed Oil Trust, 40 La. Ann. 8, 3 S. 409 (1888); Louisiana v. American Cotton Oil Trust, 1 Ry. & Corp. L.J. 509 (La. Civ. Dist. Ct. 1887); and see Thorelli, note 12 at 79 & nn.87–89.

26. People v. North River Sugar Refining Co., 121 N.Y. 582, 623–626, 24 N.E. 834 (1890); see also State v. Standard Oil Co., 49 Ohio St. 137, 185 (1892) (Ohio corporate law "requires that a corporation should be controlled and managed by its directors in the interest of its own stockholders").

27. For example, Bishop v. American Preservers Co., 157 Ill. 284, 41 N.E. 765 (1895) (corporation had no implied power to enter partnership with other corporations); American Preservers Trust v. Taylor Mfg. Co., 46 F. 152 (C.C.E.D. Mo. 1891) (same); Mallory v. Hanaur Oil Works, 86 Tenn. 598 (1888) (same; cottonseed oil trust case). See also Gould v. Head, 38 F. 886 (D. Colo. 1889), rev'd on other grounds, 41 F. 240 (C.C.D. Colo. 1890) (unlawful delegation of corporate powers to trustees; American cattle trust case).

28. State v. Standard Oil Co., 49 Ohio St. 137 (1892). See Thomas C. Spelling, *A Treatise on Trusts and Monopolies* 181 (1893).

29. 2 William W. Cook, *A Treatise on the Law of Corporations Having a Capital Stock* § 503a at 915–916 (4th ed. 1898); Ernst von Halle, *Trusts, or Industrial Combinations and Coalitions in the United States* 94 (1900).

30. Noyes, note 11 at 202; Louis Boisot, "The Legality of Trust Combinations," 39 *Am. L. Reg.* (n.s. 30) 751, 760 (1891).

31. Leathers v. Janney, 41 La. Ann. 1120 (1889); see also Holmes & Griggs Mfg. Co. v. Holmes & Wessell Metal Co., 127 N.Y. 252 (1891); Ardesco Oil Co. v. North Am. Oil & Mining Co., 66 Pa. St. 375 (1870); Treadwell v. Salisbury Mfg. Co., 7 Gray 393, 404 (Mass. 1856). See Noyes, note 11 at 204.

32. *North River*, 121 N.Y. 582, 624, 24 N.E. 834, 840, referring to New York Corporate Laws of 1884, ch. 367.

33. See Thomas R. Navin & Marian V. Sears, "The Rise of a Market for Industrial Securities, 1887–1902," 29 *Bus. Hist. Rev.* 105, 107, 109–110 (1955).

34. 49 La. Ann. 303, 21 S. 515 (1897). Noyes, note 11 at 207–208. The "business judgment" rule reinforced this power in the directors. See Chapter 6.

35. See Noyes, note 11 at 320. For example, Pennsylvania R.R. Co. v. St. Louis, Alton & Terre Haute R.R. Co., 118 U.S. 290, 309 (1885); Thomas v. Railroad Co., 101 U.S. 71 (1879). See Central Transportation Co. v. Pullman

Palace Car Co., 139 U.S. 24, 50 (1891), applying the *Pennsylvania Railroad* rule, but only because the Pullman Company, which manufactured and leased passenger cars, was not an ordinary manufacturer.

36. Noyes, note 11 at 202.

37. On the collateral transactions rule, see Chapter 25; and 1 Victor Morawetz, *A Treatise on the Law of Private Corporations* § 364 at 349, 373 (2d ed. 1886). See also Waldo v. Chicago R.R. Co., 14 Wis. 575 (1861) (railroad could not acquire real estate not along its right of way merely to increase its assets); Toll Bridge Co. v. Osborn, 35 Conn. 7 (1868) (toll bridge company may not operate a wharf for profit).

38. For example, Central Transportation Co. v. Pullman Palace Car Co., 139 U.S. 24 (1890) (condemning restrictive covenant in ninety-nine-year lease of sleeping cars under which lessor promised not to compete in sleeping-car business); Gamewell Fire-Alarm Co. v. Crane, 160 Mass. 50, 35 N.E. 98 (1893) (condemning general noncompetition agreement attending sale of patent); Strait v. National Harrow Co., 18 N.Y. Supp. 224, 231–233 (N.Y.S.Ct. 1891) (condemning noncompetition agreement attending patent acquisition and covering the entire United States except Montana). Similar cases include Western Wooden-Ware Assn. v. Starkey, 84 Mich. 76 (1890); Richardson v. Buhl, 77 Mich. 632, 43 N.W. 1102 (1889); Bishop v. Palmer, 146 Mass. 469 (1888).

39. 106 N.Y. 473, 13 N.E. 419 (1887). Other decisions upholding asset acquisitions, noncompetition agreements notwithstanding, include: United States Chemical Co. v. Provident Chemical Co., 64 F. 946 (E.D. Mo. 1894) (upholding acquisition with nationwide noncompetition agreement); Trenton Potteries Co. v. Olyphant, 58 N.J. Eq. 507 (1899) (upholding acquisition plus fifty-year noncompetition agreement); National Benefit Co. v. Union Hospital Co., 45 Minn. 272 (1891) (same); Diamond Match Co. v. Roeber, 106 N.Y. 473 (1887) (same).

40. Alfred D. Chandler, Jr., *The Visible Hand: The Managerial Revolution in American Business* 315–344 (1977). See United States v. American Can Co., 230 F. 859, 879 (D. Md. 1916), app. dism'd, 256 U.S. 706 (1921); United States v. Corn Products Refining Co., 234 F. 964 (S.D.N.Y. 1916), app. dism'd, 249 U.S. 621 (1918). See Chapter 23.

41. People ex rel. Peabody v. Chicago Gas Trust Co., 130 Ill. 268, 283, 22 N.E. 798, 800 (1889). See Frenkel v. Hudston, 82 Ala. 158, 2 S. 758 (1887); Coffin v. Ransdell, 110 Ind. 417, 11 N.E. 20 (1887). One important exception to this rule was that if the shareholders in the corporation selling the assets agreed unanimously to the sale, the corporation could take the shares of the purchasing corporation as consideration and distribute them immediately to the shareholders. Thus to the extent that asset acquisitions involved closely held corporations, or corporations with a small number of shareholders, payment could effectively be made in the shares of the purchasing corporation. See Noyes, note 11 at 228–229, 571.

42. McCutcheon v. Merz Capsule Co., 71 F. 787, 792 (6th Cir. 1896). Judge Lurton wrote the opinion. Judge Taft was on the panel.

43. Richardson v. Buhl, 77 Mich. 632, 43 N.W. 1102 (1889). 1 Arthur J. Eddy, *The Law of Combinations, Embracing Monopolies, Trusts, and Combinations of Labor and Capital; Conspiracy, and Contracts in Restraint of Trade* 616 (1901).

44. For example, when the Illinois Supreme Court condemned the glucose combination in 1899, it relied on Illinois's recently passed antitrust statute, as well as state corporate law. See Harding v. American Glucose Co., 182 Ill. 551, 615, 55 N.E. 577, 598, 620–621, 623–624 (1899). See also Boisot, note 30.

45. Bank of Augusta v. Earle, 38 U.S. (13 Pet.) 519, 588 (1839); *Paul*, 75 U.S. (8 Wall.) 168 (1869). See Alton D. Adams "State Control of Trusts," 18 *Pol. Sci. Q.* 462 (1903); 1 Morawetz, note 37 at 930–931.

46. See the diatribe by the muckraker Lincoln Steffans: "New Jersey: A Traitor State," 25 *McClure's Magazine* 41 (1905). See also People ex rel. Peabody v. Chicago Trust Gas Co., 130 Ill. 268 (1889); Valley Ry. Co. v. Lake Erie Iron Co., 46 Ohio St. 44 (1888). The rule excepted stock acquired in payment of a preexisting debt and corporations in the business of buying and selling stock, such as brokerage houses. National Bank of Jefferson v. Texas Investment Co., 74 Tex. 421 (1889). On Maryland law, see Booth v. Robinson, 55 Md. 433, 434–435 (1880).

47. *Laws of New Jersey* 344 (1866); *Laws of New Jersey* 385 (1888); *Laws of New Jersey* 265, § 4 1889; *Laws of New Jersey* 329 (1891); *Laws of New Jersey* 301 (1893). Finally, in 1897, New Jersey passed a statute denying jurisdiction to its courts to entertain liability actions against corporate officers, if the cause of action arose under the law of a different state. *Laws of New Jersey* 124 (1897). See Edward A. Keasbey, "New Jersey and the Great Corporations," 13 *Harv. L. Rev.* 198, 204 (1899); Harold W. Stoke, "Economic Influences upon the Corporation Laws of New Jersey," 38 *J. Pol. Econ.* 551 (1930).

48. See William H. S. Stevens, *Industrial Combinations and Trusts* 67–80 (1913), on holding-company provisions of New York (1892), Delaware (1899), and Maine (1901); 19 *Reports of the Industrial Commission* 598–599 (1900); Raymond Zilmer, "State Laws: Survival of the Unfit," 62 *U. Pa. L. Rev.* 509 (1914); James B. Dill, "National Incorporation Law for Trusts," 11 *Yale L. J.* 273 (1902). Dill was author of the New Jersey holding-company statute. See also Urofsky, note 21 at 164, noting that 41 states passed holding-company acts; McCurdy, note 12 at 322–323; Sklar, note 7 at 46 (170 out of 236 holding companies formed by 1898 used New Jersey law).

49. For example, McCurdy, note 12 at 330–332.

50. See Glenn Porter & Harold C. Livesay, *Merchants and Manufacturers: A Study in the Changing Structure of Nineteenth-Century Marketing* (1971); Charles R. McCurdy, "American Law and the Marketing Structure of the Large Corporation, 1875–1890," 38 *J. Econ. Hist.* 631 (1978).

51. Charles F. Bostwick, *Legislative Competition for Corporate Capital* 2 (1899).

52. See Frederick H. Cooke, *The Law of Combinations, Monopolies, and Labor Unions* 422–423 (2d ed. 1909).

53. For example, Stockton ex rel. New Jersey v. Central R.R., 50 N.J. Eq. 52 (1892); Stockton ex rel. New Jersey v. American Tobacco Co., 55 N.J. Eq. 352 (1897), aff'd, 56 N.J. Eq. 847 (1898).

54. Zilmer, note 48. On child labor and the problem of state free-riding, see Stephen B. Wood, *Constitutional Politics in the Progressive Era: Child Labor and the Law* (1968).

55. Lancaster v. Amsterdam Improvement Co., 140 N.Y. 576, 583, 35 N.E. 964, 965 (1894).

56. Rogers v. Nashville R.R., 91 F. 299, 312 (6th Cir. 1898).

57. Noyes, note 11 at 522; see also 1 Eddy, note 43 at 602–603 ("[U]nless these various conditions and limitations are specified in advance of the creation of the corporation, the legislature in a very large measure loses its power to afterwards make restrictions and limitations"); 4 Seymour D. Thompson, *Commentaries on the Law of Private Corporations* § 4100 (2d. ed. 1909) (shareholders have absolute right to transfer shares "unless the transfer is restrained by the charter . . .") (citing many cases).

58. See Marble Co. v. Harvey, 92 Tenn. 119, 20 S.W. 427 (1897); National Cotton Oil Co. v. Texas, 197 U.S. 115 (1905).

59. McCurdy, "Knight Sugar," note 12 at 334, 331.

60. United States v. E. C. Knight Co., 60 F. 306, 307 (C.C.E.D. Pa. 1894) ("[T]he American Sugar Refining Company entered into contracts . . . with the stockholders of each of the Philadelphia corporations named, whereby it purchased their stock, paying therefor by transfers of stock in its company . . .").

61. See 4 Thompson, note 57 at § 4100, citing many cases. And see Morgan v. Struthers, 131 U.S. 246, 252 (1888) (common law diversity case; "[o]ne essential feature of an incorporated joint stock company is the right of each stockholder, without restraint, to sell or transfer his shares at pleasure").

62. See Edward S. Corwin, *The Twilight of the Supreme Court* 20 (1934); Arnold M. Paul, *Conservative Crisis and the Rule of Law: Attitudes of Bar and Bench, 1887–1895,* at 182–183 (1960). Some contemporary critics of *E. C. Knight* also argued that the decision created a regulatory vacuum permitting trusts to develop free of both federal and state control. See Ardemus Stewart, "Recent Decisions," 43 *Am. L. Reg.* 88 (1895); Thompson, "Notes," note 17 at 306.

63. Noyes, note 11 at 811–812, citing Bigelow v. Calumet & Hecla Mining Co., 155 F. 869, 876 (W.D. Mich. 1907) ("The result of these two statutes [the state holding-company act and the state antitrust statute] is that power was given . . . to purchase stock . . . but the right to exercise that power in violation of the anti-monopoly statutes of the state was not given").

64. 1 Christopher Tiedeman, *A Treatise on State and Federal Control of Persons and Property in the United States* 609–610 (2d ed. 1900).

65. 1 Eddy, note 43 at 600–603, 929.

66. In re Greene, 52 F. 104 (S.D. Ohio 1892).

67. *E. C. Knight,* 156 U.S. at 13, 17.

68. 193 U.S. 197, 362 (1904). Chief Justice Fuller and Justices Holmes, Peckham, and White dissented. On the decision, see Sir Frederick Pollock, "The Merger Case and Restraint of Trade," 17 *Harv. L. Rev.* 151 (1904).

69. *Northern Securities,* 193 U.S. at 403–404. Holmes continued: "A partnership is not a contract or combination in restraint of trade between the partners

unless the well known words are to be given a new meaning invented for the purposes of this act." Id. at 410.

70. Victor Morawetz, "The Anti-Trust Act and the Merger Case," 17 *Harv. L. Rev.* 533, 534, 538, 542 (1904); Herbert Pope, "The Legal Aspect of Monopoly," 20 *Harv. L. Rev.* 167, 183–185 (1907).

71. Canfield, note 8 at 101. See also Christopher C. Langdell, "The Northern Securities Case under A New Aspect," 17 *Harv. L. Rev.* 41 (1904); J.C.G. [almost certainly the Harvard law professor John Chipman Gray], "The Merger Case," 17 *Harv. L. Rev.* 474 (1904) (arguing that *Northern Securities* decision was tantamount to condemning two people for forming a partnership).

72. Pollock, note 68 at 154; Harriman v. Northern Securities Company, 197 U.S. 244, 299 (1905); Noyes, note 11 at 695. See also G. C. Todd, "The Federal Anti-trust Act and Minority Holdings of the Shares of Railroads by Competing Companies," 22 *Harv. L. Rev.* 114, 115 (1908).

73. See Canfield, note 8 at 107.

74. United States v. Union Pacific R.R. Co., 226 U.S. 61, 86 (1912).

75. Missouri Session Acts of 1891, p. 186, § 2; Arkansas Anti-Trust Act of March 16, 1897, § 2. The original antitrust statutes of Arkansas, California, Indiana, Iowa, Kansas, Kentucky, Louisiana, Michigan, Minnesota, Mississippi, Missouri, Nebraska, North Carolina, North Dakota, Tennessee, Texas, Utah, and Wisconsin included charter forfeiture penalties. See Noyes, note 11 at 846 & n.1. See also J. Davies, *Trust Laws and Unfair Competition* 213 (1916), noting that by 1916 thirty states had passed similar provisions.

76. For example, Georgia Anti-Monopoly Act, § 2 (Dec. 23, 1896). Such provisions were upheld in Waters-Pierce Oil Co. v. Texas, 177 U.S. 28 (1900) and Hammond Packing Co. v. Arkansas, 212 U.S. 322 (1909).

77. See Harding v. American Glucose Co., 182 Ill. 551, 620–621, 623–624, 55 N.E. 577, 601–602 (1899).

78. Von Halle, note 29 at 95. Von Halle also noted that taxation laws had become more favorable to foreign corporations. Id., citing William W. Cook, *The Corporation Problem* 102–107 (1891).

79. Cook, *Corporation Problem*, note 78 at 245; Sklar, note 7 at 190–191.

80. Thomas C. Spelling, *A Treatise on Trusts and Monopolies* 220 (1893).

81. Charles F. Beach, Sr., *A Treatise on the Law of Monopolies and Industrial Trusts* 600–679 (1898); Noyes, note 11 at 762–853 (2d ed. 1909); Cooke, note 52 at 384–453.

21. The Classical Theory of Competition

1. Robert H. Bork, *The Antitrust Paradox: A Policy at War with Itself* 20 (1978).

2. For example, Thomas Arthur, "Farewell to the Sea of Doubt: Jettisoning the Constitutional Sherman Act," 74 *Calif. L. Rev.* 263 (1986).

3. See P. S. Atiyah, *The Rise and Fall of Freedom of Contract* (1979).

4. Alfred Marshall & Mary Paley Marshall, *The Economics of Industry* 2 (2d ed. 1881).

5. Alfred Marshall, *Principles of Economics* (1890).
6. Most notably Arthur Cecil Pigou, *The Economics of Welfare* (1920).
7. See Herbert Hovenkamp, "The First Great Law & Economics Movement," 42 *Stan. L. Rev.* 993 (1990).
8. The institutional developments of this transition are traced in Mary O. Furner, *Advocacy and Objectivity: A Crisis in the Professionalization of American Social Science, 1865–1905* (1975).
9. The best of these is Morton J. Horwitz, *The Transformation of American Law, 1780–1860* (1977).
10. The narrowness of explicit public policy rationales in common law decision making can be seen in a treatise such as Elisha Greenhood's *The Doctrine of Public Policy in the Law of Contracts, Reduced to Rules* (1886). Greenhood recognized only fraud, contracts to commit crimes, wagers, contracts affecting public officers, contracts promoting corruption, champerty, contracts affecting personal liberty, contracts affecting domestic relations, contracts waiving legal rights, contracts affecting public laws, and contracts in restraint of trade as being limited by public policy considerations.
11. Richardson v. Mellish, 2 Bing. 229, 252 (Ct. Com. Pl. 1824).
12. William W. Story, *A Treatise on the Law of Contracts Not under Seal* § 546 (2d ed. 1847).
13. License Tax Cases, 72 U.S. (5 Wall.) 462, 468 (1866).
14. Charles F. Beach, Sr., *A Treatise on the Law of Monopolies and Industrial Trusts* 107 (1898); Greenhood, note 10 at 684: For recognition of the unique expression of public policy concerns in the English law of contracts in restraint of trade, see 8 William Holdsworth, *A History of English Law* 56 (2d ed. 1937); Roland R. Foulke, "Restraints on Trade," 12 *Col. L. Rev.* 97, 105 (1912).
15. On "competition" in the classical tradition, see George Stigler, "Perfect Competition, Historically Contemplated," 65 *J. Pol. Econ.* 1 (1957). On "monopoly" at English and American common law, see William Letwin, *Law and Economic Policy in America: The Evolution of the Sherman Antitrust Act* 19–39 (1965).
16. Francis A. Walker, *Political Economy* 91–92 (3d ed. 1888).
17. Arthur T. Hadley, *Economics: An Account of the Relations between Private Property and Public Welfare* 64–83 (1896). See Erich Sreissler, "To What Extent Was the Austrian School Marginalist?" 160, in *The Marginal Revolution in Economics* (R. D. C. Black, A. W. Coats, C. D. W. Goodwin, eds., 1973). The Austrian economist whom Hadley relied on most was Friedrich von Wieser, particularly his *Natural Value* (Malloch trans.) (London 1893).
18. John Bates Clark, *The Distribution of Wealth* 58–78, 390–393 (1899).
19. For example, Bohn Mfg. Co. v. Hollis, 54 Minn. 223, 234 (1893) (wholesale lumber dealer who sold lumber directly to consumers not entitled to enjoin retail lumber dealers' association requirement forbidding members to deal with such wholesalers); Central Shade Roller Co. v. Cushman, 143 Mass. 353, 9 N.E. 629 (1887) (refusing to condemn incorporated association of curtain fixture manufactures designed to limit output and raise prices).

Many other cases are discussed in Herbert Hovenkamp, "The Sherman Act and the Classical Theory of Competition," 74 *Iowa L. Rev.* 1019 (1989).

20. Albert Stickney, *State Control of Trade and Commerce by National or State Authority* 157 (1897).

21. See Beach, note 14 at 121–123; Albert Kales, "Contracts to Refrain from Doing Business or from Entering or Carrying on an Occupation," 31 *Harv. L. Rev.* 193, 198 (1917).

22. English cases: *Mitchel*, 1 P. Wms. 181, 24 Eng. Rep. 347 (K.B. 1711); *Hitchcock*, 1 P. Wms. at 182, 24 Eng. Rep. at 348; 6 Adol. & E. 454, 112 Eng. Rep. 167 (K.B. 1837). American cases: McCurry v. Gibson, 108 Ala. 451, 456, 18 S. 806, 808 (1895) ("It was, at an early day, supposed that the consideration in such cases must be adequate—that is, equal in value to the restraint imposed . . ."); Pierce v. Fuller, 8 Mass. 223 (1811) (upholding naked covenant not to compete given for recited consideration of $1.00); Hubbard v. Miller, 27 Mich. 15, 25 (1873). Some courts continued to examine consideration more closely if the case involved a contract in restraint of trade. For example, Chapin v. Brown Brothers, 83 Ia. 156 (1891) refused to enforce a grocers' agreement to abandon the butter-retailing business and give it all to a single firm.

23. Navigation Co. v. Winsor, 87 U.S. (20 Wall.) 64, 68 (1873) (upholding ten-year covenant not to compete in steamship route).

24. Beach, note 14 at 107–108, citing Alger v. Thatcher, 19 Pick. (36 Mass.) 51, 54 (1837).

25. See John C. Peppin, "Price-Fixing Agreements under the Sherman Antitrust Law," 28 *Cal. L. Rev.* 297 (1940).

26. National Benefit Co. v. Union Hospital Co., 45 Minn. 272, 276 (1891). On the tendency of Gilded Age courts to confuse the types of agreements, see Herbert Pope, "The Legal Aspect of Monopoly," 20 *Harv. L. Rev.* 167 (1907).

27. Northern Securities Co. v. United States, 193 U.S. 197, 403–408 (1904) (Holmes, J., dissenting).

28. Letter of April 1910, 1 *Holmes-Pollock Letters* 163 (M. D. Howe ed. 1961).

29. 2 Arthur J. Eddy, *The Law of Combinations, Embracing Monopolies, Trusts, and Combinations of Labor and Capital; Conspiracy, and Contracts in Restraint of Trade* § 657 at 673, 674 (1901).

30. Frederick H. Cooke, *The Law of Combinations, Monopolies, and Labor Unions* 310–311 (1898; 2d ed. 1909), citing Kellogg v. Larkin, 3 Pinney 123 (Wisc. 1851); and Greenhood, note 10 at 709. Cooke also criticized Downing v. Lewis, 59 Neb. 38, 80 N.W. 261 (1899) (upholding monopoly-creating covenant not to compete in laundry business, because it was confined to a single city); San Diego Water Co. v. San Diego Flume Co., 108 Cal. 549, 41 P. 495 (1895) (upholding waterworks service division agreement because it was limited to a single city).

31. *Skrainka*, 8 Mo. App. 522, 527 (1880). See also Kales, note 21 at 205 ("the courts have made no distinction, so far as the legality . . . is concerned, between the case where the sale is to a competitor and where it is not").

32. English: Prugnell v. Gosse, Aleyn 67, 82 Eng. Rep. 919 (K.B. 1648). Amer-

ican: *Skrainka,* note 31; Lange v. Werk, 2 Ohio St. 519, 531 (1853); Dunlop v. Gregory, 10 N.Y. 241 (1851); Union Strawboard Co. v. Bonfield, 193 Ill. 421, 427, 61 N.E. 1038, 1040 (1901). Kales, note 21 at 202.

33. In re Corning, 51 F. 205, 211 (D. Ohio 1892) (dismissing indictment because defendants acted "without any attempt at any time, by contract, to control the production of the other distilleries"); In re Terrell, 51 F. 213, 215 (C.C.S.D.N.Y. 1892); In re Greene, 52 F. 104 (C.C.S.D. Ohio 1892) (whiskey trust); United States v. Patterson, 55 F. 605, 606, 641 (C.C.D. Mass. 1893) (cash register trust).

34. Diamond Match Co. v. Roeber, 106 N.Y. 473, 13 N.E. 419, 483 (1887).

35. Leslie v. Lorillard, 110 N.Y. 519, 534 (1888); Wood v. Whitehead Bros., 165 N.Y. 545, 551 (1901). See also Brett v. Ebel, 29 App. Div. 256 (N.Y. 1898).

36. English: *Mitchel,* 1 P. Wms. 181, 24 Eng. Rep. 347 (K.B. 1711); Alsopp v. Wheatcroft, [1872] L.R., 15 Eq. 59 (striking down contract because space limitation went beyond protection of party); Ward v. Byrne, 5 M. & W. 547, 151 Eng. Rep. 232 (Ex. 1839) (striking down contract limited as to time but restraining competition in all of England). American: Bishop v. Palmer, 146 Mass. 469, 16 N.E. 299 (1888) (striking down a covenant unlimited as to space); Brewer v. Marshall, 4 Green 537 (N.J. 1868) (same).

37. Nordenfelt v. Maxim-Nordenfelt Guns & Ammunition Co., [1894] A.C. 535 (upholding covenant unlimited as to space and lasting for the life of the promisor); Oakdale Mfg. Co. v. Garst, 18 R.I. 484, 488 (1894). See also Tode v. Gross, 127 N.Y. 480 (1891) (upholding a noncompetition clause attending sale of cheese factory, apparently unlimited as to territory).

38. 2 Eddy, note 29 at 818–851; Cooke, note 30 at 222–234 (3d ed. 1909); Theodore W. Dwight, "The Legality of 'Trusts,'" 3 *Pol. Sci. Q.* 592, 610–611 (1888).

39. See Sampson v. Shaw, 101 Mass. 145 (1869) (condemning concerted effort to exclude others from wheat market); Indiana Bagging Assn. v. Kock, 14 La. Ann. 164 (1849) (condemning concerted effort not to sell bagging, except with consent of majority); Stanton v. Allen, 5 Denio (N.Y.) 434 (1848). Contrast Dolph v. Troy Laundry Machinery Co., 28 F. 553, 555 (C.C.S.D.N.Y 1886), refusing to condemn a cartel because the parties "did not contemplate suppressing the manufacture or sale of machines by others." The fact that there were plenty of other "mechanics" able to make the machines would "effectually counteract any serious mischief likely to arise from the attempt of the parties to get exorbitant prices . . . ." Others are discussed in Hovenkamp, "Sherman Act," note 19.

40. United States v. Nelson, 52 F. 646, 647 (D. Minn. 1892).

41. Northern Securities Co. v. United States, 193 U.S. 197, 405 (1904).

42. For example, Seeligson v. Taylor Compress Co., 56 Tex. 219 (1882).

43. Letwin, note 15 at 95–99; Hans B. Thorelli, *The Federal Antitrust Policy: Origination of an American Tradition* 228 (1955); Bork, note 1 at 36–47.

44. People v. Sheldon, 139 N.Y. 251, 261 (1893); De Witt Wire-Cloth Co. v. New Jersey Wire-Cloth Co., 14 N.Y.Supp. 277 (Com. Pl. N.Y. 1891).

45. For example Nester v. Continental Brewing Co., 161 Pa. 473, 29 A. 102

(1894); Judd v. Harrington, 139 N.Y. 105, 34 N.E. 790 (1893); More v. Bennett, 140 Ill. 69 (1892).

46. United States v. Trans-Missouri Freight Assn., 166 U.S. 290 (1897); Cincinnati, Portsmouth, Big Sandy & Pomeroy Packet Co. v. Bay, 200 U.S. 179 (1906); Shawnee Compress Co. v. Anderson, 209 U.S. 423 (1908); Davis v. Booth, 131 F. 31, 37 (6th Cir. 1907) (upholding noncompetition clause in fish-vending business, where seller retained no interest in the business); United States v. Addyston Pipe & Steel Co., 85 F. 271 (6th Cir. 1898), modified and aff'd, 175 U.S. 211 (1899).

47. For example, Bork, note 1 at 26–30.

48. 85 F. at 281.

49. For example, Dolph v. Troy Laundry Machinery Co., 28 F. 553 (C.C.S.D.N.Y. 1886); Central Shade Roller Co. v. Cushman, 143 Mass. 353, 9 N.E. 629 (1887).

50. For example, United States v. Nelson, 52 F. 646, 647 (D. Minn. 1892) (Sherman Act case upholding price-fixing agreement); Dolph v. Troy Laundry Machinery Co., 28 F. 553 (C.C.S.D.N.Y. 1886) (upholding price-fixing and pooling agreement); Clark v. Frank, 17 Mo. App. 602 (1885) (same); Skrainka v. Scharringhausen 8 Mo. App. 522, 527 (1880) (upholding price-fixing agreement because it was limited as to time and place); Pierce v. Fuller, 8 Mass. 223 (1811) (upholding naked covenant not to compete given for recited consideration of $1.00).

51. For example, Gloucester Isinglass & Glue Co. v. Russia Cement Co., 154 Mass. 92, 27 N.E. 1005 (1891) (combination in restraint of trade legal, since it did not involve article of prime necessity); Leslie v. Lorillard, 110 N.Y. 519, 18 N.E. 363 (1888) (refusing to condemn a naked agreement not to compete); Central Shade Roller Co. v. Cushman, 143 Mass. 353, 9 N.E. 629 (1887) (disagreeing with proposition that contracts in restraint can be legal if they do not involve articles of prime necessity). Others are discussed in Hovenkamp, "Sherman Act," note 19.

52. For example, Milwaukee Masons & Builders Assn. v. Niezerowski, 95 Wis. 129, 70 N.W. 166 (1897); People v. Sheldon, 139 N.Y. 251, 34 N.E. 785 (1893); More v. Bennett, 140 Ill. 69, 29 N.E. 888 (1892); Vulcan Powder Co. v. Hercules Powder Co., 96 Cal. 510, 31 P. 581 (1892).

53. Chapin v. Brown, 83 Iowa 156, 48 N.W. 1074 (1891).

54. People v. Sheldon, 139 N.Y. 251 (1893); Morris Run Coal Co. v. Barclay Coal Co., 68 Pa. 173 (1871); Gibbs v. Baltimore Gas Co., 130 U.S. 396 (1889); Ford v. Chicago Milk Shippers Assn., 155 Ill. 166, 39 N.E. 651 (1895) (state antitrust law).

55. Dr. Miles Medical Co. v. John D. Park & Sons Co., 220 U.S. 373, 412 (1911).

56. Alfred Marshall, *Principles of Economics* 846–855 (3d ed. 1895).

57. For an analysis of cases from the turn of the century, see Albert Kales, "Coercive and Competitive Methods in Trade and Labor Disputes," 8 *Cornell L. Q.* 1 (1922).

58. Oliver W. Holmes, Jr., "Privilege, Malice, and Intent," 8 *Harv. L. Rev.* 1, 3 (1894). A simpler version had already appeared in Holmes, *The Common Law* (1881). James B. Ames, "How Far an Act May Be a Tort Because of

the Wrongful Motive of the Actor," 18 *Harv. L. Rev.* 411, 420 (1905) (If someone "should start an opposition shop, not for the sake of profit for himself, but . . . for the sole purpose of driving the plaintiff out of business," would "not this wanton causing of damage to another be altogether indefensible and a tort?").

59. Bohn Mfg. Co. v. Hollis, 54 Minn. 223, 232–234, 55 N.W. 1119 (1893); to the same effect is Mogul Steamship Co. v. McGregor, Gow & Co., 1892 App. Cas. 25. Eastern States Retail Lumber Dealers Assn. v. United States, 234 U.S. 614 (1914), quoting Grenada Lumber Co. v. Mississippi, 217 U.S. 433, 440–441 (1909) (condemning lumber cartel under state antitrust law).

60. For example, People v. North River Sugar Refining Co., 121 N.Y. 582 (1890) (condemning acquisition creating a monopoly); Cummings v. Union Bluestone Assn., 44 N.Y. Supp. 787 (N.Y.S.Ct. 1897) (emphasizing that the cartel members "controlled ninety to ninety-five per cent. of the manufactured stock sold in the state . . ."); Anheuser-Busch Brewing Assn. v. Houck, 27 S.W. 692 (1894) (condemning a cartel between "the only persons who were then competitors").

61. Cooke, note 30 at 224–225, 245–246.

62. 55 W. Va. 642, 47 S.E. 247 (1904). For example, People v. Sheldon, 139 N.Y. 251 (1893); Morris Run Coal Co. v. Barclay Coal Co., 68 Pa. 173 (1871).

63. 1 Eddy, note 29 at 466–469.

64. Pope, note 26 at 181; Victor Morawetz, "The Anti-Trust Act and the Merger Case," 17 *Harv. L. Rev.* 533 (1904).

65. As Herbert Pope observed in 1907, "under the common law decisions, the question of whether a [corporate merger] was in itself an illegal combination could hardly have arisen." Note 26 at 181–182. "If two or more competitors transferred their interests to a corporation, in pursuance of some agreement between themselves, there was an end of that transaction. No court could be called upon afterwards to decide whether that original agreement was valid or invalid, because validity meant enforceability, and there was nothing left to enforce." Id.

66. Dr. Miles Medical Co. v. John D. Park & Sons Co., 220 U.S. 373, 412 (1911) (Holmes, J., dissenting). The notion that monopolies or restraints ought to be dealt with more harshly if they involved products of prime necessity preceded the classical era. It appears to have come from the sixteenth-century statutes on regrating and engrossing, 5 & 6 Edw. VI, c. 14 (1552), which applied to "corn" or "other victual," and to "corn, grain, butter, cheese, fish or other ded . . . victuals whatsoever . . . ." See Wendell Herbruck, "Forestalling, Regrating, and Engrossing," 27 *Mich. L. Rev.* 365, 378 (1929).

67. Central Shade Roller Co. v. Cushman, 143 Mass. 353, 364, 9 N.E. 629 (1887); Queen Insurance Co. v. State of Texas, 86 Tex. 250 (1893); Gloucester Isinglass & Glue Co. v. Russia Cement Co., 154 Mass. 92 (1891); Dolph v. Troy Laundry Machinery Co., 28 F. 553, 555 (C.C.S.D.N.Y. 1886).

68. People v. North River Sugar Refining Co., 3 N.Y. Supp. 401 (Cir. Ct. N.Y. Co. 1889), aff'd, 7 N.Y.Supp. 406 (S.Ct. 1889), aff'd, 121 N.Y. 582 (1890);

see also Judd v. Harrington, 139 N.Y. 105 (1893); Santa Clara Mill & Lumber Co. v. Hayes, 76 Cal. 387, 18 P. 391 (1888). See Louis Boisot, "The Legality of Trust Combinations," 39 *Am. L. Reg.* (n.s. 30) 751, 762 (1891). Many other decisions are discussed in Hovenkamp, "Sherman Act," note 19.

69. 43 N.W. 1102, 1110, 77 Mich. 632, 658 (Mich. 1889).
70. United States v. Trans-Missouri Freight Assn., 58 F. 58, 69 (8th Cir. 1893); Dueber Watch-Case Mfg. Co. v. E. Howard Watch & Clock Co., 66 F. 637, 643, 644 (2d Cir. 1895).
71. Kales, "Contracts," note 21 at 208, citing Tuscaloosa Ice Mfg. Co. v. Williams, 127 Ala. 110, 28 So. 669 (1899); Clemons v. Meadows, 123 Ky. 178, 94 S.W. 13 (1906).
72. Gibbs v. Consolidated Gas Co. of Baltimore, 130 U.S. 396, 408–409 (1889).
73. For example, Hoffman v. Brooks, 32 (23 N.S.) Am. L. Reg. 648, 651–652 (Super. Ct. Cin. 1884); see Brown v. Jacobs Pharmacy Co., 115 Ga. 429, 437 (1902) ("What is at one time a luxury at another is a necessity . . ."). Others are discussed in Hovenkamp, "Sherman Act," note 19.
74. People v. Sheldon, 139 N.Y. 251 (1893); Cummings v. Union Blue Stone Co., 164 N.Y. 401, 405 (1901).
75. *Addyston Pipe*, 85 F. at 286. Judge Taft's statement was technically dicta, for he also held that the cartelized products, sewer and water pipes, were articles of necessity.
76. Cooke, note 30 at 255.
77. See Waters-Pierce Oil Co. v. Texas, 212 U.S. 86 (1909); Smiley v. Kansas, 196 U.S. 447 (1905); National Cotton Oil Co. v. State, 197 U.S. 115 (1905).
78. 2 Eddy, note 29 at 1011–1024. See also William L. Royall, "The 'Pool' and the 'Trust,'" 3 *Va. L. Reg.* 163 (1897); S. C. T. Dodd, "The Present Legal Status of Trusts," 7 *Harv. L. Rev.* 157 (1893–1894).
79. For example, Connolly v. Union Sewer Pipe Co., 184 U.S. 540 (1902); In re Grice, 79 F. 627 (N.D. Tex. 1897). See James May, "Antitrust Practice and Procedure in the Formative Era: The Constitutional and Conceptual Reach of State Antitrust Law, 1880–1918," 135 *U. Pa. L. Rev.* 495 (1987).
80. United States v. Trans-Missouri Freight Assn., 166 U.S. 290 (1897).
81. United States v. Joint-Traffic Assn., 171 U.S. 505, 559, 570–571 (1898).
82. Addyston Pipe & Steel Co. v. United States, 175 U.S. 211, 228–230 (1899).

22. The Rise of Industrial Organization

1. For example, Alfred D. Chandler, Jr., *The Visible Hand: The Managerial Revolution in American Business* (1977).
2. For example, Naomi R. Lamoreaux, *The Great Merger Movement in American Business, 1895–1904* (1985).
3. In England, Alfred Marshall, *Principles of Economics* 31–49 (1890); Alfred Marshall & Mary Paley Marshall, *The Economics of Industry* (2d ed. 1881). In the United States, see John Bates Clark, "Non-Competitive Economics," 41 *New Englander* 837 (1882); Clark, "The 'Trust': A New Agent for Doing an

Old Work; or, Freedom Doing the Work of the Monopoly," 52 *New Englander* 223 (1890).

4. Francis A. Walker, *Political Economy* 100 (3d ed. 1888).
5. See 3 Joseph Dorfman, *The Economic Mind in American Civilization* 88 (1949).
6. Charles F. Adams, Jr., "The State and the Railroads," *Atlantic Monthly* 360 (Mar. 1876), 691, 692 (June 1876).
7. On the influence of the German Historical School on American thought at this time, see Jurgen Herbst, *The German Historical School in American Scholarship: A Study in the Transfer of Culture* (1965); Herbst notes that some fifty-nine American economists studied in Germany between 1873 and 1905, and twenty received their Ph.D.'s there. Id. at 130. See also Joseph Dorfman, "The Role of the German Historical School in American Economic Growth," 45 *Am. Econ. Rev., Papers & Proceedings* 28 (1955); Mary O. Furner, *Advocacy and Objectivity: A Crisis in the Professionalization of American Social Science, 1865–1905*, ch. 3 (1975).
8. See David Seckler, *Thorstein Veblen and the Institutionalists* 14 (1975).
9. See "Constitution, Bylaws, and Resolutions of the American Economic Assn.," *Supp.*, Amer. Econ. Assn. Pubs. 3 (July 1889); Richard T. Ely, *Ground under Our Feet* 143–144 (1938). On the founding of the AEA, see Thomas L. Haskell, *The Emergence of Professional Social Science* 168–169 (1977); Furner, note 7 at 69–75. For example, W. S. Outerbridge, "History of the Philadelphia Gas Trust," 7 *Publications*, Am. Econ. Assn. 439 (1892); M. B. Hammond, "The Cotton Industry," 1 *Publications* (n.s.), Am. Econ. Assn. 1 (1897); William C. Stubbs, "Sugar," 5 *Publications* (ser. 3), Am. Econ. Assn. 79 (1904); S. A. Knapp, "Rice," 5 *Publications* (ser. 3) Am. Econ. Assn. 102 (1904). Others are noted in Herbert Hovenkamp, "The Antitrust Movement and the Rise of Industrial Organization," 68 *Tex. L. Rev.* 105, 110–112 (1989).
10. The European division, with some reference to the United States, is described by Eugen von Böhm-Bawerk, a leader of the Austrian theoretical school, in "The Historical vs. the Deductive Method in Political Economics," *Annals*, Am. Acad. Pol. & Soc. Sci. 249 (Oct. 1890). See E. R. A. Seligman, "Change in the Tenets of Political Economy with Time," 7 *Science* 375, 382 (Apr. 23, 1886).
11. Henry Carter Adams, "Economics and Jurisprudence," 8 *Science* 15, 16 (July 2, 1886).
12. Arthur T. Hadley, "Economic Laws and Methods," 8 *Science* 46, 47 (July 16, 1886). Henry Carter Adams responded to Hadley in "Another View of Economic Laws and Methods," 8 *Science* 103 (July 30, 1886). Other essays in the debate are reprinted in Henry C. Adams et. al, *Science Economic Discussion* (1886). Also important is Thorstein Veblen, "The Preconceptions of Economic Science" (pts. 1–2), 13 *Q. J. Econ.* 121, 396 (1899).
13. See Frank Fetter, "The Next Decade of Economic Theory," *Papers and Proceedings*, Am. Econ. Assn. 236–237 (1901); Böhm-Bawerk, note 10 at 270. See Seckler, note 8 at 18.
14. See Hovenkamp, "Antitrust Movement," note 9 at 112–114.
15. Particularly good examples are Harvard Economic Studies No. 1: William

H. Price, *The English Patents of Monopoly* (1906); No. 8: Melvin T. Copeland, *The Cotton Manufacturing Industry of the United States* (1909); no. 10: Arthur S. Dewing, *Corporate Promotions and Reorganizations* (1914) (containing case studies of several business firms). Perhaps the best known was No. 11: Eliot Jones, *The Anthracite Coal Combination in the United States* (1914). All were published by Harvard University Press.

16. United States Commissioner of Corporations, *Report of Commissioner of Corporations on the Tobacco Industry* (1909); *Report on the Steel Industry* (1911–1913). The Commissioner of Corporations also produced case study reports on the beef trust (1905), the petroleum industry (1906, 1907), the lumber industry (1913, 1914), and the International Harvester Company (1913). The FTC produced book-length reports on the book paper industry (1917), flour milling (1918, 1920), canned foods (1918), meat packing (1918), copper (1919), shoe manufacturing (1919), and grain (1920).

17. Simon Patten, *The Consumption of Wealth* (1888); William Watts Folwell, "The True Method in Political Economy," *Bulletin,* Minn. Acad. of Natural Sciences 239 (Dec. 1882).

18. Francis A. Walker, *Political Economy* 11–17 (3d ed. 1888).

19. Arthur T. Hadley, *Economics: An Account of the Relations between Private Property and Public Welfare* 23–24 (1896).

20. Jeremiah W. Jenks, "The Michigan Salt Association," 3 *Pol. Sci. Q.* 78 (1888); Jenks, "The Whiskey Trust," 4 *Pol. Sci. Q.* 296 (1889).

21. Charles E. Edgerton, "The Wire-Nail Association of 1895–1896 and Other Iron and Steel Pools," 12 *Pol. Sci. Q.* 246 (1897).

22. See Jeremiah W. Jenks, *The Trust Problem* (1900); John Bates Clark, *The Control of Trusts* (1901); Clark, *The Problem of Monopoly* (1904); Ernst von Halle, *Trusts, or Industrial Combinations and Coalitions in the United States* (1900); William M. Collier, *The Trusts: What Can We Do with Them? What Can They Do for Us?* (1900); Richard T. Ely, *Monopolies and Trusts* (1900).

23. Eliot Jones, *The Trust Problem in the United States* (1921); Myron Watkins, *Industrial Combinations and Public Policy: A Study of Combination, Competition, and the Common Welfare* (1927); Ronald Coase, "The Nature of the Firm," 4 *Economica* (n.s.) 386 (1937); Frank Fetter, "Value and the Larger Economics" (pt. 2), 31 *J. Pol. Econ.* 800, 803 (1923); Fetter, "The Economics and the Public," 15 *Am. Econ. Rev.* 19 (1925).

24. See Brief for the United States, United States v. Addyston Pipe & Steel Co., 85 F. 271 (6th Cir. 1898), aff'd, 175 U.S. 211 (1899). See also the argument of E. B. Whitney, Assistant Attorney General, reprinted in William Z. Ripley, ed., *Trusts, Pools, and Corporations* 78 (rev. ed. 1916); Brief for the United States, United States v. United States Steel Corp., 223 F. 55 (D.N.J. 1915); Standard Oil Co. v. New Jersey v. United States, 221 U.S. 1 (1911); United States v. American Tobacco Co., 221 U.S. 106, 181–182 (1911) (rule of reason required the Court to examine the history of the rise of the American Tobacco Company).

25. Board of Trade of City of Chicago v. United States, 246 U.S. 231, 238 (1918).

26. The classic argument is Milton Friedman's "The Methodology of Positive Economics," reprinted in Friedman, *Essays in Positive Economics* 3 (1953).

27. Frank Knight, "The Limitations of Scientific Method in Economics," in Knight, *The Ethics of Competition* 117, 118, 128, 144 (1935).

28. Coase, note 23.

29. Adolf A. Berle, Jr., & Gardiner C. Means, *The Modern Corporation and Private Property* (1932).

30. See the Epilogue.

23. The Fixed-Cost Controversy

1. Henry R. Hatfield, "The Chicago Trust Conference," 8 *J. Pol. Econ.* 1 (1899).

2. Henry Carter Adams, "The Relation of the State to Industrial Action," 1 *Publications,* Am. Econ. Assn. 7, 52, 59–64 (1887).

3. Francis Wayland, *Elements of Political Economy* 92–105 (1837); Thomas Cooper, *Lectures on the Elements of Political Economy* 83 (2d ed. 1830); Francis A. Walker, *Political Economy* 318 (3d ed. 1888).

4. George B. Dixwell, "Review of Bastiat's Sophisms of Protection," 11 *Bulletin,* Nat. Assn. of Wool Manufacturers 251 (1881). Dixwell is discussed in 3 Joseph Dorfman, *The Economic Mind in American Civilization* 133–134 (1949).

5. David A. Wells, *Recent Economic Changes* (1889). Wells's work is discussed in Lester Telser, *A Theory of Efficient Cooperation and Competition* 22 (1987); and Thomas S. Ulen, "Cartels and Regulation: Late Nineteenth-Century Railroad Collusion and the Creation of the Interstate Commerce Commission" 129 (Ph.D. diss., Stanford Univ. 1979).

6. George Gunton, *The Economic and Social Importance of the Eight-Hour Movement* (1889).

7. Andrew Carnegie, "The Bugaboo of Trusts," 148 *N. Am. Rev.* 141 (1889); John Bates Clark, "The Limits of Competition," 2 *Pol. Sci. Q.* 45, 55 (1887); Carroll D. Wright, "The Relation of Production to Productive Capacity," 24 *The Forum* 290 (Nov. 1897), 671 (Feb. 1898). See also Uriel H. Crocker, *The Depression in Trade and Wages of Labor* (1886) (attacking classical view that general overproduction is impossible). On Wright, see Mary O. Furner, *Advocacy and Objectivity: A Crisis in the Professionalization of American Social Science, 1865–1905,* at 44–46, 154–155, & *passim* (1975).

8. Walker, note 3; Arthur T. Hadley, *Economics: An Account of the Relations between Private Property and Public Welfare* 158, 295 (1896). In 1918 Spurgeon Bell concluded that economics "was limited more by the inadequacy of its analysis of cost than by the nature of its analysis of demand." Bell, "Fixed Costs and Market Price," 32 *Q. J. Econ.* 507 (1918).

9. See F. W. Taussig, "A Contribution to the Theory of Railway Rates," 5 *Q. J. Econ.* 438 (1891); and Taussig, *Tariff History of the United States* 316–317 (1894; 4th ed. 1898).

10. William M. Collier, *The Trusts: What Can We Do with Them? What Can They Do for Us?* 66–67 (1900).

11. See Central Trust Co. v. Ohio Central Ry., 23 F. 306 (C.C.N.D. Ohio 1885) (upholding pooling agreement), rev'd on other grounds, 133 U.S. 83 (1890); Nashua & Lowell R.R., 19 F. 804 (C.C. Mass. 1884) (same), rev'd on other grounds, 136 U.S. 356 (1890); Chicago, Minneapolis & St. Paul Ry. v.

Wabash, St. Louis & Pacific Ry., 61 F. 993 (8th Cir. 1894) (pooling permissible if designed to prevent ruinous competition). Others are discussed in Herbert Hovenkamp, "The Antitrust Movement and the Rise of Industrial Organization," 68 *Tex. L. Rev.* 105, 126–128 (1989).

12. United States v. Trans-Missouri Freight Assn., 166 U.S. 290, 329–330 (1897).

13. Charles River Bridge v. Warren Bridge, 36 U.S. (11 Pet.) 420, 436, 461, 650 (1837).

14. Morgan v. New Orleans, Mobile & Texas R.R. Co., 2 Woods 244, 17 F. Cas. 754 (no. 9804) (C.C.D. La. 1876); *Nutter,* 2 Lowell 346, 18 F. Cas. 497, 499 (no. 10,384) (D. Mass. 1874). See Continental Ins. Co. v. Board of Fire Underwriters of the Pacific, 67 F. 310 (C.C.N.D. Cal. 1895) (insurance underwriters may fix prices if purpose is to prevent ruinous competition); Central Shade Roller Co. v. Cushman, 143 Mass. 353, 364 (1887) (upholding cartel of window shade roller manufacturers designed to "prevent the injurious effects, both to producers and consumers, of fluctuating prices caused by undue competition"); Skrainka v. Scharringhausen, 8 Mo. App. 522 (1880) (upholding stone quarriers' cartel based on fear of ruinous competition); Barr v. Pittsburgh Plate Glass Co., 51 F. 33 (C.C.W.D. Pa. 1892) (approving merger as necessary to prevent ruinous competition between two firms); Diamond Match Co. v. Roeber, 106 N.Y. 473, 13 N.E. 419 (1887) (upholding merger by asset acquisition, designed to curb excessive competition). The New York decisions discussed in the paragraph are United States Vinegar Co. v. Foehrenbach, 42 N.E. 403, 148 N.Y. 58 (1895); John D. Park & Sons Co. v. National Wholesale Druggists Assn., 175 N.Y. 1, 67 N.E. 136, 139 (1903). Cases rejecting ruinous competition defenses include People v. Sheldon, 34 N.E. 785, 788, 139 N.Y. 251 (1893) ; Moore v. Bennett, 29 N.E. 888, 889 (Ill. 1892). Many others are discussed in Hovenkamp, note 11 at 129–134.

15. 172 U.S. 1 (1898); White v. City of Meadville, 155 Pa. 647, 651, 35 A. 695, 697 (1896); San Diego Water Co. v. San Diego Flume Co., 108 Cal. 549, 41 P. 495, 498 (1895). Other decisions are discussed in Hovenkamp, note 11 at 130–132.

16. Dueber Watch-Case Mfg. Co. v. E. Howard Watch & Clock Co., 55 F. 851, 854 (C.C.S.D.N.Y. 1893), aff'd, 66 F. 637 (2d. Cir. 1895); United States v. Trans-Missouri Freight Assn., 58 F. 58 (8th Cir. 1893), rev'd, 166 U.S. 290, 333–334 (1897).

17. See United States v. Joint-Traffic Assn., 171 U.S. 505, 519–523, 547–548, 569 (1898), including reporter's summary of Carter's brief for the Joint Traffic Association and E. J. Phelps's argument for the New York Central Railroad Company.

18. United States v. Addyston Pipe & Steel Co., 78 F. 712 (C.C.E.D. Tenn. 1897), rev'd, 85 F. 271, 291 (6th Cir. 1898), modified and aff'd, 175 U.S. 211 (1899). (The trial court's opinion was delivered in February, 1897, one month before the Supreme Court's *Trans-Missouri* decision was rendered; the lower court in *Trans-Missouri* had upheld the railroad cartel agreement.) See Kellogg Toasted Corn Flake Co. v. Buck, 208 F. 383, 384 (D.C.S.D. Cal. 1913); Jayne v. Loder, 149 F. 21, 28 (3d Cir. 1906).

19. United States v. Standard Sanitary Mfg. Co., 191 F. 172, 181 (C.C.D. Md. 1911); Standard Sanitary Mfg. Co. v. United States, 226 U.S. 20, 25 (1912). See also O'Halloran v. American Sea Green Slate Co., 207 F. 187 (N.D.N.Y. 1913), rejecting a ruinous competition defense in a private Sherman Act suit.

20. United States v. Great Lakes Towing Co., 208 F. 733 (N.D. Ohio 1913); 217 F. 656 (N.D. Ohio 1914).

21. United States v. Corn Products Refining Co., 234 F. 964 (S.D.N.Y. 1916), appeal dism'd, 249 U.S. 621 (1918).

22. United States v. United States Steel Corp., 223 F. 55, 93–94, 96 (D.N.J. 1915), aff'd, 251 U.S. 417, 446 (1920). See also 223 F. at 154–173, noting that the famous "Gary Dinners" held among competing steel firms before the merger, were intended by the merging parties to prevent ruinous competition. The dinners did not work; the firms persisted in undercutting the prices that were "suggested" at the dinner meetings. Thus the merger became necessary. For more on the history of the merger, see Alfred D. Chandler, Jr., *Scale and Scope: The Dynamics of Industrial Capitalism* 131–134 (1990).

23. United States v. Trenton Potteries Co., 273 U.S. 392 (1927). See Learned Hand's opinion in Live Poultry Dealers' Protective Assn. v. United States, 4 F.2d 840, 843 (2d Cir. 1924), noting debate whether per se rule still applied to cartels after 1911 *Standard Oil* decision, but concluding that it did.

24. Richard T. Ely, *An Introduction to Political Economy* 149 (1889). See also E. R. A. Seligman, *Principles of Economics* 584–586 (3d ed. 1908); Henry R. Seager, *Introduction to Economics* 160–161 (1904); Charles J. Bullock, "Trust Literature: A Survey and a Criticism," 7 *Q. J. Econ.* 167, 205–206 (1901).

25. Oswald Knauth, "Competition and Capital," 30 *Pol. Sci. Q.* 578, 587–588 (1915).

26. Bell, note 8 at 517; 2 F. W. Taussig, *Principles of Economics* 53 (1911).

27. Eliot Jones, "Is Competition in Industry Ruinous?" 34 *Q. J. Econ.* 473, 491–497 (1920); Jones, *The Trust Problem in the United States* 197 (1921); Myron Watkins, *Industrial Combinations and Public Policy: A Study of Combination, Competition, and Public Welfare*, ch. 3 (1927).

28. Bell, note 8 at 523.

29. Jones, "*Is Competition Ruinous?*" note 27 at 494.

30. Frank Knight, "Cost of Production and Price over Long and Short Periods," 29 *J. Pol. Econ.* 304 (1921); 2 Taussig, note 26 at 53–54 (3d ed. 1922); John Maurice Clark, "A Contribution to the Theory of Competitive Price," 28 *Q. J. Econ.* 747 (1914); J. M. Clark, *Studies in the Economics of Overhead Costs* 432–435 (1923); J. M. Clark, *Social Control of Business* 313 (1926). Clark developed these ideas further in a well-known essay on workable competition. J. M. Clark, "Toward A Concept of Workable Competition," 30 *Am. Econ. Rev.* 243 (1940). John Maurice Clark was the son of John Bates Clark.

31. For example, Lester Telser, *Economic Theory and the Core* 387 (1978); George Bittlingmayer, "Did Antitrust Policy Cause the Great Merger Wave?" 28 *J. L. & Econ.* 77 (1985); Bittlingmayer, "Decreasing Average Cost: A New Look at the Addyston Pipe Case," 25 *J. L. & Econ.* 201 (1982). See also

Jacob Viner, "Cost Curves and Supply Curves" (1931), in *Readings in Price Theory* 212 (G. Stigler & K. Boulding eds. 1952).

32. Edward Chamberlin, *The Theory of Monopolistic Competition* (1933).

33. Arthur J. Eddy, *The New Competition* 121, 82 (1914); Milton N. Nelson, *Open Price Associations* 45 (1922). Making the same arguments is the National Industrial Conference Board monograph, *Trade Associations: Their Economic Significance and Legal Status* 17–25 (1925).

34. For example, FTC, *Report on the Book-Paper Industry* 18 (1917).

35. Maple Flooring Manufacturers Assn. v. United States, 268 U.S. 563 (1925).

36. Franklin D. Jones, *Trade Association Activities and the Law* 30–31 (1922). See also Justice Brandeis's dissent in American Column & Lumber Co. v. United States, 257 U.S. 377, 414–418 (1921), arguing that even information exchanges about explicit prices could be competitive when firms were small, isolated, and poorly informed about market conditions.

37. For example, U.S. Dept. of Commerce, *Trade Association Activities* (1923). See Ellis W. Hawley, "Herbert Hoover and the Sherman Act, 1921–1933: An Early Phase of a Continuing Issue," 74 *Iowa L. Rev.* 1067 (1990).

38. See Arthur Burns, *The Decline of Competition: A Study of the Education of American Industry*, ch. 10 (1936).

24. Potential Competition

1. See Jeremiah W. Jenks, *The Trust Problem*, chs. 2, 4, 8 (1900); Ernst von Halle, *Trusts, or Industrial Combinations and Coalitions in the United States*, ch. 5 (1900). Somewhat more constrained was John Bates Clark, *The Control of Trusts* (1901). See Arthur T. Hadley, *Economics: An Account of the Relations between Private Property and Public Welfare*, ch. 6 (1896); Richard T. Ely, *Monopolies and Trusts*, ch. 2 (1900).

2. Albert M. Stickney, *State Control of Trade and Commerce by National or State Authority* 179 (1897); Franklin H. Giddings, "The Persistence of Competition," 2 *Pol. Sci. Q.* 62, 65 (1887); Giddings, *Democracy and Empire* 137–143 (1900); Julian M. Sturtevant, *Economics of the Science of Wealth* 64, 101–102, 241, 271, 296 (1877; rev. ed. 1886); Sturtevant, "Method in Economic Science," 1879 *New Englander* 27–28 (1879); William W. Cook, *The Corporation Problem* 237 (1891).

3. Jenks, note 1, ch. 2; Andrew Carnegie, "The Bugaboo of Trusts," 148 *N. Am. Rev.* 141, 150 (1889).

4. George Gunton, "The Economic and Social Aspects of Trusts," 3 *Pol. Sci. Q.* 385, 403 (1888) (emphasis in original).

5. Hadley, note 1 at 154, 161; John Bates Clark, "The 'Trust': A New Agent for Doing an Old Work; or, Freedom Doing the Work of Monopoly," 16 *New Englander* (n.s.) 223 (1890); *Chicago Conference on Trusts: Speeches, Debates, Resolutions, List of the Delegates, Committees, Etc.* 407 (1900).

6. J. B. Clark, *Control of Trusts*, note 1 at 70–79; Elisha B. Andrews, "The Economic Law of Monopoly," 26 *J. Soc. Sci.* 1, 5–6 (1890); see also Andrews, "Trusts According to Official Investigations," 3 *Q. J. Econ.* 117, 141–142 (1889).

7. Richard T. Ely, *Monopolies and Trusts*, chs. 4 & 5 (1900); Charles J. Bullock, "Trust Literature: A Survey and a Criticism," 15 *Q. J. Econ.* 167, 211 (1901); Bullock, "Trusts and Public Policy," 87 *Atlantic Monthly* 737–745 (June 1901); see also Charles W. Baker, *Monopolies and the People* (1889).

8. William M. Collier, *The Trusts: What Can We Do with Them? What Can They Do for Us?* 126–128 (1900).

9. John Maurice Clark, "A Contribution to the Theory of Competitive Price," 28 *Q. J. Econ.* 747 (1914). For example, Oliver Williamson, "Predatory Pricing: A Strategic and Welfare Analysis," 87 *Yale L. J.* 284 (1977).

10. See Wickens v. Evans, 3 Y. & T. 318, 328, 148 Eng. Rep. 1201, 1205 (Exch. of Pleas, 1829), enforcing a market division agreement among trunk makers, because the participants made no attempt to exclude outsiders. As a result "every other man may come into their districts and vend his goods . . . ." Dolph v. Troy Laundry Machinery Co., 28 F. 553 (C.C.S.D.N.Y. 1886). See also Kellogg v. Larkin, 3 Pinney 123 (Wisc. 1851) (upholding cartel because the market remained open to the competition of others); Frederick H. Cooke, *The Law of Combinations, Monopolies, and Labor Unions* 241 (2d ed. 1909).

11. *Nelson,* 52 F. 646, 647 (D. Minn. 1892); Dueber Watch-Case Mfg. Co. v. E. Howard Watch & Clock Co., 66 F. 637, 644 (2d Cir. 1895).

12. Queen Insurance Co. v. State of Texas, 86 Tex. 250, 274 (1893) (condemning insurance company cartel); Dueber Watch-Case, note 11 at 644; Cooke, note 10 at 256. See also Gibbs v. Consolidated Gas Co. of Baltimore, 130 U.S. 396, 408 (1889) (even partial restraints unenforceable in businesses of a public character, such as gas lighting); People v. Chicago Gas Trust Co., 130 Ill. 268, 293, 22 N.E. 798, 803 (1889) ("Whatever tends to prevent competition between those engaged in a public employment, or business impressed with a public character, is opposed to public policy and therefore unlawful"); Hooker v. Vandevater, 4 Denio 349 (N.Y. 1847) (same, common carrier).

13. Hadley, note 1 at 88, 160–161.

14. *Addyston Pipe,* 85 F. at 284, rejecting Wickens v. Evans, 3 Younge & J. 318 (Exch. of Pleas, 1829). See note 10.

15. United States v. American Can Co., 230 F. 859 (D. Md. 1916), appeal dism'd, 256 U.S. 706 (1921). See also 230 F. at 874, detailing contract with E. W. Bliss Company, under which Bliss promised not to sell can-making machinery to anyone but American Can for six years in exchange for $100,000 annually; and an output contract with Adriance Machine Company. Other quotations at 871, 875.

16. United States v. Corn Products Refining Co., 234 F. 964, 978, 989–990, 1008–1009, 1012 (S.D.N.Y. 1916), dism'd, 239 U.S. 621 (1918).

25. Vertical Integration and Resale Price Maintenance

1. See FTC, *Causes of High Prices of Farm Implements* 674–676 (1920); Eliot Jones, *The Trust Problem in the United States* 202–203 (1921). On the history

of vertical integration in the United States, see Alfred D. Chandler, Jr., *Scale and Scope: The Dynamics of Industrial Capitalism* (1990), esp. ch. 4.

2. Exclusive dealing occurs when a firm promises to deal exclusively in the goods of another firm—for example, if a gasoline retailer agrees to sell only the gasoline of a particular supplier. Tying occurs when one firm is permitted to purchase or lease a product from another firm only if it agrees to take a second product as well. For example, in the early 1900's A. B. Dick Company, a manufacturer of office machines, sold or leased mimeograph equipment only on the condition that the customers procure their paper and ink from A. B. Dick, Inc. See Henry v. A. B. Dick Co., 224 U.S. 1 (1912).

3. For example, United States v. United States Steel Corp., 223 F. 55 (D.N.J. 1915), aff'd, 251 U.S. 417, 442 (1920); United States v. Standard Oil Co., 47 F.2d 288, 310–311 (1931) (noting the "superior business position" of the vertically integrated firm).

4. For example, United States v. American Tobacco Co., 221 U.S. 106, 170 (1911) (finding that tobacco company's acquisition of suppliers of tinfoil wrappers and licorice paste had been part of attempt to monopolize the tobacco market); United States v. Corn Products Refining Co., 234 F. 964, 984 (S.D.N.Y. 1916), app. dism'd, 249 U.S. 621 (1918) (corn sweetener's purchase of candy factory found to be part of monopolization scheme).

5. William F. Willoughby, "The Integration of Industry in the United States," 16 *Q. J. Econ.* 94, 108 (1901); Alfred D. Chandler, Jr., *The Visible Hand: The Managerial Revolution in American Business* 315–344 (1977); Chandler, *Scale and Scope*, note 1, ch. 4.

6. Naomi R. Lamoreaux, *The Great Merger Movement in American Business, 1895–1904*, at 155 (1985).

7. 5 & 6 Edw. VI, c. 14 (1552) (3 Statutes at Large 588 (1811)); 4 William Holdsworth, *A History of English Law* 317–318 (2d ed. 1937).

8. 12 Geo. III, c. 71 (1772) (13 Statutes at Large 398 (1811)). However, common law prosecutions continued until an 1844 statute forbade them. 7 & 8 Vict. c. 24 (1844). See Franklin D. Jones, "Historical Development of the Law of Business Competition," 36 *Yale L. J.* 42, 43–54 (1926).

9. William W. Story, *A Treatise on the Law of Sales of Personal Property* 509 (2d ed. 1853). The principal case is Welton v. Missouri, 91 U.S. 275 (1876). See Chandler, *Visible Hand*, note 5, chs. 2 & 7; J. Willard Hurst, *Law and the Conditions of Freedom in the Nineteenth-Century United States* 44 (1956); Charles R. McCurdy, "American Law and the Marketing Structure of the Large Corporation, 1875–1890," 38 *J. Econ. Hist.* 631 (1978).

10. On resale price maintenance, see the discussion later in this chapter. On exclusive dealing, see Chicago, St. Louis & New Orleans R.R. Co. v. Pullman Southern Car Co., 139 U.S. 79, 89 (1891); Wiggins Ferry Co. v. Chicago & Alton R.R. Co., 73 Mo. 389 (1881) (upholding contract under which railroad gave all its freight transfers to one ferry company); Lenz v. Brown, 41 Wis. 172 (1876) (upholding agreement that grocer would purchase all his groceries from one wholesaler, provided that wholesaler charged as low a price as others); Brown v. Rounsavell, 78 Ill. 589 (1875) (exclusive dealing

between sewing machine manufacturer and dealer); Lightner v. Menzel, 35 Cal. 452 (1868) (same, meat market); Richmond v. Dubuque & Sioux City R.R. Co., 26 Iowa 191 (1868) (same, railroad and grain elevator company); Palmer v. Stebbins, 3 Pick. (Mass.) 188 (1825) (exclusive contract between shipper and river-boat freight carrier). English cases include Thornton v. Sherratt, 8 Taut. 529, 129 Eng. Rep. 488 (1818); Holcombe v. Hewson, 2 Camp. 391, 170 Eng. Rep. 1194 (1800). Other cases are discussed in Elisha Greenhood, *The Doctrine of Public Policy in the Law of Contracts, Reduced to Rules* 676–683 (1886).

11. United States v. Addyston Pipe & Steel Co., 85 F. 271, 287 (6th Cir. 1898), aff'd, 175 U.S. 211 (1899).

12. Jacksonville, Mayport, Pablo Ry. & Navigation Co. v. Hooper, 160 U.S. 514, 526 (1896). See Lawrence M. Friedman, *A History of American Law* 519 (2d ed. 1985).

13. 1 Victor Morawetz, *A Treatise on the Law of Private Corporations* §§ 362, 365, 393 at 347–349, 350, 373 (2d ed. 1886). See Toll Bridge Co. v. Osborn, 35 Conn. 7 (1868) (toll bridge company may not operate a wharf for profit); Waldo v. Chicago R.R. Co., 14 Wis. 575 (1861) (railroad could not acquire real estate not along its right of way merely to increase its assets); Watt's Appeal, 78 Pa. St. 370, 392 (1875) (permitting mining company to build saw mills and hotel for accommodation of those dealing with the company); Callaway Mining Co. v. Clark, 32 Mo. 305 (1862) (permitting mining corporation to operate steamboat in order to deliver coal). English cases include Lyde v. Eastern Bengal Ry. Co., 36 Beav. 16, 17, 55 Eng. Rep. 1059, 62 (1866): "If, in truth, the real object of the colliery was to supply the railway with cheaper coals, it would be proper to allow the accidental additional profit of selling coals to others; but if the principal object of the colliery was to undertake the business of raising and selling coals, then it would be a perversion of the funds of the company, and a scheme which ought not to be permitted . . .").

14. United States v. American Tobacco Co., 221 U.S. 106, 168–171 (1911). See Robert H. Bork, "Vertical Integration and the Sherman Act: The Legal History of an Economic Misconception," 22 *Univ. Chi. L. Rev.* 157, 161–162 (1954). U.S. Commissioner of Corporations, *Report on the Steel Industry* 12, 108 (1911–1913).

15. U.S. Commissioner of Corporations, *Report on International Harvester Co.* 20–37 (1913). See also Standard Oil Co. of Kentucky v. Tennessee, 217 U.S. 413 (1910) (upholding condemnation of exclusive dealing under state antitrust law); United States v. International Harvester Co., 274 U.S. 693, 704 (1927) (describing 1918 consent decree); FTC, *Causes*, note 1 at 675.

16. For example, see Donald Dewey, *Monopoly in Economics and Law*, ch. 14 (1959), which discusses exclusive dealing and tying under the heading of "law of unfair competition." See also the work by the Yale economist John Perry Miller, *Unfair Competition* (1941). FTC v. Gratz, 253 U.S. 421 (1920); Henry v. A. B. Dick Co., 224 U.S. 1 (1912); Motion Picture Patents Co. v. Universal Film Co., 243 U.S. 502 (1917) (Sherman Act); United States Shoe Machinery Corp. v. U.S., 258 U.S. 451 (1922) (Clayton Act). The Supreme

Court condemned vertical integration by railroads on the theory that the railroads were purchasing captive customers by acquiring firms such as coal producers, who used the railroads heavily. See United States v. Lehigh Valley R.R. Co., 254 U.S. 255, 259–261 (1920).

17. 1 F. W. Taussig, *Principles of Economics* 61–63 (2d ed. 1919).

18. Eliot Jones, *The Trust Problem in the United States* 66–72 (1921); Myron Watkins, *Industrial Combinations and Public Policy: A Study of Combination, Competition, and the Common Welfare* 66, 74–76 (1927). The economic basis for Watkin's theory was exploded in Ward Bowman, "Tying Arrangements and the Leverage Problem," 67 *Yale L. J.* 19 (1957).

19. Edward Chamberlin, *The Theory of Monopolistic Competition* 123 (3d ed. 1938); Henry Simons, *A Positive Program for Laissez-Faire* 20–21 (1934).

20. Arthur R. Burns, *The Decline of Competition: A Study of the Evolution of American Industry,* ch. 9 (1936). Quotations at 460–461, 422, 428–430.

21. Adolf A. Berle, Jr., & Gardiner C. Means, *The Modern Corporation and Private Property* 350–351 (1932). To the same effect is Willis J. Ballinger's TNEC monograph, with Myron Watkins and Frank A. Fetter as principal contributors, *Relative Efficiency of Large, Medium-Sized, and Small Business* (TNEC Monograph 13, 1939). The authors concluded that big business is generally less efficient than small and medium-sized business. Id. at 10.

22. Burns, note 20 at 431–432, 435. See FTC, *Wartime Costs and Profits of the Steel Industry* 32 (1925) ("the greater was the extent of integration the less was the return"); and FTC, *Prices, Profits, and Competition in the Petroleum Industry* 293 (1928) (same).

23. Frank Fetter, *The Masquerade of Monopoly* 422 (1931).

24. Ronald Coase, "The Nature of the Firm," 4 *Economica* (n.s.) 386, 390–398 (1937). Anticipating some of Coase's arguments is Lawrence K. Frank, "The Significance of Industrial Integration," 33 *J. Pol. Econ.* 179 (1925).

25. United States v. Corn Products Refining Co., 234 F. 964, 1007–1008 (S.D.N.Y. 1916), appeal dism'd, 249 U.S. 621 (1918). On the price squeeze in the aluminum industry, see Baush Machine Tool Co. v. Aluminum Co., 72 F.2d 236 (2d Cir.), cert. denied, 293 U.S. 589 (1934); and Judge Hand's celebrated opinion in United States v. Aluminum Co. of America, 148 F.2d 416, 436–438 (2d Cir. 1945). See also Donald H. Wallace, *Market Control in the Aluminum Industry* 381–390 (Harvard Economic Study, vol. 58, 1937); R. C. Cook, *Control of the Petroleum Industry by Major Oil Companies* 22 (TNEC Monograph 39, 1941); Corwin D. Edwards, *Maintaining Competition* 98, 171–172 (1949).

26. Dr. Miles Medical Co. v. John D. Park & Sons Co., 220 U.S. 373 (1911). For the history of resale price maintenance, see E. T. Grether, *Price Control under Fair Trade Legislation* (1939); E. R. A. Seligman and Robert A. Love, *Price Cutting and Price Maintenance* (1932); Claudius T. Murchison, *Resale Price Maintenance* (1919).

27. See William J. Shroder, "Price Restriction on the Re-sale of Chattels," 25 *Harv. L. Rev.* 59 (1911).

28. See Lester Telser, "Why Do Manufacturers Want Fair Trade?" 3 *J. L. & Econ.* 86 (1960).

29. See Grether, note 26.
30. For example, John D. Park & Sons Co. v. National Wholesale Druggists Assn., 67 N.E. 136, 137–138 (1903) (alleging a concerted refusal by druggists to deal only with jobbers who imposed resale price maintenance).
31. Its vestiges can be found as late as United States v. Colgate & Co., 250 U.S. 300 (1919).
32. See Chandler, *Visible Hands,* note 5 at 224–228; Thomas K. McCraw, *Prophets of Regulation* 102–108 (1984), noting Louis D. Brandeis's efforts to protect small retailers from the department stores.
33. 131 U.S. 88 (1889).
34. Even under Judge Taft's *Addyston Pipe* analysis, they should have been evaluated under the rule of reason, because they were always ancillary to the sale of goods intended for resale. See Chapter 21.
35. For example, Grogan v. Chaffee, 156 Cal. 611, 105 P. 745 (1909) (upholding resale price maintenance agreement in olive oil because of manufacturer's small market share); Dr. Miles Medical Co. v. Platt, 142 F. 606 (C.C.D. Ill. 1906) (sole owner of secret formula may dictate the price at which it is resold); Dr. Miles Medical Co. v. Jaynes Drug Co., 149 Fed. 838 (C.C.D. Mass. 1906) (same); Dr. Miles Medical Co. v. Goldthwaite, 133 F. 794 (C.C.D. Mass. 1904) (allowing an injunction to restrain interference with resale price maintenance contracts). Other decisions are discussed in Herbert Hovenkamp, "The Sherman Act and the Classical Theory of Competition," 74 *Iowa L. Rev.* 1019 (1989).
36. For example, Klingel's Pharmacy v. Sharp & Dohme, 104 Md. 218, 230, 64 A. 1029, 1030 (1906). See Wendell Herbruck, "Forestalling, Regrating, and Engrossing," 27 *Mich. L. Rev.* 365, 378–380 (1929).
37. *Dr. Miles,* 220 U.S. at 409. See Chapter 21.
38. John D. Park & Sons Co. v. Hartman, 153 F. 24, 42 (6th Cir. 1907). Lurton became an Associate Justice of the Supreme Court in 1909.
39. Continental Wall Paper Co. v. Voight & Sons Co., 148 F. 939 (6th Cir. 1906), aff'd, 212 U.S. 227 (1909).
40. John D. Park & Sons Co. v. National Wholesale Druggists Assn., 67 N.E. 136, 137 (1903); Loder v. Jayne, 142 F. 1010, 1014 (C.C.E.D. Pa.), aff'd, 149 F. 21 (3d Cir. 1906); Dr. Miles Medical Co. v. Jayne's Drug Co., 149 F. 838 (C.C.D. Mass. 1906).
41. Hartman v. John D. Park & Sons, 145 F. 358, 380 (C.C.E.D. Ken. 1906), rev'd, 153 F. 24 (6th Cir. 1907); Brown & Allen v. Jacobs' Pharmacy Co., 115 Ga. 429 (1902). See also Klingel's Pharmacy v. Sharp & Dohme, 104 Md. 218 (1906) (complaint alleging concerted refusal to deal with aggressive cutter stated a cause of action at common law).
42. Grogan v. Chaffee, 156 Cal. 611, 614, 105 P. 745 (1909). See also Ford Motor Co. v. Benjamin E. Boone, Inc., 244 F. 335 (9th Cir. 1917) (upholding resale price maintenance because defendant lacked market control); D. Ghirardelli Co. v. Hunsicker, 164 Cal. 355, 128 P. 1041 (1912) (same; state antitrust law).
43. John D. Park & Sons v. Hartman, 153 F. 24, 45 (6th Cir. 1907); John D. Park & Sons v. National Wholesale Druggists 50 N. Y. 1064, 65 (1896).

Epilogue

1. See George Stigler, "Perfect Competition, Historically Contemplated," 65 *J. Pol. Econ.* 1, 10–11 (1957), who attributes perfection of the model to John Bates Clark and Frank Knight. See John Bates Clark, *The Distribution of Wealth* (1899); Frank Knight, *Risk, Uncertainty, and Profit* (1921); Alfred Marshall, *Principles of Economics* (1890); Edward Chamberlin, *The Theory of Monopolistic Competition* (1933); Joan Robinson, *The Economics of Imperfect Competition* (1933); Adolph Berle, Jr., and Gardiner Means, *The Modern Corporation and Private Property* (1932).

2. Charles Darwin, *On the Origin of Species by Natural Selection* (1859); Jeremiah W. Jenks, *The Trust Problem* 195 (1900); Andrew Carnegie, "Wealth," 148 *N. Am. Rev.* 653, 654–655 (1889).

3. Adam Smith, *The Wealth of Nations* bk. 1, ch. 1, pt. 3 (1776). See George Stigler's important essay, "The Division of Labor Is Limited by the Extent of the Market," 59 *J. Pol. Econ.* 185 (1951).

4. See Arthur J. Cordell, "The Preface to Robinson and Chamberlin," 44 *Indian J. Econ.* 257 (1964).

5. John Stuart Mill, *Principles of Political Economy,* bk. 2, ch. 4 at 246 (1848; 1926 rep.).

6. Marshall, note 1 at V, xi, p. 513 n.1 (4th ed. 1898).

7. Gerritt Lansing, "The Railway and the State," 138 *N. Am. Rev.* 461, 462–463 (1884). See Chapter 12.

8. Marshall, note 1 at IV, xi, pp. 341, 343; V, viii, p. 464 n.1 (1890).

9. See Alfred D. Chandler, Jr., *The Visible Hand: The Managerial Revolution in American Business* (1977).

10. Jeremiah W. Jenks, *Great Fortunes; the Winning; the Using* 45 (1906); see also Jenks, *The Trust Problem,* note 2, esp. chs. 1 & 2.

11. Charles W. Baker, *Monopolies and the People* (3d ed. 1899); see also Ernst von Halle, *Trusts, or Industrial Combinations and Coalitions in the United States* (1895); Richard T. Ely, *Monopolies and Trusts* (1900).

12. Principally, Henry Carter Adams. Adams, "The Relation of the State to Industrial Action," 1 *Publications* Am. Econ. Assn. 465 (1887).

13. See Henry R. Hatfield, "The Chicago Trust Conference," 8 *J. Pol. Econ.* 1, 6 (1899); and see Chapter 23.

14. George Stigler, "Monopoly and Oligopoly by Merger," 40 *Am. Econ. Rev., Papers & Proceedings* 30, 31 (1950).

15. Jenks, *Great Fortunes,* note 10 at 46.

16. See Chapter 23; Edward Chamberlin, "The Origin and Early Development of Monopolistic Competition Theory," 75 *Q. J. Econ.* 515 (1961).

17. For example, 1 F. W. Taussig, *Principles of Economics* 206 (1911); Irving R. Fisher, *Elementary Principles of Economics* 330 (1911); Frank Fetter, *The Principles of Economics* 330 (2d ed. 1910); E. R. A. Seligman, *Principles of Economics* (4th ed. 1910). See also Ely, note 11 at 119. Most of these discussions of the monopoly price probably derived from Marshall, note 1 at 456–472 (1890). The theory was developed by Antoine A. Cournot, *Researches into the Mathematical Principles of the Theory of Wealth* (1838; trans. N. T. Bacon

1897), but did not become prominent in the English classical tradition until Marshall and after.

18. Eliot Jones, *The Trust Problem in the United States* (1921), esp. ch. 11.

19. Id. at 274–276, 535. Accord: A. S. Dewing, "A Statistical Test of the Success of Consolidations," 36 *Q. J. Econ.* 84 (1921).

20. John Maurice Clark, *Studies in the Economics of Overhead Costs* (1923); Clark, *Social Control of Business* 145, 419–425, 449–459 (1926).

21. See Joseph A. Schumpeter, *History of Economic Analysis* 1047 (1954); Piero Sraffa, "The Laws of Returns under Competitive Conditions," 36 *Econ. J.* 535 (1926); Harold Hotelling, "Stability in Competition," 39 *Econ. J.* 41, 44 (1929).

22. Under Chamberlin's theory of oligopoly, price approached the monopoly price. Chamberlin, note 1 at 54.

23. Berle & Means, note 1. See preface at vii.

24. Chandler, note 9 at 9–10, 81–187.

25. Marshall, note 1 at 641 (1890).

26. Among the most notable were Thorstein Veblen, *Absentee Ownership and Business Enterprise in Recent Times* (1923); Thomas Nixon Carver, *The Present Economic Revolution in the United States* (1925); William Z. Ripley, *Main Street and Wall Street* (1927); and Maurice Wormser, *Frankenstein, Incorporated* (1931).

27. Robert Brookings, *Industrial Ownership: Its Economic and Social Significance* 2, 4 (1925). See Thomas R. Navin & Marian V. Sears, "The Rise of a Market for Industrial Securities, 1887–1902," 29 *Bus. Hist. Rev.* 105 (1955), who describe the rise of an enormous speculative market for trust certificates. See also Richard E. Sylla, *The American Capital Markets, 1846–1914* (1975); Lance E. Davis, "The Investment Market, 1870–1914: The Evolution of a National Market," 25 *J. Econ. Hist.* 355 (1965).

28. Berle & Means, note 1 at 46.

29. See Berle & Means, note 1, preface at v & bk. 1, chs. 1–4.

30. Id. at 350–351. The discussion suggests that Berle and Means were thinking of John Maurice Clark, *Studies in the Economics of Overhead Costs* (1923), which argued that high fixed costs undermined the classical competition model. Clark's book was not cited.

31. Ronald Coase, "The Nature of the Firm," 4 *Economica* (n. s.) 386 (1937).

32. Berle & Means, note 1 at 9, 333–344, 351, 356. See George Stigler & Claire Friedland, "The Literature of Economics: The Case of Berle and Means," 26 *J. L. & Econ.* 337 (1983) (disputing notion that salaries are unrelated to profits).

33. *Time*, April 24, 1933, at 14, quoted in Robert Hessen, "*The Modern Corporation and Private Property*: A Reappraisal," 26 *J. L. & Econ.* 273, 279 (1983).

34. On Berle's participation in the move for broader securities regulation, see Joel Seligman, *The Transformation of Wall Street: A History of the Securities and Exchange Commission and Modern Corporate Finance* (1982); Michael E. Parrish, *Securities Regulation and the New Deal* (1970). On the National Industrial Recovery Act, see Ellis W. Hawley, *The New Deal and the Problem of Monopoly* (1966).

35. Chandler, note 9.
36. Arthur R. Burns, *The Decline of Competition* (1936). Quotations at 431, 441, 455. See Chapter 25.
37. Berle & Means, note 1 at 350–351.
38. See Edward Chamberlin, "Proportionality, Divisibility, and Economies of Scale," 62 *Q. J. Econ.* 229 (1948); E. A. G. Robinson, *The Structure of Competitive Industry* 44 (rev. ed. 1958). The theory can be found in John Maurice Clark's 1926 book on overhead costs. See Clark, note 30 at 131.
39. Federal Trade Commission: *Annual Report* 19 (1928); *Annual Report* 59 (1929); *Annual Report* 50–51 (1930); *Annual Report* 16, 48 (1935); *Annual Report* 48 (1936); *Annual Report* 15 (1937); *Annual Report* 11, 19, 29 (1938); *Annual Report* 12–13 (1940). Temporary National Economic Committee: TNEC, *Final Report and Recommendations* 38–40, S. Doc. no. 35, 77th Cong. 1st sess. (1941). The case law includes United States v. Yellow Cab Co., 332 U.S. 218 (1947); United States v. Paramount Pictures, Inc., 334 U.S. 131 (1948); United States v. Columbia Steel Co., 334 U.S. 495 (1948).
40. Act of Dec. 29, 1950, ch. 1184, 64 Stat. 1125, codified at 15 U.S.C. § 18 (1986). See Derek Bok, "Section 7 of the Clayton Act and the Merging of Law and Economics," 74 *Harv. L. Rev.* 226, 233–238 (1960); Herbert Hovenkamp, "Derek Bok and the Merger of Law and Economics," 21 *J. L. Reform* 515 (1988). See Brown Shoe Co. v. United States, 370 U.S. 294, 314–324 (1962).
41. See Federal Trade Commission v. F. R. Keppel & Bros., 291 U.S. 304 (1934), holding that the FTC had jurisdiction to reach unfair business practices not condemned under the antitrust laws. Wheeler-Lea Amendment, Act of Mar. 21, 1938, ch. 49, 52 Stat. 114, § 4, codified at 15 U.S.C. § 52 (1986).

Index